BEING
RIGHT

BEING RIGHT

Conservative Catholics in America

Edited by

Mary Jo Weaver & R. Scott Appleby

Indiana University Press
Bloomington • Indianapolis

The paper used in this publication meets the minimum requirements of
American National Standard for Information Sciences—Permanence of
Paper for Printed Library Materials, ANSI Z39.48-1984.

Manufactured in the United States of America

Library of Congress Cataloging-in-Publication Data

Being right : conservative Catholics in America / edited by Mary Jo
    Weaver and R. Scott Appleby.
        p.   cm.
    Includes index.
    ISBN 0-253-32922-1 (hard). —ISBN 0-253-20999-4 (pbk.)
    1. Catholics—United States—History—20th century.   2. Catholic
Church—United States—History—20th century.   3. Conservatism—
United States—History—20th century.   4. Church and social
problems—Catholic Church.   I. Weaver, Mary Jo.   II. Appleby, R.
Scott, date.
BX1406.2B45   1995
282'.73'09045—dc20   95-6665

1 2 3 4 5 00 99 98 97 96 95

CONTENTS

PREFACE
Working on Being Right

Appleby, R. Scott, Ph.D. Divinity School, University of Chicago, 1985; Professor of History, University of Notre Dame; Director of the Cushwa Center for the Study of American Catholicism; Associate Director of the Fundamentalism Project of the American Academy of Arts and Sciences, University of Chicago, 1988–95; Louisiana roots, southwest Chicago neighborhood; writes about American modernism and worldwide fundamentalism; young, liberal, Americanist.

Weaver, Mary Jo, Ph.D. University of Notre Dame, 1973; Professor of Religious Studies and Women's Studies, Indiana University; grew up in the preconciliar church in a small town in Ohio; writes about European modernism and American Catholic feminism; middle-aged, liberal, feminist.

When we put it this way, we can see why some people might wonder how we came to work on a long-term project on right-wing American Catholics. The research questions that eventually led to this book started with "Catholic fundamentalism," a phrase we began arguing about in 1988. By then, Appleby had embarked on his work for the Fundamentalism Project at the University of Chicago and had helped to gather an international group of scholars to locate and define family resemblances in an impressive array of modern religious fundamentalisms. Weaver, finding an increasing number of conservative Catholics in her courses at Indiana University, had begun to wonder if the triumph of liberal Catholicism—a perspective that dominated most books on American Catholicism—was as clear and certain as it seemed. Both of us were aware of a spate of articles in popular Catholic magazines about Catholic fundamentalism and were interested to discover what it might mean if approached from a less partisan perspective.[1] The first volume from the Fundamentalism Project[2] had a long essay on Catholic fundamentalism by Bill Dinges and James Hitchcock, and Appleby was invited to the College Theology Society meeting in 1989 to explain this new phenomenon. At the same meeting, Weaver was part of a plenary panel on Catholic fundamentalism, meant to define it and alert society members to its nuances.

So, we met again, this time with a clearly shared interest, but aware of our rather different perspectives. Whereas Weaver insisted that there was no such thing as Catholic fundamentalism, Appleby thought that there was, even though he admitted it was not as clear a fit as in some other cases. As scholars of American religious history, we were both aware that *fundamentalism* was a word with a very specific American evangelical context. We had each read the great interpreters of Protestant fundamentalism and realized that fundamentalists shared a set of different but not unrelated qualities: a relationship to end-of-the-world speculation dating back to the nineteenth century;[3] membership in a "diverse federation of co-belligerents united by their fierce opposition to modernist attempts to bring Christianity into line with modern thought";[4] participation in a faction *within* evangelicalism and not a movement distinct from it;[5] total commitment to the doctrine of biblical inerrancy, seeing in the Bible the key to all their religious and political beliefs;[6] and in continuity with the American populist tradition of early republican Christianity.[7]

We differed about how Roman Catholicism might fit into these generic categories, but both recognized that Catholics are generally uninterested in end-of-the-world speculation and/or the second coming of Christ. They are, furthermore, historically ignorant about the Bible and waste no energy defending its inerrancy. Unlike evangelicals, Catholics are not given to emotional expressions of religious belief, and seldom do they profess to be drawn to a spirit of democracy in religion. At the same time, it was clear to us that there was a significant body of American Catholics united in their opposition to *modernity*, a word that could be expanded to include postconciliar "abuses," pro-choice rhetoric, insufficient respect for papal authority, failure to obey Catholic teaching about artificial birth control, the tendency to lose touch with the great voices of the "Catholic revival" in the 1930s and 1940s, an abandonment of the devotional tradition of the church, and a disregard for the sound conclusions of scholastic theology. Since our understanding of religion suggested to us that it is generically conservative, we wondered if momentum favored an organized group of right-wing Catholics. Could they effectively change the direction American Catholicism has been moving for the past thirty years? Furthermore, if Protestant fundamentalism is, to borrow a simile from Michael Lienesch's recent book, "like a comet" because it is dramatic, returns periodically over the religious landscape, and never dies, were we seeing in conservative Catholicism a predictable expression of protest against modernity?[8]

In 1991, with funding from the Lilly Endowment, Weaver began an exploratory study about conservative American Catholics. Appleby was thoroughly immersed in worldwide fundamentalism, more convinced than ever that there were generic similarities in a variety of international religious settings yet still uneasy about how Catholics fit into the pattern. We were, by then, in continual communication about our work and quite able to imagine a collaborative project that would draw our interests into a coherent study. Weaver's exploratory project was designed to lead to a second, long-term grant that would enable us to work together.

To her colleagues, Weaver's new project was a peculiar departure from her previous work on Catholic feminists. She heard the same cautions about this undertaking that she had heard about prior projects: these people (conservatives and/or feminists) are "marginal" or, worse yet, "extremists" who are not really worthy of study. And she was aware, herself, that she was in troubled waters because she was a postconciliar Catholic, a convinced feminist, and a dedicated pluralist trying to understand people who objected to the postconciliar church and saw feminism and/or pluralism as the Antichrist. She began her study, therefore, by immersing herself in the most traditional setting she could find: her Uncle Charles, a fervent watcher of the Eternal Word Television Network, a peaceful anti-abortion demonstrator, totally obedient to the pope, surrounded by like-minded friends, invited her to spend a week with him in Akron, Ohio. She made no secret of her own views, but neither did she spend much time discussing them. Rather, she told her uncle and his friends that she was there to understand what worried them, what they hoped for in the future, and what made them sad or angry in the contemporary church.

As she spent hours listening and taking notes on her laptop computer, she could not help remembering using a similar strategy when she first began to write about Catholic feminists. She tried, without success, to imagine a constructive dialogue between feminists and these ardent conservatives, but saw only that American Catholics inhabit several different mental universes that appear to be inexorably out of touch with one another. As she discussed her own reservations with Appleby, she found that they both saw in the disjunctions of modern Catholicism a reluctance to deal with history.

Thirty years ago, nearly *all* American Catholics were "fundamentalists" in the sense that we were shaped by a post-Tridentine mentality, marked by practices judged by the culture to be esoteric, and devoted to supernaturalism. We had an ambiguous relationship to American culture, forced to stand outside of it in some ways, yet convinced that we upheld truly American values over against our Protestant compatriots who attended church irregularly, got divorced, and were soft on communism. If there was such a thing as Catholic fundamentalism, therefore, it seemed to us that it had always been there, and had, in fact, been one of the shaping experiences of our own religious lives.

What could we learn from Catholic conservative voices of opposition? Do those voices, which echo in the halls of our collective memory, have the power to raise nagging doubts about the wisdom of assimilation? How could we construct a project that would allow us to hear those voices in their own terms? The first thing we had to jettison as we wrote our grant proposal was the word *fundamentalism* in relation to Catholics. As Weaver attended meetings of conservative Catholic sisters, scholars, students, and critics, she found that Catholic conservatives—not a monolithic group by any means—thoroughly resisted the word *fundamentalism* and preferred to describe themselves as orthodox or traditional. Some simply said that they were faithful or Roman, with a decided stress on those adjectives.

Our collaborative grant, "Being Right: Conservative American Catholics," was funded by the Lilly Endowment as a three-year project in which we gathered a group of scholars and conservative activists together for what we hoped would be constructive conversation about the future of the American Catholic Church. At our first meeting in May 1992, we invited historians, theologians, sociologists, and representatives of various conservative Catholic organizations to discuss our tentative agenda. Working from her exploratory grant-year notes, Weaver presented a wide range of right-wing Catholic groups, periodicals, agendas, and questions that she and Appleby thought would define the coming project. It was our first learning experience.

The conservatives in the group were quick to tell us that many of the groups we hoped to study were "marginal" and did not represent what they perceived as the "center" of American Catholicism where they located themselves. Here we were, coming from our own perspectives, as sympathetic as we could be, and the first thing they wanted us to recognize was that *they* were not the people needing an explanation, we were. In effect, they said, "If we are what you were, *you* are the ones who must account for yourselves." At the same time, many of them were appalled that we had not invited certain other people, and that we were including scholars who were not particularly sympathetic to their views. While that first meeting was not acrimonious, it was lively, and we spent three days redesigning the project. Some members decided to remain as observers with the option to withdraw after the next meeting; others were clearly enthusiastic about what we might finally produce collectively. Appleby and Weaver spent a day after the meeting implementing the suggestions and designed the October gathering to meet most of the suggestions offered in May.

Our compromise with their critique lay in the recognition that we should try to explain the last thirty years of American Catholic life as it was experienced by those we were calling conservative American Catholics. How did American Catholics get to the point where they needed adjectives to describe themselves? Why is it no longer enough, as it was in 1955, for someone to say that he or she is a Catholic? Why do we now, in 1995, meet Catholics who are "recovering," "communal," "cradle," "practicing," "Tridentine," "conciliar," "feminist," "orthodox," "Roman," "American," "disgruntled," "liberal," or "conservative"?

Andrew Greeley, in an article in the Sunday magazine section of the *New York Times* (10 July 1994, pp. 38–41), claims that Catholicism has not declined because 25 percent of the American Catholic population say that they are Catholic. His figures are based on a survey in which data gatherers called a national sample and asked whether they were Catholic. If they said "Yes," they counted. That certainly works, but is it really that easy? Thirty years ago, those responding positively to the question had to say what they *did:* they fasted at appointed times, went to Mass regularly, went to confession at least once each year, obeyed their priests and bishops, sent their children to Catholic schools, were familiar with various devotional practices, followed the recommendations of the Legion of Decency, and were drenched in supernaturalism. Had that assemblage of markers been reduced to saying "Yes" to a survey question?

This book is our attempt to provide in detail the substance of this sensibility and to show some of the directions it has taken in one sector of American Catholicism in the thirty years since the Second Vatican Council. We are looking back at a generation of American Catholics who describe themselves in traditional terms and asking what they have been doing. We want to explore the mental universe of this group and to make it possible to understand what has happened to their hopes. We are also, of course, trying to understand ourselves as we try on various adjectives qualifying or expanding what we mean when we say that we are Catholics in the modern world.

NOTES

1. The first person to suggest the phrase "Catholic fundamentalism" was probably Gabriel Daly in an article on integralism, "Catholicism and Modernity," *Journal of the American Academy of Religion* 53 (1985): 773–96. The articles in the popular press were usually meant to warn Catholics about a resurgence of militant conservatism in the church. See, for example, "Who Are the Catholic Fundamentalists," *Commonweal* 116 (27 January 1989): 42–47. The January/February issue of the *New Catholic World* was devoted to this topic, as were the 27 September 1986 issue of *America* and the May 1988 issue of *Theology Review*. A column by Peter Hebblethwaite, "A Roman Catholic Fundamentalism," *Times Literary Supplement*, 5–11 August 1988, p. 866, is an example of an article full of useful information but written from a decidedly partisan (antifundamentalist) perspective.

2. Martin E. Marty and R. Scott Appleby, eds., *Fundamentalisms Observed* (Chicago: University of Chicago Press, 1991).

3. Ernest Sandeen, *The Roots of Fundamentalism: British and American Millenarianism, 1800–1930* (Chicago: University of Chicago Press, 1970).

4. George Marsden, *Fundamentalism and American Culture: The Shaping of Twentieth-Century Evangelicalism, 1870–1925* (New York: Oxford University Press, 1980), p. 4.

5. James Davison Hunter, *Evangelicalism: The Coming Generation* (Chicago: University of Chicago Press, 1987).

6. James Barr, *The Scope and Authority of the Bible* (Philadelphia: Westminster Press, 1980).

7. Nathan Hatch, *The Democratization of American Christianity* (New Haven: Yale University Press, 1989).

8. Michael Lienesch, *Redeeming America: Piety and Politics in the New Christian Right* (Chapel Hill: University of North Carolina Press, 1993).

ACKNOWLEDGMENTS

We wish first of all to thank the Lilly Endowment for its support of this project. Jeanne Knoerle and Fred Hofheinz have been gracious foundation officers and steady friends throughout the past four years. Our colleagues at Indiana University, the University of Chicago, and the University of Notre Dame have read parts of the manuscript and have been encouraging with their responses. Jeff Walker, John Haas, and Martin Connell served ably at various times as research assistants. Walker, who arranged the details of our meetings over a two-year period, deserves special praise.

This project might not have taken shape had not Mary Jo's uncle Charles McDowell and his family invited her to spend a week in Akron, Ohio, talking to a dedicated community of Catholics distressed by dissent and anguished by perceived abuses of the Second Vatican Council. As the design of this book moved from grassroots discontent to institutional embodiments of conservative American Catholicism, Uncle Charles and his friends were left behind, but their freedom of spirit and unfailing kindness cannot easily be forgotten.

As we shaped this book and tried to include the most representative groups, we were advised by more people than we can possibly name. Still, some of them deserve special mention: Ralph McInerny and Marvin O'Connell at the University of Notre Dame, Monsignor Eugene V. Clark and Patricia Puccetti Donohoe at the Homeland Foundation in New York, Andrew Greeley, David Schindler, Anne Roche Muggeridge, Stephen Tonsor, James Varacalli, Dominic Aquila, and Bishop James Hogan were generous with their time and helpful with their advice. Although we realize that this book may not please all of them, and admit that we did not always follow their counsel, we nonetheless appreciate their kindness and their constant courtesy.

We are grateful to the members of the "Being Right" seminar who met for conversation and mutual correction over a two-year period. Some of their contributions were advisory rather than written: William Shea, Philip Gleason, Martin Riesebrodt, and Orlando Espín were important members of the discussion. The contributors to this volume signed on for a two-year stint and met their obligations with good will. Benedict Ashley, Mike Cuneo, Allan Deck, Bill Dinges, Helen Hull Hitchcock, Jim Hitchcock,

Joe Komonchak, Jim Sullivan, George Weigel, and Sandie Zimdars-Swartz were good companions along this unmarked trail.

The actual physical production of this book has rested, for the most part, on the able shoulders of Barbara Lockwood at the Cushwa Center: she worked with two different computer systems, made changes, did the formatting, and otherwise got the manuscript ready for the press. Jenny Mobley at Indiana University handled the accounting needs of the grant with accuracy and dispatch. Alice Falk, who was responsible for proof-reading, was her usual unflappable self, doing perfect work in record time.

Finally, we thank our families and friends for their support. Peggy Appleby kept track of Ben, Paul, Clare, and Tony while Scott tracked conservative Catholics. Mary Jo would not manage as well without the support of friends like Robyn Wiegman, Mary Favret, David Brakke, and Andrew Miller. For her, too, Luke Johnson has been a constant source of E-mail hilarity, while Don Gray and Susan Gubar have been there with good scotch and sage advice throughout.

BEING
RIGHT

Introduction

Who Are the Conservative Catholics?

MARY JO WEAVER

Readers familiar with American Catholic history in the twentieth
century will recognize the major themes of this volume and not be surprised to see that the Second Vatican Council (1962–65) and the dissent
surrounding the birth control encyclical, *Humanae Vitae* (1968), quickly
became rallying points for Catholics. In this volume about *conservative*
Catholics, these two events are mentioned—sometimes along with liturgical change—in almost every chapter. Oddly, these chapters contain
relatively few references to the political, economic, and social contexts that
formed the background music of the 1960s and that often help to explain
the need of some people to resist what they perceive as never-ending and
often destructive change.

Vatican II occurred within the context of the war in Vietnam, the Cold
War, the emergence of the third world, new technologies, and other frac-
tious events. Its implementation in the United States coincided with late
civil rights activity, urban riots, the assassinations of Martin Luther King
and Robert F. Kennedy, the Watergate scandal, youthful rebellion, and the
rise of a counterculture associated in the popular mind with women's liberation, sex, drugs, and rock and roll. The overall sense of disintegration
voiced by many of the conservatives in this book, therefore, may seem too
rooted in ecclesiastical or theological contexts, with insufficient attention
paid to the larger cultural environment. If this is the case, then perhaps the
groups and individuals that make up this book tell us something about the
isolation many conservatives have felt in the wake of Vatican II.

It also may be true that right-wing Catholics share a posture of resistance to modernity that allows them to assume a common cultural context. If they think the larger political or economic background simply needs to be opposed, then they might prefer to put their contextual stress on theological, ecclesiastical, and liturgical matters. Whatever the reasons, the conservative Catholics presented in this book think of themselves and their approaches as normative. Conservative American Catholics in general do not believe that their concerns require explanation. As the title of William D. Dinges's chapter on the traditionalist movement says, "We are what you were." The challenge of accountability, they believe, rests with those who have changed, whose hold on their Catholic identity is not as firm as conservatives think it should be.

Although most of the Catholics portrayed in this volume are not traditionalists in the Lefebvrist sense, they do share with them an important perspective: they believe that they have held steady while the world around them has moved. The markers that identified their Catholicism have shifted since the Council. It is not surprising to read, for example, in James Hitchcock's chapter that he *finds himself* on the right, defined more by a condition than by an action. Some of the conservatives in this volume are like drivers on a highway that runs through Baton Rouge, Louisiana: they enter traffic on the left and, without changing lanes, pass through several intersections that move them to the center and then, finally, to the far right. Bewilderingly, they find themselves in a location quite different from where they started and hasten to point out that they have not moved.

Conservative Catholic Identity

If I were to combine interview notes from the many different conservative Catholics I have talked with over the last four years, I could come up with a composite personality who would be in his or her mid-fifties, a second- or third-generation ethnic who attended Catholic schools through college, and who married and reared a family in the traditional Catholic manner. If I asked that person to explain what has happened to the church in his or her lifetime, I imagine I would hear something like the following:

"I was brought up in a church that was alive with the supernatural. God was present in the tabernacle, the saints were part of my life, the mystical body of Christ defined my place in the universe. We had 'community,' as they say today—we helped one another and shared our burdens—but we did not have to talk about it all the time. The church then was an unambiguous source of authority and moral guidance at every stage of my life. The family, the church, and the school worked together to see to it that we all kept the faith.

"I found my identity in an American Catholic community that was well-defined. We knew who we were, and we understood that there were clear boundaries between us and others. We were not necessarily hostile to the outside world—even though it had been pretty hostile to our parents and grandparents—but we knew that it was not our true home. The liturgy conspired to keep us conscious of a transcendent destiny, and if we were more focused on death than our non-Catholic neighbors, that was as it should be. We were confident in ourselves as Catholics, as members of the true church.

"As we gained more power and influence in the world, as we became better-educated and made more money, we were sometimes accused of being arrogant. Maybe we were. Mostly, however, we were *innocent.* We accepted the claims of the church without question because it anchored us: we knew what was right and wrong for ourselves (and for others). It was not smugness so much as it was a profound confidence in our relationship with the supernatural. Our superiority seemed clear and natural to us because we knew that we had the truth amid many different attempts to define it. Being Catholic was a comfort and a challenge.

"But look what has happened. In the short span of my adult life, all of this has changed. My church experienced the most dramatic upheaval of its last five hundred years. At the time of Vatican II, I did not worry: I trusted the church and the magisterium and so approached the Council with optimism and a spirit of exuberance, as most Catholics did. I was ready for renewal and reform, but what I got was revolution. In the aftermath of the Council, we Catholics lost our identity, our innocence, and the basis for our self-confidence.

"Almost overnight, all the markers that distinguished us from non-Catholics seemed to erode. Our innocence about the supernatural and our relationship to it, our confidence in the church as the embodiment of God's will, were swallowed up in historical criticism and moral relativism. Furthermore, a variety of radical movements—feminism chief among them—located justice, right reason, and salvation not in God but in the human person.

"I recognized that this lost identity would be the legacy of Vatican II in 1968 when, for the first time in memory and in American Catholic history, a group of prominent American Catholics publicly treated the church as if it were any other human institution and got away with it. They criticized the church on academic and secular grounds, preferring those terms to revelation, and they asserted their right to dissent and to form their own opinions on a variety of matters. Shockingly, they were not punished. Indeed, many of them were rewarded with lucrative positions in elite institutions of American Catholic life, for example, in universities and publishing houses.

"It seems to me that for the past thirty years, the core of Catholic identity has been lost. These people who dissent, who have adopted other sources of authority as their guide for moral life and liturgical consciousness, have thrown away the crowning glory of Catholicism. The genius of the church has always been its ability to shape Catholic identity formed in faith and measured in obedience to the teaching church. I do not want to return to the nineteenth century, or to the 1950s, but I am alternately heartbroken and angry at what has happened and deeply conflicted about what to do about it."

Giving Voice to a Conservative Perspective

The purpose of this book is to demonstrate in detail the substance of this sensibility, and to describe some of the forms it has taken in the generation following the Council. By paying attention to Catholic conservatives in their own terms, we hope to sketch the details of a mental universe that, in some respects, feels alienated from itself in spite of its claim to have been faithful to the church. The efforts of the conservative Catholics portrayed in this book are sometimes heroic, sometimes pathetic attempts to respond to this sense of alienation and rejection.

In the middle of the fourth century, St. Jerome described the aftermath of the Council of Nicaea. "The church woke up one day and groaned to find itself Arian," he lamented. Many of the conservative Catholics in this volume believe that they can say something similar about the aftermath of Vatican II: "The church woke up in 1968 and ached to find itself pluralist." What can they do now if, as they believe, the institutional church has turned liberal in ways that go beyond anyone's imagination before the Council? What does it mean to have been a liberal before the Council, and then find oneself a "conservative" because of what the church has done to itself?

This volume explains what happened from a conservative vantage point. Although we have not been able to include all the modulations of the conservative Catholic voice, we believe that we have gathered a representative sample. Some of the authors identify themselves as conservatives and write about their experience and their attempts to respond to the alienation they find in their lives. Others are scholars who are interested in some aspect of conservative Catholicism but are not in any way identified with it. All of the authors have been part of a two-year process of engagement and dialogue with one another, presenting their papers for discussion and opening themselves to criticism.

The book has been designed to provide three different perspectives. It begins with a set of contextual essays that attempt to place contemporary conservative American Catholicism within its broad ecclesiastical, historical, and moral contexts. One author questions whether a conservative/liberal axis is a useful way to understand modern Catholicism. The second set of essays are written from an "insider's" vantage point by people who are partisans of the positions they describe. In conversations with colleagues who do not share their perception of Catholicism, these authors were asked to make their positions as clear and forceful as possible. The final four chapters were written by scholars interested in some manifestation of conservative Catholicism; the authors are sympathetic to their subjects, but the critical questions they bring to the groups they investigate are different from those raised by the insiders. Their essays are based on extensive field work and on group discussions which helped them to recognize nuances of their own biases. The essays in the second and third parts of the book tend to be more descriptive than evaluative because we were trying to gather reliable information about dimensions of Catholic life about which opinions are presently, for the most part, formed in polemical contexts.

Part of the merit of this book lies in the process of its fruition. Because we wanted to ensure that conservative Catholics were able to speak in their own terms, Scott Appleby and I tended to accept most of their suggestions about the composition of the group and the general subject matter of the essays. When we began to sketch out this project, we had an idea of what issues were important, but we had to realize that however important they might have been to *us*, they were not necessarily the things that our group members recognized as crucial. There are certain ideas and groups, therefore, that one might expect in a book such as this that are not included in this volume. My early classification system included six broad categories: European movements with a presence in the United States; embodiments of traditional Catholicism; groups organized to fight abortion or feminism; education or intellectual movements; liturgical protest movements; and miscellaneous manifestations of the Catholic conservative spirit.

European Movements

As we mentioned in the preface, Scott and I went to the first meeting with a list of items that we wanted to investigate and to work into a coherent system. For example, we wanted to know about the origins and intentions of European movements with a presence in the United States. What challenges did they face as they attempted to fit into the American cultural milieu? We wondered what made them attractive to American Catholics and whether a pluralist context changed their theology or their purpose. We identified four such movements—Opus Dei, the Knights of Malta, Communio e Liberazione, and the Lefebvrists—but were persuaded to include only one of them in this volume, the traditionalist followers of Marcel Lefebvre.

Although we agreed that the Knights of Malta and Communio e Liberazione were either so thoroughly European or so esoteric that we could exclude them from a book on American Catholicism, we were disappointed not to include Opus Dei. Founded in Spain in 1928, this organization has a reputation for secrecy which many people find disturbing, and it has a unique status in the Catholic Church by way of being a personal prelature of the pope, answerable not to local bishops but only to the Vatican. It is a lay movement which aims to promote piety among the laity by appealing to well-educated, highly disciplined, profoundly committed Catholics who, in their ordinary jobs, can penetrate society in ways not open to priests.

Opus Dei is surrounded by controversy, partly because of its supposed influence at the Vatican, partly because of its vigorous practices of mortification. The beatification of its founder, José Maria Escriva de Balanguer, triggered a flood of negative and hostile articles from liberal Catholics and added to the near-impossibility of finding good, dispassionate accounts of the organization. Most of those who write about Opus Dei are partisans working energetically for it or against it. Its adherents say that it is a pious lay movement working to further the aims of the church, whereas its critics claim that it is a political movement—especially active in Latin America—that displays undiluted sinister intentions.

Traditional Catholicism

Our second classification drew a number of groups together united in their desire to foster some aspect of a preconciliar Catholic identity or to defend the church from internal and external enemies. We were interested in their purposes and their influence, their episcopal support and their relation to American political movements. Our tentative list included the Blue Army of Mary and the numerous offshoots of Marian piety that we thought were growing increasingly apocalyptic; Vox Sacerdotalis, an English organization of priests vehemently dissatisfied with the present state of the church; the Institute for Religious Life, founded to provide traditionally minded nuns with an alternative to the Leadership Council for Women Religious; a variety of youth groups, including Miles Jesu, St. Paul's Outreach, and Legionnaires of Christ, whose very existence belied the notion that conservative Catholics were mostly middle-aged malcontents; the Wanderer Forum, an incorporated foundation whose energies are spent alerting its members to the dangers of "neomodernism" in the contemporary church; the Catholic League, founded to oppose discrimination against Catholicism in the media; and Catholics United for the Faith, a lay organization founded in 1968 to oppose dissent and pluralism within the church.

Space constraints prevented us from including all of these groups and forced us to make some choices about how to represent these voices of traditional Catholicism. Rather than profile the Blue Army of Mary, for example, we chose to include a chapter on Marian devotion attentive to new apparition sites in the United States. Sandra L. Zimdars-Swartz, who has written compellingly about Marian devotion from La Salette to Medjugorje, focused her attention on two popular new sites of Marian apparition. Her essay for this book discusses what draws people to make pilgrimages and what differentiates modern seers from earlier ones.

When we looked collectively at the other groups in this category, we concluded that a chapter on Catholics United for the Faith would be our best choice. James A. Sullivan, vice-president of CUF, joined us partway through our process with the blessings and approval of his organization. I had met Jim during the first grant year and was eager to have him take part in this undertaking, but was not sanguine about it. Several years earlier I had been disinvited from giving the John Courtney Murray Lectures at the University of Toledo because the local CUF chapter objected to my work on Catholic feminism and to the fact that I had signed a statement in the *New York Times* in 1983 calling for more discussion about abortion among Catholics. I was happily surprised, therefore, when Jim agreed to participate in the shaping of this book. The fact that his contribution was made with the encouragement of his board of directors showed me that one cannot judge a national organization on the basis of a local behavior. It may also convey a certain evolution in CUF even in this decade.

It should be noted that a book such as this one necessarily omits hard-nosed conservatives, those whose own positions prevent them from dialogue with what they may perceive as "the enemy." Some of the groups that have not been included in this book, therefore, chose not to work with us, believing, perhaps, that their positions might be compromised by their participation. For example, I had hoped originally to write a chapter on the Institute for Religious Life, established in 1974 to "promote authentic religious life as taught by the Vatican Council." The institute has now been replaced by the Council of Major Superiors of Women to provide a clear alternative to the Leadership Council of Women Religious, the group that represents a majority of American nuns. The history and controversy surrounding the formation of this group, made up of sisters who wear the religious habit, follow the original intentions of their founders, and obey the pope in all matters, would have been an important chapter in any book attempting to trace a conservative Catholic sensibility.

I was particularly interested in the institute—and its intellectual forum, the Consortium Perfectae Caritatae—because my earlier work on feminism in the Catholic Church identified American nuns as leaders in the Catholic feminist movement. I wanted, therefore, to be able to understand those sisters who perceive the Leadership Council of Women Religious to be made up of rebellious, disobedient women touched, if not driven, by feminism. Part of my research during the first grant year included trips to institute conventions and conversations with sisters and priests gathered there. Bishop John Hogan, retired ordinary of the Altoona/Johnston diocese and a director of the institute, has maintained a cordial phone relationship with me over the last few years, but many of the sisters I wanted to interview simply refused to speak to me. A number of them had read or heard about Donna Steichen's caricature of my work in her book *Ungodly Rage,* and believed that I was a neopagan, goddess-inspired abortion activist. As one sister said in a letter to me, "I was told that you were dangerous. . . . In an earlier age you would have been excommunicated. . . . We have nothing in common."

Groups Organized to Fight Abortion and Feminism

One theme that cuts across almost all conservative Catholic groups is their rejection of abortion as a viable option and their activism in pursuit of some means to curb what they see as a murderous practice. Because they perceive a pro-choice position as inexorably linked with feminism, they often oppose initiatives that, as they see it, infect the church with feminist consciousness. It is not clear to me how many anti-abortion groups are active in the American Catholic Church: the back page of *The Wanderer* regularly runs ads for Our Father's House, Aid for Women, Des Plaines Pro Life, and other such organizations, but they are usually appeals for funds. Media-famous groups such as Lambs for Christ, the Pro-Life Action League, and Operation Rescue are important actors on the national stage, and along with peaceful demonstrators such as Free Speech Advocates, Catholics United for Life, and Women for Faith and Family, they represent an important segment of conservative Catholic energy.

We have included one essay on anti-abortion activism and one chapter on an antifeminist alternative for Catholic women, but these issues are also important aspects of other organizations represented in this book. For example, in his essay on neoconservatives, George Weigel shows that the broad set of issues addressed by his colleagues include significant efforts to curb abortion in the United States and to oppose the ways in which radical feminism may influence the American Catholic bishops. James Hitchcock's chapter on the Fellowship of Catholic Scholars, Sandie Zimdars-Swartz's work on Marian apparitions, and James Sullivan's description of Catholics United for the Faith all exhibit a sensitivity to these issues.

The aspect of anti-abortion activism represented in this book is that of Catholic militancy. Michael W. Cuneo, who has done extensive field work with members of this group, has provided a profile of their history and development that links their work with reverence for the church's position against artificial contraception. Although his essay represents but one specific manifestation of anti-abortion activity—omitting such things as neoconservative lobbying efforts, for example—it is an important chapter precisely because so little has been written about it. The discussions in the last two years that were the most acrimonious and difficult were all centered on this area, proving once again that constructive discussion about abortion is probably impossible in the American Catholic Church.

The antifeminist chapter of this book was written by Helen Hull Hitchcock, founder of Women for Faith and Family. Because this topic is a particular interest of mine, I had hoped to include other notable antifeminist women in the discussion in order to complement Helen's perspective. I tried, for example, to interest Anne Roche Muggeridge and Janet Smith— fervent critics of the liberals in the church and ardent defenders of *Humanae Vitae*—in this project, but was told by both of them that, as they saw no resolution to our controversies, they did not want to participate. As Anne told me in a telephone conversation, "There is no possibility that you will find that we *are* right." My reply, that neither was there any chance that we would find that they are "wrong," did not mollify her. My conversations with her have always been cordial and helpful, mostly because she makes the inherent limitations of this project quite clear. From her perspective, if we cannot agree on first principles—that the church possesses absolute truth and that our job is to follow its teachings—there is no point in talking.

Helen Hull Hitchcock represents what she believes to be a significant group of Catholic women in her essay about Women for Faith and Family. Although she does not make antifeminism the primary focus of her chapter, Women for Faith and Family was clearly founded in order to give traditional Catholic women the means to oppose feminist-dominated discussions about the now-defunct U.S. bishops' pastoral on women in the church. When Helen and I first met in Indianapolis, we were, naturally, wary of one another, but we developed a working relationship that eventually led to her strong statement on behalf of Catholic women who, when they felt excluded and betrayed by conversations about "women in the church," organized a significant voice of opposition.

Educational/Intellectual Movements

One group of conservative Catholics can be gathered around what they perceive as a crisis in Catholic education or intellectual life. We identified several initiatives that we thought worthy of attention, including a growing Catholic enthusiasm for home schooling; postconciliar Catholic colleges founded to provide genuine Catholic education for the next generation; newly invigorated Catholic universities such as the Franciscan University of Steubenville; professional societies such as the Fellowship of Catholic Scholars; and conservative Catholic institutes, whether free-standing ones such as the John Paul II Institute for Marriage and Family, or those founded within existing universities, such as the Ignatius Institute at the University of San Francisco. In this category we also included a list of conservative Catholic periodicals and publishing ventures that are meant to nourish a traditional understanding of the faith.

A book dedicated to educational questions would have included chapters on all of these matters. We have tried to cover as many of them as possible by including a chapter on the Fellowship of Catholic Scholars by James Hitchcock, and my chapter on newly founded Catholic colleges. We have included a short, annotated list of conservative Catholic periodicals as an appendix.

We did not include a chapter on the Franciscan University of Steubenville because we were not convinced that Catholic Charismatic Renewal, which is the undergirding inspiration for the rehabilitation of Steubenville, fits into the general plan of the book. The charismatic movement is quite traditional in terms of obedience to the magisterium, and at the same time quite nontraditional in its Pentecostal prayer forms and assumptions.

Liturgical Groups

When I began my first grant year, an old mentor told me that I would get the most heartfelt observations about the state of contemporary Catholic life by asking people what they thought about the liturgy. That is true. The most painful conversation I had during that year was with a woman in Akron, Ohio, who said that she had not been able to take her family on vacation since the Council for fear that they would be unable to find an appropriate church for Sunday worship. Terrified of "clown Masses" and liturgical dance, she had stayed home, lamenting the loss of the Latin Mass and worrying about the future of a church that allows experimentation and deviance in the most important part of her life. *The Wanderer* is replete with columns about Latin Mass celebrations in the United States, and the most obvious candidate for inclusion in this book was an essay on the preconciliar liturgy.

Although we could have included a chapter on the demise of older devotional forms, or on the approved *Novus Ordo* Latin Mass, we chose to ask Bill Dinges to follow up his work on various manifestations of the Lefebvrist movement in the United States. In his chapter, he includes the history of the movement and the ways in which it has fractured and taken on new life in a variety of organizations, including the Society of St. Pius X, the Priestly Fraternity of St. Peter, the St. Pius V Society, and Independent Latin Mass Priests. Other liturgical concerns, for example, resistance to sex-inclusive language in the Mass, appear in other essays, notably in Helen Hull Hitchcock's chapter on Women for Faith and Family.

Miscellaneous Conservative Initiatives

We realize that more than one book on Catholic conservatives is necessary to capture the broad range of activities and ideas represented. Some of the initiatives we have excluded are small and not clearly effective, such as the Couple to Couple League, founded by John Kippley to support those who believe that acceptance of *Humanae Vitae* is crucial to one's identity as a Catholic. Some of them are small and relatively esoteric, including Legatus, the group of Catholic CEOs founded by Domino's Pizza mogul Thomas Monaghan. Others, such as the Eternal Word Television Network, are impressive manifestations of a preconciliar spirit, but have not been accessible to us. Finally, other conservative Catholic initiatives, such as the one presented to me by a retired history professor—that very soon Opus Dei would found a "real" Catholic university in the United States, a combative institution for the training of cadres to embody the genuine spirit of Vatican II—are not yet visible.

Shared Perspectives

When we began this project, we thought that all the people we wanted to include had some level of discomfort with the Second Vatican Council or its aftermath. Although many of the groups represented in this book welcomed the Council and continue to see it as a watershed moment in the history of Catholicism, they share a basic unhappiness about the ways Vatican II has been implemented in the last thirty years. In his essay about the Council, Joseph A. Komonchak sketches two negative reactions to it. On the one hand, he says, one can find those extremists who reject the Council altogether and judge all popes since Pius XII to be illegitimate. Their numbers are few, but the basis of their position has had sufficient energy to reify into a complicated set of positions. On the other hand, he describes the reform-minded conservatives whose discomfort lies in the ways the Council was implemented. Although the responses he sketches are not equally shared by those represented in this book, his essay shows that the Council itself was perhaps the most important event dividing conservative and liberal Catholics in the last thirty years. To return to an earlier point, he shows how certain individuals and schools of thought have, perforce, become conservative even though they themselves have not moved.

James Sullivan, in his chapter about Catholics United for the Faith, and George Weigel, writing about the neoconservative movement in American Catholicism, both make it clear that conservative Catholics are those who do not have problems with the Council itself, but react vigorously to the ways that Council documents have been implemented in the last thirty years. Sullivan says that the documents are good. They provided the founding impetus for CUF, which is now in the paradoxical position of criticizing episcopal implementation even as it strives to support Catholic obedience and reverence for authority. Weigel agrees about the essential goodness of the documents, paying particular attention to the "Declaration on Religious Freedom," but works to oppose the ways they have been used by radical feminists and others as an excuse to go wild in the name of reform. His chapter notes that neoconservatives are especially worried that this unbridled radicalism has infected the National Council of Catholic Bishops.

If we look at general American Catholic reactions to the Council, it would probably be safe to say that many Catholics are unhappy with the postconciliar status quo. Conservatives are upset in different ways than are progressives and are animated by resistance and opposition. Benedict M. Ashley's chapter situates contemporary ethical debates within a modern Thomistic context, and explains the anguish of conservative Catholics who have been seriously disappointed at the lack of moral leadership since the Council. From a different vantage point, Allan Figueroa Deck argues that the whole fragmentation of Catholics into liberal and conservative camps is pointless in a Hispanic context. For him, a possible solution to the recovery of a genuine Catholic identity lies in the recovery of an earlier concept of tradition, a way of being Catholic that Hispanic American Catholics possess precisely because they were evangelized before the Council of Trent and therefore were never divisively shattered by its aftermath.

Scott Appleby's chapter places the debates of this book within the historical context of Americanism within the U.S. Catholic Church. In showing how American Catholics, conservatives as well as liberals, affirm a basic compatibility between American values regarding human nature and society and those presented by their church, he identifies the foundational assumptions that unite "right" and "left," however fractured they may be about pressing questions of a pastoral nature. The groups and individuals represented herein probably have a complicated array of reactions to "parish life," and present diverse challenges to their pastors. Although this volume tends to concentrate more on institutional issues, several authors notice the concrete ways in which pastoral issues have galvanized conservative responses.

Mapping American Catholicism

This book is an attempt to look clearly at some of those responses. At the same time, we hope that in sketching a particular sensibility, we can make a first step toward a larger mapping project that will attempt to take stock of American Catholicism at the end of the twentieth century. We hope in the future to be able to offer a similar sketch of liberal American

Catholics and, eventually, to encourage constructive conversations that belie Robert Wuthnow's dire assessment that as liberals and conservatives come to know more about one another, they find it impossible to engage in any dialogue whatsoever, preferring to glare at one another across an unbridgeable chasm. Historically, the Catholic Church has been able to open itself to varied and sometimes threatening voices, which have led it to new understandings of itself.

As cartographers, we have not tried to impose an a priori grid on the chapters in this book. Rather, in gathering a group of conservative partisans and nonconservative scholars, we have allowed the project to develop on its own terms. This volume is a collection of essays by some American Catholics who agree that they are conservatives—people for whom the conservative/liberal continuum makes sense—and by historians and sociologists whose work has taken them to various conservative settings. This particular axis is not meant to be exhaustive for people who would be considered conservative in a larger sense, i.e., people of traditional piety, loyal to the magisterium, and shaped primarily by an older supernaturalism. Everyone represented in this book is self-consciously conservative. Many are clearly countercultural, though in different degrees.

We recognize that these chapters present one slice of the larger movements they sometimes represent. Each chapter in the last two sections, therefore, begins with a prologue outlining a larger context of understanding and activity. One of the principles guiding our selection of material has been the fact that many of these groups have not been written about very much. When we had to make choices, we chose groups that often do not appear in studies of American Catholicism—Women for Faith and Family, Catholics United for the Faith, the Fellowship of Catholic Scholars, and neoconservatives—and had them described by people who claim to represent them. We have also included marginal movements or initiatives—the Lefebvrists, new Marian apparitions, militant anti-abortion activists, and newly founded Catholic colleges—and asked scholars who have done field work in these areas to report and evaluate their findings. The contextual essays that begin the book could serve as well for a book on liberal American Catholics: the ecclesiastical context of the Second Vatican Council, the Americanist face of public Catholicism, the moral context of secular humanism, and the Hispanic context of a more ancient understanding of tradition serve to remind us that we are living in a period of immense change in the Catholic Church.

PART I
Contexts

1

Interpreting the Council
Catholic Attitudes toward Vatican II

JOSEPH A. KOMONCHAK

Introduction

Whether or not they began before the Second Vatican Council, none of the conservative Catholic movements and organizations (and indeed very few other Catholic groups) can be studied today without taking into account their views of what James Hitchcock called "the most important event within the Church in the past four hundred years."[1] There are very few features of everyday Catholic life, from the central elements of its preaching and worship to the most peripheral of its etiquettes, that were not affected by the Council or at least by the changes said to have been introduced as a consequence or implementation of it. This is true both of the church's internal life and of its relationship to the "others": other Christians, other religions, unbelievers, "the world" in general. The everyday social form that the church had assumed in the previous century and a half was so rapidly transformed after the Council's close that Emile Poulat could remark that the church had changed more in a decade than it had in the previous century: "The Church of Pius XII was closer to that of Pius IX than to that of Paul VI."[2] The transformation can be illustrated by a single controversy: reactions to Paul VI's encyclical on birth control,

Humanae Vitae, issued less than ten years after the death of Pius XII. Something happened.

A great deal of what happened was officially authorized. The Mass and the other sacraments underwent reforms that often, for example, in the introduction of vernacular languages, went far beyond what the Council had mandated.[3] Other changes saw the near-abrogation of the law of Friday abstinence, the reform of Lenten fast regulations, new orientations in catechesis, the establishment of diocesan and parochial councils, the spread of lay ministries, and the encouragement of ecumenical conversations and cooperation. From a theological or canonical perspective, none of these changes was revolutionary, but many of them had more dramatic psychological and sociological consequences than the word *reform* suggests. The everyday self-consciousness of Catholics was altered, as were the ordinary processes of the church's internal activity and its action in the world.[4]

Once the genie of reform was let loose by the Council, it proved impossible to keep it confined within officially approved limits. The literature of conservative Catholics laments the decline in traditional popular devotions, the abandonment of distinctive clerical and religious dress, the political activities of clergy and religious, women's abandonment of hats in church, the massive departures from the priesthood and religious life, the decline in membership and even the dissolution of Catholic professional associations, the abandonment of Gregorian chant and its replacement by Protestant hymns or by music that imitates popular musical styles, the collapse of the unitary neoscholastic method and language of theology, the spread of dissent (particularly after the publication of *Humanae Vitae*), and the movement for the ordination of women. Growing up Catholic in the postconciliar period is now so different that a teacher has to explain many of the symbols and rubrics, gestures and rules that once characterized a quite distinctive Catholic subculture.

The changes in Roman Catholicism, in other words, were so profound that a Catholic movement or organization, even if it had wished to remain the same, would have found itself after the Council in a changed church and in an altered relation to the world. Groups with primarily devotional interests, for example, faced the new emphasis on the liturgy as the center of Catholic piety and the effects of the Council's statement that all devotions be evaluated in the light of their relationship to the liturgy.[5] Marian groups were confronted not only with the reorientation of the theology of Mary found in the last chapter of *Lumen Gentium* (Vatican II's Dogmatic Constitution on the Church) but also with the Council's withdrawal from the antimodern and apocalyptic attitude toward the modern world that often had inspired them. Catholics with primarily world-oriented purposes had to face the challenges represented by the Council's new approach to the world and its method of understanding and dialogue rather than of suspicion and condemnation.

A study of movements and organizations founded before the Council, then, must pay attention to the impact of the Council and its aftermath on their constitution, purposes, and membership. Many of the conservative Catholic groups formed after the Council were established in order to oppose, if not Vatican II itself and its new orientations, at least the dramatic changes in the everyday life of the church that accompanied the implementation of the Council's reforms. Before an analysis of opposition to the Council and/or to its impact is offered, it may be useful to consider a typology of interpretations of Vatican II and to set the contemporary debate in the context of the drama of the Council itself.

The Interpretation of the Council

A typology of interpretations of the Council, with all the risks of oversimplification that ideal types involve, might first identify two extremes. The progressive interpretations of the Council work with a sharp, almost black-and-white, disjunction between the preconciliar and postconciliar church. Dismissive adjectives characterize the former: it was triumphalistic, legalistic, hierarchical, patriarchal, ghetto-like, clericalistic, irrelevant, and obsessive-compulsive. Pope John XXIII opened the church to allow the Spirit to blow across the dead bones of Ezekiel's vision. At the Council the church finally made the accommodations to modernity it had long stubbornly resisted. If there has been confusion since, it is because an intransigent minority, which engaged in rearguard actions at the Council and thus forced compromises to be introduced into its texts, continues to resist the directions of the Spirit who inspired the Council.

The traditionalist interpretation of Vatican II makes use of a similar disjunction between pre- and postconciliar Catholicism but reverses the appreciations. The popes from Gregory XVI to Pius XII had acutely recognized and rightly condemned the apostate and even demonic character of the liberal modernity that was thwarting Christ's right to reign over society and culture. The church had effectively constructed itself as an antimodern subculture with the tight organization and inspiring vision that an army of reconquest requires. All this was weakened if not destroyed by the Council, where the church surrendered its distinctive vision of the world and its role in it and where the lines of authority were fatally loosened. The consequences of this surrender to the church's archenemy are everywhere visible today.

These two interpretations of the Council and its impact leave a lot of room for mediating positions, some of which will be described below. It is worth pausing for a moment, however, to consider certain features of the two views here typified. They agree on a number of points. Both assume a sharp contrast between two historical epochs; each sees the Council as a dividing line between two distinct kinds of Catholicism; both identify the point at issue as the church's relation to the modern world. They differ less on the details of what happened than on its interpretation and evaluation.

While the differences between these two views derive a good deal of their passion from events that followed the Council, it is important to note that such differences characterized a good deal of the drama of the Council itself. Vatican II was not a peaceful event. It unfolded as a confrontation, even a battle, and those who witnessed it will remember with some vividness that the outcome was by no means secure.

The main conflict concerned the adequacy of the preconciliar church's attitudes and strategies in its encounter with the modern world. After Pope John XXIII appointed the preparatory commissions, a struggle began about the very nature and direction of the Council. The struggle was particularly evident in three areas: pastoral practice, theology, and ecclesiastical structures. With regard to the church's pastoral practice, it was a struggle between those who thought that relatively minor adjustments were sufficient and those who wished the Council to undertake a major rethinking of its redemptive role in the world. In terms of the church's articulation of its faith, it was a struggle between defenders of classical scholastic method, terminology, and emphases and those who thought that classical theology needed to be broadened and deepened by a "return to the sources" and that a biblical and patristic orientation and expression would be more comprehensible to contemporaries. In terms of the church's structures, it was a struggle between those who favored the highly centralized and uniform system that had developed in the previous century and those who envisaged a decentralization of authority that would enhance the role of bishops and encourage local adaptations and initiatives.

In all three struggles, both sides claimed to be interested chiefly in the church's proper and effective response to contemporary needs and challenges. They differed sharply in the identification of those needs and challenges and so, necessarily, in what the church's *aggiornamento* must entail. But in the two years of the Council's preparation, on each of these three points it was the defenders of the status quo who prevailed.

The dramatic character of the Council, therefore, particularly in its first session, lay in the fact that fortunes were reversed in less than two months. The defenders of the status quo were roundly defeated by the assembled bishops. The Council accepted in principle a reform of the liturgy that would be quite thoroughgoing and profound. The classically articulated texts prepared by the Theological Commission were severely criticized and in effect discarded as models of what the Council should say and how it should say it. And the men who had dominated the preparation of the Council gave way to a new group of leaders who emerged from the ranks of the proponents of greater change in the church. All these decisive changes were ratified between the first two sessions when Pope Paul VI assumed the papacy and the direction of the Council.

These reversals were so sudden that it is not surprising that they were widely interpreted as something like a *coup d'église*. Throughout the Council the majority of bishops were "progressive," the minority "conservative," and the last three sessions of the Council confirmed the decisions made at the first session. Still today, the best way to approach the conflict that defined the conciliar drama is by comparing what Vatican II would have said or done if it had simply rubber-stamped the official texts prepared for it with what it actually did and said in its sixteen documents. The contrast is dramatic.

When the conciliar reforms began to be implemented, and when the spirit of reform began to spread far beyond officially authorized changes, it was natural that the conflicts would continue. Within the first decade after the Council's close in 1965, numerous books and articles appeared with titles indicating that something more than "reform" was underway. Many of the changes introduced, both official and unofficial, were presented as implications of the Council. Even the official reforms were often urged on the people by appeals and explanations that disparaged the pre-conciliar church: "We're going to treat you like adults, not children, from now on." Astonishingly rapid and superficial reviews of church history were not uncommon, as when people spoke of the end of the Counter-Reformation, of Tridentine Catholicism, or of the Constantinian era.[6]

Not surprisingly, similar claims were often made in support of changes that were not officially authorized. (One hopes that an example cited by an elderly nun was not too common: A priest held a rosary in his hands in the pulpit, told the people: "You don't have to say this anymore," and broke the rosary, scattering the beads on the floor.) When no explicit basis for a change could be found in the conciliar documents, an appeal was often made to "the spirit of the Council," that is, either to what the Council's actual achievements pointed toward or to what the Council "would have done" had it not been frustrated by an intransigent minority.

It was not long after the Council closed that "the spirit of Vatican II" began to be invoked in order to relativize the Council itself, as at a meeting of Concilium in 1970, which launched an appeal to go "beyond Vatican II for the sake of Vatican II." A year earlier, a defense of dissenters from *Humanae Vitae* gave a good expression of the ideas behind this slogan. Vatican II was said to have wrought a "revolution," to have marked "the end of an ecclesiological era and the inauguration of a new one." But now, only four years after it closed, the Council's documents are said to have been "dated" on the first day after solemn promulgation. Theologians cannot be content with "a rote memorization of, and literalist conformity to, the conciliar teachings and directives." To require theologians to refer only to "the letter" of Vatican II, these liberal theologians argued, would run the danger that "the *spirit* of Vatican II might be ignored." Vatican II's teachings have to be recognized for what they are: "formulations which express, for the most part, the maximum capacity of that time but which do not preclude future, on-going developments beyond the categories of Vatican II itself."[7]

If the assumptions behind the "liberal" presentation of Vatican II's work were resisted during the Council itself, conservative opposition to them increased as the church began to change after it closed. The titles of many books published in the decades since the Council include words such as *crisis, decomposition, decay,* and *apostasy;* the authors employ metaphors such as madness, betrayal, and desolation.[8] For the authors of such works, the drama of Vatican II was a trauma.

The "Naive Optimism" of Vatican II

The various renderings of the Council make it difficult to know precisely what is meant by the phrase "Vatican II," which is often used by both liberals and conservatives as a mantra. In a narrow sense, the term refers to an event that occurred between 1962 and 1965 and to the sixteen documents it produced. A broader sense includes the officially approved reforms meant to implement the Council's decrees, and a still wider sense includes also the unofficial reforms and the impact on the church of both sets of changes. When "the spirit of the Council" is invoked, however, things become so broad as to be nebulous. What precisely is meant by the term *Vatican II* is one of the chief problems faced by any effort to interpret and evaluate the Council today.

One might consider the case of Michael Novak, the American Catholic intellectual who wrote a very good and sympathetic book on the second session of the Council.[9] Twenty years later, however, he was moved, one suspects not simply by his ideological pilgrimage but also by postconciliar developments, to make the following extraordinary claim:

> The very meaning of Catholicism as a coherent people with a coherent vision has been threatened. What the barbarian invasions, centuries of primitive village life [*sic*], medieval plagues and disease, wars, revolutions, heresies and schisms had failed to do, the Second Vatican Council succeeded in doing. It set in motion both positive forces and forces that squandered the inheritance of the church. It set aside many proven methods and traditions. It fostered some experiments that have worked and some that decidedly have not.[10]

The last three sentences in this quotation contain qualifications that make the indefensible generality of the main sentence all the more remarkable. "The Second Vatican Council" in that sentence does not, it seems, refer to the actual Council and its sixteen official texts but to what was made of it in the postconciliar period.

The example of Novak points up the relationship between one's interpretations of the Council and one's judgments about the church's relationship to the modern world. Here the criticism, which comes from both left and right on the ideological spectrum, is that the Council's attitude toward the modern world, particularly in *Gaudium et Spes* (the Pastoral Constitution on the Church in the Modern World), displayed a "naive optimism." From the left the criticism is that the Council worked within a framework defined largely by the challenges and problems of the encounter with the liberal modernity of the Northern Hemisphere. The "modern world," in the singular, was taken to mean the world that liberalism had created, and so eager was the Council to show that the church could have something to say to it and something to learn from it that it failed to address the failures of liberal modernity, in particular the price at which it achieved its progress, a price paid by the exploited classes and countries of the world. This criticism is often found among representatives of political theology and of liberation theology.

Criticism of the Council's naive optimism can also be found in people quite opposed to such orientations. Joseph Ratzinger's development on this issue is instructive. As early as 1966, Ratzinger was arguing that the Council failed to stress sufficiently that between the world and the church there must always be a passage through the Cross. "An orientation of the

Church towards the world which would mean a turning away from the Cross would lead not to a renewal of the Church but to its decline and eventual decay." If Ratzinger stops short here of attributing this view to the Council itself, he describes Pope John's vision as "a theology of hope which sometimes seems to border on naive optimism."[11] By 1975 Ratzinger was saying:

> The text [Gaudium et Spes] and, even more, the deliberations from which it evolved breathe an astonishing optimism. Nothing seems impossible if humanity and church work together. The attitude of critical reserve toward the forces that have left their imprint on the modern world is to be replaced by a resolute coming to terms with their movement. The affirmation of the present that was sounded in Pope John XXIII's address at the opening of the Council is carried to its logical conclusion; solidarity with today seems to be the pledge of a new tomorrow.[12]

Finally, in his famous 1984 interview, Ratzinger was attributing the breakdown within the church not only to "latent polemical and centrifugal forces" therein but also, outside the church, "to the confrontation with a cultural revolution in the West: the success of the upper middle class, the new 'tertiary bourgeoisie,' with its liberal-radical ideology of an individualistic, rationalistic and hedonistic stamp."[13] This criticism is now fairly widespread and played an important role in the discussions and even in the final report of the extraordinary session of the Synod of Bishops in 1985.

Opposition to *Dignitatis Humanae*

"Naive optimism" is too mild a criticism of the Council for others who consider its chief fault to be its capitulation to the liberal assumptions of modernity. This critique characterized Archbishop Marcel Lefebvre's movement and groups even more extreme than his (see below), and it is spreading among some American Catholics.

For these critics, the most questionable conciliar document has always been Vatican II's Declaration on Religious Freedom (*Dignitatis Humanae*). In it, they believe, the Council abandoned the constant teaching of modern popes, particularly their condemnation of religious freedom and endorsement of the ideal of the Catholic confessional state. The basic reason why the Council must be rejected is that it reversed the attitudes and strategy that had characterized the church since the Renaissance and Reformation and particularly since the French Revolution. Capitulating to the very liberalism the church had always and correctly opposed, it introduced into the church the principles of the French Revolution:

> Liberty is the religious liberty we spoke of above, which gives error rights. Equality is collegiality with its destruction of personal authority, of the authority of God, the pope, the bishops; it is the law of numbers. Fraternity, finally, is represented by ecumenism.
>
> Through these three words the revolutionary ideology of 1789 has become the Law and the Prophets. The Modernists have achieved what they wanted.[14]

For Lefebvre the internal corruption of the church since the Council was a natural consequence of its surrender to the external enemy:

> All the popes have refused the Church's marriage with the Revolution, an adulterous union from which can come only bastards. The rite of the New Mass is a bastard rite, the sacraments are bastard sacraments: we no longer know if these sacraments give grace or do not give grace. The priests who come out of the seminaries are bastard priests; they do not know who they are; they do not know that they were made to go up to the altar, to offer the sacrifice of Our Lord Jesus Christ, and to give Jesus Christ to souls.[15]

For Lefebvre, the Council itself must be blamed for turning away from certain political alliances the church had made in opposition both to liberalism and to socialism. Opposed to both these classic enemies, Lefebvre regretted the disappearance of the confessional Catholic state as well as the Council's refusal formally and explicitly to condemn communism.[16]

Most American Catholics have taken pride in *Dignitatis Humanae,* not only because of the insistence of their bishops that the Council address the issue of religious freedom, but also because of John Courtney Murray's role in its elaboration. It was not the French but the American Revolution that was of primary importance to them, and they saw in the conciliar text a vindication of Murray's argument that the American political experiment differed from the European and could be shown to be compatible with Catholic doctrine on church and state because it was not based on or justified by the secularist ideology that informed the French experience in particular. Lefebvre's obsession with "the principles of 1789" seemed then foreign to American Catholic sensibilities.

Recently, however, one notes a tendency on the part of some American Catholics to call this once-common view into question. There is the relatively mild form of those who dispute Murray's reading both of the classic

Catholic teaching and of the American experiment and thus his argument for their compatibility. More radical is the suggestion that *Dignitatis Humanae* did not in fact alter Catholic teaching and strategy at all. Most radical is the argument that the American political experiment is in fact incompatible with Catholic teaching because it is contrary to the ideal of the Catholic confessional state.[17]

On this issue of the church's relation to the modern world, then, Catholics differ as widely as they do with regard to matters internal to the church. Critiques of the Council's response to modernity come from both ends of the political spectrum. At the fairly moderate center are those who accept the Council precisely as a long-overdue but not uncritical accommodation to liberal modernity, in both its economic and political aspects, a stance that needs to be followed up and defended against both rightist and leftist critics of the liberal experiment. In the United States, for example, these critics unite in arguing that people such as Richard Neuhaus, Michael Novak, and George Weigel make an idol of the American economic and political experiment. The continuing debate over the validity and success of John Courtney Murray's project has pertinence here.

Researchers should be alert to the connections between political orientations and attitudes toward the Council. On both right and left the political orientation often determines how people view the state of the church.[18] Whatever *odium theologicum* still rankles today, one sometimes thinks, is mainly driven by *odium politicum*.

The spectrum of attitudes of conservative Catholic groups toward the Council is as broad on the right as it is on the left, and it is not helpful to lump them all under a single rubric. Criticisms of "the Council" may be motivated by a simple restorationist desire to return to the attitudes and strategies of Gregory XVI, Pius IX, and Pius X, by concern about the decline of favorite devotions, by disdain for the banality of liturgical translations or practices, by perceived misinterpretations of the conciliar texts, or by fear that the church is losing a sense of its distinctive identity and contribution. Theological and social scientific interpretation of conservative criticisms of "the Council" will have to be alert to such differences. Nevertheless, two broad categories suggest themselves: those who reject the Council altogether, and those who object to the ways in which the conciliar documents have been implemented.

Rejection of the Council

At what one hopes is the extreme are the sedevacantists, people who judge the Second Vatican Council to have so departed from the tradition as to have taught heresy. By their reasoning, the popes who have approved and endorsed its teachings are heretics. In promulgating the documents of the Council, that is, Paul VI ceased formally to be pope. His subsequent acts being therefore invalid—including his appointments of cardinals and his rules for future papal elections—the conclaves that elected his two successors were also invalid. The present pope, in addition, has himself ratified Vatican II and *Dignitatis Humanae* and therefore forfeited any valid claim to the papacy. The Apostolic See, therefore, is vacant, and pretenders to it need not, indeed must not, be obeyed.[19]

A variation on this theme is that a massive and satanic fraud was perpetrated on the church under Pope Paul VI. The real pope was held a prisoner somewhere in the Vatican, while an actor, who had had a not altogether successful plastic surgery (one ear was poorly done, and besides, his voice gave him away), posed as Montini. The source of this "information" is unclear. Archbishop Lefebvre said it came from a person possessed by the devil,[20] but Veronica Leuken claims to have received it during an apparition of the Blessed Virgin at Bayside on September 27, 1975.[21] A milder version of this theory has it that Paul VI was not responsible for his actions, because he was a drugged prisoner of a curial cabal.

Although he had no great love of Paul VI, who, he said, "caused more damage to the church than the Revolution of 1789,"[22] Lefebvre was not willing to go quite that far. The last two versions he found too simplistic because they overlooked Paul VI's liberal sympathies. He stopped just short of endorsing the sedevacantists' argument, wondering whether in thirty years there might be discovered "statements of this pope that are absolutely contrary to the church's tradition."[23]

As William Dinges notes in chapter 10 of this volume, the sedevacantists do not appear to have a great following in the United States. Yet Lefebvre's followers continue to make the case that the Council has produced a disaster for the church. Michael Davies's book on the Council, which made Lefebvre a hero, ended with these lines: "If any attempt is to be made to assess the cost of the Council in spiritual terms then all that can be done is to adapt the words of Tacitus and state: 'When they create a wilderness they call it a renewal.'"[24] In another book, Davies echoes Lefebvre's argument that Vatican II betrayed classic doctrine on church and state.[25]

In the Bayside apparitions and in other extreme American rejections of the Council, the motivation appears to be primarily the spread of abuses in the church. A list of these was supplied in a publication called *The Apostasy* in 1974:

> We want the Catholic Mass and the priests of God, not the "Meal" and the updated "Presidents." We want the organ and the Gregorian

Chant, not folk songs and guitars. We want the House of God, not houses where young people fondle each other at the "kiss of peace." We want adoration and reverence. We believe in the Gospel, not in Godspell; we adore Christ the Lord, not Jesus Superstar. We want our nuns to be true spouses of Christ, humble in appearance, their eyes cast down, and fully covered; not mini-skirted hussies with permed hair, lipstick, shapely calves, and see-through blouses. And we want our priests to wear the Roman collar and the cassock, not a tie with a suit. We want to be able to address them as "Father," not as "Fred" and "Bill."[26]

The same publication offered its readers a "Catechism of Current Catholicism," written by its theological advisor, in order to trace such abuses to their source in Vatican II. The postconciliar crisis is described as the infiltration of the church by her enemies: modernists, Communists, Freemasons, and, "behind them all," Zionists.[27] Their aim is to destroy her traditions, particularly of worship. They infiltrated the church at Vatican II, where "liberal bishops, indoctrinated by their traitorous theologians . . . voted for 'modernizing' the Church *(aggiornamento)* under the pretext of 'Ecumenism.'" Popes John XXIII and Paul VI were unwitting parties to this movement. Neither papal nor a general Council's infallibility is compromised, however, since Vatican II avoided solemn definitions. Christ remains present to his church, but he did not promise that the church would always prosper; in fact, he foretold "a great apostasy to precede Antichrist and the Second Coming of Our Lord." After the Council, furthermore, the validity of some sacraments is doubtful because of faulty vernacular translations, particularly of the words of consecration in the Mass. Under these circumstances, Catholics must remain faithful to the ancient tradition, repent, say the rosary daily, and consecrate themselves to the Immaculate Heart of Mary. "In a word," the "Catechism" warns, "heed at last the message of Fatima."

The idea that popes and bishops were the unwitting dupes of modernist theologians is not uncommon among such conservative critics of the Council. For this view many rely on their own reading of *The Rhine Flows into the Tiber,* a history of the Council written by Ralph Wiltgen, a Divine Word priest with ties to the "Coetus Internationalis Patrum," a group of conciliar bishops organized by Lefebvre and others and an implacable foe of any concessions to collegiality, ecumenism, or religious freedom. Wiltgen's thesis is that what the Council became and did was in large part due to the activities of bishops and experts from Germany, Austria, Switzerland, France, Holland, and Belgium. In itself this is an unexceptionable historical thesis, but, as Wiltgen acknowledged in a preface to a reprinting, it has been used by critics of Vatican II, from whom he seems to wish to distance himself, "who charge that the Council's 16 documents have been vitiated, even invalidated by pressure groups."[28]

The nondogmatic character of Vatican II is another point emphasized by critics of the Council who stop just short of rejecting it entirely. Because the Council deliberately abstained from issuing any formal condemnations of heresies and from making dogmatic definitions, the conciliar positions with which they disagree can be dismissed on the grounds that Vatican II claimed only "pastoral" authority. The Catholic doctrine of the infallibility of "doctrinal" councils is thus left intact. This helps to explain Lefebvre's fury when Paul VI said that Vatican II was as important a council as Nicaea and when Cardinal Ratzinger insisted that its authority equals that of Trent and Vatican I. The critics who use the Council's deliberately pastoral character in order to escape its authority reflect an understanding of *pastoral* that was defended by a minority at the Council. This minority distinguished the "pastoral" from the "dogmatic" and even from the "doctrinal"; they understood it to mean little more than the practical applications which bishops and priests would make of the dogmatic decisions that are the proper work of the Council itself. The conciliar majority did not accept this disjunction and attempted a presentation of the faith that was at once doctrinal and pastoral, that is, both faithful to the Gospel and expressed in a way that can be understood and appreciated by contemporaries. Ironically, the heirs of the opponents of a "pastoral" Council now stress this characteristic in order to escape its authority.

Defenders of the "Real" Council against the "Para-Council"

Much closer to the center of the conservative Catholic spectrum are those who defend the Council's documents and reforms but insist that Vatican II must be carefully distinguished from the mythological Council imagined by some conservatives and zealously promoted by progressives. Historian James Hitchcock was one of the first American Catholics to set out this position. In a book published in 1971, he argued that Vatican II had in fact met almost all of the expectations entertained by liberal Catholics in the early 1960s. "There is no honest way of calling the Council a failure," he wrote.[29] Yet within five years of the Council's close, "radical" Catholics were regarding it as at best a starting point, now quite inadequate, for sets of reforms that Hitchcock believed posed threats to the integrity and vitality of Catholic Christianity. He spoke of "the failure of *aggiornamento*" and placed blame on both "rigid reactionaries" especially in the hierarchy, "who never believed in reform and did little to implement it," and "radical innovators with little commitment to historic Catholicism who nonetheless had a disproportionate influence in the reform movement." Naturally, he concluded, "these two extremes have constantly fed on each other, each serving as a bogey which gives the other a certain credibility."[30]

In this and a subsequent book (1979), Hitchcock concentrated his attention on the "radical innovators." A regular theme in his survey of the postconciliar crisis of identity in the church is the contrast between what the Council actually said and what was being advocated by the radicals. He identified one of their typical modes of argument:

> Much innovation in the Church has been legitimized in the following manner: (1) appeals to the decrees of Vatican II. When certain of these decrees are discovered to be rather conservative, this shifts to (2) appeals to the "spirit" of Vatican II, which did not get embodied in all the decrees, or to (3) the "spirit of Pope John," whose intentions were so radical that the Council did not begin to probe them. When faced with the traditionalism of this Pope on many questions (see *The Journal of a Soul*), refuge can be sought in (4) Scripture, whose authority exceeds that of all popes and councils. When inconvenient passages about hell or physical resurrection are brought forward, these are explained as peculiarities of the Semitic mind and the burden is shifted to (5) the needs and beliefs of modern man.[31]

The disregard of the actual texts of the Council "in favor of an amorphous 'spirit of Vatican II' which can be made to mean anything anyone wants it to mean" is a regular theme in Hitchcock's second book. "Virtually every ecumenical council has been followed by a crisis, usually stemming from the refusal of a major segment of the Church to accept its decrees," he contends. "The Second Vatican Council is perhaps the first council to be followed by a crisis in which its teachings have been distorted into meanings contrary to their original intention."[32]

Hitchcock's view, echoed in North America by George A. Kelly and Anne Roche Muggeridge, is shared by some of the Europeans who played important roles in the Council. Henri de Lubac, for example, was one of the theologians who helped prepare the Council's escape from the narrow theological and ecclesiological system that prevailed in Rome particularly during the last decade of the pontificate of Pius XII.[33] Although de Lubac was a member of the Preparatory Theological Commission, he found himself to be a target of one of its decrees. He helped convince bishops at the first session of the Council that the texts prepared by that commission needed to be radically redrawn. By the end of the Council, however, de Lubac began to have doubts about the interpretation and direction some bishops and experts were attempting to give to the Council. Subsequent events only confirmed de Lubac's concern, and in 1968 he gave a speech at St. Louis University in which he noted several widespread distortions of the Council. He later found a term for the phenomenon, by contrasting "the Council and the para-Council."[34]

By the "para-Council" de Lubac meant what the Council *should have said,* according to its liberal interpreters. According to him, the proponents of this para-Council sought a change in the church that involved not simply *aggiornamento* but "mutation," a difference "not of degree but of nature." After the Council, de Lubac lamented, the liberals became the darlings of the media, through which they vigorously promoted their para-Council, "which often deserved the name of 'anti-Council.'" The para-Council's advocates, de Lubac charged, dismiss as an internal contradiction any actual conciliar statement that does not support their desired program of reform. They reject the Council's efforts at synthesis as political compromises, which must be exposed if one wishes to get at the Council's "true" meaning. The bishops at Vatican II, whose deep "intuitions" were inhibited by "old habits of thought," articulated this "true" meaning imperfectly, thereby leaving the full task to theologians. The bishops were timid as well as inarticulate: they feared that the Christian people were not yet ready for great leaps forward. In addition, the conciliar documents bear the marks of the decade in which they were written and should not be expected to be pertinent in all particulars to later moments of a rapidly changing history. According to the paraconciliarists, de Lubac complained, the enduring validity of the Council is "not found in the contents of the documents, in the letter, but is entirely contained in its orientation, its spirit." It was thus an "open" Council, inspired by a spirit of renewal with unlimited applications.

De Lubac noted that the para-Council had particularly distorted *Gaudium et Spes* in favor of a radical view of the church expressed in several "nebulous slogans." To move from a centuries-long infancy to adulthood, the church must undergo a "radical revolution" and give up the idea that she is "the depositary of the truth." The para-Council demands that she become secularized, democratize her structures, and downplay her interior life. De Lubac is perhaps most distressed by para-Council interpretations of the actual Council that portray it as a triumph of progress over tradition. He insists that the Council's achievements, so far from being a rejection of tradition, were made possible by the recovery of the great tradition effected by decades of scholarship before the

Council. What the Council rejected was the quite modern ecclesiastical and theological system that was confused with tradition in the last two centuries. Mistaken interpretations of the Council reflect a disdain for tradition that leaves the church with no independent basis on which to confront the modern world, whose lead and agenda it is thus forced to follow wherever these may go. The para-Council's near-monopoly on journalistic accounts of the Council, de Lubac argued, has rightly led many Catholics to oppose the Council itself.

Cardinal Ratzinger agrees with much of de Lubac's analysis of the postconciliar situation, but adds an interesting question which serves to ground a typology of interpretions of the Council: Which conciliar texts should be hermeneutically central? Ratzinger favors the Constitutions on the Liturgy, on the Church, and on Divine Revelation, texts in which the return to the sources had the most effect and which must serve as the solid doctrinal center to which all the other texts, especially those concerned with the church's relation to the world, must always be referred. To this view he contrasts an interpretation that sees an arrow of progress that starts from the retrograde texts officially proposed for the Council's deliberations, moves upward in the dramatic repudiation of those drafts at the first session, and ascends still higher in the doctrinal texts on the liturgy, the church, and divine revelation. But since these texts were so influenced by the situation from which the Council was trying to free the church, the arrow streaks higher toward the pinnacle of the conciliar achievement in the texts that discuss the church's relation to the world, particularly the Constitution on the Church in the Modern World and the Declarations on Non-Christian Religions and on Religious Freedom. The conciliar arrow continued its flight, however, and after the Council produced political theology and the various forms of liberation theology. On this view, in other words, the secret of the Council's achievement is to be found in an epochal movement, for which the texts that reflect the return to the sources represent only an early stage, toward a new engagement with the world, one that must be renewed ever again, in accordance with new demands and challenges.[35]

It is important not to confuse, as a careless journalism often does, de Lubac's or Ratzinger's interpretations of the Council with those that simply reject Vatican II. The latter often read the Council as having been hijacked during its course by liberal bishops and theologians; the former also seem to think the Council was hijacked, but after the fact and by those who quite misrepresented what it actually accomplished. Whether one agrees with this assessment or not, one must certainly acknowledge that it differs from that of a Lefebvre, as the archbishop finally had to admit when he led his people into schism. For Lefebvre, the church needs to be liberated from Vatican II; for de Lubac and Ratzinger, the church needs to be liberated from the distortion that has often been confused with the Council, and the best way to accomplish this is a return to the real Council and its real spirit.

This interpretation of the Council thus represents a third position between the traditionalists' rejection of the Council and a certain progressive interpretation of it as the "new Pentecost," when the Spirit was again allowed to breathe life into the dry bones of preconciliar Catholicism. This middle position might be called a "reformist" interpretation because of its insistence that the popes and bishops never wished for a revolution to produce a new church, but a spiritual renewal and pastoral reform of the church. This judgment of conciliar intentions is surely correct: the popes and bishops did not anticipate, much less desire, what in many ways became, at least in certain areas of the world, something like a revolution in everyday Catholicism. And there is certainly a need to rescue the "genuine" Council from the mythologized event that has been and still is invoked on behalf of changes that never entered the minds of the conciliar members.

On the other hand, it is not clear that the question of the causality of the Council can be answered simply by examining the intentions of the popes and bishops. Choices and actions often have consequences never intended by their authors. De Lubac and Ratzinger give insufficient attention to the fact that what theologically and canonically might be mere reform can, at least in certain circumstances, be psychologically and sociologically quite revolutionary. I have argued elsewhere that in fact the Council itself took certain steps that, whatever the intentions of the bishops and popes, were revolutionary in their potential consequences. Among these choices were the more positive or at least more nuanced attitude toward the modern world, the call to update and reform the church, and the renewed emphasis on the local church.[36]

Others who were at least as deeply involved in the work of the Council as were de Lubac and Ratzinger do not share their views either of the Council's achievement or of the postconciliar period. Differences existed among the progressive theologians at the Council, differences that were kept submerged at the beginning of Vatican II, when it was important to maintain a common front against the defenders of the preconciliar system. The differences began to become visible, particularly in the last session of the Council, when the system had been defeated and it was now necessary to say and to decide what should take its place. (Perhaps one might compare this to what happened with Solidarnösc in Poland, united against the entrenched system, fractured when freedom came.) Disagreements surfaced, for example, over the texts on the church's relation to the world, not simply because the major doctrinal texts had already been promulgated, but chiefly because a suspicious and condemnatory attitude toward the modern world had largely inspired the preconciliar system and the Catholic identity it promoted and defended, and because major differences in method distinguished even theologians who shared a desire to overcome that modern system by a recovery of the tradition in order to promote the church's redemptive role in the modern world. One of Joseph Ratzinger's earliest assessments of the Council included precisely the contrast between incarnational and eschatological views of the church's relation to the world and made clear his own preference for the latter.[37]

Conclusion

Any study of the Catholic right today must include the effort to locate its various expressions in the context, at least, of the history of the church over the last fifty years: the preconciliar church, the Council itself, and the postconciliar period. Ideally the various expressions would be seen also against the backdrop of a larger history of at least 150 years, during which the church's self-realization was inextricably linked to the great economic, social, political, and cultural developments of modern history. Close study of the debates that marked the preparation of the Council, of the drama of its crucial first session, and of the discussions that produced its documents reveals that the real confrontation concerned less differences in doctrine and practice in themselves than opposed positions on the attitudes and strategies the Catholic Church had assumed toward the principles and movements that had inspired and shaped the modern world. It was the latter positions, I believe, that not only explain in good part the differences on matters of emphasis and language in doctrine and on questions of practice (e.g., on the vernacular in the liturgy) but also illumine the differences among the "progressive" majority which were largely hidden during the Council itself but whose reappearance in the postconciliar period complicates the "map" of contemporary Catholicism.

NOTES

1. James Hitchcock, *Catholicism and Modernity: Confrontation or Capitulation* (New York: Seabury Press, 1979), p. 75.

2. Emile Poulat, *Une Eglise ébranlée: Changement, conflit et continuité de Pie XII à Jean Paul II* (Paris: Casterman, 1980), p. 41.

3. The Council's Constitution on the Sacred Liturgy set out basic principles for reform but left their implementation to a postconciliar commission. Pope Paul VI gave this body considerable latitude for its work, and the extent and character of the reforms it introduced—e.g., the

full use of the vernacular, the reform of the Mass, the creation of new eucharistic prayers, etc.—have been read by many postconciliar groups as a betrayal of the Council itself.

An example of how criticism of one postconciliar development can lead to an indictment of the Council itself is provided by "The Truth about Communion in the Hand," which appeared in the *Crying in the Wilderness Newsletter,* Autumn 1993: "Though Communion in the hand was not mandated by the Second Vatican Council, what WAS 'canonized' by Vatican II was 'Ecumenism'— this false spirit of counterfeit unity that had been previously condemned by the Church . . . —this movement of Catholics becoming more buddy-buddy and huggy-huggy with other religions, and especially with Protestants. . . . The ecumenical spirit became the primary formative principle in the whole range of the new liturgical forms established since the Council. This is why the new liturgy so closely resembles a Protestant service."

4. Joseph A. Komonchak, "The Local Realization of the Church," in G. Alberigo, J. P. Jossua, and J. A. Komonchak, eds., *The Reception of Vatican II* (Washington: CUA Press, 1987), pp. 77–90.

5. One thinks of First Friday and First Saturday devotions, the Infant of Prague, Christ the King, the Miraculous Medal, Forty Hours, etc.

6. To cite three examples from a book on Catholic radicals in the late 1960s: "The kids and I felt that for the first time in a thousand years we were building community around the altar" (quoting D. Berrigan). "The Catholic Church can be compared to a zoo of wild beasts, held in captivity for over a millennium, whose bars Pope John removed." "From the time of the French Revolution the Church had lived in political exile, doling out medicine for the metaphysical blues and for individual salvation." See Francine du Plessix Gray, *Divine Disobedience: Profiles in Catholic Radicalism* (New York: Vintage Books, 1972), pp. 73, 94, 101.

7. Charles E. Curran et al., *Dissent in and for the Church: Theologians and Humanae Vitae* (New York: Sheed and Ward, 1969), pp. 100–101.

8. See Louis Bouyer, *The Decomposition of Catholicism* (Chicago: Franciscan Herald Press, 1969); Dietrich Von Hildebrand, *Trojan Horse in the City of God* (Chicago: Franciscan Herald Press, 1967); Louis Coache, *Vers l'apostasie générale* (Paris: La Table ronde, 1969); Philippe Brunetière, *L'Eglise en panique* (Paris: Desclée, 1970); Bernard Fay, *L'Eglise de Judas* (Paris: Plon, 1970); Renaud Dulong, *Une église cassée* (Paris: Editions economie et humanisme, 1971); John Eppstein, *Has the Catholic Church Gone Mad?* (New Rochelle, N.Y.: Arlington House, 1971); L. Francis Hardy, *L'Eglise trahie* (Paris: Nouvelles editions latines, 1972); Jacques Ploncard d'Assac, *L'Eglise occupée* (Vouille: Diffusion de la pensée française, 1975); Joseph Patrick James McGaughan, *Vatican II: A Satanic Victory* (Hicksville, N.Y.: Exposition Press, 1980); Ralph Martin, *The Crisis of Truth* (Ann Arbor, Mich: Servant Books, 1982); Francesco Spadafora, *La tradizione contro il Concilio* (Rome: Volpe, 1989); Anne Roche Muggeridge, *The Desolate City: Revolution in the Catholic Church* (San Francisco: Harper and Row, 1986).

9. Michael Novak, *The Open Church: Vatican II, Act II* (New York: Macmillan, 1964).

10. Michael Novak, *Confession of a Catholic* (San Francisco: Harper and Row, 1983), p. 8.

11. Joseph Ratzinger, "Catholicism after the Council," *The Furrow* 18 (1967): 17–18.

12. Joseph Ratzinger, *Principles of Catholic Theology: Building Stones for a Fundamental Theology* (San Francisco: Ignatius Press, 1987), pp. 380–81.

13. Joseph Ratzinger, *The Ratzinger Report: An Exclusive Interview on the State of the Church* (San Francisco: Ignatius Press, 1985), p. 30.

14. Lefebvre's last book (*Lettre ouverte aux catholiques perplexes* [Paris: Michel, 1985], p. 132) borrowed heavily from an analysis of liberalism prepared in 1924 for a meeting sponsored by the Apostolic League for the Return of Nations to the Christian Social Order. See A. Roussel, *Liberalisme et catholicisme. Rapports présentés à la "Semaine Catholique" en Février 1926 sous les auspices de la Ligue Apostolique, pour le retour des Nations à l'ordre social chrétien* (Paris: Aux Bureaux de la "Lingue Apostolique," 1926.

15. Lefebvre, *Lettre ouverte aux catholiques perplexes,* p. 148.

16. In a number of circles, the rumor continues to be believed that Pope John XXIII made a deal with Soviet authorities: if they allowed the Russian Orthodox Church to send observers to

the Council, he would make sure that the Council did not condemn communism. This view is regularly repeated in North America by the leader of the *Fatima Crusader.*

17. See Solange Hertz, *The Star-Spangled Heresy* (Santa Monica: Veritas Press, 1993); Michael Davies, *The Second Vatican Council and Religious Liberty* (Long Prairie, Minn.: Neumann Press, 1993); and Donald J. D'Elia and Stephen M. Krasen, eds., *We Hold These Truths and More: Further Catholic Reflections on the American Proposition—The Thought of Fr. John Courtney Murray and Its Relevance Today* (Steubenville: Franciscan University Press, 1993).

18. Hitchcock, *Catholicism and Modernity,* pp. 150–79.

19. See M. L. Guérard des Lauriers, "Le Siège apostolique est-il vacant?" *Cahiers de Cassiciacum* 1 (Nice: Association Saint-Herménégilde, 1989): 5–111. St. Hermenegilde was chosen as sponsor of the association that publishes this journal because in 586 she was decapitated for refusing to receive communion from an Arian bishop. Guérard des Lauriers was a brilliant Dominican priest, with a doctorate in mathematics, who taught at Le Saulchoir for many years and then at the Lateran University in Rome. An opponent of "the new theology" in the mid-1940s, he became so convinced of the argument he advanced in this cahier that he had himself ordained a bishop by a schismatic bishop in Spain.

20. Marcel Lefebvre, *Ils l'ont découronné. Du liberalisme á l'apostasie: La tragédie conciliaire* (Escurolle: Ed. Fideliter, 1987), p. 224.

21. See *Michael Fighting,* October–December 1975, which quotes the Virgin as telling the seeress that this was done so that Cardinals Casaroli, Benelli, and Villot, who also kept the pope drugged, could take over the papacy. Our Lady also speaks of photographs, and on the back page of the sheet appear three photographs, one of Paul VI, the other two of the impostor. Whoever sent this to me was kind enough to circle the right ear, apparently to indicate where the surgeon's skill had failed him.

22. Lefebvre, *Lettre ouverte aux catholiques perplexes,* p. 198.

23. Lefebvre, *Ils l'ont découronné,* pp. 223–24.

24. Michael Davies, *Pope John's Council* (New Rochell, N.Y.: Arlington House, 1977), p. 259.

25. Davies, *The Second Vatican Council and Religious Liberty.*

26. "An Open Letter to the Bishops," *The Apostasy,* September 1974, p. 13. This mimeographed newsletter, edited in Valley Cottage, New York, by John B. Fragale, ceased publication with this issue, apparently affiliating itself from then on with the Orthodox Roman Catholic Movement.

27. The hoary theme of a Jewish-Masonic conspiracy, much loved by intransigent modern Catholics, appears often in traditionalist Catholic circles. The notorious anti-Semitic work published during the Council by the pseudonymous Maurice Pinay, *The Plot against the Church* (Los Angeles: St. Anthony Press, 1967, 1982), is still in print and regularly offered for sale in advertisements in their literature.

28. Ralph M. Wiltgen, *The Rhine Flows into the Tiber: A History of Vatican II* (Rockford, Ill.: TAN Books, 1985), p. 1.

29. James Hitchcock, *The Decline and Fall of Radical Catholicism* (Garden City, N.Y.: Image Books, 1972), p. 24.

30. Ibid., p. 29.

31. Ibid., pp. 61–62.

32. Hitchcock, *Catholicism and Modernity,* pp. 28, 33; see also pp. 64, 75–76, 181, 228.

33. Henri de Lubac, *At the Service of the Church* (San Francisco: Ignatius Press, 1993).

34. Henri de Lubac, *A Brief Catechesis on Nature and Grace* (San Francisco: Ignatius Press, 1984), pp. 235–60.

35. Joseph Ratzinger, *Principles of Catholic Theology: Building Stones for a Fundamental Theology* (San Francisco: Ignatius Press, 1987), pp. 378–79, 390.

36. Joseph A. Komonchak, "Interpreting the Second Vatican Council," *Landas: Journal of Loyola School of Theology* 1 (1987): 81–90.

37. Ratzinger, "Catholicism after the Council," pp. 3–23.

2

The Triumph of Americanism
Common Ground for U.S. Catholics in the Twentieth Century

R. SCOTT APPLEBY

"Conservative" American Catholics tend to be concerned, perhaps more than "liberal" Catholics, with preserving or defending Roman Catholic orthodoxy ("right belief"). The conservative contributors to this volume, for example, whether they see themselves as being "far right," "right," or "center-right" on an ideological map of contemporary Catholicism, all speak of a crisis in postconciliar Catholicism. They differ among themselves on the meaning and source of the crisis, but their concerns can be traced back to a sense that Catholics have lost, or are in the process of losing, a shared faith.

George Weigel, a neoconservative Catholic, laments what he and his colleagues see as a crisis of belief. Their concern is supported by polls showing that a majority of American Catholics no longer believe in such core doctrines as the real presence of Christ in the Eucharist.[1] Catholics United for the Faith, represented here by its vice-president, James Sullivan, sees the situation as rooted in a crisis of authority. CUF has, accordingly, focused its energies on stifling dissent from the authoritative teaching of the magisterium, and on promoting that teaching among the laity. At times, CUF seems to be addressing liberal or moderate bishops: act like bishops and enforce Roman teaching![2] Conservative American Catholic scholars, represented in these pages by James Hitchcock and Father Benedict Ashley, might argue that the crisis goes to the question of identity. According to this diagnosis, American Catholicism is losing its soul and will, because it has already lost its mind. Faith and discipline erode under the relentless pressure of American pluralism and voluntarism, a cultural setting in which Catholics, like other Americans, can and do choose and construct an identity from a plethora of possibilities. And Catholics became like other Americans, runs the argument, when Catholicism squandered its rich legacy of Thomistic thought, which was the source of its metaphysical, intellectual, and cultural distinctiveness in the United States.

While Vatican II is seen as the immediate catalyst of the contemporary crisis, its roots in this country go back to the turn-of-the-century controversy over Americanism and modernism. In that earlier crisis, the two heresies were woven together in a web of papal denunciations of the modern world. The pope who condemned Americanism in 1899, Leo XIII, had warned Catholics against embracing American-style pluralism and voluntarism as norms for the universal church (*Longinqua Oceani,* 1895). Pope Leo's critique of American society encompassed its economic doctrines as well; in *Rerum Novarum* (1891), the premier Catholic social encyclical that defended the "inviolable" human right to own private property (contra the socialists), the pope had also condemned unrestricted economic competition and the excesses of capitalism following from it. Among the debilitating products of unrestrained capitalism, in the pope's view, were the spiritual temptations it introduced into society. On a number of fronts, therefore, the United States seemed to pose a serious challenge to Roman Catholic teachings on society, state, and religion. Thus it is hardly surprising to discover that the Vatican theologians who penned Pope Pius X's 1907 condemnation of modernism saw "the synthesis of all heresies" as the theological expression of Americanism.[3]

For conservative Roman Catholics at the turn of the twentieth century, America was fast becoming the symbol and embodiment of the irreligious forces opposing the worldwide church and the orthodoxy it defended. (The reader who is familiar with contemporary church politics will note that this attitude is alive and well in the Vatican of the late twentieth century.) At the turn of the twentieth century, however, the Roman Catholic Church in the United States was still considered a mission church, a status reflecting its social organization in immigrant enclaves, and reinforcing its dependence on Rome. The conservative prelates and priests of the U.S. church were therefore quick to rely on Rome's authority to set the terms of the faith, define its boundaries, and enforce discipline. As American citizens, they were reluctant to criticize openly the principle of church-state separation, but they did support the condemnations of Americanism and modernism, and they did not presume to lecture Rome on the virtues of the American experiment in ordered democracy.[4]

Times have changed. An ultraconservative or traditionalist Catholic, someone such as the Lefebvrists profiled in chapter 10 by William Dinges, might look back over the course of "the American century" and make the following observations: Modernism was condemned, but returned—in the guise of the religious liberty, collegiality, and ecumenism (the *Liberté, Egalité,* and *Fraternité* of the French Revolution, according to Archbishop Lefebvre) that were elevated to the status of orthodoxy in the decrees of Vatican II. Liberal elites in the American church were instrumental in this triumph of modernism. Among other things, they helped to overturn the intellectual guardian of orthodoxy, neoscholastic Thomism, in favor of a confusing pluralism of theological method. Thus did the American and French liberals triumph—all the while embracing Americanism, an updated form of Gallicanism. As a result of their victory, the true church is in eclipse, preserved only by a sacred remnant.

What I find interesting about this critique is that it falls on deaf ears in the American Catholic Church of the 1990s, even among the majority of conservative and neoconservative Catholics. The outlook of the traditionalist—specifically, the linking of certain kinds of political philosophy and theological error—reflected the orthodox school of thought for much of the twentieth century. In the postconciliar era, however, most American Catholics, of the right as well as the left, balk at any suggestion that the foundational political principles of the United States contain heretical or even troubling theological implications for Catholics. Only the extremists of right and left, in fact, continue to agree with the proposition, taken for granted by a majority of American Catholics in the early decades of this century, that Roman Catholic and American visions of human nature and society are not easily reconciled, and may in some important regards be irreconcilable.

The shift in attitudes is important for understanding the landscape of conservative American Catholicism today. We are in an unprecedented situation in the sense that liberals and conservatives, despite their important differences and vehement disagreements, share a basic orientation and set of assumptions about the United States and its worthiness as a model for the Roman Catholic Church. The conservatives, as we shall see, tend to apply the lessons learned in two hundred–plus years of U.S. political and economic history to Roman Catholic social doctrine, while the liberals tend to apply Americanist insights to the ecclesiology, or internal governance, of the church itself. Nonetheless, the tacit agreement to lift up the American experiment as exemplary, even revelatory, is striking to the historian. Even the original Americanists did not go this far.

How did this state of affairs come to pass? And what are its implications for the Roman Catholic Church in the United States?

The answer to the first question lies in the decoupling of Americanism and modernism over the course of the twentieth century, and the consequent "liberation" of American Catholic public philosophy, social ethics, and theological self-understanding from the encompassing and well-integrated theological system of neoscholasticism.[5]

By the "decoupling" of Americanism and modernism, I mean that the basic convictions and tendencies associated with Americanism were acquitted of charges of guilt by association with modernism. The rehabilitation of Americanism—the renewal of American Catholic confidence in the orthodoxy of church-state separation, confessional pluralism, and religious voluntarism—occurred first within the American neo-Thomist revival (1920s–1950s) and then, definitively, in the collapse of the neoscholastic system (1960s). Some of the original Americanists, like those few American priests accused of modernism, had challenged neoscholasticism in its role as the exclusive philosophical and theological expression of Roman Catholic orthodoxy. Five decades passed, however, before other systems of thought actually threatened to displace neoscholasticism. Catholic intellectuals and officials whose careers fell between 1910 and 1960 (roughly, that is, between the condemnations of modernism and the reforms of Vatican II) guaranteed their orthodox credentials by avoiding theology and philosophy that was not "protected" under the canopy of neoscholasticism. It would not do, after all, for the American church to be cast continually under a shroud of suspicion.[6] From midcentury on, however, the vast majority of Catholics living in the United States saw no contradiction between what John Courtney Murray called "the American proposition,"[7] on the one hand, and their Catholic faith, on the other.

As long as neoscholasticism reigned supreme, internal discord over "orthodoxy" was not a pressing problem for the American church. When neoscholasticism collapsed around the time of the Council, however, the old fears of modernism arose again in some quarters, and ideological camps hardened as American Catholic intellectuals and activists jockeyed for position to lay claim to the historic Catholic legacy.[8]

On the map labeled "American Catholicism in the Twentieth Century," then, we see a building confidence in a public expression of Catholicism that embraces American ideals unapologetically if not uncritically. To borrow David J. O'Brien's terminology, we see the return of a "republican style" of Catholicism, first evident in the episcopacy of John

Carroll (1790–1815), in which the church defines itself through an interior, privatized piety, on the one hand, and a mutually correcting, public
dialogue with non-Catholic Americans, on the other. With the movement
of the majority of American Catholics into the middle class, the republican style came to overshadow if not eclipse the "immigrant style" of the
right, associated with devotional Catholicism, and the "evangelical Catholicism" of the left, associated with radical Catholics such as Dorothy
Day, the Berrigans, and Thomas Merton, among others.[9]

This is not to say that the immigrant and evangelical styles of Catholicism have no role in the contemporary public debate. This would be
impossible, given the enormous growth and importance of the Hispanic
American and Asian American Catholic communities in recent decades,
and the incorporation of an evangelical perspective in the social teachings
of the U.S. bishops in the 1980s. Nonetheless, advocates of the immigrant
and evangelical styles have often found themselves outside looking in, dismissed by the resurgent republican Catholics (especially, it seems to me,
by the conservatives and neoconservatives). On the map charting the engagement of Catholics in the American public order, in other words, those
who ignore the Americanist heritage, or who continue to link it to modernism or to some other form of incorrect belief, are often cast as marginal
figures. Indeed, the Americanist center of U.S. Catholicism has grown
very large indeed, encompassing figures as diverse as John Courtney
Murray, Charles Curran, George Weigel, Jay Dolan, Rosemary Ruether,
William F. Buckley, Jr., Michael Novak, Mary Jo Weaver, Helen Hull
Hitchcock, James Hitchcock, Dennis McCann, and countless others, all
of whom, as Roman Catholics living in the United States, have entered
into the kind of mutually respectful dialogue with American culture that
Rome warned against in the late nineteenth century. Those who directly
challenge the neo-Americanist assumptions—from Stanley Hauerwas and
Michael Baxter on the left to David Schindler and traditionalist Catholics on the right—sometimes see their criticisms incorporated by the
neo-Americanists. But the interpretive paradigm of the neo-Americanists
remains intact.[10]

The second phase of Americanism, or neo-Americanism, began around
the time of "the Murray project," as it is called by its self-appointed in-
heritors of both right and left. Like the earlier form of Americanism, it
entailed a search for a suitable *theological* foundation for an Americanist
public philosophy.[11] In the emergence of neo-Americanism, the Jesuit
scholar John Courtney Murray was a key figure in that he worked firmly
within a neoscholastic framework while privileging, for the purpose of establishing a viable public philosophy in a pluralist American society, its

natural law/human reason/consensus-building elements. By contrast, the explicitly theological elements of neoscholasticism were concerned with preserving the priority of faith, the revealed law (as interpreted authoritatively not by the reasonable "public" but by the magisterium), and the exclusive truth claims of Catholicism. These explicitly theological concerns were not seen to be central to the unfolding public conversation, in part because their prominence might threaten to lend a sectarian cast to the project. Murray in no way denied this pole of neoscholasticism; indeed, his best-known collection of essays, *We Hold These Truths,* opens with his assertion that the real question is not Catholicism's compatibility with American democracy, but vice versa.[12] In an important sense, furthermore, Murray's "republican Catholicism" was ultimately transformationist, in keeping with the "evangelical style."[13]

Yet even as Murray wrote, the neoscholastic canopy protecting Americanism was collapsing under the pressure of biblical theologians, liturgists, and historical critics who deemed it to be, even in its more historical and nuanced neo-Thomist expression, still too ahistorical and metaphysical to be of much use in an empirical, existentialist age. As a result of the unraveling of neoscholasticism, the republican-style Catholics of the post-conciliar era have had to develop suitable public theologies to complement their political philosophies.[14]

The observation that contemporary liberals and conservatives share a set of assumptions that may be termed *Americanist* requires a brief review of the first appearance of Americanism, in order to see how today's neo-Americanists have appropriated this historical experience. It is safe to say that the neo-Americanists reject any linking of their projects to modernism or neomodernism. The first Americanists, however, were unable to avoid this linkage.

The Historical Meanings of Americanism

On January 6, 1895, Rome promulgated *Longinqua Oceani,* Pope Leo XIII's encyclical to the American hierarchy congratulating it on the "giant strides" made by the church in religious matters and noting that the United States provided a social environment in which Catholic sodalities, schools, clergy, and religion in general "are in a flourishing condition." Leo acknowledged that the church, "unopposed by the Constitution and government of your nation, fettered by no hostile legislation, protected against violence by the common laws and the impartiality of the tribunals, is free to live and act without hindrance." Nonetheless, he warned, "it would be very erroneous to draw the conclusion that in America is to be sought the type of the most desirable status of the Church, or that it would be universally lawful or expedient for State and Church to be, as in America, dissevered and divorced." Despite its hearty condition, Leo continued, the church would be in even better shape if, "in addition to liberty, she enjoyed the favor of the laws and the patronage of the public authority."[15]

Four years later, in 1899, the same pope issued *Testem Benevolentiae,* a letter to Cardinal Gibbons of Baltimore indicating his disapproval of "the opinions which some comprise under the head of Americanism," for these opinions raise "the suspicion that there are some among you who conceive of and desire a church in America different from that which is in the rest of the world." The erroneous opinions and "principles" of the so-called Americanism Pope Leo XIII reduced to one proposition: "In order the more easily to bring over to Catholic doctrine those who dissent from it, the Church ought to adapt herself somewhat to our advanced civilization, and, relaxing her ancient rigor, show some indulgence to modern popular theories and methods."[16]

The next sentences of the encyclical are particularly important in establishing the fact that Rome perceived theological as well as cultural and political elements in Americanism:

> Many think that this is to be understood not only with regard to the rule of life, but also to the doctrines in which the *deposit of faith* is contained. For they contend that it is opportune, in order to work in a more attractive way upon the wills of those who are not in accord with us, to pass over certain heads of doctrines, as if of lesser moment, or to so soften them that they may not have the same meaning which the Church has invariably held. Now, Beloved Son, few words are needed to show how reprehensible is the plan that is thus conceived, if we but consider the character and origin of the doctrine which the Church hands down to us. On that point the Vatican Council says: "The doctrine of faith which God has revealed is not proposed like a theory of philosophy which is to be elaborated by the human understanding, but as a divine deposit delivered to the Spouse of Christ to be faithfully guarded and infallibly declared."[17]

The consequences of this error, the pope continued, included the implicit denial that "the Apostolic See . . . has constantly adhered *to the same doctrine, in the same sense and in the same mind.*"[18] (Indeed, this "denial" was voiced by European modernists and their American Catholic admirers at St. Joseph's Seminary in Dunwoodie, New York.)[19] Finally, the pope

criticized the supposed preference of the Americanists for active over pas-
sive virtues, and the tendency to eschew "all external guidance" and to
rely instead on the indwelling Spirit. According to Americanism, "the
Holy Ghost pours greater and richer gifts into the hearts of the faithful
now than in times past; and by a certain hidden instinct teaches and
moves them with no one as an intermediary."[20] This position would be
elaborated and condemned again, eight years later, as "vital immanence"
in Pope Pius X's encyclical on modernism.[21]

The first historians of Americanism, writing in the 1940s and 1950s,
adopted Cardinal Gibbons's 1899 strategy of response to these papal
warnings: these are indeed serious errors, and no one in America holds
them, least of all Isaac Hecker, founder of the Paulists, or his admirers in
the hierarchy. Thomas McAvoy, for instance, flatly denied any necessary
connection between Americanism and modernism, and made a distinction
between the dangerous doctrines condemned in *Testem Benevolentiae,* on
the one hand, and "true" Americanism—the particular way of being and
acting of Catholics in America—which was completely unrelated to the
condemned heresy. McAvoy, writing at a time when American Catholics
were concerned to demonstrate their patriotism to American Protestants,
further denied that simple American patriotism was implicated in the
papal encyclical. It was true, of course, that the so-called Americanists had
called for a thoroughly Americanized church and had opposed German
nationalist parishes and schools in the United States and the sending of a
(foreign) apostolic delegate from Rome. In some cases, such as Archbishop John Ireland's embrace of the Faribault-Stillwater plan, they had
also seemed willing to negotiate with and even praise the U.S. public
school system, in apparent disregard for the Third Plenary Council's call
for a separate system of Catholic parochial schools. Despite these and
other controversies associated with the liberal bishops, the real problem
originated in Europe, McAvoy insisted, where elements of true Americanism had been abstracted and transformed into a theological program
worthy of censure. But the pope had in no sense condemned the American system of government or "the American way of life"; to the contrary,
he had explicitly omitted from rebuke "the conditions of your common-
wealths, or the laws and customs which prevail in them."[22]

The Synthesis of All Heresies

Both Americanism and modernism were condemned in broad strokes
that indicted no one in particular but covered "almost everyone who was

not dead," as one liberal Catholic ruefully put it. The two heresies were seen by their opponents as inextricably linked, with Americanism being the cultural, political, and ecclesiopolitical expression of modernism's theological and philosophical project. The Americanists' acceptance of religious liberty, church-state separation, and scientific scholarship encouraged other American priests to rethink important aspects of theology and doctrine. Among other innovations, the Americanists inspired the turn to nonscholastic methods of doing theology. They themselves, however, did not intend for Catholic priests and scholars simply to conform their thinking to political and religious currents in the United States. Ultimately, as their speeches and writings demonstrate, the Americanists sought to transform American society. The American Catholic modernists, by contrast, focused their attention not on the transformation of American society, but on the internal reform of the church itself.[23]

It was in this sense of his hope for Catholicizing America that Cardinal Gibbons called Isaac Hecker a "true child of the Church" and supported critical scholarship.[24] His episcopal allies, John Ireland and John Lancaster Spalding, were prominent proponents of the effort to adapt Catholicism to the modern age so that it might transform the modern age.

Much like early Protestant liberals who endorsed Darwinian natural selection without fully understanding its implications for the faith, Ireland was confident about the possibility of reconciliation between democracy and magisterium, religious faith and scientific method. He promoted the building of a synthesis between the ancient faith and modern thought but did not foresee the risks involved. The volatile combination of forceful progressivism and incomplete scientific understanding blinded Ireland to the implications of his rhetoric and undermined his prestige at Rome. He gave unwitting encouragement, time and again, to men and ideas that the Vatican condemned. On the eve of the promulgation of *Testem Benevolentiae,* for example, he described Hecker as "providential" in his demand for a new form of Catholic spirituality suited to modern America.[25] In 1892 he publicly praised Alfred Loisy and supported his new review of biblical criticism, *L'Enseignment biblique,* identifying it with the highest aspirations of Catholic theology. And in 1896, Ireland applauded the American priest John Zahm's major work *Evolution and Dogma,* an attempt to reconcile the two. He was to regret each of these endorsements.[26]

John Lancaster Spalding, bishop of Peoria, felt more comfortable in discussing the nuances of modern philosophy and theology, and was determined to resist the dominance of Roman neoscholastics in the intellectual affairs of American Catholicism.[27] As a leader of the Americanists, he protested the appointment of a permanent apostolic delegate to the

United States. American Catholics, he wrote, "are devoted to the Church; they recognize in the Pope Christ's Vicar, and gladly receive from him the doctrines of faith and morals; but for the rest, they ask him to interfere as little as may be." Spalding endorsed church-state separation in America and urged that the church "adapt herself to all forms of government . . . with their differences of laws, customs, education and sentiment."[28] He assailed the notion that medieval Catholicism had achieved the ideal relationship between church and state, or faith and reason. During his inaugural address at the laying of the cornerstone for Catholic University on May 24, 1888, Spalding opined: "Saint Thomas is a powerful intellect but his point of view in all that concerns natural knowledge has long since vanished from sight . . . and so when we read the great names of the past, the mists of illusions fill the skies, and our eyes are dimmed by the glory of clouds tinged with the splendors of a sun that has set."[29] Catholic scientists and theologians must be willing, if necessary, "to abandon positions which are no longer defensible, to assume new attitudes in the face of new conditions."[30] James Driscoll, the Sulpician president of St. Joseph's Seminary in New York, consulted with Spalding in implementing a "curricular pluralism" in the seminary, with an eye to introducing students to European higher biblical criticism and to the writings of Loisy, Tyrrell, and other "modernist" thinkers.[31]

The U.S. priests who dabbled in modernism were also self-styled Americanists. John Zahm, a Holy Cross priest and professor of chemistry and physics at Notre Dame, taught that the *idea* of Darwinian evolution, properly understood, posed no obstacle to the faith of the Catholic. The encouragement he received from Gibbons, Ireland, and Spalding was not enough to shield Zahm from his opponents in the Vatican and in the American church who linked his advocacy of evolution theory and modern science to his "uncritical acceptance of American values." Curial officials resented Zahm's penchant for ecclesiastical intrigue and his support of the Americanists.[32] In this sense it was hardly a coincidence that the decree banning *Evolution and Dogma* was followed four months later by the encyclical condemning Americanism.

By the turn of the century, neoscholastic church officials began to perceive Americanism and evolutionism as aspects of a larger historical movement that challenged their positions of privilege in the church, insofar as it threatened to overturn the philosophical and theological assumptions upon which the institutional system of their era was founded. In the view of Salvatore Brandi, S.J., the editor of *La Civiltà Cattolica*, Zahm embodied the link between Americanism and evolutionism.[33] As an evolutionist he adopted a new and dangerous way of thinking about church and world—a new "episteme." It was Zahm's methodology that troubled Brandi most about *Evolution and Dogma*. Zahm took as a starting point not deductions from revealed truth but "unbiased" inductions from empirical data. He promised a "synthesis" of these inductions and the "authentic" teaching of the Catholic tradition. He interpreted Scripture critically, assigning different levels of authority to different passages and scientific competence to very few. And he claimed that the defined teachings of the church on these matters were few in number, which allowed him to proceed liberally in most questions.[34]

Most egregious to Brandi was Zahm's grounding of his positions in the authority of the church fathers and medieval scholastics. Brandi wrote that Zahm's mistakes reflected an insufficient training in neoscholasticism: "Because he does not seem to be familiar with Thomistic philosophy, he has misinterpreted these principles and for this reason he cites and makes application of them incorrectly."[35] To propose that Thomas had condoned the theory of bodily evolution was to introduce an undesirable pluralism of interpretation into the reading of scholasticism. Zahm had attempted to do the same with the fathers and with the Bible. This approach threatened the neoscholastic monopoly on the interpretation of these sources.[36]

In the first decade of the twentieth century, other American priests followed Zahm's "trajectory of modernism." Two of these left the church as self-proclaimed modernists. Both were initially attracted to Catholicism by the thought of Hecker and encouraged by the Americanist bishops. Both the Paulist, William L. Sullivan, and the Josephite, John R. Slattery, came to reject neoscholasticism after studying the writings of European modernists. Both men, finally, were Americanists who shared an optimistic assessment of science, a passion for republican ideals, and faith in "the conclusions of the higher criticism."

"According to Catholic authorities," Slattery wrote, "the antidote of modernism lies in Rome, the episcopate, and scholasticism. To look beyond any one of them is to be a modernist."[37] Because Americanists valued democracy and freedom of thought, speech, and religion, Slattery wrote, they favored a theological model of revelation as an ongoing phenomenon open to all people and not restricted to a clerical elite. Were it developed sufficiently, the Americanist ecclesiology would be based on the belief in the Divine Spirit as immanent in the community, and would see the church as always engaged in the dynamic process of development. The curialists, on the other hand, were concerned with preserving the lands and political powers inherited from an age of despotism and monarchy; and neoscholasticism provided a theoretical framework in which elitism and the concentration of power in the hands of the few made sense. Thus Slattery argued that "the letter on modernism is a political document."[38]

Paulist priest William Sullivan also joined the Americanist "movement." For Sullivan the essentially moral questions of government, liberty, and authority framed the new, American Catholic understanding of the work of the Infinite Spirit. Thus Americanism was the necessary prerequisite for modernism, which wed the political principles of the Americanists to the critical study of church history, theology, philosophy, and exegesis. Americanism affirmed the possibility of options in matters that the Americanists considered to be nonrevealed and thus subject to change (e.g., the proper relationship between church and state); modernism provided the theological vindication for this position by locating it in nonscholastic yet wholly authentic traditions of Catholic thought. "We know what the American Spirit is in the political and social order," he wrote in *Letters to His Holiness.* "Translate it into the religious order and you have Modernism at its best and purest."[39] Note the connection in Sullivan's mind between "simple patriotism" and a revolutionary Catholicism:

> Americanism is a word that connotes patriotism. It seems to embrace all that is indigenous to this republic and is typical of it; and whatever becomes of Biblical criticism or the philosophy of dogmatic conformity, the mass of Catholics in this country will not be un-American. So the *Testis Benevolentiae* [*sic*] which laid Rome's solemn disapproval upon Americanism, was not received with enthusiasm, and raised indeed in some quarters a levity not far removed from disdain. It surely loosened rather than tied more firmly the bonds uniting America to Rome.[40]

In Sullivan's view the modernists, adherents of liberalism, were opposed by the Romanists, defenders of the church-controlled state. The absence of coercion of religious belief under the U.S. Constitution was, however, the surest way to realize the possibility of genuine religious freedom, which was, for Sullivan, "a genuine Catholic value." The Romanists did not, obviously, believe their own theological claims that human reason, aided by grace, could attain to the good and true without coercion. They perpetuated a system of internal government and a corresponding political philosophy inimical to the true spirit of Catholicism and of the gospel of Jesus alike. Sullivan wrote:

> Here then is the Romanized Catholic Church appealing to the American people, asking them to embrace its teachings as the pure Gospel of Christ, and yet saying: "Not only have I a theological, but a political creed. Of that political creed one of the tenets is that church and state should be united. The opposite opinion is a damnable error. . . . Therefore you Americans, ere you perfectly find

Christ, must most firmly hold that your Constitution is fatally de-
fective, since it is opposed to the union of church and state." What
shall we say of this be we Catholics or not? What can we say except
this: that it is akin to blasphemy that a religion should have any political creed whatsoever . . . that a religion which demands a weakening
of loyalty to country before it baptizes us into salvation is obstructing
the cause of Christ. . . . To such has the Papacy descended![41]

Sullivan felt that Americans would never fully accept a system in which
"the will of people, priests and bishops counts, as such, for nothing." Just
as the papacy desired to determine state policy, so did it seek the unques-
tioning subordination of the processes of critical thought to its own
preconceived ends. Thus, anti-Americanism in questions of government
manifested itself as antimodernism in questions of intellectual investigation.

Sullivan and Slattery had indeed traveled a long way from Ireland's
buoyant embrace of American values. Yet both men, early in their careers
as would-be Catholic apologists, cited the archbishop's speeches as preparing the way for theologically innovative scholarship.

The Neo-Americanists: "Liberal" and "Conservative" Centrists

Eight decades later, Ireland was being invoked by another defender of
Catholic Americanism. George Weigel opens his 1989 book, *Catholicism
and the Renewal of American Democracy,* with an invocation of the
Americanist tradition and "John Ireland's dream."[42] Like Ireland, Weigel
and his neoconservative colleagues Michael Novak and Richard John Neuhaus seek to inform "the American experiment" with a Catholic vision. Yet
Weigel distances himself rapidly from other neo-Americanists—"the liberal
Catholic establishment" and "the Catholic Left"—who would advocate
that Roman Catholicism reinvent itself as a democratic institution. "Calls
for 'taking America seriously' that confuse the deliberative processes and
structures of governance appropriate to a political community with the deliberative process and structures of governance to the community of faith
involve a category error of considerable proportions," Weigel warns.[43]

The ideological opponents of the neoconservatives include American
Catholics who advance the argument for a democratic Catholic Church.[44]
In so doing, Rosemary Radford Ruether, Eugene Bianchi, and their
colleagues attempt a dual recovery of "the roots of modern democratic
theory," on the one hand, and biblical and traditional teachings within
Catholic Christianity which provide warrant for the democratization of

ecclesial structures, on the other. These Catholics are sharply critical of the failures of American-style democracy, including its close ideological iden-tification "with free market capitalism of a form that is generating vast injustice between a small elite of wealthy people and a vast underclass of impoverished people."[45]

Yet like the neoconservatives, the liberals accept as normative for church and society the principles and freedoms associated with the found-ing of the United States and incorporated into official church doctrine in *Dignitatis Humanae*. They participate in and applaud the work done on social ethics and the general direction of the U.S. bishops' social teachings on the nuclear arms race, the conditions necessary for peace, and the re-quirements of economic justice for all peoples. At the same time, these liberal neo-Americanists argue that the Catholic Church's witness to American and Christian ideals is radically compromised by its own anti-pluralist and antidemocratic structures. The hierarchy fails fully to recog-nize, they complain, that "democratic, participatory forms of government are more appropriate for the expression of respect for persons and safe-guarding against abusive relationships than hierarchical and monarchical systems of government that treat the governed as rightless dependents."[46]

Neoconservative Catholics protest, in response, that they are not un-critical of democratic capitalism. Michael Novak has recently reminded his readers, for instance, that his early writings contain thorough cultural cri-tiques of American society that need not be rehashed in an era when such cultural critiques are legion.[47]

The neo-Americanists of the right and left share a grounding in "the American experiment in ordered liberty," but disagree on the nature of its significance for the Catholic Church. Whereas the neo-Americanists of "the left" believe that apostolic authority resides in the Spirit-inspired community of baptized Catholics, those of "the right" prefer, they say, "a complex process of discernment, reflection, debate, and prayer within boundaries established by ancient and authoritative texts and monitored by an authoritative magisterium."[48] Nonetheless, the neoconservatives share the liberals' hope that the Catholic Church will learn from the example of the United States. "The future development of Catholic social teaching could be significantly enhanced," Weigel urges, "by taking America *more* seriously" than church tradition has heretofore done, "and taking it more seriously precisely as a morally grounded social, cultural, and political experiment in democratic pluralism."[49]

Rather than create participatory structures within the church itself, the Catholic neoconservatives have created their own distinctive mode of ecu-menical and interreligious conversation with evangelical Protestants and conservative American Jewish intellectuals. The neocons seek to develop a public theology to support the American political philosophy, as they interpret it, and the "democratic capitalism" of the United States. In this project they rely on the moral guidance of the magisterium, although they also selectively criticize its teachings. Ruether and Bianchi note, however, that conservatives and neoconservatives exempt the hierarchy from historical development and fail to challenge the assumption that the church "has always possessed a centralized monarchical and hierarchical form of government" which is "divinely mandated and unchangeable." Conservatives, they write, "must begin to ask the hard questions about the relationship between historical realities and theological and ethical norms."[50]

For both camps, however, democracy is not just one option among others. Catholic neoconservatives see history as developing providentially in a democratic direction, but they also insist that historical developments accrue legitimacy and authority only through the endorsement of the magisterium. In part this is why Neuhaus, Novak, and Weigel heartily celebrate the recent social encyclicals of Pope John Paul II, which they interpret as providing official recognition of the victory of democratic capitalism over atheistic socialism, along with a long-overdue baptism of the former.

The liberal camp, placing its faith in the work of the transcendent Spirit in the believing community, seeks its own transcendent reference. While the question of "good" church government "seems to us not fundamentally different from the question of what would be 'good' forms of social and political order generally," theirs is a theological and not simply a secular claim, for "it is based on the premise that the God who is revealed in Jesus Christ is not other than the God who created the world." Thus, they argue, their proposal for democratizing the church is more than a utilitarian or politically motivated adaptation to current conditions. It is also based on normative premises, namely "a Spirit theology [which] accepts historical and personal factors as part of an ongoing process. In this outlook, God is immersed in the historical process, helping us continually to rethink and reform the shape of the church."[51] The liberal neo-Americanists also claim, like Weigel, that their theological approach involves not just *aggiornamento* but also *ressourcement.*[52]

Other comparisons could be drawn, but the major point is clear: both liberals and neoconservatives have been formed in similar ways by the American experience. Indeed, it is difficult to imagine how an effective public theology could be constructed without its theologians reflecting, as well as critically engaging, the prevalent assumptions of the public culture. Yet the neoconservatives' willingness to adapt Catholic particulars to the requirements of republican discourse is one marker setting them apart from other Catholics who are usually seen as falling somewhere to the right of center. For example, Novak, Neuhaus, and Weigel have been engaged in a debate, carried on in the pages of *Communio* (North American edition, edited by David Schindler) and *Crisis*. Schindler initiated the debate with a long and complex attack on NNW, as he calls them. To rehearse the particulars of the debate, which runs now into hundreds of printed pages, is unnecessary: in essence, Schindler accuses the neoconservatives of being religious liberals in conservative dress. They accept definitions of the human person, and other "ontological" ideas, derived from American philosophical traditions which rest on "assumptions [that] carry a logic which will work itself out in history, in a way not entirely governed by the intentions of the ideas' originators." To adopt these Enlightenment-era philosophical premises is already to depart from the accumulated wisdom of Catholic tradition. "The ontological and spiritual meaning carried in the Church's great tradition of Christology has social-cultural implications," Schindler writes, and one cannot depart from this great tradition without thereby endangering the "full scope of orthodoxy." The neocons are naive, he charges, in thinking that they can separate institutions from ideologies, to use Novak's formula, and reinvigorate the former with the spirit of (resourced and updated) Catholicism. Institutions are not so easily divorced from their ideological meanings. Thus the neoconservatives' proposals, despite their express intention to the contrary, "serve liberal society better than they serve Catholic social thought." Although offered in the name of pluralism, Schindler observes, the project of NNW has actually colluded with the "monism of the American way of life," that is, "the homogenization of Protestantism, Catholicism, and Judaism in terms of America's underlying logic of liberalism and democratic capitalism."[53]

As for the liberal neo-Americanists, they must face their own radical critics who claim that they, too, "have capitulated to the ethos of American liberalism."[54] In addition, both broad camps of contemporary neo-Americanists must face tormentors on the right for whom the old charge of modernism is ready-made.

The Synthesis of All Heresies Redivivus

"Up until now, an astonishing thing has been taking place," writes Fr. Robert D. Smith. "To the best of my knowledge, every biblical commentary written in English for a Catholic audience in the twentieth century has been engaged in promulgating the modernistic dogma of universal salvation, promulgating the idea that there does not exist in the teaching of Christ any teaching about a coming final Judgment, in which all men are to be separated permanently into the damned and the saved." The modernists "win . . . at least in their own minds" by explaining away Christ's words as hyperbole, figures of speech not meant to be taken literally. While this interpretation is "laughable," Smith says, it finds a ready audience among Catholic academics, liberal priests, and even some confused bishops. The popularity of the modernists is particularly galling and inexplicable, he concludes, because their commentaries are all "dull" and deadening to faith.[55]

While this response to "modernist" biblical criticism could have been lifted from any number of antimodernist tracts written in the United States in the first decade of the twentieth century, it appeared originally in the January 21, 1993, issue of *The Wanderer*. The theme is numbingly redundant in the postconciliar literature of Catholic ultra-conservatives and traditionalists: the apostasy of the present age and the general "desolation" of the Roman Catholic Church stem from the destructive resurgence of the modernist "movement."

The postconciliar crisis of Catholic faith, according to this line of reasoning, was created by the triumph of liberalism at Vatican II. Traditionalists especially, as distinct from conservatives, blame the "poorly planned and mismanaged Council" for opening up the church internally to the transforming principles of modernity. A council that was supposed to reinvigorate pastoral application of unchanging Catholic doctrine had ended by entertaining a new (and mortally dangerous) paradigm for Catholic self-understanding—a paradigm first sketched decades prior by the modernist Alfred Loisy, who had the temerity to challenge Roman supernaturalism and suggest that the truths of the Catholic faith develop in time and over time, in the fragile custody of fallible human interpreters. For traditionalists, therefore, the real problem of postconciliar Catholicism, in short, was not merely liberalism but its atheistic alter ego, modernism.

In the 1960s, a new wave of antimodernism appeared, featuring analysis strikingly similar in tone and content to that of the early twentieth century.[56] In these writings the crisis of postconciliar Catholicism is interpreted as a battle between belief and disbelief in which new ideological configurations are likely. The Anglo-Catholic *New Oxford Review*, for example, advertised itself in 1982 as "a Catholic journal that is written for both laity and clergy, and focuses its fire on the modernists while maintaining open doors to Evangelicals, Pentecostalists, and the Eastern Orthodox," and touted a regular column by James Hitchcock which provided "a running account and interpretation of the epic battle shaping up between the Holy Father and the modernists."[57]

The postconciliar wave of antimodernism found an early elaboration in *The Battle for the American Church* (1979), in which Msgr. George A. Kelly used antimodernism as an interpretive lens to view the struggle for ideological hegemony in U.S. Catholicism. Kelly states clearly what was at stake for conservative Catholics in the immediate aftermath of the Council. The conflict over the proper interpretation of Vatican II is essentially a "battle of ideas" for "control of the lives of the faithful accomplished through control of Church machinery itself. . . . It is 'ideas' that ultimately will prevail in the Church." Yet ideas "eventually find favor with power brokers of one kind or another" and ultimately become "pawns in a game" for institutional power. Responsible Catholics must therefore be willing to enjoin the "guerrilla-type warfare going on inside the Church."[58]

Kelly echoes a theme first developed in the papal condemnations of modernism: the true threat of modernism is a threat to doctrine, to right belief, and to the supernatural worldview which sustains it. "The issues at stake are the correctness of Catholic doctrine and the survival of the Catholic Church as a significant influence in the life of her own communicants," Kelly writes. "A large segment of the Church's middle management—teachers, editors, administrators—has come to have suspicion of teaching effort that appears to be narrowly Catholic. Indeed, concentration on Catholic doctrine is no longer greeted in some Catholic circles, even as a *pluralistic option*."[59]

In Kelly's analysis, Alfred Loisy and Hans Küng stand as exemplars of the first and second waves of modernism, respectively, and he posits a direct link between them. In subjecting Catholic documents, including the Scriptures, to the historical-critical method, Loisy first revealed the atheistic trajectory of the modernist project, and Küng's postconciliar project confirms the lesson. In this Loisy-Küng understanding, divine revelation is no more than the "progressive education" of men, proportioned to human reason and to the condition of peoples to whom it was (is) addressed; accordingly, revelation as a body of thought cannot be discussed apart from the human experience from which it derived. Loisy ultimately argued that Christianity had no fixed "core" of beliefs or doctrines that stood outside of time and culture. Likewise, Küng's *On Being a Christian* draws on Catholic sources selectively and in a highly ideological fashion. In Küng's method, those Catholic sources that emphasize Christ's humanity are lifted up, while the supernatural elements are muted. Much in the style of Thomas Jefferson's portrayal of Jesus as the Enlightened Natural Law Ethicist, Küng dismisses all miracles and doctrines that cannot be given a natural explanation. The "Küng methodology," Kelly fears, is being employed in the postconciliar era by other Catholic scholars around the world, and particularly in this country.[60]

The charges of modernism in the postconciliar church continue to appear today in some conservative and traditionalist publications. Yet it would be inaccurate to suggest that these charges represent the nature of the criticism most frequently leveled at the neo-Americanist center of contemporary public Catholicism. Indeed, the most effective and visible criticisms usually come from positions within that amorphous, shifting, and relatively inclusive "center," when "liberals" and "conservatives" trade barbs and, at times, compliments.

Conclusions

I

Keeping our imaginary map in mind, we can see that the Americanist ethos has survived in the dominant form of public Catholicism in a republican style. Despite its internal diversity and polemical tendencies, this form of public Catholicism provides a playing field shared by liberals and conservatives alike. It has supplanted the preconciliar neoscholastic system as the interpretive framework within which American Catholic bishops and "professional Catholics"—women religious, priests, lay ministers, Catholic historians, theologians, ethicists, public philosophers, and the like—carry on the apostolic work of the church.

Most traditionalists and conservatives, however, do not concentrate their energies on postconciliar public Catholicism, but on questions internal to the life of the church. Neoconservatives take the lead in advocating public Catholicism in a conservative mode, though they ordinarily have the support, if not active collaboration, of many scholars and leaders in the conservative scholarly societies and organizations. Many conservative Catholics cling tenaciously to a view of the church as primarily a spiritual, sacramental communion rather than a "servant," a "herald," or even a public "institution," to invoke Avery Dulles's well-known ecclesiological models. When we consider the internal life of the church, in other words, the configuration of the players on the map changes. Here the "center-left" liberals, in their concern about the internal governance of the church, find themselves contesting the same terrain not only with the public Catholics of neoconservative mind, but also with conservative organizations such as CUF, Opus Dei, and the fledgling Catholic colleges described in chapter 12 by Mary Jo Weaver.

As on the map of public Catholicism, the prescriptions of liberals and conservatives differ greatly one from the other. But both liberals and conservatives understand that the majority of American Catholics—while they may be aware of the highlights of the internal Catholic debate over American social ethics and public philosophy, and take notice of major events such as the bishops' pastoral letters—are nonetheless engaged in different and pressing questions of a pastoral nature. How is the local church to be "governed" or "led in minstry"? What is to be the role of women in the ministries of the church? How are priests and ministers to be held accountable to their congregations? How are Catholics to understand sacraments, Scripture, worship, their own spiritual traditions?

Accordingly, we must ask whether public Catholicism has anything to offer to the church in its internal life of grace and religious experience. For all of its smugness and metaphysical aloofness, the neoscholastic system certainly did. Philip Gleason writes:

> The conviction that the Catholic faith was rationally grounded, and that there were appropriately certified specialists somewhere who could perform the required demonstration of that fact, became a hallmark of the American Catholic mind in the generation before the Second Vatican Council. Indeed that conviction itself took on the quality of faith. . . .
>
>   . . . Consider, for example, the intense devotionalism, the piety, the drive for personal sanctity—all coupled with deep loyalty to the Church—that was so conspicuous a feature of Catholic life in the preconciliar era. Many other factors no doubt played a role in the development of this vigorous spirituality: the devout traditions of an immigrant-derived people; the reforms of Pius X regarding frequent reception of Holy Communion; systematic efforts to stimulate piety through parish missions, novenas, public recitation of the rosary, and so on. But putting faith on so solid a footing surely contributed, perhaps indispensably. Knowing what they believed, having confidence in the truth of those beliefs, and seeing an intimate connection between their faith and the Church with her treasury of grace, Catholics could throw themselves with loving abandon into the search for personal holiness through assistance at Mass, reception of the sacraments, attendance at devotional exercises, spiritual reading, and of course private prayer. A highly rationalistic understanding of faith thus paradoxically made possible, indeed encouraged, an emotional, even fideistic, practice of the faith.[61]

Do the concerns of conservative, neoconservative, or traditionalist Catholics—most of whom are white, middle-class, third- or fourth- generation Americans reacting in some fashion to the Second Vatican Council—reflect the preoccupations of contemporary American Catholics under forty years of age, or speak to the popular religious experiences of hundreds of thousands of Hispanic American and Asian American Catholics? In other words, does public Catholicism provide the same kind of canopy that neo-scholasticism did for generations of American Catholics "keeping the faith"?

Recognizing the validity of such questions, and expressing their desire for the preservation of orthodoxy, the neo-Americanists of the right as well as the left have sought to construct public theologies that incorporate "evangelical" or "devotional" styles of piety. One of the major differences, in fact, between Americanists and neo-Americanists has been the ability of the latter to begin the long and complex process of providing a historical and theological grounding or "justification" for Catholic public philosophy at the close of the twentieth century. The hope is for an inclusive public theology and a style of public Catholicism that is faithful to the abiding Catholic truth claims while being informed by postconciliar insights concerning revelation, theological method, and the relationship between the discursive mode of religious authority, on the one hand, and public philosophy, on the other.

Ironically, as in the first episode of Americanism a century ago, today's Americanists constitute an elite group moving in a somewhat rarefied religious and political culture unlike that of ordinary Catholics. The same could be said, of course, about the mostly clerical upholders of the neo-scholastic tradition. But postconciliar conservative Catholicism has been less willing (and increasingly unable) to ignore the contributions of women and American minorities, of lay Catholics as well as priests; and many conservative spiritual groups draw upon the rich and diverse expressions of popular religion in the United States. The advent of "local theologies" indicates an awareness that the ongoing American Catholic conversation about our "experiment in ordered liberty" must occur in many places beyond the seminary and the academy. Otherwise, the conversation will remain abstracted from the true center of the faith, the lived experience of the Catholic people. The difficulties facing public Catholicism, conservative as well as liberal, in crafting a theology that invigorates and appeals to popular Catholic religious sensibilities is a topic demanding sustained attention.

II

In reviewing the passage from Americanism as a heresy, phantom or otherwise, to Americanism as the basis for a renewed public Catholicism, we might ask: How did we arrive at this point? Let me summarize my answer by referring to three "decouplings." First, as I have argued, "the true Americanism" escaped the turn-of-the-century attempt to depict it, alongside modernism, as a virulent modern heresy. The charge of a link between Americanism and modernism did re-emerge in the 1960s with the collapse of the neoscholastic synthesis that had preserved patriotic Americans and defenders of the First Amendment from the charge of "liberalism" or "modernism." But the new accusations did not carry the day in an era inaugurated by Pope John XXIII's ban on heresy-hunting.

This first decoupling—the separation of Americanism from modernist atheism and materialism—was enhanced by a second one, namely, the implicit separation of natural law discourse from its underpinning (or overarching) theological system. In the postwar debates about religious freedom and church-state separation, the neoscholastic thinkers Joseph Clifford Fenton and Francis J. Connell argued relentlessly with John Courtney Murray about the proper interpretation to be given to the American proposition. During a particularly heated point in his conflict with Murray, Monsignor Fenton, editor of the *American Ecclesiastical Review*, ran an article reminding the faithful of the pernicious effects of theological modernism: "The common basis of the false doctrinal Americanism and of the Modernist heresy is, like doctrinal indifferentism itself, ultimately a rejection of Catholic dogma as a genuine supernatural message or communication from the living God Himself."[62] These charges were not directed at Murray by name, and he was vindicated eventually from suspicions that he was not sufficiently orthodox. Nonetheless it might be argued that Murray's legacy, variously interpreted by supporters on all points of the ideological spectrum, was the decoupling of neoscholastic public philosophy from its own theological premises. This was, to be sure, an unintended consequence of "the Murray project."

Finally, a third "decoupling" was going on in international Catholicism even as American Catholics took refuge from modernism in public philosophy. The sociologist Gene Burns describes the separation of Roman Catholic social teaching from the magisterium's (more explicit and thus more binding) doctrines on personal faith and morals. "Indeed, one of the more interesting developments in Catholicism since the Second Vatican Council has been the ambiguous conciliar doctrine on Church decision-making authority and Church commitment to social and political issues, leading different sectors of the Church to question different parts of the ideological structure," he writes. "Ideologically, the last quarter century has been a particularly ambiguous and contentious period in the Church's history, partly due to the legacy left by the council and partly due to the development of new resources and greater autonomy by Catholic groups challenging Vatican dominance."[63]

In this development, ideological space was created for experimentation in the application of Roman Catholic social doctrine, even prior to the acknowledgment and (partial) acceptance of pluralism in the fields of personal morality and religious belief. In this way public or social Catholicism became an arena for creative thinking and the working out of problems in the church's confrontation with modernity. It also became, as Burns points out, an arena of ideological fragmentation and of shifting power relations within the institutional church. For better or worse, this describes the reality of our current situation thirty years after the Second Vatican Council.

NOTES

1. In 1993 a Gallup poll found that only 30 percent of American Catholics believe that when they receive communion they are actually receiving the body and blood of Christ. Only 21 percent of Catholics under the age of fifty believe in the real presence, while 24 percent believe that Christ becomes present in the bread and wine only if the recipient believes this to be so.

2. Cf., for example, James V. Schall, S.J., "The Spirit of *Veritatis Splendor,*" *Lay Witness* 15, no. 9 (June 1994): 1–6.

3. This point is developed and supported in my *Church and Age Unite! The Modernist Impulse in American Catholicism* (Notre Dame, Ind.: University of Notre Dame Press, 1992), chap. 4.

4. Cf. James Hennesey, S.J., *American Catholics: A History of the Roman Catholic Community in the United States* (New York: Oxford University Press, 1981), pp. 200–201.

5. On the ecclesiological functions of neoscholasticism, from a theological viewpoint, cf. Gabriel Daly, *Transcendence and Immanence: A Study in Catholic Modernism and Integralism* (Oxford: Clarendon Press, 1980); from a sociological viewpoint, see Lester R. Kurtz, *The Politics of Heresy: The Modernist Crisis in Roman Catholicism* (Berkeley: University of California Press, 1986), pp. 167–89.

6. On the strengths and weaknesses of the neoscholastic system, see Philip Gleason, *Keeping the Faith: American Catholicism Past and Present* (Notre Dame, Ind.: Notre Dame Press, 1987), pp. 166–72.

7. On this term, see the foreword to John Courtney Murray, *We Hold These Truths: Catholic Reflections on the American Proposition* (Kansas City, Mo.: Sheed and Ward, 1960, pb 1988).

8. On the emergence of the various traditions within social Catholicism, cf. Charles E. Curran, *American Catholic Social Ethics: Twentieth-Century Approaches* (Notre Dame, Ind.: Notre Dame Press, 1982).

9. David O'Brien, *Public Catholicism* (New York: Macmillan, 1989), pp. 243–52.

10. In this regard one might consider *The Challenge of Peace,* the U.S. bishops' pastoral letter, which adopts an "evangelical Catholic" approach when addressing members of the church, and a "republican Catholic" mode of discourse and reasoning when addressing the general public.

11. There has been, likewise, a historical rendering of each phase of Americanism, with Thomas McAvoy, *The Great Crisis in American Catholic History* (Chicago: H. Regency Co., 1957), ably representing the first wave and Jay Dolan, *The American Catholic Experience* (New York: Doubleday, 1985), representing the second phase. On the Americanist historiographical tradition, see Philip Gleason, "The New Americanism in Catholic Historiography," *U.S. Catholic Historian* 11 (Summer 1993): 1–18.

12. Murray, *We Hold These Truths,* pp. ix–x.

13. Cf. David Hollenbach, S.J., "Public Theology in America: Some Questions for Catholicism after John Courtney Murray," *Theological Studies* 37 (June 1976): 290–303.

14. In the last fifteen years or so there have been an impressive array of sophisticated projects toward this end. Cf., for example, Michael J. Himes and Kenneth R. Himes, O.F.M., *Fullness of Faith: The Public Significance of Theology* (Mahweh, N.J.: Paulist Press, 1993), and John A. Coleman, *An American Strategic Theology* (New York: Paulist Press, 1982).

15. Pope Leo XIII, *Longinqua Oceani,* quoted in John Tracy Ellis, ed., *Documents of American Catholic History* (Milwaukee: Bruce, 1956), pp. 517–18.

16. Leo XIII, *Testem Benevolentiae,* ibid., pp. 561–62.

17. Ibid., pp. 554–55.

18. Ibid. Italics in original.

19. Appleby, *Church and Age Unite!,* chap. 4.

20. Pope Leo XIII, *Testem Benevolentiae,* in Ellis, p. 557.

21. Appleby, *Church and Age Unite!,* introduction.

22. Pope Leo XIII, *Longinqua Oceani,* in Ellis, p. 516.

23. On the connection between Americanism and modernism, cf. Margaret Reher, "Americanism and Modernism: Continuity or Discontinuity?" *U.S. Catholic Historian* 1 (Summer 1981): 87–103.

24. In 1889, for example, Italian canon Salvatore di Bartolo published a book translated into English as *Criterions of Catholic Truth.* At his request Gibbons reviewed it, writing that it would surely "strengthen faith and remove prejudices" of those who considered Catholicism to be inimical to modern thought. John Tracy Ellis, *The Life of James Cardinal Gibbons, Archbishop of Baltimore, 1834–1921,* 2 vols. (Milwaukee: Bruce Publishing Company, 1952), vol. 2, p. 101.

25. Ireland's introduction to Elliott's *Life of Father Hecker* was reprinted in Felix Klein, *Americanism: A Phantom Heresy* (Crawford, N.Y.: Aquin Book Shop, 1951), pp. xiii–xxi.

26. Marvin O'Connell, *John Ireland and the American Catholic Church* (St. Paul: Minnesota Historical Society Press, 1988). Also see James H. Moynihan, *The Life of Archbishop John Ireland* (New York: Harper and Brothers, 1953), p. 110. Alfred Loisy reflected on Ireland in *Memoires pour servir a l'histoire religieuse de notre temps* (Paris: E. Nourry, 1930–31).

27. David Francis Sweeney, *The Life of John Lancaster Spalding, First Bishop of Peoria, 1840–1916* (New York: Herder and Herder, 1965).

28. John Lancaster Spalding, "Catholicism and A.P.A.ism," *North American Review* 154 (September 1894): 284.

29. Spalding, "Address at the Dedication of Catholic University," quoted in Sweeney, *The Life,* p. 171.

30. Quoted in John Tracy Ellis, *The Formative Years of the Catholic University of America* (Washington, D.C.: American Catholic Historical Association, 1946).

31. Spalding was quickly identified in Rome as a troublemaker. Denis O'Connell politely understated the case when he suggested that "Bp. Spalding is not considered strongly attached to Rome nor to Roman training." Cardinal Simeoni, the prefect of the Congregation of the Propaganda, warned Archbishop Corrigan of New York that Spalding's cornerstone speech "contained many unusual and not very sound ideas." And Spalding's testy response to *Testem Benevolentiae,* given in the Church of the Gesu in Rome, incited the opposition of the Jesuits, as did his friendship with Loisy, Lucien Laberthonniere, Friedrich von Hügel, and George Tyrrell. Tyrrell found Spalding's lectures "in sympathy with all that is best and most Catholic in modern thought." See Baron von Hügel to Percy Gardner, April 25, 1903, in Baron von Hügel, *Selected Letters, 1896–1924* (London: n.p., 1927), pp. 120–21.

32. Gilbert Français, C.S.C., to Rev. John Zahm, C.S.C., 10 November 1898, John Zahm Collection, University of Notre Dame archives.

33. "Leone XIII E L'Americanismo," *La Civiltà Cattolica,* ser. 17, vol. 5 (18 March 1899): 641–43.

34. "Evoluzione e Domma," *La Civiltà Cattolica,* ser. 17, vol. 5 (7 January 1899): 34–49.

35. Ibid., p. 41.

36. Ibid., pp. 42–48.

37. Slattery, "How My Priesthood Dropped from Me," *The Independent,* July 1906.

38. Ibid. Slattery wrote: "[Rome] has lost, and lost forever, her once universal hold on the state, the family, the university, the school, and the workshop. Her face is toward the setting sun, and humanity faces ever the morning. She will die hard. . . . In a similar way the old frameworks— law, civilization, Christianity serve to keep Rome before the eyes of the world. Men put life where there is none. . . . Rome knows full well that she is at least moribund. But she ever looks for that resurrection which seemed in sight under scholasticism, got its first set-back in the Renaissance, its defeat in the Reformation, and its divorce from the state in the American Revolution."

39. William L. Sullivan, *Letters to His Holiness Pope Pius X* (Chicago: Open Court, 1910), p. xvii.

40. Ibid., pp. xiv, xv.

41. Ibid., p. 134.

42. George Weigel, *Catholicism and the Renewal of American Democracy,* p. 1.

43. George Weigel, "Catholicism and the American Proposition," *First Things* 23 (May 1992): 42.

44. Eugene C. Bianchi and Rosemary Radford Ruether, eds., *A Democratic Catholic Church: The Reconstruction of Roman Catholicism* (New York: Crossroad, 1992).

45. Ibid., p. 12.

46. Ibid.

47. Michael Novak, "Schindler's Conversion: The Catholic Right Accepts Pluralism," *Communio* 19 (Spring 1992): 150.

48. See chapter 6.

49. Weigel, "Catholicism and the American Proposition," pp. 38–44.

50. Bianchi and Ruether, *A Democratic Catholic Church,* p. 7.

51. Ibid., p. 35.

52. Curran, "What Catholic Ecclesiology . . . ," in ibid., pp. 94–95. See also Jay P. Dolan, "The Desire for Democracy in the American Catholic Church," also in ibid., p. 116.

53. David L. Schindler, "Christology and the Church's 'Worldly' Mission: Response to Michael Novak," *Communio* 19 (Spring 1992): 164–78.

54. Both the neo-Americanists "on the right" and those "on the left" find themselves under attack from the so-called far right and far left, respectively—on basically the same grounds, namely, of compromising the integrity of the Catholic worldview by accommodation to the "alien," "secular" culture of America. Dennis P. McCann reports on such an attack by Stanley Hauerwas, who chides McCann, Ruether, Charles Curran, Richard McBrien—and George Weigel and Michael Novak—for forgetting "the importance of being Catholic." In a commentary that echoes many of its kind, Hauerwas charged that the attempts of these individuals to craft a viable, ecumenical public theology has led to a "confusion . . . typical of the intellectual leadership of mainline Protestantism" and has produced "a style in social ethics that is but a pale imitation of secular humanism." Dennis P. McCann, "Natural Law, Public Theology, and the Legacy of John Courtney Murray," *The Christian Century,* 5–12 September 1990, p. 801.

55. Fr. Robert D. Smith, "A Religion without Salt," *The Wanderer,* 21 January 1993, p. 2.

56. *The Wanderer* is a rich source of this rhetoric, with antimodernist columns appearing with regularity after the Council. The theme is also taken up eventually by the *National Catholic Register, Fidelity,* and assorted diocesan newspapers.

57. "Support the Pope," advertisement, *The Wanderer,* 14 October 1982; see also James Hitchcock, "The Papal Break with Liberal Protestantism," and Joseph Fessio, S.J., "Behind the Pope's Crackdown," in *New Oxford Review* (March 1980).

58. Msgr. George A. Kelly, *The Battle for the American Church* (Garden City, N.Y.: Image Books, 1981), pp. 37, vii.

59. Ibid., p. viii.

60. The payoff to Kelly's rehearsal of the historical precedent set by Loisy takes the form of a warning and an admonition: Do not rest content in the courage of Pius X and his successors in

banishing modernists from the church, for these and similar condemned opinions have been res-urrected in contemporary Catholicism. The first official warning of modernist resurgence, Kelly notes, came in 1950 when, one month after he issued his infallible declaration on Mary's assump-tion, Pope Pius XII issued the encyclical *Humani Generis,* in which he listed fifty-six errors against the faith moving through the corridors of Catholic seminaries and universities—doubts about transubstantiation and the real presence of Christ in the Eucharist, the inspiration and in-errancy of Scripture, original sin, the relevance of the church, and its authority to define faith and morals.

61. Gleason, *Keeping the Faith,* p. 170.

62. Joseph Clifford Fenton, "The *Sacrorum Antistitum* and the Background of the Oath against Modernism," *Ecclesiastical Review* 143 (October 1960): 249–50.

63. Gene Burns, *The Frontiers of Catholicism: The Politics of Ideology in a Liberal World* (Berkeley: University of California Press, 1992), p. 15.

3

The Loss of Theological Unity
Pluralism, Thomism, and
Catholic Morality

BENEDICT M. ASHLEY, O.P.

Nothing has contributed more to the postconciliar polarization of "conservatives" and "liberals" than the opening the Second Vatican Council gave to "pluralism" in theology. The notion that there are many valid perspectives on religious truth implies that these perspectives cannot be reduced to a single, objectively true theology and seems to contradict the biblical "one Lord, one faith, one baptism" (Eph 4:5).[1] Of course, pluralism in theology does not necessarily imply pluralism in faith, but will it not inevitably result in a split within the Catholic Church?

For the last thirty years, following the close of the Second Vatican Council in 1965, liberals in the American church have misconstrued the meaning of pluralism in such a way as virtually to equate it with "dissent." By the Council's definition, pluralism implies an openness to a variety of approved theological methods, all contributing to the constant renewal of orthodox Catholic teaching. It is not an invitation to dissent from such teaching. Nonetheless, Father Charles Curran and a number of his colleagues challenged the actual content of the authoritative teaching of the magisterium on the occasion of the promulgation of *Humanae Vitae,* Pope Paul VI's 1968 encyclical reaffirming the ban on artificial means of contraception. The Washington, D.C., press conference held by the dissenters was heavily publicized, and in such a way as to depict rebellious theologians as being on equal ecclesiastical footing with the bishops themselves. The American media specialize in this kind of coverage of public events—reportage in which crucial distinctions are seldom explained (or understood) by the press or television reporters. In this case the failure to emphasize the substantive difference between academics working in a university setting and bishops acting in service to the universal church had a profound leveling effect, and seemed to legitimize dissent as merely one of the ways of fulfilling one's role as a Catholic—much the way voting fulfills one's role as citizen of a democratic republic.

In this episode the Americanization of the Catholic experience took an unfortunate turn, for the controversy over *Humanae Vitae* opened the floodgates for a tidal wave of public dissent from official Catholic teaching—on abortion, homosexuality, the exclusion of women from ordination, and a host of other issues. From 1968 to the present day, the Catholic press (in periodicals such as *America, Commonweal,* and the *National Catholic Reporter*) has joined the secular media in giving equal play to the ideas of dissenters and bishops; some conservatives would argue that the coverage of "popular" theologians and academic dissenters is far more extensive than that given to the bishops, the church's official teachers. Every controversial opinion held by this or that theologian or by an author hawking his or her new book is held up as the latest and therefore the most important "development" in American Catholicism. (Some of these "experts" are ex-priests, ex-nuns, or even ex-Catholics.) In this context, conservative Catholics worry, it is very difficult if not impossible to preserve the authentic markers of Roman Catholic identity.

Defenders of theological pluralism attempt to soothe these conservative fears by pointing out that in the first millennium of the church there were many diverse theological traditions, notably those of the Eastern churches and of the Latin church, and earlier still those of Jewish and Gentile Christianity.[2] While some of these led to schism and heresy, they argue that theology had not yet developed as a systematic discipline distinct from the pastoral tradition of the faith, leading to the confusion of theological differences and faith differences. Therefore, in the High Middle Ages, when theology became an academic discipline within the new universities, rival schools of theology such as the Thomists and the Scotists were recognized by church authorities as different yet equally orthodox.[3] Thus medieval scholasticism seems to offer proof that pluralism in theology can exist in the unity of the faith and be fruitful for the church.

To this defense of pluralism, conservative Catholics reply that scholastic theologians never claimed, as do today's liberal theologians, a right to dissent from the decisions of the papal and episcopal magisterium, to which they remained strictly subordinated. Moreover, they say, scholastic pluralism degenerated into the factionalism of the Late Middle Ages and the nominalism that prepared the way for the "heresies" of the Reformation and the splintering of the church into denominations. According to some conservative Catholics, then, the record of theological pluralism has been on the whole very negative, reaching its climax in the relativism of "modernity," which today seems to be the chief foe of Christianity.

It is therefore hardly surprising that many conservative Catholics in the United States would like to see a return to Thomistic unity in Catholic education. They point out that the "Catholic Revival" in the period between the two world wars was based on this unity of outlook. The recovery of Europe after World War II and the defeat of communism, they remind us, were encouraged by social encyclicals based on Thomist principles. Finally, the preparations for Vatican II were led by theologians largely of Thomist formation, and the great expansion of Catholicism in the United States was largely based on a Catholic school system following Thomist principles. Contrasting these successes to the present confusion and division within the church, conservatives call for a return to the path marked out by Pope Leo XIII in his 1879 encyclical *Aeterni Patris*.

What many conservative Catholics today recall nostalgically as "Thomism," however, was actually a post-Tridentine eclecticism almost as Cartesian as it was Thomistic. Nonetheless, a version, or rather versions, of the thought of St. Thomas Aquinas dominated Catholic culture in the five decades of the twentieth century preceding the Second Vatican Council. Conservative Catholics lament the fact that this unifying dominance of Thomistic thought quickly collapsed after the Council. Why did it collapse? What are the consequences of this collapse for contemporary Roman Catholicism in the United States? This chapter provides some answers to these questions from the perspective of a Thomist Catholic moral theologian. We begin with a brief overview of the history of the fortunes of Thomism as a system unifying Catholic thought, education, and practice, illustrating along the way the diversity inherent in Thomism itself. This diversity is particularly relevant when we consider twentieth-century theological developments and the event of Vatican II as a watershed in the history of Thomism as a cultural and intellectual basis for Catholic culture. Accordingly, the chapter provides a description of three main schools of Thomism in this century. Finally, we conclude by assessing the impact of the pluralism seemingly endorsed by Vatican II on Thomism itself and on Catholic thought, education, and practice in the United States.

Thomism in the Modern Era: An Overview

In the post-Enlightenment era of modernity, secular humanism—the religion of humanity—has come to dominate the technologically advanced world. Of course, secular humanists ridicule the idea that their views constitute a set of dogmas comparable to those of a religion. Do they not advocate freedom of conscience, opinion, and speech? Do they not promote unrestricted pluralism? Conservatives, however, see ample evidence that the elites who control the universities and the public media have established secular humanism as the "theology" of the United States, replacing the former hegemony of Protestantism.

While secular humanists claim to advocate freedom of religion, they in fact enforce the privatization of all religions except secular humanism; i.e., they exclude them from the public sphere on the grounds that in a pluralist society, advocacy of a position other than the secularist faith amounts to an "imposition of one religion on others." Conservatives who formerly saw communism as the greatest enemy of Christianity now wonder whether secular humanism will prove even more dangerous because of its ability to disguise its suppression of religion by its pluralistic or libertarian slogans.

Conservative Catholics who share this critique of pluralism and secular humanism recognize four phases of the church's efforts to find a successful strategy for survival in the hostile or at least indifferent milieu of secular modernity. The first phase, during and following the French Revolution, was shocked reaction, ending in the compromise with Napoleonic tyranny and hopes for monarchical restoration to defend the church. This reactionary phase survives today with the Lefebvrists.

The second phase was that of Pius IX and Vatican I, in which the church sought to formulate a clear position on the relation of faith and reason to church authority. The church condemned certain theologies of good intention but erroneous formulation such as fideism, traditionalism, rationalism, and idealism. In this period the "Roman School" of theology positioned itself against Germanic culture with its remarkable development of romanticism and idealism. (Ironically, one of the chief personages of the Roman School was the German Thomist Joseph Kleutgen.) Germanic culture, the Romanists suspected, had been at the root of the Protestant movement and continued to Protestantize Catholicism. This suspicion was exacerbated by the Kulturkampf of governments seeking to establish state control over the church.[4]

The third phase of the church's battle against secular modernity was inaugurated by the decision of Pope Leo XIII to adopt a general program of dialogue with modern democratic government and to abandon any hope for monarchical restoration. Leo promulgated social encyclicals advocating positive solutions for the social evils that had arisen from modernity's advance, and advocated a uniform Christian education based on the tradition of scholasticism, especially on the philosophy and theology of St. Thomas Aquinas.[5]

In order to present the Catholic faith to the modern world, the church required a philosophy and a theology free of the idealism, rationalism, and fideism present in so many systems of thought developed during the Enlightenment.[6] While Pope Leo, in his encyclical *Aeterni Patris,* spoke of "scholastic thought" in its whole breadth, thereby including the medieval form of pluralism, he was emphatic in recommending the thought of Aquinas. He did not mean to limit Catholic theology to the past, because he explicitly insisted on the updating of Thomism. He certainly supposed that the good points of other scholastic thinkers would be assimilated to Thomism, but there is no doubt that he was giving priority to *one* system of theology in preference to all others, as the most suitable instrument in expounding the Christian faith.

Finally, from Leo XIII to the Second Vatican Council, twentieth-century popes have taken steps to promote Thomism and to defend its hegemony vis-à-vis other systems. Pius X, for example, went so far as to approve the *Twenty-four Theses* which were to define authentic Thomism as against certain eclectic systems claiming its name.[7] Nevertheless, Thomism, even prior to the Second Vatican Council, divided into a number of radically different interpretations and was opposed from several other perspectives.[8] The principal sources of opposition to Thomism in the decades extending from Vatican I (1870) to Vatican II (1965) were modernism, "the new theology," theologies generated by the new biblical criticism, and process theology.

Modernism, condemned by Pope Pius X in 1907, was an inchoate movement of liberal Catholic theologians and biblical critics, most of them priests, who resisted late-nineteenth-century neoscholasticism as a narrowing of the Catholic tradition which excluded the mystical-experiential mode of theology and closed the door to historical-critical research. The proponents of the Théologie Nouvelle, a twentieth-century school of thought originating in France, advocated return to the patristic base of theology, particularly the Augustinian tradition, instead of scholasticism. Both of these "movements," as well as other liberal theologians and philosophers, followed the historical-critical method in biblical exegesis, which exposed the weakness of the scholastic understanding of the Bible and further undermined the neoscholastic dominance of Roman Catholic thought. Process theology, especially as presented by the influential French Jesuit Pierre Teilhard de Chardin in the 1940s and 1950s, criticized Thomism as presenting a fixed, nonevolving world.

Although Vatican II gave unqualified approval to none of these tendencies, it certainly did not check them. Indeed, the "spirit of the Council" was invoked by a new generation of innovators, including Marxist-inspired liberation theologians and feminist theologians who developed a "hermeneutic of suspicion" based on the assumption that theologies reflect the economic and power concerns of different classes.

Because the Council fathers did not want to restrict theological efforts to the framework of Thomism, they contented themselves with recommending St. Thomas as the guide of systematic theological education,[9] and ignored the philosophical question. Subsequently, however, under Pope John Paul II, the Congregation for the Doctrine of the Faith has had to moderate opposing tendencies, especially in the field of moral theology. The writings of John Paul II, as in the recent encyclical *Veritatis Splendor,* reflect a Thomism which seeks to assimilate some of the methods and emphases of modern phenomenology, even as it avoids and occasionally condemns the excesses of modern Catholic theology. Thomism has in fact played such a conservative role since its recovery and renewal in the nineteenth century.

The Recovery of Thomism

The common impression that Thomism was the standard of Catholic theology and philosophy from the thirteenth century to Vatican II is seriously mistaken.[10] By the nineteenth century, Thomism was largely a memory clouded by the Enlightenment's contempt for the Middle Ages and "monkish superstition" (as Gibbons was fond of saying). The philosophy that had replaced it was generally a form of Cartesianism, often in the version of G. W. Leibnitz (d. 1716) or of Christian Wolff (d. 1754). By the end of the eighteenth century, theology had taken on a positivistic cast in which history rather than theory dominated. Some thought Thomism useless or even dead. The story of its re-emergence and eventual re-enthronement is one made dramatic by the exigencies of history.

Since Thomism was a heritage jealously guarded by the Dominican Order, it was endangered when the French Revolution and Napoleonic Wars pushed the Dominicans to the brink of extinction. In the first quarter of the nineteenth century, however, the Italian Vincentians and later certain Jesuits became advocates of a renewed Thomism. Thus Joseph Pecci (for a time a Jesuit) and his brother Giacchino, the future Leo XIII, were introduced to the thought of Aquinas and became convinced that the medieval scholastics and especially Aquinas provided a philosophical and theological synthesis that was thoroughly Christian yet capable of forming a solid point of departure from which to meet the problems of the modern world.

When Leo XIII became pope, he implemented this program in 1879 through the encyclical *Aeterni Patris*. It did not propose a simple return to the thought of the thirteenth century but explicitly urged Catholic philosophers and theologians to abandon obsolete questions and disputes and to use scholasticism and especially the work of Aquinas as a way of dealing positively with modern problems and discoveries. This confronted the church with the double problem of retrieving the authentic thought of St. Thomas and finding the element of truth in modern thought and then reconciling them.[11]

To advance his program, Leo XIII urged the founding of a center of Thomistic studies at the University of Louvain, headed by Fr. Désiré-Joseph Mercier (1881–1926).[12] The evolution of views at this Institut Superieur de Philosophie is evident in the textbooks written there and widely used to promote an updated Thomism, never quite free from the influence of Leibnitz and Wolff. In the United States, however, Leo's program was only gradually implemented.[13] In Jesuit colleges and universities, the form of neoscholasticism associated with the Jesuit Francisco Suarez (d. 1617) prevailed for many years. Elsewhere, the Thomism was largely that of Louvain.

In the late 1920s, scholarly reviews such as the Jesuit *Modern Schoolman* and the *New Scholasticism* (1927), the journal of the newly founded American Catholic Philosophical Association, challenged the historic authenticity of the thought of St. Thomas, as it had been rendered by the vague "Neo-Scholasticism." A basic question was raised: Is Thomism a consistent (although critical) development of Aristotle's thought, or a fundamentally different system? Non-Aristotelian Thomism divided into two main schools, the Existential and the Transcendental, the former rejecting any attempt to synthesize Thomism and Kantianism, the other proposing such a synthesis. Thus there emerged three main tendencies in twentieth-century neo-Thomism: Existential Thomism, Transcendental Thomism, and Aristotelian Thomism.

Existential Thomism

In the United States, the Existential Thomists, led by Etienne Gilson and centered at the Pontifical Medieval Institute of Toronto, formed the most influential school before Vatican II and are still generally received in America as the standard interpreters of the Angelic Doctor.[14] Gilson was a historian of philosophy who saw Thomism primarily as a theology shaped by a unique metaphysics. He gave little attention to Aquinas's commentaries on Aristotle's physical works, which he thought did not express Aquinas's own views. Nor did Gilson give much attention to the ethical or the strictly theological aspects of Aquinas's work. His stress was on the uniqueness of Aquinas's metaphysics, which he believed was constructed on a fundamentally different basis from that of Aristotle or any modern philosophy.[15] Gilson saw the unifying principle in Thomism as the act of existence (*esse*) known not conceptually but by an act of judgment enunciating that *being is not necessarily material.* This judgment founds a metaphysics independent of natural science or the other special disciplines, which are not strictly "philosophy." Gilson argued that the tradition of classical Thomistic commentators such as Cajetan and John of St. Thomas had obscured the importance of *esse* and hence was not an authentic guide to interpreting the Angelic Doctor.

At the same time Gilson admitted a kind of legitimate pluralism of philosophy and theology in the church, because, as he showed in his brilliant studies of St. Augustine, St. Bonaventure, and Duns Scotus, other systems can be constructed, valid on their own terms but having different aims than Thomism. Only Thomism, however, can fulfill the function of a "central" *philosophia perennis.*[16]

Transcendental Thomism

The Transcendental Thomists, led by Josef Maréchal, S.J.,[17] also see Thomism primarily as a metaphysics. But they claim that for Thomists to refuse to face the critical question raised by Descartes and Kant dooms any positive approach to the achievements of modern thought and culture and prevents the church from speaking to the modern world in terms it can understand. Maréchal held that Aquinas had developed a system which was valid in its own right, independent of Kantianism, but he believed that there was implicit in that system insights which Kant developed into an alternative and complementary system. According to Maréchal, a Thomist can accept Kant's system once it has been subjected to appropriate corrections.[18]

The Transcendental Thomists, in explaining their acceptance of Kant, begin with the fact that Aquinas broke from the Platonic tradition of abstracting knowledge entirely from any basis in the material world; indeed,

Aquinas explicitly accepted the Aristotelian principle that all knowledge comes from the senses. Yet the Platonic tradition was formidable. Plato held that the certitude and stability of intellectual knowledge cannot rest on sense knowledge because the material world is in constant flux. For Plato, the source of certitude was found not in the material world but in the ideal forms innate to the intelligence. For Augustine and many of the medievals, intellectual knowledge was a divine illumination. The followers of Duns Scotus further freed metaphysics from any dependence on the actual world by basing it on the univocal concept of Being and its modes, including the singularity of every substance. (Although this concept was derived by abstraction from sense knowledge, it gave access to the realm of *possibility*, not of actuality.)

Inaugurating the modern era of philosophy, Descartes revived the notion of innate ideas, while Hume and the empiricists attacked the distinction of intelligence from sense and, opting for sense knowledge, denied all certitude. Kant, in order to save the certitudes of mathematics and science, then revived the Platonic view that certitude depends on intelligence, but rooted this not in innate ideas but in innate logical categories by which sense data have to be organized to be intelligible. These categories are said to be a priori or "transcendental" to sense experience.

The Transcendental Thomists accept this Kantian notion and therefore ask whether in Aquinas's epistemology there is any room for such an a priori element in knowledge.[19] Aquinas teaches, they note, that in judgment the intelligence reflects on its own act; it not only knows but *knows that it knows*.[20] Thus the Transcendentalists can make their central claim, namely, that metaphysical certitude presupposes the subject's self-knowledge of the dynamism of its own acts. This self-knowledge transcends—is not dependent on—any particular data derived from the senses.

Although he denied that he was a Transcendental Thomist, Bernard Lonergan, S.J., elaborated this claim and admitted the convergence of his thought with Maréchal's. Lonergan's "cognitional theory" analyzed the way various kinds of objective truth are reached in the various special disciplines. At the metaphysical level, he argues, the mind attains perfect self-possession and perceives that its innate dynamic tendency to endless questioning implies the existence of the Absolute Truth, God, and the necessary truth of metaphysical principles. Thus metaphysics is *virtually* independent of sense knowledge and is in a sense *innate*, although in the human being sense experience is necessary to actualize it. Lonergan, however, seems to endorse a Platonizing metaphysics which denies the Aristotelian (and Thomistic) notion of a relative stability in the flux of material objects—a stability which makes it possible for sense knowledge to ground true certitude. Critics of Transcendental Thomism hold that the Platonizing interpretation of Aquinas is false.[21]

American Catholic conservatives have been suspicious of Transcendental Thomism in its theological applications and generally look back to the domination of Existential Thomism as the golden age of a unified Catholic thought. They see the theology of Karl Rahner as opening the way to a dangerous subjectivism and eclecticism. The real question, however, is whether either interpretation of Thomism provides a sufficiently radical critique of the secular humanist worldview, based as it is on modern science, to serve the purpose for which Leo XIII revived Thomism. Can the church enter into effective dialogue with secular humanism if the church has not honestly faced the problems raised by science?

Aristotelian Thomism

Aristotelian Thomism, promoted by William H. Kane, O.P., of Aquinas Institute, River Forest, Illinois,[22] and Charles De Koninck of Laval University,[23] is based on Aquinas's discussion of the sciences in his *Commentary on Boethius De Trinitate* q. 5 and 6 and in his philosophical commentaries on Aristotle.[24] In these works Aquinas holds that Aristotelian epistemology entails a plurality of scientific disciplines formally independent of each other and each with its own proper first principles, methodology, and type of truth and certitude. Metaphysics is First Philosophy—a reflection over all the *presupposed* special disciplines to distinguish and coordinate them according to the principles and causes common to them all. This First Philosophy studies the immaterial principles of all the things that are objects of the special sciences, principles that are known analogically only by arguments from effects to cause based on truths established by the special sciences.

Perhaps the most influential and creative Thomist on the American scene prior to Vatican II was Jacques Maritain.[25] He is generally considered an Existential Thomist, but he is perhaps better classed as an Aristotelian because his *chief d'oeuvre, The Degrees of Knowledge,*[26] dealt with the plurality of disciplines and placed metaphysics as the culmination, not the foundation, of knowledge. Yet Maritain was so impressed by the way the modern sciences have developed independently of any sound metaphysics to guide them that he felt it necessary to propose a new type of science, formally distinct from the philosophy of nature by the fact that it was not *dianoetic* or essential but *perinoetic* or merely accidental. This perinoetic knowledge is gained through models and hence should be subdivided into *empirio-metric* science using mathematical models, and *empirio-schematic* science using nonmathematical models.[27] While dianoetic knowledge can attain certitude, perinoetic knowledge remains merely probable. Hence natural philosophy is stable truth, while modern natural science is ever-changing.

Maritain does not seem to have realized that knowledge through models, which does indeed play a very large role in modern science, would have been interpreted by Aquinas not as a new type of *scientia* but as a *dialectical* part of the single science of natural philosophy.[28] For Aristotle and Aquinas, dialectic forms a necessary part of any science but does not stand on its own. Thus Maritain continued to isolate the certitude of metaphysics from any direct influence of modern science, which he considered merely probable. Hence little difference was perceived between his position and Gilson's. Furthermore, Maritain grounded metaphysics on an intuitive judgment that being *qua* being is not material.

The Aristotelian Thomists, on the other hand, took the position that natural science proves the existence of an Absolute First Cause which is nonphysical, as well as relative first causes that are nonphysical, of which the human intelligence is an instance.[29] Thus "being" is not exclusively material being or mathematical being but also must include immaterial beings of which the First Cause is the ultimate principle. Thus while every scientific discipline is about being, only First Philosophy considers being in its full (analogical) extension, precisely as being.

Aristotelian Thomists accuse the Transcendental Thomists of failing to show that the being studied by metaphysics is objectively real. Because the Transcendentalists depict being as mental being, say the Aristotelians, they remain imprisoned within the Cartesian subject and never attain to the objectively real. The Aristotelians also believe that the Existential Thomists have likewise failed to face the critical problem—finding a secure ground for metaphysics—since they suppose that being is not merely physical being, but do not establish the conditions for such a judgment in sense knowledge.

Transcendental and Existential Thomists point to the collapse of Aristotelian science in the face of modern science (which claims only probable knowledge). The triumph of modern science rendered invalid any physical proof of God or the immateriality of the human intellect, which therefore can be established with certitude only by a metaphysics independent of natural science. The Aristotelians reply that this refutation is based on an outmoded history of science.[30] Modern research has shown a fundamental continuity between Aristotelian and modern science, which has been masked by wrong interpretations of modern science based largely on Hume or Kant. The fundamental principles presented in Aristotle's *Physics* and *De Anima,* on which the proofs of immaterial existents are based, have been confirmed, not refuted, by modern science, and the correction of the more particular aspects of his scientific worldview does not invalidate these principles but is normal in science.

For the Aristotelian Thomists, then, the collapse of Thomism has been due to the fact that the other varieties of Thomism evaded the challenge of the natural sciences and attempted to develop a metaphysics having no roots in science. As a result, these varieties of Thomism were not able to engage secular humanism, which rests on a natural science interpreted in empiricist or Kantian terms.[31]

Preconciliar American Catholic Education

How did these various schools of Thomism influence the American church educationally? The Jesuits and Dominicans represent the clearest and most influential trends. A comprehensive account, however, would have to give prominent attention to the history of Thomism at the Catholic University of America, where Dominicans played some role and where many of the professors at Catholic institutions of higher learning did their doctoral studies. Still, at the college and university level, the Society of Jesus has been by far the predominant influence in American Catholic education. St. Ignatius Loyola required the members of his society to have a Thomistic education in philosophy and theology, but from the seventeenth century this meant Thomism as synthesized with Scotism by Francisco Suarez.[32]

The Jesuit tradition of education for the laity was strongly influenced by the humanism of the Renaissance with its emphasis on logic, rhetoric, and the Latin and Greek classics, although in the United States this had to be adapted to American conditions. Because Catholic collegians had been thoroughly instructed in the catechism in the parochial schools, only a course in apologetics or in church history was required at the college level. Catholic education was supposed to confirm laity in their faith so that they would be able "to give reason for the faith that is in them" in their secular vocation. Theology was for the clergy.

The Order of Preachers looked on Thomism as their proper possession, but in the United States they owned only one university, Providence College in Rhode Island. In the 1930s, however, the Dominicans realized an opportunity in the growth of women's colleges operated by congregations of sisters intent on training their own members as well as young laywomen. The Jesuits had a monopoly on men's education, but the women's colleges remained open to Dominican theologians. The question then arose as to what type of religious education they should provide young women.

The answer was most eloquently formulated by Father Walter Farrell, O.P., who argued that to make religious education respected at the college level, it should be taught as scientifically as other disciplines. But religious knowledge as a science, according to Aquinas, is theology, the *Regina Scientiarum*. Hence, all Catholic college students should learn theology as a science, or, better still, as a "wisdom." For Farrell, however, theology was practically identical with the *Summa Theologiae* of St. Thomas. The study of Scriptures was auxiliary, since Aquinas had already distilled the substance of the Bible and other disciplines in his scientific theology. Thus, under Dominican tutelage, many women's colleges (and some for men not under Jesuit direction) during the thirty years before the Council provided their students with courses systematically covering the entire *Summa*. Furthermore, these students were required to take an extensive range of Thomistic philosophical courses to prepare them for theology.

Farrell and his colleagues, however, recognized that a textual study of the *Summa* presupposed a depth of preparation and motivation which only Latin and a seminary setting could make possible. Consequently the Dominicans produced textbooks digesting the *Summa,* first Farrell's own brilliantly written *Companion to the Summa* in four volumes and then the *College Theology* texts, edited by Francis Cunningham, O.P., and published by the Priory Press. The Thomism of these works was substantially that taught by the redoubtable Reginald Garrigou-Lagrange of the Angelicum in Rome, faithful to the Dominican commentators of Aquinas, and heavily metaphysical in its emphasis, but little affected by historical study or the controversies of interpretation described above. Thus a whole generation of college-educated sisters and Catholic laywomen were well acquainted with the theology of St. Thomas, presented clearly but largely with little reference to current problems or intellectual trends in modern society.

In their zeal, the Dominicans believed that the laity at large should also have the opportunity to learn the wisdom of the Angelic Doctor. In all three provinces of the order in the United States, chapters of a Thomist Association were formed under lay leadership but with an itinerant faculty of Dominican fathers who provided the membership on Sundays with a monthly Mass, sermon, and lecture. The lectures systematically covered the *Summa* through the entire course, which took several years. The laity in attendance were usually professional people, teachers, lawyers, and physicians.

In the meantime the Jesuits also were developing more extensive religious requirements in their colleges and universities along lines which they considered more suited to the needs and interests of the laity. After World War II, the Jesuit philosophical programs abandoned Suarez for Existential Thomism and theology programs became *kerygmatic*. This term indicated the influence of the European liturgical and catechetical movement propagated by the works of Josef Jungmann, S.J., and of the patristic and biblical studies in which European Jesuits were then playing a prominent part.

American Dominicans saw these tendencies as mere eclecticism which would not provide students with anything substantial. They were only vaguely aware of the European movements in which Dominicans such as Yves Congar, M.-D. Chenu, and Edward Schillebeeckx were also playing a significant part, and the direction that Vatican II took was quite surprising to most of them. The decline in the women's colleges, the changes in the sisters' congregations, and the general move in Catholic colleges and universities to cut back on requirements in philosophy and religion resulted for Dominicans in a major re-employment of their apostolates, with far fewer men in teaching. The same trend, however, took place in the Society of Jesus, because their new generation turned toward the social apostolate. This shift has resulted in a postconciliar laity in whose education the influence of the thought of St. Thomas is much more modest.

"Traditional" Morality

Although it is not unusual to hear conservative Catholics wish for a return to "traditional moral theology," it is not always clear what they mean by this phrase. Many of them seem not to realize the disparity between authentic Thomism and the legalistic version of moral theology that predominated in the preconciliar church. Whereas the moral theology of Thomas Aquinas is teleological, treating the morality of human acts in relation to the ultimate end of the human person, the theology of the preconciliar moral manuals was deontological and legalistic, basing the morality of human acts on the will of the legislator. Whereas Thomistic moral theology emphasizes the development of character (virtue) through good action, the moral theology of the manuals reduced virtue to obedience to law, and emphasized casuistry. The manual theology was dominant in the preconciliar Catholic parochial schools in which most present-day conservatives were educated. Many conservative Catholics, therefore, equate the approach of the manuals with the authentic Catholic tradition, not realizing that it is merely one expression thereof.

Let us consider briefly the development of and challenges to the manual tradition. Before Vatican II, the seminary training of priests in the United States was uniformly based on manuals of moral theology first written by Jesuits and patterned on the work of St. Alphonsus Ligouri in the eighteenth century. These manuals were constantly updated as to particular detailed problems and moral controversies, but their methodology and the bulk of their contents were traditional. Although these manuals reflected to a degree the various theological traditions in which the authors were trained, notably the Dominican, Franciscan, Jesuit, and Redemptorist schools, the practical conclusions were almost totally convergent. Open, controversial questions had largely been closed by directives of the magisterium.

This remarkably uniform and technically detailed view of Catholic moral life was communicated to the laity through catechisms, through instruction in the Catholic schools, and through Sunday sermons, often scheduled systematically to cover the Ten Commandments. These moral standards were enforced by the practice of regular confession in which penitents were required to confess all their grave sins in species and number. No one who had committed a grave sin dared to receive the Eucharist or the other sacraments without first going to confession under pain of sacrilege. Moreover, sermons were frequently directed to urging Catholics not to remain in mortal sin even for an hour, since they might die at any time and be condemned forever to hell if they did not receive absolution.

The theoretical basis of the post-Tridentine moral theology developed in the manuals can be traced to the period of transition from the High Middle Ages to the Renaissance. Duns Scotus taught that morality is based not on the requirements of human nature as such but on the commands of God or of human authorities in church or state delegated to act in God's name. Scotus was simply taking up one strand of the Christian tradition going back to the Ten Commandments. This legalism or voluntarism, merely proposed by Scotus, was systematically developed by William of Ockham and the nominalists and came to dominate the late medieval moral theology against which Luther protested. In moderated form it was taken up by Francisco Suarez and became the dominant mode of moral thinking promoted by the Society of Jesus. In order to carry out the reforms of Trent, the Jesuits first produced the manuals of the type just described to assist them in their promotion of regular confession.

Such a voluntaristic system of morality is liable to degenerate into a minimalism or pettifogging casuistic legalism that finds loopholes in every moral law. In the grip of such a system, those of good will are likely to be enmeshed in scrupulosity and neurotic guilt, and those of bad will in cynical rationalizations for their sins. In the history of the United States church there have often been areas of behavior in which church teaching has been rigorously applied, and others in which it has been conveniently ignored. In the South, discrimination against blacks in schools, in seating in church, in order of communion, and in marriage was often practiced in Catholic churches without comment. The support by Catholics of corrupt politicians was common. Catholics were often indifferent to questions of social justice while enforcing a severe sexual morality on women, yet winking at its violation by men.

One of the main effects of the Thomist revival was to raise serious questions about this "traditional" moral theology, which, as we have seen, was far from purely Thomistic in its structure. Even before Vatican II, historical studies of Thomism led Catholic moralists to demand a revision of the classical moral manuals. Conservative intellectuals today find themselves accused of failing to accept the personalism of Vatican II, of ignoring human historicity, and of "physicalism" or "dualism." Yet they generally favored the revision of the old manual moral theology but rejected the novel moral methodologies proposed as replacements, such as proportionalism, which reduces moral judgment to a single "principle of proportionate reason," namely, whether in a human act the proportion of positive values prevails over that of its negative values. As *Veritatis Splendor* points out, this theory conflicts with the view of the magisterium, defended by conservatives, that some human acts are morally evil per se and hence that some concrete negative moral norms are binding in all circumstances without exception; e.g., it is always objectively wrong to intend abortion or suicide.

Such new methods of moral theology gained wide acceptance through the predominant influence of Karl Rahner, S.J.[33] For the conservative wing of American Catholicism, of course, Existential Thomism remains the chief intellectual support, although there is growing interest in Hans Urs von Balthasar's thought, which rests more on the Augustinian tradition.[34] Yet Rahner's Transcendental Thomism appeals to the romantic pole in secular culture. Supplemented by the theology of Bernard Lonergan, S.J., Rahner's approach has become profoundly influential in the United States.[35]

Rahner's theology is both comprehensive and profound. It flows from Maréchal and the phenomenologist Martin Heidegger, although it is always respectful of the thought of Aquinas. Rahner admitted his avoidance of the scientific question in an interview given not long before his death:

Certainly, the theologian has ultimately only one thing to say. But this one word would have to be filled with the mysterious essence of all reality. And yet each time I open some work of whatever modern science, I fall as theologian into no slight panic. The greater part of what stands written there I do not know, and usually I am not even in the position to understand more exactly what it is that I could be reading about. And so I feel as a theologian that I am somehow repudiated. The colorless abstraction and emptiness of my theological concepts frightens me. I say that the world has been created by God. But what is the world—about that I know virtually nothing, and as a result the concept of creation also remains unusually empty. I say as a theologian that Jesus is as man also Lord of the whole creation. And then I read that the cosmos stretches for billions of light years, and then I ask myself, terrified, what the statement that I have just said really means. Paul still knew in which sphere of the cosmos he wanted to locate the angels; I do not.[36]

Pluralism and Dissent: The Decline of the Moral Authority of the Church

The problem with this type of theology becomes acute when we move from the dogmatic area of theology to the moral.[37] Vatican II's liturgical reforms disturbed many conservative Catholics and led extremists to deny the validity of the sacraments performed by the new rites. The Council's ecumenical outreach disturbed others and led extremists into the Lefebvrist schism. Yet the main source of concern for conservative Catholics since the Council has been the decline of the moral authority of the church. In this decline the rise of dissent, as mentioned earlier, played a powerful role.

Conservatives are alarmed by what they see as a collapse of Christian moral standards in the church and a disastrous compromise with liberal Protestantism and still worse with secularism. Nor is their concern unsupported by the fact that today there is widespread neglect of confession, that in some places (against the admonitions of the Vatican) it has been largely replaced by "general absolution" without individual confessions, and that it is common to see all attending Mass receive communion, although it is well known that many present neither live according to the moral teaching of the church nor have gone to confession. Furthermore, there is constant complaint from parents that even in Catholic schools their children are not being given detailed moral instruction, do not know the catechism, are unaware of the gravity of mortal sin. Also, there is widespread resistance among priests and religious educators to the Vatican's requirement of early confession for children. Finally, sermons are seldom given on the importance of confession, the gravity of mortal sin, or the danger of hell. Even the doctrine of purgatory is often left unmentioned, so that at funerals the grieving family is prayed for but not the deceased, who is assumed unquestionably to be already in heaven.

Pierre Hegy reports a study which shows that between 1963 and 1990, the percentage of Catholics attending church at least once a week fell from 71 percent to 40.5 percent.[38] In 1972, 21 percent of Catholics saw nothing wrong in premarital sex; by 1990, the number had risen to 44 percent. In 1987, 70 percent of Catholics surveyed said "yes" in answer to the question, "Can one be a good Catholic without going to church every Sunday?" Sixty-eight percent said "yes" to the question, "Can one be a good Catholic without obeying the church's teaching on birth control?" Thirty-nine percent responded "yes" to the same question about abortion. Hegy thinks that these figures suggest a shift from both the conservative and liberal models of the church to an "evangelical" model of "empowerment" in which the church becomes a "movement" rather than a controlling organization. For conservatives, certainly, this seems simply a disaster.

These new and vague moral standards of the left wing of the church, conservatives note, receive ecclesial sanction not from the pronouncements of the Vatican, which are automatically regarded as negativistic, "controlling," reactionary, outmoded, and sure to be liberalized in due time, but from the so-called *sensus fidelium* and from the "distinguished theologians" of the "mainstream" whose expertise makes them more trustworthy than the often incompetent clergy. It appears to many conservatives that the American bishops overemphasize politically correct social justice issues whose solutions they admit are a matter only of human opinion and not of divine revelation, while speaking softly about issues of personal morality, especially sexual morality, where there is clear-cut biblical teaching. They suspect that this too is a compromise with secular liberalism.

Much of the blame for these erosions of traditional teaching and morality is laid on Rahner and his disciples. To conservatives it appears that traditional Catholic morality has been replaced by a new system in which there is only one obligation stressed, the Great Commandment of love of God and neighbor, but what this "love" consists in, other than a vague sentiment, is left to the individual conscience. The standards of "individual conscience" seem to conservatives to be relative, shifting, and based largely on pragmatic, secular standards determined by the laws of the United States, by popular psychology, and by "politically correct" notions current in the media. Conservative theologians have vigorously opposed the methodology of moral judgment based on "the principle of proportionate reason" which purports to be a "development" of Transcendental Thomism, on the grounds that it contradicts both Aquinas and the Catholic moral tradition.

The conservatives' accusations have centered in the United States chiefly on the writings of two influential moral theologians, Father Charles Curran and Richard A. McCormick, S.J. For both, the controversy over *Humanae Vitae* and the papal condemnation of contraception was the occasion for proposing revisions of the traditional methodology of moral theology. Curran was a student of Fr. Bernard Häring, a distinguished scholar in the tradition of the eighteenth-century Redemptorist school of moral theology characterized by a moderate voluntarism and legalism typical of the post-Tridentine church. Häring's *The Law of Christ* has been widely used in seminaries in the Vatican II period, because of its efforts to combine this traditional theology with an emphasis on the primacy of charity. His later writings are marked by a great concern for compassionate pastoral casuistry. Curran, working from the same attitude, has never attempted a new systematization of moral theology, but seeks only to open the discipline to the resources of modern psychology, sociology, and history so as to assist pastoral casuistry or decision-making. In doing so, however, he has felt it necessary to question moral norms which Catholic tradition has regarded as absolute.

Curran has promoted a novel theory of moral decision called "a theology of moral compromise," according to which acts that would be objectively immoral by natural law if there had been no original sin can in our fallen state in some cases become objectively moral. Curran accused traditional natural law theory (as reflected in *Humanae Vitae* and other Vatican pronouncements on sexual questions) of being "physicalistic" or "biologistic" because it makes the nature of the physical act rather than the moral intention of the agent the determinant of morality. Curran, like Häring, retains the general framework of Thomistic natural law theory but has tried to reconcile it with what he calls "contemporary Christian experience." But has he found a nonarbitrary method to distinguish in this "experience" between what is authentically Christian and what is simply a reflection of American culture dominated by secular humanism? His dissent from papal teaching on many points, especially in the field of sexual morality, led after twenty years of controversy to the declaration by the Vatican Congregation for the Doctrine of the Faith that he was not functioning as a "Catholic theologian," and to his consequent dismissal from the theology department of the Catholic University of America. Richard A. McCormick, S.J., is a student of John Connery, S.J., a moralist of unquestioned orthodoxy in the Jesuit casuistic tradition. As editor of "Moral Notes" in the prestigious scholarly journal *Theological Studies,* McCormick became an advocate of proportionalism. McCormick's application of this method of moral decision-making to complex problems in medical ethics has led him to criticize many positions of the magisterium in this field.

Proportionalism flows out of Rahner's Transcendental Thomism and his meta-ethics, which were deeply colored by the phenomenology of Heidegger and his colleague Max Scheler.[39] For Scheler there are absolute moral values which by a moral sense we grasp transcendentally (i.e., a priori), but their categorial application to concrete moral decisions is a creative act for which there can be no absolute rules. In Europe, well-known moralists such as Joseph Fuchs, S.J., Bruno Schüller, S.J., and Peter Knauer, S.J., have proposed proportionalism as a methodological theory. Conservatives are convinced that in application it has been the source of much of the dissent from traditional moral norms concerning extramarital sex, contraception, homosexual practice, remarriage after divorce, abortion, euthanasia, etc.

In the United States, Curran and McCormick have been quite influential in promoting proportionalism among the main Catholic publishers of scholarly books and magazines. They have strongly influenced teaching in many seminaries and schools of theology. The 1977 report of a task force of the Catholic Theological Society of America, *Human Sexuality: New Directions in American Catholic Thought,* was an extreme yet significant example of this influence.[40] Its criticism by the National Conference of Catholic Bishops was largely ignored.

The writings of Curran and McCormick have been so influential in American seminaries and among American priests that conservatives generally believe that a significant percentage of priests no longer regard moral pronouncements of the Vatican as normative for their pastoral practice. Rather, many priests follow the writings of liberal moral theologians on the presumption that "the church will change on these questions as she has always done" to catch up with the enlightened views of American democracy. With Curran they feel that such views reflect the *sensus fidelium,* the "Christian experience of the laity" which is the authentic church, while the magisterium is simply trying to defend its power. Conservatives, on the other hand, see the popes as the preservers of traditional morality against the liberal theologians and wish only that they would act more decisively against them.

So widely accepted has proportionalism been in the United States that theologians who have criticized it have been stereotyped automatically as conservatives. Thus the Dominicans Kevin O'Rourke, Brian Millady, and myself, and laymen theologians Russell Hittinger, John Haas, and Mark Johnson have argued that proportionalism justifies acts which are contradictory to the ultimate end of human nature known to us through philosophical and theological analysis. Germain Grisez, William E. May, and John Finnis, who do not accept certain important aspects of Thomistic moral theory, have likewise argued that proportionalism attempts to justify acts that violate one of the several basic and self-evident goods of human nature. The Jesuits John Connery and Thomas O'Connell judge proportionalism to be casuistically arbitrary and unworkable; and the "Augustinian" school of Dietrich von Hildebrand, while agreeing with Max Scheler's notion of the distinction between transcendental values and categorial norms, has maintained that moral ideals can be realized by divine grace, in all circumstances.

Conservative Catholics characterize the moral views of Curran as reflecting the "situationism" or "contextualism" popular in liberal Protestantism. They suspect that these theories are hardly more than academic rationalizations of moral compromise. Liberals in turn charge conservatives with hypocrisy for decrying the decline of sexual morals while remaining indifferent to the questions of social justice. Conservatives reply that this liberal stress on "social justice" is a hypocritical strategy for shifting attention from responsibility for one's personal behavior to a specious concern for social problems over which Catholics in a secular society have little or no control. Moreover, conservatives point out that they are more consistent than the liberals, since conservatives generally support the Vatican in both its conservative stand on personal morals and its liberal stand on social justice, while the liberals support it only on the latter positions and dissent from it on the former.

The Future

It remains to be seen how the criticism of proportionalism and situationism presented in Pope John Paul II's 1993 encyclical *Veritatis Splendor* will be received, and whether it will assist in promoting a less polarized moral thinking among Catholics. Deeper questions will likely persist, however, including those about moral authority ("Who has the right to decide what is moral and immoral?") and the grounds of authority ("On what is this judgment based?").

In the postconciliar era, the fragmentation of Thomism and the general pluralism in theology have meant that the center of authority is often contested. J. A. DeNoia, O.P., has pointed out that Vatican II had two aspects: *aggiornamento* (updating) and *ressourcement* (return to the sources), but that in the public media the emphasis has been only on the former.[41] It is hardly surprising, therefore, that the Extraordinary Synod of 1985, an effort by the magisterium at *reaccentramento* (recentering), was seen by the liberal press as a retrenchment.

Today moderate conservatives ask for a recentering which does not reject the need for updating but puts equal emphasis on a return to the sources. This does not mean a revival of the narrow neoscholasticism of the manual tradition, but a recovery of the whole heritage of Christian tradition. To such a *ressourcement,* conservatives believe, St. Thomas Aquinas will contribute his great gift for *reaccentramento*. Moderate conservatives believe that Aquinas, freed from some of the misinterpretations I have described, will provide a model for the church to accept the pluralism of modern culture without losing the plenitude of its own tradition. Their intellectual efforts seek to transform that hope into reality.

NOTES

1. See Avery Dulles, S.J., *The Craft of Theology: From Symbol to System* (New York: Crossroad, 1992), pp. 124–26, for a summary of the bewildering number of theological trends since Vatican II. For problems this raises with the very notion of theology, see David Tracy, *Blessed Rage for Order: The New Pluralism in Theology* (New York: Seabury Press, 1975).

2. See Jean Daniélou, *A History of Early Christian Doctrine,* vol. 1, *Theology of Jewish Christianity;* vol. 2, *The Gospel Message and Hellenistic Culture* (London: Darton, Longman, Todd, 1964).

3. For the different views of the nature of theology in the High Middle Ages, see Yves M.-J. Congar, *A History of Theology,* trans. and ed. Hunter Guthrie, S.J. (Garden City, N.Y.: Doubleday, 1968), pp. 85–143, and William C. Placher, *A History of Christian Theology: An Introduction* (Philadelphia: Westminster Press, 1983), pp. 140–61, who speaks of the "fragile synthesis" of the High Middle Ages.

4. For a more positive appreciation of the Germanic theology of this period, see Thomas F. O'Meara, O.P., *Church and Culture: German Catholic Theology, 1860–1914* (Notre Dame, Ind.: University of Notre Dame Press, 1991).

5. He explained this last step in the encyclical *Aeterni Patris* (1879). Translation in Victor B. Brezik, C.S.B., ed., *One Hundred Years of Thomism: Aeterni Patris and Afterwards—A Symposium* (Houston: Center for Thomistic Studies, University of St. Thomas, 1981), pp. 173–98.

6. See Marcia Colish, "St. Thomas in Historical Perspective: The Modern Period," *Church History* 44 (1975): 445.

7. See Edouard Hugon, O.P., *Les Vingt-Quatre Thèses: Principes de Philosophie,* 9th ed. (Paris: P. Tequi, 1946).

8. Gerald A. McCool, S.J., *Catholic Theology in the Nineteenth Century: The Quest for a Unitary Method* (New York: Crossroad, Seabury, 1977), and *From Unity to Pluralism: The Internal Evolution of Thomism* (New York: Fordham University Press, 1989); Georges Van Riet,

Thomistic Epistemology: Studies concerning the Problem of Cognition in the Contemporary Thomistic Schools, 2 vols. (St. Louis: B. Herder Book Co., 1963); and Helen James John, *The Thomist Spectrum* (New York: Fordham University Press, 1966).

9. "Then by way of making the mysteries of salvation known as thoroughly as they can be, students should learn to penetrate them more deeply with the help of speculative reason exercised under the tutelage of St. Thomas." *Optatam Totius,* n. 16.

10. See Thomas J. A. Hartley, *Thomistic Revival and the Modernist Era* (Toronto: Institute of Christian Thought, University of St. Michael's College, 1971), with extensive bibliography pp. 90–106; Leonard E. Boyle, O.P., "A Remembrance of Pope Leo XIII: The Encyclical Aeterni Patris," comment by James A. Weisheipl, O.P., in Brezik, *One Hundred Years,* pp. 7–27; and Giovanni Felice Rossi, *La Filosofia nel Collegio Alberoni e il NeoTomismo,* Monografie del Collegio Alberoni, 25 (Piacenza: Collegio Alberoni, 1961), and *Il movimento neotomista piacentino inizato al Collegio Alberoni da Grancesco Grass nel 1751 e la formazione di Vincenso Bussetti* (1974), in the series directed by Antonio Piolanti, Biblioteca per la Storia del Tomismo (Pontificia Academia Teologica Roma, Città del Vaticano).

11. The work of publishing a critical text of Aquinas's *Opera Omnia* (the Leonine edition) is, after more than one hundred years, still in progress! Remarkable efforts by scholars such as Denifle, Mandonnet, Haureau, Wulf, Gilson, Chenu, Congar, and Van Steenberghen have largely succeeded in putting Aquinas into his historical context, but no up-to-date synthetic history of Thomism and its influence has been written. As to the fundamental grounds and unity of Aquinas's system, there is wide divergence.

12. See Louis de Raeymaeker, *Le Cardinal Mercier et l'Institut Superieur de Philosophie de Louvain* (Louvain: Publications Universitaires, 1952).

13. See Gerald A. McCool, S.J., "The Tradition of Saint Thomas in North America: At 50 Years," *The Modern Schoolman* 65 (March 1988): 185–206. John S. Zybura, ed., *Present-Day Thinkers and New Scholasticism: An International Symposium* (St. Louis: B. Herder and Co., 1926); and Jesse A. Mann, "Neo-Scholastic Philosophy in the United States of America in the Nineteenth Century," *Proceedings of the American Catholic Philosophical Association* 33 (1959): 127–36.

14. For Gilson's biography, see Lawrence K. Shook, C.S.B., *Etienne Gilson* (Toronto: The Pontifical Institute of Medieval Studies, 1984); and Armand G. Maurer, "The Legacy of Etienne Gilson," in Brezik, *One Hundred Years,* pp. 28–44.

15. For Gilson, Aquinas's philosophy, though formally distinct from Christian theology, could never have been established except on the basis of the biblical revelation of God as the "I AM," and hence it deserves the name "Christian philosophy." James A. Weisheipl, O.P., in his comment on Leonard Boyle's article in Brezik, *One Hundred Years,* pp. 24–25, says that the term *philosophia Christiana* (which has given rise to endless controversy) does not occur in the official publication of *Aeterni Patris* or in its title and received currency only through its translated versions.

16. *The Christian Philosophy of St. Augustine* (New York: Random House, 1960); *The Christian Philosophy of Saint Bonaventure* (New York: Sheed and Ward, 1938); *Jean Duns Scot: Introduction à ses positions fondamentales* (Paris: Vrin, 1952). The centrality of Thomism is argued in his major work, *The Unity of Philosophical Experience* (New York: Scribner's, 1937).

As for the efforts of Transcendental Thomism to reconcile Aquinas and Kant, Gilson held that these are based on the false Cartesian epistemological question which, once taken seriously, inevitably ends in idealism and skepticism. Related to this school is the work of Cornelio Fabro, who emphasized the doctrine of various degrees of "participation" in *esse* as central to Thomism, but credited it to Plato, not Aristotle. See Cornelio Fabro, *La nozione metafisica di partecipazione,* 2nd ed. (Turin: Societa Editrice Internazionale, 1950). See also L.-B. Geiger, *La participation dans le philosophie de saint Thomas* (Paris: Vrin, 1942).

17. His principal work is *Le Point de départ de la métaphysique,* 5 vols. (Paris: Desclée De Brouwer, 1944–49, originally 1922–26); see Van Riet's *Thomistic Epistemology,* vol. 1, pp. 236–71, on the influence on Maréchal of Maurice Blondel, *L'Action* (Paris: Alcan, 1893),

rev. ed. (Paris: Presses Universitaires de France, 1950), translated by Oliva Blanchette as *Action: Essay on a Critique of Life and Science of Practice* (Notre Dame, Ind.: University of Notre Dame Press, 1984); also McCool, *From Unity to Pluralism*, pp. 87–113.

18. Maréchal, *Le Point de départ*, vol. 5, pp. 66–71.

19. Some draw support from the historic fact that Aquinas was obviously also influenced by the Platonic tradition drawn from Augustine and the Plotinian Pseudo-Dionysius. On this topic see Robert J. Henle, S.J., *St. Thomas and Platonism* (The Hague: Martinus Nijhoff, 1956).

20. *Quaestiones Disputatae de Veritate*, 1, a.9.

21. For an evaluation by an Existential Thomist, see Robert J. Henle, S.J., "Transcendental Thomism: A Critical Assessment," in Brezik, *One Hundred Years*, pp. 90–116.

22. See the article of James A. Weisheipl, O.P., in the festschrift for W. H. Kane, O.P., in Weisheipl, ed., *The Dignity of Science* (Washington, D.C.: The Thomist, 1961), and my essay "The River Forest School of Natural Philosophy," in R. James Long, ed., *Philosophy and the God of Abraham: Essays in Memory of James A. Weisheipl* (Toronto: Pontifical Institute of Medieval Philosophy, 1991), pp. 1–16.

23. For De Koninck's view, see "The Unity and Diversity of Natural Science," in Vincent E. Smith, ed., *The Philosophy of Science* (Jamaica, N.Y.: St. John's University Press, 1961), pp. 5–24.

24. Oddly, Gilson held that these commentaries do not express Aquinas's own philosophical convictions, but it is now generally conceded that they are in fact Aquinas's defense against those of his day who considered his adoption of Aristotelianism dangerous. See James A. Weisheipl, O.P., *Friar Thomas D'Aquino* (Garden City, N.Y.: Doubleday, 1974), pp. 281–85. Also John M. Quinn, O.S.A., *The Thomism of Etienne Gilson: A Critical Study* (Villanova, Pa.: Villanova University Press, 1971), pp. 94–124, and S. Elders, "S. Thomas D'Aquin et Aristote," *Revue Thomiste* 88 (1988): 357–76.

25. See Donald A. Gallagher, "The Legacy of Jacques Maritain," in Brezik, *One Hundred Years*, pp. 45–60.

26. Translated by Gerald B. Phelan (New York: Scribner's, 1959); see also Joseph W. Evans, "A Maritain Bibliography," *The New Scholasticism*, 46, no. 1 (January 1972): 118–28.

27. See his *Degrees of Knowledge*, pp. 21–70, 136–201; *The Philosophy of Nature* (New York: Philosophical Library, 1951), reviewed by William H. Kane, O.P., *The Thomist* 16 (1953): 127–31; and "The Philosophy of Nature," in *Science and Wisdom* (New York: Scribner's Sons, 1940).

28. See my *Aristotle's Sluggish Earth* (River Forest, Ill.: Aquinas Institute, 1957).

29. For current debate see John F. X. Knasas, *The Preface to Thomistic Metaphysics: A Contribution to the Neo-Thomist Debate on the Start of Metaphysics* (New York: Peter Lang, 1990).

30. See James A. Weisheipl, O.P., *The Development of Physical Theory in the Middle Ages* (New York: Sheed and Ward, 1959) and *Nature and Motion in the Middle Ages*, ed. William E. Carroll (Washington, D.C.: Catholic University of America Press, 1985); for Wallace, *Causality and Scientific Explanation*, 2 vols. (Ann Arbor: University of Michigan Press, 1972–74), pp. 176–83; *From a Realist Point of View* (Washington, D.C.: University Press of America, 1979); *Galileo and His Sources* (Princeton: Princeton University Press, 1984); and *Galileo, the Jesuits, and the Medieval Aristotle* (Hampshire, Great Britain: Variorum Press, 1991).

31. See my article "Thomism and the Transition from the Classical World-View to Historical-Mindedness," in *The Future of Thomism*, ed. Deal W. Hudson and Dennis W. Moran, Preface by Gerald A. McCool, S.J. (Notre Dame, Ind.: University of Notre Dame Press, 1992), pp. 109–22.

32. For what follows see George Ganss, S.J., *St. Ignatius' Idea of a University* (Milwaukee: Marquette University Press, 1956), and the numerous works of Walter Ong, S.J.

33. Some of the difficulties in Thomistic moral theology which this trend felt were in need of revision are explained by Michael Bertram Crow, "Thomism and Today's Crisis in Moral Values," in Brezik, *One Hundred Years*, pp. 74–89.

34. James O'Donnell, S.J., *Hans Urs von Balthasar* (Collegeville, Minn.: Liturgical Press/Michael Glazier, 1992), pp. 3–5, lists as the main influences on Balthasar Henri de Lubac, S.J., Erich Przywara, S.J., and the mystic Adrienne Speyer.

35. The process theology of Teilhard de Chardin might have moved American theology into deeper engagement with science, but it proved too superficial to maintain much influence. For an appreciation of Rahner, see Ann Carr, *The Theological Method of Karl Rahner* (Missoula, Mont.: Scholars Press for American Academy of Religion, 1977); for a criticism see Fergus Kerr, O.P., *Theology after Wittgenstein* (Oxford: Basil Blackwell, 1986), pp. 3–27, and Avery Dulles, *The Craft of Theology* (New York: Crossroad, 1992), p. 132.

36. Karl Rahner, "The Experiences of a Catholic Theologian," *Communio* 11, no. 4 (1984): 412.

37. Rahner did not write much about moral theology, but his few essays on the foundations of ethics were quite influential.The fundamental essay is "On the Question of a Formal Existential Ethics," in *Theological Investigations*, vol. 2 (Baltimore: Helicon Press, 1963), pp. 217–34.

38. Pierre Hegy, "'The End of American Catholicism?'—Another Look," *America* 168, no. 15 (1 May 1983): 4–9.

39. Scheler's chief work is *Formalism in Ethics and Non-Formal Ethics of Value: A New Attempt toward the Foundation of an Ethical Personalism,* trans. M. S. Frings and R. L. Funk (Evanston, Ill.: Northwestern University Press, 1973). For discussion see Alfons Deeken, *Process and Permanence in Ethics* (New York: Paulist Press, 1974).

40. Anthony Kosnick, ed., *Human Sexuality: New Directions in American Catholic Thought* (New York: Paulist Press, 1977).

41. "American Theology at Century's End: Postconciliar, Postmodern, Post-Thomistic," delivered at a symposium at the University of St. Thomas in Rome, 4–5 May 1990.

4

"A Pox on Both Your Houses"
A View of Catholic Conservative-Liberal
Polarities from the Hispanic Margin

ALLAN FIGUEROA DECK, S.J.

> *Liberal Christianity encountered*
> *modernity, accepted much of it, and*
> *now, instead of directing, inspiring*
> *and renewing it, it has almost*
> *disappeared within it.*
> *—Langdon Gilkey*[1]

Efforts to understand contemporary Roman Catholicism in the United States are often marred by the failure to take into account the massive presence of new constituencies. Historians who have focused on the European immigrant story—the *terminus a quo*—often celebrate the "coming of age" of the church in the years following the Second World War, paying little attention to the Catholic population and the history of the Southwest. Modern interpreters, who concentrate on the tensions between Catholicism and modern culture, or who take an ecclesiastical approach to American Catholicism, often concentrate on middle-class or mainstream issues, ignoring the "new" Catholic populations that constitute a significant portion of the church in many eastern and midwestern cities. In both cases, those whose lives and concerns tend to be ignored are Hispanics, a group that now constitutes more than 35 percent of the American Catholic population.

When critics and interpreters find controversies between conservative and liberal Catholics, therefore, or notice wide disparities of viewpoint in newspapers such as *The Wanderer* and the *National Catholic Reporter,* they take as their point of departure a mainstream reality that they have helped to create. The liberal/conservative debate reflects diverse points of view and cleavages among mainline United States Catholics who, regardless of which side they are on, occupy the territory of secular, modern North Americans.

Rapid change in the cultural and social class makeup of U.S. Catholics demands that we now address the issue of the "second wave," the *terminus ad quem.* Where is United States Catholicism going? What becomes of today's passionate liberal-conservative clashes as the "new Catholics" come into their own? There has been a tendency to freeze the analysis on the moment of mainstreaming, while failing to notice that the river has moved on. This chapter explores the relevance and significance of conservative-liberal polarizations, from within an emerging new perspective, that of the burgeoning Hispanic Catholic communities. Their distinctive heritage and style of acculturation, occurring *at this moment* and not some other in U.S. history, make past interpretations of the immigrant reality, the so-called immigrant analogy, inadequate for grasping the meaning and import of their presence.[2]

David Hayes-Bautista, Mario Barrera, and other Hispanic researchers have begun to detect a distinctive pattern of Hispanic assimilation for the United States. Hispanic immigrants are assimilating to the North American milieu, yet the speed at and the degree to which they do so contrasts them with previous immigrant groups. A notably higher retention rate for language, religion, and attitudes toward family are among the factors highlighted in recent studies. Mario Barrera uses the term *re-traditionalization* to refer to the conscious effort on the part of U.S. Hispanics to be North American in a new way.[3]

If indeed that is the case, then U.S. Hispanics may represent a new way of being North American, of being "modern" and Catholic. Their tradition's encounter with modernity, distinct from that of Euro-American conservatives and liberals, may offer another road for Christianity in the global village of the coming millennium. This chapter explores that possibility.

Who Are the Hispanics?

In the period since 1945, the Hispanic[4] presence in the Catholic Church has dramatically risen in both national and global terms. Approximately 35 percent of the worldwide population of Roman Catholics are found in Latin America.[5] More than one-third of U.S. Roman Catholics are Hispanic, and if projections are met, half of all U.S. Roman Catholics will be of Hispanic origin sometime in the early years of the coming millennium.[6] For many decades the Hispanic presence was viewed as a regional reality, relevant, perhaps, to the Southwest and California but of little moment elsewhere. Yet by the 1980s, significant Hispanic populations were to be found in every major city of the United States. The largest concentrations of U.S. Hispanics are found in five states: California, Texas, Florida, New Jersey, and Illinois. Twelve archdioceses or dioceses of the United States have an Hispanic Catholic population in excess of 50 percent. Fifty-five percent of all dioceses reporting had some form of Hispanic ministry. Surprisingly, Hispanics constitute 60 percent of the Catholic community in places such as Yakima, Washington, and 15 percent of the Catholic population in Alaska.[7] Diocesan seminaries are admitting Hispanic students in larger numbers than ever before. Approximately a third of the diocesan seminarians in California and Texas are Hispanics.[8]

Perhaps one of the reasons for the marginality of Hispanic concerns in both the church and society at large despite the overwhelming evidence of their presence is the diversity of the various groups—24 million strong today—lumped under the term *Hispanic* or *Latino*. Historically the Mexicans and their progeny were the people in question. Unrelenting immigration from every conceivable Latin American nation, however, has contributed to an unprecedented diversity of national origin. To that must be added serious differences in regard to social class status and level of assimilation. It has therefore become more difficult to generalize about Hispanics, a term used only in the United States, since "Hispanics" or "Latinos" do not really exist in the various Latin American nations, where such an umbrella term is unnecessary.[9]

Nevertheless, there are grounds for asserting a commonality of purpose and destiny for these peoples: the perdurance of the Spanish language, their Catholic ethos, and, as theologian Virgilio Elizondo points out, the *mestizo* experience (racial mingling of Iberians, Native Americans, and Africans) that most of the Hispanic cultures in question have undergone. The underlying cultural unity of the Hispanic American peoples has been noted by Mexican educator José Vasconcelos in his concept of the *raza cósmica,* the "cosmic race," generated over five hundred years of Catholic Hispanic civilization in the Americas. Despite the growing diversity of the Hispanic communities with the coming of large numbers of Central American and Caribbean immigrants and the upward social class mobility of second and third generations, 60 percent of the Hispanic population continues to be of Mexican origin. The U.S. Bureau of the Census maintains that the situation will remain so for the foreseeable future, and significant numbers of these people, particularly the newest immigrants, are socioeconomically deprived.[10]

In assessing the reality of the U.S. Catholic Church in the closing decade of this century, it becomes increasingly urgent to factor in the data and perspectives corresponding to this emergent, youthful force. The considerable diversity of the Hispanic groups in terms of social class, level of assimilation, and English language acquisition suggests that generalizations about the so-called Hispanic reality must be taken with caution.

More important, the idea that Hispanics will acculturate in the same way the Irish, Germans, and Italians did is inadequate. The Hispanic presence cannot be grasped simply in terms of the traditional "immigrant analogy," as David Hayes-Bautista has demonstrated.[11] Interpretations coming out of Latin America today indicate that Latin Americans are certainly being affected by the "acids of modernity." British social scientists William Rowe and Vivian Schelling have shown, however, that the popular masses in Latin America are maintaining several premodern popular traits and cultural values.[12] Their findings are somewhat reminiscent of those of Hayes-Bautista, who was looking at U.S. Hispanics.

Consequently, there is a need to acknowledge the distinctiveness of Latin American popular cultures as they interact with the dominant North American culture. It cannot be presumed that they are simply going the way of previous immigrant cultures. As the Hispanics go, so goes a major part of the U.S. Catholic Church. Insight into U.S. religion is therefore seriously limited by the failure to address the implications of this remarkable trend.[13]

Major obstacles, however, stand in the way of carrying out this pressing new task. There is a notable dearth of research on the subject. Mainstream Catholic writers, while acknowledging the sea change, have generally preferred to bracket it. Only now has a "critical mass" of Hispanic writers, such as those represented by the Academy of Catholic Hispanic Theologians of the United States (ACHTUS) or La Comunidad of the American Academy of Religion (AAR), begun to engage academia with research interests, writing, and teaching in this field. For the first time, Hispanic religious thinkers rooted in the context of the United

States, not imports from Latin America, are entering into a dialogue with the U.S. Catholic mainstream.[14]

It therefore is not only fitting but increasingly necessary that Hispanic perspectives be taken toward most of the pressing issues facing the churches. Typically, interpreters ignore Hispanics. A case in point is Richard John Neuhaus's treatment of the "American Catholic moment." He exults over the mainstreaming of Catholicism in America and its new-found influence while ignoring one-third and the fastest-growing part of that church. I have criticized him and other participants in this debate for disregarding the Hispanic presence, for giving the impression that the U.S. Catholic Church "has now arrived."[15] It may have arrived, but another train, as it were, is leaving the station. And with few exceptions, mainstream U.S. Catholic thinkers are not yet running to get on this one.

Consequently, I have chosen to address an issue previously unexplored: Hispanic Catholic traditionalism in relationship to its mainstream, U.S. Catholic counterpart. The pioneering work of William D. Dinges provides a framework for understanding the nature and scope of traditionalism among mainstream U.S. Catholics who are middle-class and Irish, Italian, German, or Slavic in ethnic origin. The Fundamentalism Project, directed by Martin E. Marty and R. Scott Appleby, places the discussion about traditionalisms in the context of international movements of religious reaction in Asia, the Middle East, and Latin America.[16] Finally, this book is taking a deeper and more critical look at the phenomenon within U.S. Catholicism.

When speaking of traditionalism in the Hispanic context, one is not referring primarily to the specific kind of traditionalism, profiled in Dinges's chapter of this book, that revolves around dissatisfaction with the reformed liturgy. Nor does it refer to concerns regarding the legitimacy of the current pope such as those of the sedevacantists discussed in the chapter by Joseph Komonchak. United States Hispanic groups with such interests are virtually nonexistent. Rather, what is meant by Hispanic traditionalism is simply the orientation to the traditional, often pre–Vatican II, even pre-Tridentine spirit of Catholicism which has perdured among Hispanics but without that strident ideological edge characteristic of U.S. Catholic traditionalists discussed elsewhere in this volume. This chapter steps outside the mainstream to view the reality of Catholic conservatism and traditionalism from the margin and from a cross-cultural angle.[17]

Hispanic Catholicism is uniquely positioned to be a test case and a bridge between the official Catholicism of the West (of which mainstream U.S. Roman Catholicism is a notable expression) and the many "local" Catholicisms that fall outside that mainstream.[18] Popular Hispanic American Catholicism is but one of those local Catholicisms: others can be found in Asia, Africa, and the Pacific Islands. Catholic conservatism in the period since the Second Vatican Council has raised a number of concerns that may also relate to the process by which local churches interact with the modern, Western hegemonic church in its various manifestations: as the conservative Roman or papal church, the church of European Catholic intellectuals, and the U.S. liberal-progressive church. My goal is to explore the wider, global meaning of traditionalism in a study of the confrontation between diverse cultures and social classes, between modern and premodern worldviews, between first and third world Catholicisms.

Tradition: Rediscovering a Deeper Current

In what sense may one speak about an Hispanic religious conservatism or traditionalism? In a certain sense it is inappropriate to use the words *tradition* or *traditionalism* in their current, popular meanings. Theologian Orlando Espín shows how a contemporary Roman Catholic understanding of tradition is grounded in post-Tridentine theologies which made hard and fast distinctions between teachings, beliefs which pertain to faith, and other beliefs commonly held but based more on local custom and popular devotion. The modern dialectical imagination subjected this rich blend of Catholic practices and experiences to the cool, calculating eye of critical reason in a heretofore unprecedented manner.[19] Tradition with a capital *T*—namely, the official doctrinal and dogmatic pronouncements of the hierarchy—came to overshadow *traditio* as it was commonly understood for the first sixteen hundred years of Christianity:

> It is indeed amazing that until 1546 Christian *traditio* included, without much reflective distinction at the everyday level, both the dogmatic declarations of the councils of antiquity as well as pilgrimages and devotional practices that often had as ancient a history as Chalcedon. If arguments could be made to the effect that some medieval theologians were indeed making distinctions between traditions of one sort or another before Trent, it can also be shown that at the magisterial and popular/pastoral levels these distinctions were not accepted at all or were assumed at best to be "theological opinions" that did not represent the commonly held faith of Christians.[20]

It is tradition in this broader and more subtle sense that is foundational for Hispanic American Catholicism because the Catholic faith came to Latin America two generations before the Council of Trent. Furthermore, its mandates were promulgated in an exceedingly gradual (and often incomplete) way in the Spanish colonial empire.[21] Today's Hispanics are the product of intense cultural encounters among Spaniards, pre-Columbian peoples, and enslaved Africans, a foundational experience that reinforced the popular sacramental, open-ended understanding of tradition first communicated by the Spanish missionaries. To grasp how this understanding of tradition functions, one must look at the Catholicism of the people, the popular Catholicism of Latin America, not the standard, normative, official religion of their theologians, clergy, or educated elites:

> Hispanic popular Catholicism is the product of a "sacramental" worldview. Rural, traditional, family-oriented societies were its matrix. On the other hand, it can be argued that post–Vatican I (and probably post-Enlightenment) Roman Catholicism has been deeply influenced by a rationalist worldview, more at home in an urban, modern, individualist setting. These two worldviews have survived next to each other for some time . . . at times in conflict. Each of these worldviews have produced distinctive ways of understanding Christianity, even within the same Western Catholic tradition.[22]

Anglo-European Catholicism of the nineteenth century, in contrast, is decidedly the product of post-Tridentine and post–Vatican I trends in church history. The operational understanding of tradition in this Euro-American Catholicism is the relatively refined doctrinal, systematic understanding of the faith that one would expect of a literate, upwardly mobile middle class. Insofar as it is Catholic, that approach to the faith continues to be analogical or sacramental. Nevertheless the cultural hegemony of Protestantism in the United States has certainly influenced Catholics in the direction of dialectical imagination, one that, to use Andrew Greeley's words, "sets God over against the world and its communities and artifacts."[23]

The point to be made here is that "tradition" has been imbued in the modern, Western world, in mainstream European and U.S. Catholicism, with the historical baggage of modern, post-Enlightenment culture. The move away from an analogical and sacramental understanding of Christian sources toward an ever more scientific apprehension sets the stage for the polarization of American Catholicism into liberal and conservative camps. Rigidly defined confessions and doctrines and critical written texts have become the stuff of theological reflection and religious studies. Fixation with texts and precise formulations served to narrow the vast tradition and stifled the pluralism of premodern Christianity. Donald N. Levine calls modernity's underlying discomfort with pluralism "the flight from ambiguity."[24] G. Macy speaks of this trend in terms of Christian history:

> The different Christian groups have a single, common past that reaches from the time of the apostles to the time of the reformation. Each of the different groups emerging from that past can find its roots there because the past which Christians have inherited is a *pluralistic* past. What was lost in the Reformation was not just Christian unity, but toleration of pluralism.[25]

The vast premodern tradition includes the beliefs of the people, doctrines, dogmas, confessions, and certainly the effects of those beliefs on Christian piety.[26] Contemporary Catholic theology is attempting to retrieve tradition in this broader sense. In a synthetic effort to get to the heart of tradition, Avery Dulles, outlining the contemporary *status questionae,* maintains that theologians such as Yves Congar contributed to the development of a highly dynamic concept of tradition. According to Dulles, the Second Vatican Council in its Constitution on Divine Revelation (*Dei Verbum*) understood tradition in an inclusive, complex way, referring to it as "the way in which the Church perpetuates and transmits to all generations all that it is and all that it believes."[27] Dulles thus argues that creativity is a constitutive element of tradition.

I am suggesting, therefore, that the implicit, popular Hispanic understanding of Catholic tradition has something in common with that tradition's pre-Tridentine forms. Accordingly, emphasis is placed more on *traditio,* the process of handing on the values and beliefs of a community (especially in an imaginative way through symbol, ritual, and story). The *traditum,* the specific content of that belief, its cognitive, rational, dogmatic expression, is given less importance. Interestingly, this "premodern" approach to tradition may also be congenial to a Vatican II understanding of the same which has moved away from the more rigid, static approaches of the past 450 years. As a result, the polarization of the Catholic community into rigid ideological camps does not capture the imagination of Hispanics.

If conservatives and liberals tend to disagree with one another with regard to Vatican II, Hispanics can also lay claim to a different interpretive trajectory. Langdon Gilkey provides a useful analysis of the Council in which Hispanics can recognize themselves. Gilkey writes that liberal Protestants and modernists in the nineteenth and twentieth centuries subjected the Christian tradition to the most rigorous and relentless kind of analysis, "de-mythologizing" almost everything. In an effort to make itself comprehensible to the modern world, Christianity was stripped of its fire, its mystique and mystery. Protestants began this "destruction derby" in the eighteenth century, says Gilkey. Catholics got on the bandwagon at the end of the nineteenth century and crested at the Second Vatican Council. A profound crisis, entailing the movement away from a symbolic, truly "theological" approach to God and the understanding of the faith, has followed in the wake of this process.[28]

Gilkey believes that the resolution of Christianity's current impasse is to be found in a rediscovery of the role of symbol as principal conveyor of Christian tradition. The solution is not to be found in what today's conservatives seem to be suggesting, that is, assent to ever more conceptually clear doctrines. Nor is the path of the liberals—the critical/historical relativization of Christian beliefs—any more helpful. Some of the same elements found in traditional Hispanic Catholicism—a sense of being part of a universal community of faith not limited to one's race, ethnicity, or social class; a sense of being a people, a community, part of something larger than one's individual existence; and a sacramental sense, an orientation toward symbol, ritual, and myth—are exactly the elements Gilkey recommends for a restructured and renewed Catholicism.[29] For Gilkey, the sacramental character of the Catholic ethos is especially important:

> Catholicism has had a continuing experience, unequalled in other forms of Western Christianity, of the presence of God and grace mediated through symbols to the entire course of ordinary human life. Three elements of this continuing experience of grace are important in this connection: the sense of transcendent mystery; . . . the communication of this experience through a wide range of symbols—material, sensuous, aesthetic, active, verbal, and intellectual; and the sense of the utter importance of this "sacramental" communication of grace for each stage and each crisis of ordinary human beings in the world.[30]

Hispanic popular Catholicism, while not usually falling into heterodoxy, is fundamentally a system of symbols with an exceedingly undeveloped formal doctrine or theology. Perhaps it can be compared in some ways to the Eastern Catholic tradition, whose theology, while certainly more developed than its Hispanic counterpart, especially in its use of the decrees of ecumenical councils, has placed more emphasis on the functional, sacramental, and liturgical aspects of Christian life than on its intellectual comprehension. There is a principle of *lex orandi, lex credendi* working in both Eastern and Hispanic Catholicisms: the "liturgy" in Hispanic Catholicism is not limited to the official one. To it Hispanic piety adds an almost bewildering range of rites, symbols, and customs lifted from the repertoire of the cultures and races with which it has mingled over five hundred years.[31]

Hispanic Catholic Tradition: Beyond Modern Traditionalism

While the Hispanic tradition may at times manifest some of the qualities of a Euro-American traditionalism, it generally avoids such a pitfall
because its "texts" are more performative, symbolic, graphic, and affective than literary and literal. This difference has to do with the fact that
Hispanic cultures are at various levels of adaptation to the culture of
modernity. While the impact of literacy and modern consciousness is profound and the forces of modernization are unavoidable, the ancient,
premodern roots of Hispanic American cultures remain quite vital. The
Catholicism of U.S. Hispanics has been less "tainted" by the culture of
modernity. As members of the urban working class or as *campesinos* (rural
peasants), Latin American Catholics experience illiteracy, lack of mobility,
and serious socioeconomic limitations, all of which have specific consequences. First, as is often true of oral cultures, the role played by the
imagination is primary. A reflexive, cognitive, individualized awareness of
the "objective," historical, social, political, economic, and cultural underpinnings of their religion is generally lacking. Second, cultural and
religious meaning is communicated not by the articulate print medium,
by discrete, easily retrievable, objective sources (books, catechisms), but
by polyvalent symbols and traditional rituals whose meanings are not
readily accessible to rational analysis. The departmentalization and fragmentation of knowledge characteristic of modern cultures has yet to occur
or has only partially occurred in the Hispanic world. The symbols are
therefore organic. They strike a chord deep in the identity and collective
memories of a people. They are conveyed not with rational objectivity and
coolness but with subjectivity and affective heat. The symbols and rituals
are the heritage of a community, a collectivity. They are not the domain
of experts endowed with scientific know-how and disconnected from the
mythos of the people, their root metaphors and stories.[32]

A premodern appreciation of religion is necessarily traditional in the
above sense. It is embodied in the teachings of elders, in art, music, and
popular refrains. It is communicated orally. As Walter Ong has explained,
oral cultures are traditional: cultural meaning is conveyed through repeatedly recited formulae.[33] Knowledge is communicated from person to
person, identified with the authority who emits it. Oral communication
therefore is highly personalized and internalized, coming from within the

speaker, and is received aurally, inwardly, by the hearer. Communication is from an "inside" (the speaker) to another "inside" (the hearer); consequently, knowledge is not stripped from the person of the knower. It is not there waiting for the reader as in the case of books. Rather, it is buried in the collective memory and performed by those authorized to speak the word. Yet oral communication, the basis of religious discourse in traditional cultures, is not individualist; that is, it is not the communication of an individual's insights, perceptions, or bright ideas. Rather, it is the sacred communication of the ideals of a community held together for survival by competent authority. The message's validity is derived from its organic relation to the structure of plausibility developed by the culture. The religious message is usually localized, literally rooted in the land, in the local community. And religion is the heart of that plausibility structure, that "order of factuality" Geertz explains in his article on religion as a cultural system.[34]

Hispanic Catholicism, moreover, reflects some extremely deep currents in oral culture and religion. This is due not only to the medieval, baroque Catholicism of the original evangelizers of the sixteenth century, but also to the ancient currents of pre-Columbian and African religions and cultures. Their symbols were successfully transferred from their original non-Christian contexts into explicitly Christian ones by a process of substitution.[35]

The relative, limited success of "official religion" in penetrating the masses of Hispanic America was, nevertheless, an important factor in the transformation of the people's religion, in opening that religion up to the "new" trends of theology, of learning agendas proposed by official teachers. The official Catholicism of bishops, religious, and theologians exists side by side with the people's religion to this very day. Historically in Latin America the influence of religious elites (theologians, clergy, hierarchy) was mitigated by difficulties of travel, political divisions, lack of formal educational opportunities, illiteracy, and extreme social class divisions. Consequently the "little traditions" (to use anthropologist Robert Redfield's term) held their own quite well in the face of the "big Tradition." The pre-Tridentine attitude of Latin America's first evangelizers also made them more flexible, more "pluralistic" than was possible as the post-Tridentine mentality gained strength over the subsequent centuries.

While the acids of modernity continue to eat away at the premodern world of Hispanics—especially those who find themselves in the United States, the paragon of modernity—it has not totally, even now, done away with what Paul Ricoeur calls the "first naiveté."

Orlando Espín provides a seminal articulation of the encounter between the traditional religion of Hispanics with Euro-American religion: "Today, the encounter between Euro-American and Hispanic Catholicisms frequently produces conflict. Modern logic tells symbol it must yield to the claims of positive reason, while symbol tells logic that it has lost its poetic reason and perhaps its heart."[36]

By almost any measure there is something "conservative" about the ritual and symbolic world of Hispanic Catholics. It is not perceived as the religion of "people in the know." It is obscurantist, medieval, and premodern, replete with superstition. It possesses neither rational articulation nor internal coherence, and is closely identified with the lower socioeconomic classes. It is perceived as sentimental and grossly emotional. Cultural anthropologists, not theologians, study it and do ethnographic studies reminiscent of those done on "primitive religions." Social psychologists may study popular religiosity in a Freudian key as a manifestation of neurosis. Social activists may find it "alienating" and interpret it in Marxian fashion as an opiate. Consequently the people's religion is subjected to various reductionist theories, explained away and ultimately dismissed.

Insofar as educated U.S. Catholics subscribe to the myths of modernity, especially to the myth of progress, it seems inconceivable that the popular religion of uneducated masses could be perceived as anything less than backward. Liberals will be most disturbed by this form of Catholicism because it does not reflect the internalized individualism of mainstream U.S. Christianity, with its emphasis on personal appropriation and cognitive/rational awareness of the faith. Steeped in symbol and ritual, especially in a constellation of images and practices centered on the Virgin Mary, Hispanic Catholicism seems to be a "throwback" to some other time.

Modern conservatives, however, while being delighted with Hispanics' devotion to Mary, their ready acceptance of and even devotion to hierarchical figures such as the pope, and their traditional attitudes toward divorce, abortion, and homosexuality, may find the Hispanic sense of moral *epikeia*, the highly personalized applications of received norms, and inconsistencies of their religious practices unacceptable. Conservatives can find serious fault with the open-ended character of popular beliefs, the lack of a dogmatic content and closure on their understanding of the tradition. The traditional Hispanic sense of devotion to the pope may appeal to the Catholic traditionalist until he or she realizes that this too is of a piece with the Hispanic hierarchical world, in which symbols of authority are given great importance for the sake of the community and its well-being or survival. It is said, for instance, that Pope John Paul II's journeys to Mexico were among his most successful, in that huge numbers—literally millions—of ordinary people came out to see and cheer him. These Mexican Catholics have very little formal understanding of their faith. Much less do they know exactly what this pope is teaching. In a sense it makes no difference because he is a symbol. What he stands for is hardly commensurate with his speeches and theological views. He is part of a people's way of life that is meaningful. His importance revolves around his role in the community, and that is why he must be respected, even revered. Devotion to the pope is not the result of the logical application of the doctrine of the Petrine office to this or that papacy. That devotion is part of a bigger communal and aesthetic pattern that goes far beyond the discrete, controlled, cognitively grasped world of either Western liberals or conservatives. Theologian Roberto S. Goizueta attempts to ground the distinctiveness of Hispanic religiosity and speaks of the historical praxis of U.S. Hispanics in these terms:

> The community implicit in praxis is not, however, the modern Western community, understood as a voluntary association of atomic individuals; rather it is an organic reality in which the relationship between persons is not only extrinsic but, at a more fundamental level, intrinsic as well. In and through praxis, the intrinsic unity of person, community and God is affirmed. In the praxis of the modern Western subject, the subject has ontological priority; in the praxis of U.S. Hispanics community has ontological priority, for it gives birth to subjectivity.[37]

Goizueta's insights help explain why the Hispanic Catholic sense of tradition makes it a *tertium quid* in terms of current conservative-liberal controversies regarding such issues as women's and gay rights, authority in the church, and liturgical reform. Goizueta shows how Hispanic attitudes toward something as basic as authority, toward grassroots communities and hierarchical institutions, differ from those of modern, mainstream North Americans. He gives the example of the opposition or dualism that North American commentators on Latin America (right- and left-wing) see in the base ecclesial communities, the so-called popular churches, on the one hand, and the institutional church, on the other.

> Boff . . . warns us against any attempt to understand Latin American popular Catholicism, with its emphasis on grass-roots communities, as an alternative to the institutional church. . . . The fundamental difference between the traditional European church and the emer-

gent third-world church is not one of structure but of social praxis. In fact, . . . the structural differences are complementary.[38]

Authority is in general viewed positively in Hispanic American cultures because it is an integral dimension of community particularly in the context of survival. In modern Western democratic cultures, it is understandably viewed with suspicion as a potential infringement on individual well-being.

Conclusion

So far this discussion of mainline and Hispanic tradition and traditionalisms has taken the United States and Europe as the context for contrast and comparison. What occurs in the United States, however, may have bearing as well on a larger confrontation occurring at the global level. Third world religions, not only third world local Catholicisms, are involved in a momentous encounter. Insight into the encounter in the United States may shed light on the global process.

It makes no sense to transfer conservative/liberal antagonisms onto third world peoples, to suggest that eventually they will get to where the moderns are. Polycentrism is a reality of today's world. The neuralgic point is modernity, the confrontation with modernity. Third world peoples in general tend not to perceive and interpret the world in the same way that modern Westerners do. They have been less influenced by literacy. They are less individualistic, less enamored of univocal concepts of truth and universal rationality, less fascinated with the knowing subject in isolation from others.[39] The programmatic ideal of modern Western civilization—its conceptualist, ahistorical methodologies, its faith in technique and universal pragmatic reason—is increasingly called into question. Hispanics are surely influenced by these trends, but many, even those thoroughly immersed in North American culture, are not capitulating to them.

To the extent that U.S. Hispanics remain outside the Western mainstream and continue to exhibit in their *mestizo* Catholicism the symbolic orientation of their African and indigenous progenitors and their premodern medieval and baroque Spanish ancestors, to that extent their tradition will stand in sharp contrast with other Catholic traditions and traditionalisms. As that Catholicism seeks to inculturate the faith in global contexts, its current forms, etched out in bold relief and sometimes made to appear static, will evolve. Hispanic tradition may then become a helpful link with the Catholic past as well as with the future, with the peoples of the third world, with a new polycentric intellectual culture.

This seems possible and appropriate given the unique character of Hispanic Catholicism, nurtured over five centuries in the Americas on the multiracial and multicultural roots of Spaniards, Indians, and Africans and now passing through an influential but not necessarily decisive, modern Anglo-Americanizing phase. Consequently, as Hispanics attain more visibility both in the U.S. Catholic Church and in the broader society, their presence offers perspectives on the faith and the world that go beyond or prescind from current conservative-liberal polarizations.

NOTES

1. Langdon Gilkey, "The Crisis of Christianity in North America," in Jeff F. Pool, ed., *Through the Tempest* (Minneapolis: Fortress Press, 1991), pp. 7–8. Gilkey considers U.S. Catholicism part of mainline, liberal Christianity. See p. 7.

2. I explore the need for an Hispanic perspective on U.S. Catholic Church history in greater detail in A. F. Deck, "At the Crossroads: North American and Hispanic," in Roberto S. Goizueta, ed., *We Are a People* (Minneapolis: Fortress Press, 1993), pp. 1–20.

3. See David E. Hayes-Bautista, Aida Hurtado, R. Burciaga Valdez, and Anthony C. R. Hernández, *Redefining California: Latino Social Engagement in a Multicultural Society* (Los Angeles: UCLA Chicano Studies Research Center, 1992). Also Mario Barrera, *Beyond Aztlan: Ethnic Autonomy in Comparative Perspective* (Notre Dame, Ind.: University of Notre Dame Press, 1988), especially chap. 5, "Post-Movement Trends," pp. 45ff.

4. The term *Hispanic* is used in this essay, although other writers may prefer the word *Latino.* Both are umbrella words used to refer to all peoples of Latin American origin in the United States.

5. See "Catholic World Statistics," in the *Catholic Almanac for 1993* (Huntington, Ind.: Our Sunday Visitor Publishing, 1993), p. 367.

6. See Joseph P. Fitzpatrick, "The People: Demographics," in T. Howland Sanks and John A. Coleman, eds., *Reading the Signs of the Times* (New York: Paulist Press, 1993), p. 27.

7. See "Hispanics" in the *Catholic Almanac for 1993,* pp. 488f.; also A. F. Deck, "Hispanic Ministry," in Sanks and Coleman, *Reading the Signs of the Times,* pp. 168–76.

8. See *Seminary Forum,* Autumn and Winter 1992 (Washington, D.C.: CARA, the Center for Applied Research in the Apostolate, Georgetown University), for the most current seminary enrollment statistics by ethnicity.

9. For the most complete history of United States Hispanic Catholics in the twentieth century, see Jay P. Dolan, Gilbert Hinojosa, Jaime Vidal, and Allan Figueroa Deck, eds., *The Notre Dame History of Hispanic Catholics in the U.S.* (Notre Dame, Ind.: University of Notre Dame Press, 1994).

10. See Bureau of the Census, 1989, U.S. Dept. of Commerce, *Current Population Reports: Population Characteristics,* series P20, #431; also *The Hispanic Population in the United States: March 1988* (advance report); and series P20, #421 for 1990 data.

11. David Hayes-Bautista synthesizes his findings regarding the perdurance of distinctive Hispanic American values among U.S. Hispanics in "Mexicans in Southern California," in Abraham F. Lowenthal and Katrina Burgess, eds., *The California-Mexico Connection* (Palo Alto, Calif.: Stanford University Press, 1993), pp. 131–46.

12. William Rowe and Vivian Schelling, *Memory and Modernity: Popular Culture in Latin America* (London: Verso, 1991). Rowe and Schelling's focus is the relationship between popu-

lar culture, on the one hand, and modern and high cultures, on the other, within Latin America. They show how popular culture, which in many ways is the dominant culture of Latin America, has adapted to and survived the onslaughts of modernity without totally succumbing to some generalized forms of modernity. See pp. 1–15. For another recent analysis of Latin American Catholicism, see political scientist Daniel H. Levine, *Popular Voices in Latin American Catholicism* (Princeton: Princeton University Press, 1992).

13. This is the point made by several experts speaking before the U.S. bishops on 16–17 June 1989 at their annual meeting at Seton Hall University. See Bishop Raimundo Peña, "Opening the Door to Life in the Church," *Origins* 19, no. 12 (17 August 1989): 193f.

14. The dearth of U.S. Hispanic publications is only now being addressed. Dolan et al., *The Notre Dame History of Hispanic Catholics in the U.S.,* is an example of the growing effort to fill the void. Associations such as ACHTUS are also making headway in this regard. For the background of ACHTUS, see A. F. Deck, "Introduction," in Allan Figueroa Deck, ed., *Frontiers of Hispanic Theology in the United States* (Maryknoll: Orbis Books, 1992), pp. ix–xxvi; also Arturo Bañuelas, "U.S. Hispanic Theology," *Missiology* 20, no. 2 (April 1992): 275–300.

15. Two recent collections on the topic of American Catholicism, with contributions by leading Catholic commentators such as Richard McBrien, J. Bryan Hehir, Catherine L. Albanese, Richard John Neuhaus, and Joe Holland, are Joseph F. Kelly, ed., *American Catholics* (Wilmington, Del.: Michael Glazier, Inc., 1989), and Joe Holland and Anne Barsanti, eds., *American and Catholic: The New Debate* (South Orange, N.J.: Pillar Books, 1988). The Hispanic presence simply does not appear in these works. John A. Grindel, in *Whither the U.S. Church?* (Maryknoll: Orbis Books, 1991), apologizes for dedicating only two pages to the Hispanic reality: "The overview of the present situation of the Catholic Church in the U.S. offered here is primarily an overview of the white, Anglo-Saxon Catholic Church. . . . Given the rapidly growing number of Hispanics in the U.S. Church this absence is more than regrettable. However, to a great extent, the data regarding Hispanics does not exist" (p. 83).

16. William D. Dinges and James Hitchcock, "Roman Catholic Traditionalism and Activist Conservatism in the United States," in Martin E. Marty and R. Scott Appleby, eds., *Fundamentalisms Observed* (Chicago: University of Chicago Press, 1991), pp. 66–141. This is the first volume in the series produced by the Fundamentalism Project. For an analysis of Latin American fundamentalism, see Jorge E. Maldonado, "Building 'Fundamentalism' from the Latin American Family," pp. 214–39, and Susan Rose and Quentin Schultze, "The Evangelical Awakening in Guatemala: Fundamentalist Impact on Education and Media," pp. 415–51, in Marty and Appleby, eds., *Fundamentalisms and Society: Reclaiming the Sciences, the Family, and Education* (Chicago: University of Chicago Press, 1993).

17. The reality of fundamentalisms conceived of globally in the Fundamentalism Project is pursued here in a cross-cultural and cross-social-class key with Hispanic cultures as primary referent. Mainline Catholic conservatism, traditionalism, and fundamentalism, detailed in other chapters of this book, provide points for comparison and contrast.

18. Robert J. Schreiter details the process by which local theologies emerge from local churches in *Constructing Local Theologies* (Maryknoll: Orbis Books, 1985). Stephen B. Bevans cogently describes various models that function in doing local theology in *Models of Contextual Theology* (Maryknoll: Orbis Books, 1992).

19. Andrew M. Greeley, "Do Catholics Imagine Differently?" in *The Catholic Myth* (New York: Charles Scribner's Sons, 1990), pp. 41–46. For an example of how Hispanic popular religiosity and official Catholicism relate analogically and not dialectically, that is, in a nondichotomizing manner, see Robert E. Wright, "If It's Official, It Can't Be Popular? Reflections on Popular and Folk Religion," *Journal of Hispanic/Latino Theology* 1, no. 3 (May 1994): 47–67.

20. Orlando O. Espín, "Pentecostalism and Popular Catholicism: Preservers of Hispanic Catholic Tradition?" *ACHTUS Newsletter* 4, no. 1 (Spring 1993): 10.

21. See José Oscar Beozzo, "Evangelization and History," *Lumen Vitae* 33 (1978): 281–82; also Enrique Dussel, *Historia General de la Iglesia en América Latina* (Salamanca: Ediciones Sígueme, 1982), p. 482.

104   ALLAN FIGUEROA DECK, S.J.

22. Espín, "Pentecostalism and Popular Catholicism," p. 12.

23. Greeley, "Do Catholics Imagine Differently?" p. 46.

24. Donald N. Levine maintains that the flight from ambiguity is one of the basic features of modern culture. Contrary to popular and even academic convictions, he contrasts the *rigidity* of modern cultures with the *flexibility* of traditional ones in *The Flight from Ambiguity: Essays in Social and Cultural Theory* (Chicago: University of Chicago Press, 1985), pp. 1–43.

25. G. Macy, *The Banquet's Wisdom: A Short History of the Theology of the Lord's Banquet* (Mahwah, N.J.: Paulist Press, 1992), p. 14.

26. Pelikan's all-embracing approach in *The Christian Tradition* contrasts markedly with that of Adolf von Harnack in *History of Dogma*. Harnack, a liberal nineteenth-century Protestant, conflates dogma with the richer notion of tradition. He limits tradition to (1) articulate, authoritative formulations of the faith and (2) religious customs logically derived from these formulations. Contemporary American and European traditionalisms are driven by these same concerns as well as by the spread of literacy. Easy access to the printed word and the decline of orality in the modern world have given doctrinal formulations an "etched in granite" quality never before possible. See Jaroslav Pelikan's several volumes titled *The Christian Tradition: The History of the Development of Doctrine* (Chicago: University of Chicago Press, 1991); also Adolf von Harnack, *History of Dogma,* 7 vols. (New York: Russell and Russell, 1958).

27. Avery Dulles, "Tradition and Creativity in Theology," *First Things,* November 1992, p. 22.

28. Langdon Gilkey, *Catholicism Confronts Modernity* (New York: Seabury Press, 1975).

29. Peter W. Williams provides a now standard text on popular religion in the United States among several different ethnic/racial groups and denominations. His typology is quite relevant to Hispanic popular religion. See his *Popular Religion in America* (Chicago: University of Illinois Press, 1989), pp. 10–19. For a detailed view of U.S. Hispanic popular Catholicism, see Jaime Vidal, "Popular Religion among the Hispanics in the General Area of the Archdiocese of Newark," in *Presencia Nueva* (Newark: Office of Pastoral Research, Archdiocese of Newark, 1988), pp. 237–352.

30. Gilkey, *Catholicism Confronts Modernity,* p. 20.

31. See María Rosa Icaza, "Prayer, Worship and Liturgy in a U.S. Hispanic Key," in Deck, *Frontiers of Hispanic Theology in the United States,* pp. 134–53. Orlando O. Espín shows how a theology, in this case a theology of grace, can be derived from this popular religion in "Grace and Humanness: A Hispanic Perspective," in Goizueta, *We Are a People,* pp. 133–64.

32. Marcello de Carvalho Azevedo outlines the salient features of modernity in its encounter with Christianity today in *Inculturation and the Challenges of Modernity* (Rome: Gregorian University Press, 1982).

33. Walter J. Ong, *The Presence of the Word* (New York: Simon and Schuster, 1967), especially chap. 2, "Transformations of the Word," pp. 17–22.

34. Clifford Geertz, "Religion as a Cultural System," in *The Interpretation of Cultures* (New York: Basic Books, 1973), pp. 90–91.

35. A classic description of this remarkable process of evangelization is found in Robert Ricard, *The Spiritual Conquest of Mexico* (Berkeley: University of California Press, 1966).

36. Espín, "Pentecostalism and Popular Catholicism," p. 13.

37. Roberto S. Goizueta, "Rediscovering Praxis: The Significance of U.S. Hispanic Experience for Theological Method," in Goizueta, *We Are a People,* p. 64.

38. See Roberto S. Goizueta, "United States Hispanic Theology and the Challenge of Pluralism," in Deck, *Frontiers of Hispanic Theology in the United States,* pp. 2–3.

39. Much has been written in the field of interreligious dialogue regarding this encounter. Michael Amaladoss, an Indian missiologist, has written a lucid exposition of this encounter and the shifts in paradigms it requires in modern Westerners. See his *Making All Things New: Dialogue, Pluralism and Evangelization in Asia* (Maryknoll: Orbis Books, 1990).

PART II

Insider Perspectives

5

Catholics United for the Faith
Dissent and the Laity

JAMES A. SULLIVAN

Prologue

Catholics United for the Faith is an association of lay Catholics dedicated to advancing and defending the teachings of the Catholic Church through the proper implementation of the documents of the Second Vatican Council. Founded in 1968, during the tempestuous period of dissent from Pope Paul VI's encyclical banning artificial birth control *(Humanae Vitae)*, CUF bears the impress today of Vatican II and the scorch marks of the ecclesial fires of the late 1960s and early 1970s. In a certain sense, CUF also reflects the mind of Paul VI, for the organization was founded as a conscious response to this pope's call for "inner personal and moral renewal."[1]

It is a commonplace in theological discussions that the twentieth century is the age of the laity. While some have questioned whether the great vision and testament to the laity drafted at Vatican II has, in fact, "arrived," the present age is considered by many to be a unique time of lay involvement.[2] It is within this framework of general lay activism that the story of CUF has been written. Since CUF was created as a group endeavor, it also falls under the rubric of the "group apostolate" encouraged by Vatican II.[3]

The purpose of this prologue is briefly to indicate where CUF might be located on a religious/cultural "map" of contemporary Catholic movements. Although it is a lay activist group, CUF does not necessarily share the spirit of many so-called lay activist movements today. The term *activism* may be broadly interpreted.[4] For example, some lay activist groups have exhibited a "bitter zeal" (to quote St. Benedict) which is, in CUF's eyes, counterproductive.[5] Furthermore, some groups strike an occasional politicizing tone in an attempt to establish an "us vs. them" mentality, which is opposed to CUF's ultimate aims—despite the unfortunate fact that some of our own chapters have occasionally adopted this mindset. In its self-understanding, CUF is marked by loyalty to Rome and by a spirit of cooperation with Catholic religious authorities.

To set themselves apart from activist tendencies which they reject, CUF members have attempted to follow a three-part program featuring prayer as the chief and indispensable element, complemented by study of the content of the Catholic faith (as expressed most authoritatively in documents issued by the magisterium), and by action, when and where appropriate. The concern of CUF, to put it another way, is that action be informed by prayer and study. The emphasis on spiritual formation and the constant reading of Scripture as well as the documents of Catholic tradition endows CUF with a meditative and contemplative character which sets the organization apart from many other lay endeavors.[6]

While CUF did not see its mission as identical to that of the right-to-life movement, there was considerable affiliation and interchange between CUF and the nascent pro-life movement. In 1972 CUF published *Respectable Killing,* a book strongly critical of the abortion movement, authored by CUF executive director Kenneth Whitehead. In addition, individual members of CUF, including chapter chairpersons, served in local pro-life groups. At times, CUF chapters opted to dedicate large portions of their resources and time to pro-life activities,[7] while certain notable personalities in the pro-life movement have credited CUF as a source of inspiration for their efforts.[8]

Despite this occasionally close alliance between CUF and the right-to-life movement, several other concerns, including liturgical and catechetical works, have occupied CUF, ensuring that its overall efforts would not be limited to this one important issue. Sometimes it has been assumed that CUF, in defense of Catholic truth, would take responsibility for responding to public attacks of an anti-Catholic nature occurring in published works or in the media. This role, however, is handled by the Catholic League for Religious and Civil Liberties, with offices in New York City. Certainly any Catholic apostolate or group could come forward and defend the integrity of the Catholic Church, yet the Catholic League handles such issues on a formal basis, with a staff of litigators. Thus we regularly refer callers who are concerned with possible instances of libel to the league offices.

Closer to home, in matters more parochial, attention has been recently focused on the rights of the faithful as they deal with other members of the church on the diocesan or parish level. Here the questions concern due process and redress in church tribunals. In these cases, the St. Joseph Foundation in San Antonio, Texas, provides information and expert opinions. Even in cases where our own members might seek a canonical opinion, we forward their concerns to the St. Joseph Foundation or a competent canon lawyer. There is concern that an overly "litigious" spirit may come to color the dealings with members inside the church. In this respect, CUF leaders have warned of an excessive "problem orientation"— a near-obsessive preoccupation with dissent and liturgical deviations.[9] Yet a strictly quietist approach is also inadvisable. To renounce the process of canonical redress would be to turn against the very mechanism established by the church. It would also betray an undue obsequiousness and perhaps signal an unspoken capitulation to elements of clericalism, which has by no means been rooted from the church.

Since the Council we have also observed a "restorationist" reaction, which sees in Catholicism a religious bulwark against modernity. This reaction is perhaps the opposite of ultraprogressivism or what Maritain termed "kneeling before the age." The restorationist spirit is a psychological and social stance which prefers in all things the *stile antico*. Such thinking includes a distaste for Vatican II and an appraisal of the last twenty-five years as entailing a departure from Catholic truth. CUF, while seeking to support the kind of doctrinal and moral conservatism we find in Pope John Paul II's restatement of the reality of intrinsically evil actions in *Veritatis Splendor*, nonetheless resists integralist attempts to depreciate the importance of Vatican II and the late-twentieth-century popes.

In the mid-1970s, Karl Keating, a former lawyer turned apologist, founded Catholic Answers, another organization situated in proximity to CUF on the religious/cultural map. This organization has focused on competition with evangelical Christians by explaining Catholic doctrines and encouraging cradle Catholics to evangelize. Through books, tapes, pamphlets, and a monthly publication, *This Rock*, Keating has concentrated on the field of apologetics, an area which many CUF members believe to be undercultivated in the postconciliar period.[10]

Because apologetics implies the "defense and explication" of Catholic teaching, there was a natural intersection between the work of Catholic Answers and that of CUF. Yet the overlap has been welcome and demonstrates how various apostolates can have common pursuits but different missions. When we receive queries about Jehovah's Witnesses or Mormonism, or about recondite matters which relate to separated Christian communions, we direct them to Catholic Answers.

In two additional ways, CUF differs from other conservative Catholic organizations. First, CUF has made it a priority to understand and explicate church teaching about the contemporary role of the laity. We are attentive to the "theology of the lay state." CUF is thought of as a conservative association. The idea of forming a Catholic group which would not operate as an arm of the hierarchy (the older Catholic Action model), however, struck many conservative Catholics as radical. Yet CUF has always accepted the radical rethinking of the lay state as part of its mission.

Second, CUF was conceived not merely as a vehicle for ideas and teaching but also as having a real communitarian dimension. This dimension is expressed by the gathering into chapters. Of course, other conservative groups on the map have adopted the chapter model—one thinks of the Catholic League for Religious and Civil Liberties and the Latin Liturgy Association. Yet the group affiliates spawned by these organizations were considerably smaller and less an integral feature of the overall operations than was the case in the experience of CUF, which at present has 140 chapters.

Origins

On August 17, 1968, at the St. Paul Hotel in St. Paul, Minnesota, two priests and ten laypersons gathered for the purpose of establishing an organization to be called Catholics United for the Faith.[11] They made plans to launch the new group through editorial statements in *Triumph* magazine and in the Catholic weekly *The Wanderer* (September 12), dispatching press releases to the Religious News Service, the National Catholic Welfare Council, and the Associated Press. The founders formed an ad hoc advisory committee and created a self-perpetuating board of directors, including L. Brent Bozell, Michael Lawrence, Alphonse Matt, Sr., Alphonse Matt, Jr., and H. Lyman Stebbins. Stebbins, away in Europe, was the only designated board member who was not present at the meeting. Yet by the time of the first public press conference, held at the Mayflower Hotel on September 26, Stebbins would be named by the others as acting president. Because of his importance in the founding of CUF, especially with regard to his grasp of the message of Vatican II concerning the laity and his own reading in Catholic sources, it is necessary to know something of the background of H. Lyman Stebbins.

As the spiritual founder of CUF, Lyman Stebbins was hardly born to the role. In fact, his origins and background made him a most unlikely architect of a conservative Catholic association. Stebbins was born September 3, 1911, the son of Rowland Hart and Marion Lyman. His father had left Wall Street to become a theatrical producer and was responsible for bringing a string of plays to Broadway, including Marc Connolly's *Green Pastures* and *White Horse Inn,* which introduced Kitty Carlisle to the New York stage. The family was landed Episcopalian, extending back to Rowland Stebbins, who left Ipswich, England, in 1624 and died in Northampton, Massachusetts, in 1671. Lyman's great-grandfather, Henry George Stebbins, was president of the New York Stock Exchange and one of the founders of the Metropolitan Museum of Art.

Lyman was educated at St. Paul's in Concord and then at Yale. The Yale years were lived without any particular religious identity; the nominal Episcopalianism of his childhood had given way to a moral and spiritual vacuity.[12] Upon graduation, he fulfilled family expectations and entered the brokerage house of DeCoppet and Doremus.

In 1942, while seeking a volume by C. S. Lewis, Stebbins happened into a Sheed and Ward bookstore in Manhattan. From this point forward, he began a reading romance which led him into the Catholic Church. One of the first volumes which captured his attention was *The Things Which Are Not Caesar's,* by the French Thomist Jacques Maritain. The Maritain volume was crucial in enlarging Stebbins's view of the papacy. The book's disclaimer, that the author "withdraws in advance anything which would contradict the teaching of the Church," convinced Stebbins that intellectual excellence and submission to religious authority were not mutually exclusive. After taking instruction from Paulist father Vincent Holden in New York, Lyman Stebbins was received at the Jesuit's Farm Street Church in London in 1946.

During the 1950s and early 1960s, Lyman led a life of semi-retirement and solitude as a Benedictine oblate. He was drawn to the singing of the divine office and Gregorian chant in company with his brother and sister oblates or with the religious of the monastery at Mount Savior, Elmira, New York, or the Convent Regina Laudis in Bethlehem, Connecticut. Under spiritual direction, he commenced a "novitiate of the spiritual life," adapted to the conditions of a layman. This contemplative focus was given a further theological and philosophical depth through contact with Catholic scholars Baldwin Schwarz and Dietrich von Hildebrand. Stebbins served as friend and "editor" to both of these men, editing certain of their works for a wider English-speaking audience.[13] Stebbins's vocation to the contemplative dimension, as well as his grounding in Catholic sources, moved the founding members of CUF to request that he carry the standard for CUF at the Washington press conference.

In 1968 the church was in a state of siege. Even writers sympathetic with the Catholic left wrote of "revolution in the church" and "the maelstrom of dissent." The crisis was precipitated by *Humanae Vitae,* which reaffirmed the church's ban on artificial birth control. Cardinal Patrick O'Boyle encountered opposition from "the Washington Nineteen," diocesan priests drawn from the Association of Washington Priests, a voluntary Vatican II study group of which Fr. James Corriden was chairman. Fearing that they would not counsel penitents to form their consciences according to the letter of the encyclical, O'Boyle had no choice but to face them directly.

Yet the cardinal's problems were not limited to his own diocesans. At Catholic University (where the cardinal sat as chancellor), Rev. Charles Curran organized a public act of dissent from the encyclical and held his own press conference on July 30, 1968, at Caldwell Hall. Brandishing aloft a list of more than six hundred Catholic college and university teachers who disagreed with *Humanae Vitae,* Curran captured the moment for the party of dissent.[14] Lost in the furor over *Humanae Vitae,* however, was the fact that other papal pronouncements were being contested— *Sacerdotalis Celibatus* in particular, Pope Paul VI's 1967 encyclical on priestly celibacy, and the *Credo of the People of God,* published in June 1968. As Professor James Hitchcock was to remark, the dissent paid to *Humanae Vitae* was a talisman of deeper disagreement over the teachings of the ordinary magisterium of the church.

The founders of CUF were preoccupied with this issue of dissent and sought to address it in a unified group effort. Quite fortuitously, the recently concluded Second Vatican Council had urged the formation of private associations of the laity. For Lyman Stebbins, the conciliar texts relating to the laity were crucial; far from ducking these documents, he was looking for a way to concretize the call to the laity, and found it in the explosion of dissent in the summer of 1968. Stebbins and the other founders of CUF were able to harness their opposition to the Curran party by taking the kind of concerted group action that the Council proposed.

At the press conference of September 26, Stebbins said:

> Publication of Pope Paul's encyclical *On Human Life* has occasioned unprecedented controversy in the Catholic Church in America. The Catholic faithful of this nation, immigrants from many countries, have had virtually only one common bond, their faith. The distinctive mark of this faith, historically, has always been the unstinting loyalty

American Catholics have shown to the Holy Father. There are some indications that this loyalty is now threatened; that there are Catholics who wish to break the doctrinal bonds that unite Rome with America. Catholics United for the Faith has been organized to combat this tendency. We assume before anything else that Catholics are Roman Catholic; that doctrinal fidelity to the teachings of the Holy Father is indispensable to the faith.[15]

The immediate origins of Catholics United for the Faith thus involved a forthright effort to counter the rising current of dissent to the papal magisterium, and to incarnate that resistance within a framework outlined by the Council documents themselves.

The Nature of CUF

In pursuit of its mission, CUF has encountered opposition from various quarters. In the 1970s, for example, two chapters in North Carolina and Georgia drifted into the Lefebvrist camp. As a consequence, their charters were revoked by International CUF. In these cases some individuals may have assumed that CUF was a "traditional" group, and that each and every salvo against modernity would be in the CUF spirit. This is not the case, of course, and the decoupling of chapters is proof that International CUF means to be scrupulous in regard to those who would wish to exploit CUF for their own purposes. Nevertheless, this extremist form of traditionalism has entered the chapters enough times to give a kind of preconciliar patina to our efforts, in the view of some observers.

Nonetheless, the problem of CUF's purported "reactionary" status says something about its critics. In a 1987 article in *America,* M. Timothy Iglesias, while finding CUF "not as wicked and dangerous as some of its opponents assume," nevertheless sees CUF as intent upon founding "a conservative utopia" supported by a "rationalistic" theological methodology and a "Hobbesian" sense of authority. He bemoans the group's preoccupation with *Humanae Vitae,* suggesting that CUF's defense of the encyclical as normative for Catholics is simply CUF's "canon within the canon." Furthermore, Iglesias maintains that CUF's excessive attachment to legitimate authority effectively undercuts the possibility of "theological interpretation," since all questions are settled by authority.

By way of response, we might state that dissent is endemic in the United States. The right to dissent has been normalized by so many theologians ("responsible dissent"), and adopted by so many of the baptized as a way of being mature and coresponsible, that CUF's opposition to it in the name of the magisterium strikes many as antediluvian. The "dissenting sociological mainstream" may define the norm of Catholicity from a behavioral point of view. From the evangelical perspective, however, the majority opinion is not always compatible with the truth of the Gospel. In the present situation, in which a liberal or dissenting posture has commandeered "the center," CUF appears conservative, but its alleged conservatism should be evaluated according to the teachings of the papal magisterium, the Council itself, and the enabling documents coming from the Roman Curia. Are we further to the right than the magisterium on contraception, women's ordination, abortion, or ecumenism? How do we fare vis-à-vis *Familiaris Consortio, Dignitatis Mulieris, Centesimus Annus, Lumen Gentium,* and *Inaestimabile Donum?* How does attachment, nay, even Talmudic zeal, for these documents make us narrow? In short, criticism of CUF is often based on our refusal to accept the soft middle ground of "managed dissent."

Although Newman's understanding of the development of doctrine is embraced by CUF's founders, the role of theological interpretation may have been insufficiently stressed. Yet three points need to be kept in mind. First, our outreach was more modest. We sought to be an aid to our members on the level of parish catechetics, not the higher reaches of theology. Secondly, since the apostolate was family-oriented, issues involving the transmission of life (*Humanae Vitae*), the Sunday liturgy (*Inaestimabile Donum* and *Domenicae Cenae*), and education in chastity preoccupied our attention. As a catechetical resource, we were led away from more rarefied concerns to the bread-and-butter issues. Also, the founders of CUF, and other conservative Catholics generally, believed that the higher reaches of theological scholarship were compromised.[16]

Nevertheless, theological development has had its part to play in CUF. In establishing itself as a lay organization, to be led by lay people, CUF was in advance of many in the church in 1968. As a matter of orthopraxis, CUF was defying older, conservative patterns of clericalism, which assumed that the laity must seek a sanction from church authority in order to function.[17] We were not unmindful of Congar's writings on the laity, for instance, nor of the distinction between the ministerial priesthood and the priesthood of the faithful. Indeed, in the pages of *Lay Witness,* our publication, we sought to give a specific focus to the theology of the lay state by fleshing out precisely what the priestly, kingly, and prophetic roles might be in the lives of the laity.[18]

One of the charges leveled at CUF is that it acts as a watchdog over abuses, reporting perpetrators to episcopal authority or to Rome. Nobody likes a whistle-blower, so goes the adage, and CUF members have become adept at (some would say excessively preoccupied with) uncovering deviations from the rubrics. Some bishops are said to be cool to CUF members. Pastors are said to be irritated when confronting parishioners who maintain that the CUF documentation service has provided them with church documents that tell against practices permitted in the local church. What we have found at this office, however, is the all too common retort from parish priests that some exemption from church law permits them to have things their own way. In such instances, CUF members often find themselves in a position of being "talked down to" by priests who seek to evade the letter of church law by resorting to a kind of pre-emptive clericalism. By their own authority, they will permit what often is, in fact, a departure from the rubrics.

Yet some people affiliated with CUF have sought to use the norms and discipline of the church as a stick to flail somebody. Querulousness and haggling are to be deplored in every instance. The counsel given in *Lay Witness* and in addresses by the founder and other officers, that the truth be pursued in charity, has been delivered in order to blunt such intemperate actions.[19]

In other cases, certain CUF members misjudged the severity of problems in the church. If a teacher or director of religious education on the parish level was dissenting from a teaching of the church, some of our members presumed that church authority would move immediately to rectify the situation, even removing the teacher if necessary. When such an outcome failed to materialize, however, many grew frustrated. Letters were sent to Rome. Curia offices were petitioned, in the hopes that Rome could fix what was not being fixed on the level of the local church. The reaction among some petitioners was acute anger. Yet the approach of the International Office was to counsel that the root cause of the problems assailing the church was a spiritual malaise, a falling away from the fullness of the faith. In such an analysis, the heart of the matter lay well beyond an administrative "fix-it" approach. Nevertheless, CUF was not about to abandon members in the field. The CUF office attempted to speak directly to liaison committees of the NCCB or to Rome, acting on behalf of members whom we judged to be rightly aggrieved in a particular matter. Fielding grievances from our own members while seeking to be a conduit for the resolution of pastoral problems brought to our attention placed an enormous burden on the resources of a ten-member staff. It also brought out a dimension of activity at the International Office, hardly understood by many outside observers, that of the sympathetic listener.

A further charge related to the accusation of hostility to theological inquiry is the perception that CUF is a *fundamentalist* or *integralist* organization.[20] Such a charge often carries with it the presumption that CUF has a "political agenda" in spite of "disclaimers" from the International Office. We claim political neutrality, especially in areas where the magisterium has specifically acknowledged a plurality of political options which might be applied in a given instance. Actually, the present political order in the United States, with mainline Democrats seemingly incapable of breaking ranks in order to vote against abortion, has given Catholic lay apostolates a kind of Republican patina, inasmuch as civic action on behalf of the unborn has made bedfellows of Catholic Democrats and conservative Republicans.[21]

While it is certainly true that some CUF members also hold strong conservative political views, other members are unpersuaded by arguments for supply-side economic growth and see a much wider role for government, a role defensible in principle through papal social teachings.[22] There have even been attempts to link CUF with European-based apostolates and to suggest that we had sympathies for throne-and-altar regimes or pro-fascist governments. Yet such a link is unfair, inasmuch as CUF deliberately sought to steer a separate course and to allow no entanglements with *ancien régime* movements.[23]

This charge of fundamentalism, however, runs deeper than merely suspecting CUF of a right-wing political agenda. Fr. John A. Coleman proposed the view that Catholics United for the Faith had launched a "campaign" to downplay its "papal fundamentalism" by suggesting that the progressivist Fr. Richard McBrien had invented the term (*fundamentalist*) in order to deflect attention away "from his own dissenting views on papal authority." This claim has a measure of truth. While CUF denies the fundamentalist label, we certainly do feel that many dissenting theologians have sought to assert their own "centrist character," thereby making Catholics who accept the more controversial norms of the church appear "right-wing" by comparison. We would argue that this kind of "centrism" is more tactical, a matter of commandeering the middle.[24]

The Influence of Cardinal Newman

The accusation of fundamentalism attributed to CUF provides an opportunity to reflect on the role that Cardinal Newman has played in the religious imagination of CUF. Newman's works became the staple of Stebbins's literary diet when he entered the church, and they have helped to give a balance to our activities and our outlook since 1968.

During the 1950s and early 1960s, Stebbins immersed himself in the works of Newman. As the Second Vatican Council renewed the call for the group apostolate, Stebbins considered creating a group that would embody the élan of the Oxford Movement.[25] Along with a strong "ecclesial sense," the Oxford "conspirators" had an intellectual orientation centered on church history and the recovery of the writings of the fathers. Stebbins wished to replicate this combination as an antidote for the strong centrifugal tendencies that were at work in the church in the 1960s. In Newman, Stebbins found an emblem for church unity, a vision of the church as a reality overarching private opinion, a bulwark against the vagaries of religious individualism. "New creeds," Newman wrote in *Sermons on Subjects of the Day*, "private opinions, self-devised practices, are but delusions. . . . Vehemence, tumult, confusion, are no attributes of that benignant flood with which God has replenished the earth. That flood of grace is sedate, majestic, gentle in its operation." In one of the first brochures issued by CUF, Newman was quoted at length:

> Trust the Church of God implicitly even when your natural judgment would take a different course from hers and would induce you to question her prudence or correctness. Recollect what a hard task she has; how she is sure to be criticized and spoken against, whatever she does; recollect how much she needs your loyal and tender devotion; recollect, too, how long is the experience gained in 1800 years; and what a right she has to claim your assent to principles which have had so extended and triumphant a trial.[26]

Stebbins and the other founders hoped that the erudite traditionalism of Newman could be disseminated by a core group of committed Catholics (a new group of "conspirators") and become a leaven in the church in America.

Unity would not be achieved, however, unless the issue of authority was squarely confronted. The current crisis in the church, as seen by Stebbins, was a crisis of faith and a crisis of authority. Again, Newman was the guide:

> The most obvious answer, then, to the question why we yield to the authority of the Church in questions and developments of faith, is, that some authority there must be if there is a revelation given, and other authority there is none but she. A revelation is not given, if there be no authority to decide what it is that is given.[27]

> Faith and obedience . . . are not divided one from the other in fact. They are but one thing viewed differently . . . viewed as sitting at Jesus's feet it is called faith; viewed as running to do His will, it is called obedience.[28]

Elsewhere in this volume, George Weigel seeks to elevate the discussion beyond the issues of authority, indicating a desire to bypass the current logjam reflected in left/right polarization. "The theological approach we seek to advance would, we believe, shift the debate from the question beloved of both left and right—'Who has authority in the church?'—to the more evangelical (and far less narcissistic) question, 'What is authoritative for the church?'"[29] There is much to be said in favor of Weigel's view; certainly a response along the lines of Newman's *Development of Doctrine* would favor inquiry into the sources of revelation (Scripture and tradition). Nonetheless, theological scholarship would necessarily need to be evaluated by the magisterium, a point specifically adverted to in *Dei Verbum* #10. Germain Grisez provides that soupçon of clarification CUF would wish to add to Weigel's analysis. Grisez remarks:

> Plainly the magisterium has a great deal more to do than just ascertaining a consensus. The magisterium has the authority to decide—not in the sense of choosing but in the sense of judging—what belongs to revelation. It is not the word of God; revelation is complete in Jesus. But what is revealed must be unfolded and effectively communicated in each age. For this work to be accomplished without deviation from divine truth, the magisterium exists to receive, guard and explain that truth which the church as a whole infallibly believes.[30]

Newman addressed a nineteenth-century situation which seemed perfectly congruent with the religious fragmentation of the 1960s. "To a cultivated mind . . . religion will commonly seem to be dull, from want of novelty. Hence excitements are eagerly sought out and rewarded," Newman wrote. "New objects in religion, new systems and plans, new doctrines, new preachers, are necessary to satisfy that craving which the so-called spread of knowledge has created. The mind becomes morbidly sensitive and fastidious; dissatisfied with things as they are, desirous of change *as such,* as if alteration must of itself be a relief."[31] The times seemed to war against Newman's desire to hold fast to the ancient ways, while "the cult of obsessive contemporaneity," Christopher Derrick's aphorism for the age, seemed to Stebbins and the CUF founders the precise problem gripping the church.

Challenges from the Far Right

The spectacle of dissent or theological progressivism was not the only nemesis; there was also the matter of attacks on CUF by the "traditionalists." This concern emerged almost from the beginning, inasmuch as the *Missa Pauli VI* was promulgated in 1969, the year following CUF's inception. No sooner had CUF sought to counter theological liberalism (the particularly Americanist distrust of authority in religious matters) than it faced another threat among its own members from another direction, that of theological *integralism*. The flashpoint was the opposition to the New Order of Mass.[32]

E. William Sockey, executive director of CUF from 1977 to 1985, reflecting on the crisis, observed:

> Since CUF was founded to support, defend, and advance the efforts of the teaching church, it found itself squarely in the middle of a controversy with members and chapters divided over what action to take. Some urged CUF to form an alliance with Archbishop Lefebvre's Society of St. Pius X and other "traditionalist" groups in order to defend the Faith. However, unswerving loyalty "to the Pope, and thus to the Church, and thus to Christ" was one of the founding principles of the CUF apostolate. Thus even before all the facts in the matter were known, CUF pledged its complete fidelity to the pope, and consequently found itself being attacked along with the pope by those who should have been among the church's strongest champions.[33]

A major plank in CUF's response to the inroads of Lefebvrism was the book *The Pope, the Council and the Mass: Answers to Questions "Traditionalists" Are Asking,* coauthored by CUF officers James Likoudis and Kenneth S. Whitehead. The book had the effect of discomfiting various Catholics who had imagined that CUF subscribed to a policy of "no enemies to the right." Yet the organization was not about to countenance a secessionist movement that would contest with the pope. The pope's supreme authority was at stake in the issue of the revision of the liturgy. Some who resisted the *Novus Ordo* claimed that the revisions were not about faith and morals but were matters of administration. Viewed this way, respectful disagreement with enactments from Rome was possible. What was missing from this perspective, however, was the understanding that "not only in matters pertaining to faith and morals, but also in matters pertaining to the discipline of the Church," it was to be acknowledged that "the Roman Pontiff had full and supreme power of jurisdiction over the whole Church" (Vatican Council I, *Dogmatic Constitution of the Church of Christ Pastor Aeternus,* #3). This same teaching was repeated at Vatican II and also amplified in *Lumen Gentium,* #18 and #22, where the exercise of the Roman primacy takes place in conjunction with the bishops throughout the world.

While some traditionalists sought to draw a line between faith and morals on the one hand and jurisdiction on the other hand, others acknowledged the pope's general jurisdiction but questioned whether his authority could extend to establishing a revised order of Mass. These latter appealed to Pope St. Pius V's Apostolic Constitution *Quo Primum*, issued in 1570 to establish the Tridentine Mass. Pius had enjoined clergy to conform to "Our recently published Missal." "They must not in celebrating Mass," Pius went on, "presume to introduce any ceremonies or recite any prayers other than those contained in this Missal." Yet the authors of *The Pope, the Council and the Mass* observed that such an injunction was disciplinary in nature, meant to enforce uniformity in the Tridentine Mass. They observed that Pius V had not specifically mentioned that future popes would be bound by his enactments. Indeed, Fr. Josef Jungmann was cited, approvingly, to show that some changes were introduced by subsequent popes, as in Pope Urban VIII's (1634) rewording of the rubrics, or Clement VIII's revision of some of the biblical chant pieces in the Mass.

In handling other objections of the Tridentinists—viz., that the *Novus Ordo* had resulted in a "Protestantization" of the Mass, that Vatican "officials" were responsible for a kind of subversion of the authentic understanding of the Mass, or that the English rendering of the Latin *pro multis* as "for all" constituted a heretical introduction into the rite of consecration—CUF clearly separated itself from those unwilling to accept the Mass of Paul VI. While the extent of defections from the CUF fold over support of Pope Paul VI is unclear, the decision had the benevolent effect of discouraging many Catholic conservatives from allying themselves with Lefebvre. It also served to solidify CUF's credibility among some of the bishops and the clergy, who realized that we were fully ready to put the good of the church ahead of partisan or constituent concerns.[34]

Closely allied to the revisions in the Mass was the whole question of tradition. Since the party resisting the *Novus Ordo* had declared themselves "traditionalists," it was important to define precisely what the word *tradition* meant in a Catholic context. CUF felt it curious, to say the least, that we would appear to be taking issue with those claiming the mantle of "tradition." On this point CUF maintained:

> Catholic Tradition is something guarded and preserved *in the Church;* Catholic Tradition, in the true sense, is not merely what we think it is or ought to be; certainly it is not just what we may have been accustomed or used to; it is, finally, what the Church decides that it is; the Church herself, not private persons, is the judge of what belongs to the unchangeable Catholic Tradition and what does not.[35]

This understanding of tradition has had a chastening effect on many who have come to CUF to have their own predilections nourished. While most in CUF have had that true *sensus fidelium,* an authentic grasp of the faith, some thought us to be a "conservative federation," about the business of furthering any ecclesiastical endeavor that was "rightist." However, from the beginning CUF adopted Newman's dictum or prayer, "Trust the Church of God implicitly . . . even if your natural judgement would take a different course."[36] Whatever managerial pitfalls or administrative shortcomings may have arisen within the ranks over the past twenty-five years, the apostolate has never wavered from the fundamental axiom, "to think with the church." Even in disciplinary matters, where it might be possible to doubt the practical wisdom of a church directive (e.g., allowing communion in the hand or altar girls), there was never any challenging of the authority of the church to bind or decide a matter.[37]

One of the reasons for the imperfect appropriation of the nature of tradition by those who would otherwise be our doctrinal compatriots is the tendency to see tradition from only one point of view. That is, tradition means on the one hand "doctrines to be held." Yet from another point of view, tradition refers to the organ or mode of transmission of those doctrines, namely, the magisterium or teaching authority of the church. In *The Catholic Encyclopedia* (1912), Jean Bainvel wrote that the Greek term *paradosis* ("tradition") contains this twofold meaning of tradition. The failure to concentrate attention on the organ of transmission—wanting doctrine *without the magisterium*—may place the individual in the position of arbiter, an incipient Protestant style. Thus Pope Paul VI declared that Archbishop Marcel Lefebvre was closer to the sixteenth-century Reformers than one would ever imagine.

From this vantage point, it is not so difficult to see that church progressives and church traditionalists have much in common. They both want the freedom to stand outside the church and to assay church doctrine unhampered by the living teaching agency of the magisterium. While progressives would revise or replace dogmatic statements and the meaning traditionally ascribed to such dogmas by the magisterium, traditionalists tend to reify dogma in a way that does not admit of the need of the magisterium to assist in any development. This latter position has the effect of making the traditionalists a *petite* magisterium. CUF eschews both positions, because it insists that it is not possible to be a Catholic and to stake out a position ahead of, in advance of, or separated from the living teaching authority of the church. Rather, it is vital for everybody to "think with the church," which means thinking "inside of the church."

Numbered among the "norms of ecclesiality" set forth by Pope John Paul II in his apostolic exhortation *Christifideles Laici* (#30) is "*The witness to a strong and authentic communion* in filial relationship with the pope, in total adherence to the belief that he is the perpetual and visible center of the unity of the universal Church, and with the local Bishop, 'the visible principle and foundation of unity' in the particular Church, and in 'mutual esteem for all forms of the Church's apostolate.'" This norm, enunciated on December 30, 1988, simply reaffirmed the orientation of all Catholics, whether as individuals or in groups, to adopt a filial relationship with church authority.

In a good number of U.S. dioceses, however, the educational machinery, operating under the presumed consent of the bishop, would often give a rostrum to theologians and speakers who directly contested one or another official teaching of the church. Since CUF members took seriously the principles of the apostolate to defend and advance the teachings of the church, they found themselves seemingly on the wrong side of the local bishop. In such cases, many questions emerged as to how negotiations might proceed in such a way that the bishop could be alerted to the public record of theologian X, who was about to speak under diocesan auspices. CUF chapters were advised not to demonstrate outside diocesan facilities, although they were encouraged to bring their misgivings in the form of questions to the CUF public address or workshop. At all times, this office insisted that the ecclesial bonds between the bishop and the faithful not be broken. Lyman Stebbins observed:

> What is a layman to do if he cannot avoid seeing that his own bishop is misrepresenting (when he is not simply denying) the manifest mind and intention of the Supreme Authority? And what if a lay member of CUF were to feel that the democratic process in the Church, so spoken about since the Council, was not available to them in regard to the bishops: they cannot "throw the rascals out" as all warm blooded, political Americans always want to do?[38]

After mentioning various avenues of recourse open to the laity, including a "respectful and short letter to the bishop," a short note to the apostolic delegate or to the appropriate congregation in Rome, Stebbins added that "the conclusion is that the role of straightening out the bishops is not given to us . . . instructing bishops is not one of our assigned tasks."

Concerned about talk of an "American Catholic Church," of incipient schism or de facto schism, CUF has made every effort to mute a kind of ultramontanism which would suggest that the Catholic owes allegiance to

Rome but "not to those bishops." Without denying apparent breaches between Rome and particular U.S. bishops, CUF has taken steps to lessen an "us vs. them" attitude and to solidify a right orientation of the faithful with the bishop. A house dossier was compiled, entitled "Papal Teachings on the Obligations of the Laity to the Bishops." Including the span of time from Pius IX's 1854 encyclical *Neminem Vestrum* to John Paul II's apostolic exhortation *Christifideles Laici*, article 30, the purpose of these extracts is to foster a filial loyalty to pope and bishop as the only course in which the lay apostolate could thrive.[39]

Other Contested Issues

Besides matters of doctrine and liturgy, CUF has gained notoriety for its opposition to programs of sex education (also called family life programs) which have been introduced into Catholic schools. Our willingness to be an advocate for parents opposed to the introduction of formal sex education curricula put us at odds with school principals and in some cases with pastors and bishops. Along with other parents' groups, CUF has opposed two of the major family life curricula now being used in the U.S., the Benziger Family Life Program and the New Creation program, published by William C. Brown. By and large CUF has found the pedagogical approach in both series to be invasive and intrusive, threatening the kind of delicacy which needs to be preserved in discussions of sex. Indeed, the very concept of formalized classroom instruction in human sexuality in Catholic schools is fraught with problems, as we see it, including the danger of eliding into a secularized approach which emphasizes contraceptive sex. In addition, many Catholic schoolteachers dissent from the church's norms on sexuality themselves, thus becoming uncertain trumpets for their students.

Recently, programs have been created which seek to affirm the decision of young people to be abstinent from sex until marriage. With some mild reservations as to graphics and pedagogy, CUF has supported these efforts to promote chastity. In a very generalized way, the officers and membership of CUF find the large classroom setting to be the least appropriate forum for communicating the importance of sex. The fact that so many Catholic educators want to pursue family life education through programs, however, gives the school a primacy in this area. Pope John Paul II commented specifically on this trend to reduce the role of parents in the formation of their own children when he addressed the U.S. bishops in Los Angeles during his 1987 visit.

> From time to time, the question of sex education, especially as regards programs being used in schools, becomes a matter of concern to Catholic parents. The principles governing this area have been succinctly, but clearly, enunciated in *Familiaris Consortio*. First among these principles is the need to recognize that sex education is a basic right and duty of parents themselves. They have to be helped to become increasingly more effective in fulfilling this task. Other educational agencies have an important role, but always in a subsidiary manner, with due subordination to the rights of parents.[40]

The present position of the magisterium, therefore, would be to accord the school a role while emphasizing the preeminence that parents have in the area of sex instruction.[41] It is a matter of discerning the signs of the time, however, as to whether in fact some schools do not have the order inverted.

Membership

The CUF membership is determined by a simple process of running labels. We mail to a list of approximately 11,300 labels (10,800 domestic and 500 foreign). We estimate that roughly 30 percent of our member labels include married couples, which would bring our total membership to 15,000. As far as our numbers are concerned, we seem to be replicating ourselves with an annual increase of about 200 new members. In 1976 our membership was listed at 13,000, and that figure has remained a benchmark, with yearly increases to bring it to its current level.

When the apostolate was established in 1968, it was presumed by many, if not all, of the organizers that there would be a mighty groundswell of lay support which would vault our membership into a sizable five-figure number, perhaps a six-figure number. As things developed, the realization dawned that such a scenario would not be forthcoming. Indeed, Stebbins preferred biblical images of the mustard seed to the thronged hosts of the Philistines. In his personal correspondence he was quite vigorous in soliciting support and membership in CUF, yet this was done on a person-to-person basis rather than in the form of a campaign. Maritain's "poor temporal means," a term describing the way contemporary Christians might confront the world's worldliness, had an influence on Stebbins and on CUF. The day-to-day dealings with members and friends are more the fare of the *anawim*. The nun from Regina Laudis writes to wish us well; she recalls the John Deere tractor that Mr. Stebbins had provided the abbey. A student calls looking for help with a term paper; a would-be seminarian wants our opinion on a particular seminary.

Limiting our membership growth was the urgency with which many Catholics moved into pro-life work, which became the dominating commitment for them. While Catholic pro-lifers were aware of CUF and invariably supportive of what we were trying to do in the classroom and in the sanctuary, they found themselves overextended. Some of these people would have been sure assets to CUF as potential chapter organizers and members. On the other hand, the pro-life effort in other places worked to increase CUF membership as various chapters took up pro-life activity as a central chapter initiative. In Delaware, Long Island, and Florida, to name three key regions, CUF chapters have been instrumental in shouldering pro-life work.

Because CUF is oriented to a doctrinal and intellectual formation in the faith, it has tempered a purely "activist" dimension. People have come to CUF very anxious "to get started," with a particular action to be staged, perhaps a confrontation with a theologian. While we applaud the prospect that error might be confounded by the truth, it is also gratifying to know that CUF members in a position to address a dissenting theologian are thoroughly grounded in the faith, and in the church's spiritual exercises. Moreover, the love for the church which the CUF founders saw embodied so clearly in Newman seemed to be in a recessive state in America in the 1960s and 1970s. CUF president James Likoudis has said that "the erosion of the faith among Catholics in America, even among some practicing Catholics, was much more widespread than the original founders had imagined."[42]

Data on the social background of our members are hardly scientific. We have conducted no demographic studies. It would be useful to learn the educational background of the members, however, because CUF is to a large extent a part of a flowering of American lay Catholicism. Most of our older members, converts and cradle Catholics alike, have followed a similar course in the church to that of CUF founder Lyman Stebbins; that is, they have read themselves into their strong adherence to the teaching church. Many of our original members came into contact with theological studies well before the conciliar period, through the translations and published works of Sheed and Ward and the Catholic Book Club. This lay theology was often of the "night school" variety, that is, apart from formal theological course work. Thus, CUF really represents a movement of the *plebs Christi* to take coresponsibility for thinking theologically. In CUF we find an erudition that is not the product of formal theological training but is stimulated by love of the church and a vocation to study her doctrinal sources.

CUF encourages members to affiliate with CUF chapters. There are 125 chapters, 111 in the U.S. and Canada with 5 regional directors. CUF activity flourishes in Australia as well, with 8 chapters, and in New Zealand, with 3. We have national directors in both countries. There is a CUF chapter presence in Myanmar, Ghana, and Sri Lanka. In the distribution of members and chapters, CUF has seen a rapid growth in California and the Pacific Northwest. California lists more than 600 CUF members, with Michigan, Ohio, Pennsylvania, and Texas each numbering more than 400 members. Our chapters are formed by individuals who are committed to the principles of CUF as articulated in the Chapter Formation Manual as well as the monthly publication, *Lay Witness*. The chapter chairman is the leader of the local CUF chapter, and a great amount of outreach of International CUF is accomplished by this individual ambassador. The chairman speaks on behalf of CUF, organizes the chapter meetings, serves as a liaison with the local media and the diocesan press, and on occasion attends regional meetings with other chapter chairmen.

Over its history, CUF has been well served by the chapter format. Lyman Stebbins saw the chapter as a spiritual nucleus, where the primary focus would be the formation in holiness of the individual members. It was also hoped that the chapter could become a focal point of orthodox Catholic witness, and this led naturally to the idea of conferences and invitations to speakers.

CUF was responsible, for instance, through its Michigan chapters, for sponsoring the appearance of Cardinal Silvio Oddi, then prefect of the Congregation of the Clergy. Cardinal Oddi spoke on "The Rights of the Catechized to the Truth." His appearance and reaction to it in Catholic circles in the U.S. are the subject of discussion in Kenneth Briggs's book *Holy Siege*. Christopher Derrick, Germain Grisez, James Hitchcock, and Herbert Ratner, M.D., are some of the Catholic lay leaders who have spoken under CUF auspices.

In a few instances, chapters have moved outside the perimeter of CUF's moderate orthodoxy to invite speakers who have a high "conservative" profile yet depart from discipline or the teaching of the church in some matter. A chapter in the Washington, D.C., area invited Fr. Nicholas Gruner as a keynote speaker in 1992. When informed by the local chapter about the invitation, the International Office asked the chairman to disinvite the speaker. The recalcitrant chairman refused and the chapter was dissolved, even as they went forward with the conference. In other cases, CUF chapters have obtained speakers who were resolutely Catholic from the dogmatic standpoint yet remained indisposed, psychologically at least, to the *Novus Ordo*. This writer remembers contesting from a podium in Ohio with one such speaker, having to bring the speaker's address to a shorter ending. In Atlanta and Raleigh, powerful Lefebvrist currents led to the suppression of chapters by the International Office in New Rochelle.

But the record of troublesome chapters is far outweighed by the stability and balance brought to the CUF enterprise by its many fine chairmen. In Memphis, then-Bishop Stafford was won over, frankly, by the demeanor and charity of the chapter members. In Charlotte, then-Bishop Donahue was impressed by the chapter's dedication to catechetics and allowed them use of a chancery building for meetings. As ordinary in Cincinnati, Cardinal Bernardin celebrated Mass at a CUF convention. These instances remark a type of collaboration between CUF members and the hierarchy which has helped ensure doctrinal and liturgical stability in the apostolate.

In recruiting new members, CUF relies to a great extent on the help of the local chapter; yet increasing visibility on the part of the officers and the president of CUF, Jim Likoudis, has drawn new attention to the association. Likoudis has been featured on the Phil Donahue show (opposite Geraldine Ferraro) on the subject of Catholics and abortion-voting politicians; while Geraldo has sought the voice of Catholic orthodoxy in various programs by featuring Mr. Likoudis on topics such as clerical sexual abuse of minors and discussions of priestly celibacy.[43] In a period of time when many Catholics imagine that the requisite evangelical style is one of tepidity or temporizing, it seems to have fallen to CUF to present the teachings of the church in a clear voice. While it might at first be thought that Geraldo and James Likoudis represent an odd pairing, the fact is that the media are looking for a directness—a *respondeo dicendum*—that they do not necessarily find from Catholic voices that speak in a measured "bureaucratese."

In the past, CUF has attempted to establish chapters on college campuses. A brochure was drawn up in the late 1970s entitled "CUF on Campus," but the demands on a small staff to keep up communication with chapters already in operation forced the collegiate plan to be considered merely a "great idea" awaiting another day. In 1994, however, property was purchased near the Franciscan University of Steubenville for the H. Lyman Stebbins Center for Lay Formation. One of the principal ambitions of this new facility will be a headquarters for outreach to college and university students. Thus the campus idea continues to occupy the attention of International CUF.

CUF's capacity to reach new members has been helped immeasurably by the publication of elementary school catechetical books, the Faith and

Life Series. Conceived in 1985 as a joint enterprise of Catholics United for the Faith and Ignatius Press, the series has been an extension of CUF's original commitment to catechetics. In this case, however, the challenge was not to critique preexisting material but to create an elementary religious education series. Faith and Life has brought a whole new category of members into the fold. These younger parents, many in their thirties, will remark to us that they were themselves the "victims" of the emotive and psychological approach to catechetics which prevailed in the postconciliar years, and they find themselves on the rebound, desperate for doctrine for their children. While this phenomenon of orthodox and younger parents has ensured a new generation of committed members for CUF, the response to our series inside official catechetical circles in the United States has been far from enthusiastic.

In the diocese of Tyler, Texas, Faith and Life was judged to be "pre–Vatican II" in ecclesiology, sacramental theology, and imagery. The diocesan director of education was not content merely to list what she thought to be weaknesses in the text. At length she suggested that the child's "right to comprehend the faith" was threatened by an approach which was overly "intellectual and dogmatic" while being "extremely cognitive." The art reproductions in the text were praised, but the methodology was criticized severely.[44] The Diocese of Norwich inveighed against the series as "print-heavy, with medieval and other archaic artwork." The art, said the director of catechetical ministry, would have "a potentially frightening effect on young children." The Diocese of Columbus found the imagery of God the Father to be "mainly that of a Lawgiver, Judge, and masculine." Our Christology was upbraided for being "almost entirely a 'Christology from above,'" while the anthropology was said to be "dualistic" with a "strong emphasis on original sin."

Needless to say, we felt that there was a high degree of invective in these critiques (especially the buzzwords such as *print-heavy, cognitive,* etc.) not without certain valid criticisms of our books. The criticisms leveled against Faith and Life, however, tell much about the state of religious education. Where we are roundly condemned for being "cognitive," we insist that we are returning to a necessary intellectual focus. What appears to some DREs as "archaism" in religious art finds plenty of secular advocates at universities and auction houses. From our perspective it seemed essential to restore pride in sacred art, for cultural as well as pedagogical reasons. The irony of contemporary religious education is that there well may be more antipathy to Western culture in Catholic schools than in secular universities. At almost every juncture, religious education professionals were criticizing precisely those elements which we thought to be necessary, even remedial (i.e., emphasis on content, religious art graphics, and the concentric over the linear approach).

While many diocesan religious education offices seemed to unite against Faith and Life, events took a surprising turn in the Arlington, Virginia, diocese. Approximately one-quarter of the pastors of the diocese protested evaluations of catechetical material done by the Office of the Director of Catechetics. In letters to Mr. Lloyd LaMois, the pastors questioned the sharp disparity between reviews of the Benziger and Sadlier series (which received ratings of 2.9 on a scale of 3) and that of Faith and Life (which was given 0.00). Another letter, this time from thirty-one associate pastors, also took issue with the evaluation committee, while protesting an apparent takeover of the catechetical enterprise by diocesan committee people from the priests themselves. Many of these disgruntled priests argued that contemporary catechetics is in a thralldom over methodology yet pays little regard to content or doctrine. A great many of the assistant pastors were themselves using the Faith and Life Series and resented a move by the Education Office to preempt use of the books.

The revolt of the Arlington pastors may signal a number of changes on the horizon. Priests who had traditionally left the teaching role to parish professionals are now reasserting themselves as primary catechists in the parish. DREs and mainline Catholic publishing houses such as Benziger, Sadlier, and Silver Burdett, which have had a tight grip on catechetics in most parishes, may now find themselves in competition with a growing segment of orthodox parents and priests. These latter find Faith and Life more to their liking.

The very vehemence with which religious educators opposed Faith and Life gave us reason to think that we had touched the exposed nerve of mainstream catechesis. We had collided with powerful interests in the Catholic Church in the United States who seemed hardly capable of dealing with the cognitive falloff in elementary school students.

The collision course pitting parents (in need of orthodox catechesis) with diocesan professionals more inclined to a dialogic kind of catechesis in many ways defines the current crisis in religious education in this country. The history of the CUF apostolate over the last ten years has been taken up with this struggle. In so many different parishes and dioceses in the U.S., a scenario is acted out wherein a group of parents, desirous of more doctrine in the religious ed program, approach the DRE with a request that the Faith and Life Series be introduced. The concerned parents are told invariably that the series is not approved by the diocese or that it has been found wanting *pedagogically*. Faith and Life may well be "the Everest" among all other catechetical offerings, as Peter Kreeft maintains, yet it is resisted by any number of diocesan educators, the true power brokers in catechetics.

Although Faith and Life has faced inordinate difficulties on the diocesan level, it has become the catechism of choice for a large percentage of Catholic home schoolers. The tide of home schooling has influenced CUF membership; many Catholic home schoolers who felt disenfranchised have found CUF to be a vital support. By obtaining texts from the Faith and Life Series and, later, by joining local CUF chapters, these parents have seen the wider possibilities of formation and study of the faith.

In peering into the future and trying to envision the kind of audience that would find a natural fit with our work, CUF leadership is convinced that a broad-based catechetical effort is required. With the success of the Faith and Life Series came numerous requests that we undertake a high-school program. Parents and students who had grown up with Faith and Life were requesting a secondary-school series. Such an effort is now underway. We receive a continuous stream of calls relative to the RCIA program, requesting our recommendation of an adult catechism. Parents of children enrolled in parish confirmation classes wonder if we have a manual for confirmation which they might use to assess their child's course of study. Recently, Faith and Life has been translated into Lithuanian and Vietnamese, indicating that CUF's catechetical resources may be useful on an international scale. CUF members involved in parish Scripture studies call repeatedly to ask our opinion of resources and commentaries which are being used.

In other words, there seems to be a wide range of catechetical concerns, from preschool issues to adult study of the faith. Hardly a reclusive conservative who shuns contact with priest and people, the average CUF member is inclined to be involved at the parish level. Criticisms which we have received about parish RCIA, Bible study, or adult education are coming from our own members who are enrolling in these very programs. Our membership is engaged in a diversity of catechetical and sacramental areas, and is committed to working within the local church. There is every reason to envision the future CUF apostolate as a player in parish and diocesan life. This contact with the parish will leaven our members, but it may also bring a renewed respect for CUF and an attentiveness to church teaching on the part of the local parish.

In the face of a literal avalanche of requests regarding instructional materials, it seems improbable that CUF could turn its back on catechetics. The very real practical question remaining is how much CUF can accomplish in the way of publishing and producing its own catechetical materials. An ambitious publishing agenda would seem to put this apostolate in a very promising position to attract new members, especially as education is taken up at the parish level, but also occurring increasingly in homes via the computer revolution and the home schooling movement.

Present publishing schedules include *Lay Witness,* originally begun in 1978 to address topical and noteworthy themes while also providing material of an in-house nature related to our chapters and their activities. Today *Lay Witness* is one reason why CUF has sustained itself and gained a following. The editorial position has always been to follow rather carefully the expressed teaching of the magisterium, while inviting an occasional theological piece of interpretation from an approved author. *Lay Witness* has also been the vehicle by which aspiring Catholic writers have reached a wider audience. Inasmuch as the emphasis has been to address important theological concerns (yet in a way accessible to a wide Catholic readership), the publication has helped to guide the apostolate toward a deepened faith, not neglecting the scholarly dimension when required. In this way, it serves to inform all the members, while indirectly deflecting criticism that CUF may be about a "fundamentalist" retrenchment.

From 1973 to 1975, Executive Vice-President Kenneth Whitehead coordinated a massive effort among all the CUF chapters in response to the draft proposal of the *National Catechetical Directory*.[45] Published in 1977 as a booklet, *Man Does Not Live by Experience Alone,* this fifty-page analysis became a classic rejoinder to the school of "experiential catechesis," which was then the dominant model for religious education in the U.S. This analysis set the tone for critiques of other catechetical series which issued from the CUF office, and also defined the direction in which the yet-to-be-published Faith and Life Series would proceed. Since that time other books and booklets have been produced: *The Pope, the Council and the Mass; Blessed by the Cross: Five Portraits of Edith Stein; St. Therese of Lisieux: Doctor of the Church?* and *The Popes' Teaching on Sex Education.* President Jim Likoudis authored *Ending the Byzantine-Greek Schism,* a contribution to ecumenical discussions ongoing between Rome and the Orthodox Church. Plans are underway for a high-school series as well as booklet-length treatments on the liturgy and sacred scripture.

In plotting the course of future growth for CUF, we face the bugbear of funding, the perennial heartbreak hill of nonprofit organizations. While CUF is the recipient of some support from foundations, that amount is relatively small, constituting about 18 percent of our total budget. The vast bulk of operating income is derived from consistent small donations from our members. CUF's target audience includes a large segment of young families with children in catechetical instruction (some of whom are extended beyond their means with tuition costs), people who are hard-pressed to support with dollars an organization to which they are also deeply committed. Likewise, CUF's documentary service provides an enormous amount of reprint and photostatic services, which require staff time but remunerate the organization only marginally in income. The production of the Faith and Life Series has helped to offset the year-long struggle to maintain our member services, operating costs, and printing bills. Yet each fiscal crisis has been surmounted, and CUF feels confident in planning for the future.

Conclusion

The present situation in the church in the United States seems to offer bright spots and shadows. This ambiguous condition will have an impact on the CUF apostolate. Dissent from authentic teachings of the magisterium remains endemic. People practice a kind of pick-and-choose Catholicism, a situation which places the believing Catholic in a minority role. In such a context, CUF will continue to exhort its members to a full adherence while counseling them to charity, magnanimity, and prayer where the faith commitment around them seems to lapse. Inner personal and moral growth will be a remedy when institutional supports are not forthcoming.

On a more promising front, the younger generation of Catholics have a different attitude toward church authority. Their formative years were not spent at Dayton University or Catholic University, where rebellion against papal encyclicals was considered *de rigueur* for educated Catholics. The press in Denver for the last papal visit seemed struck by the lack of confrontation between John Paul II's reassertion of the church's teaching on contraception, abortion, and divorce, and the youth in attendance. In order to thrive, Catholicism requires a level of *communio* or institutional peace. Yet from CUF's perspective this ecclesiastical peace is the fruit of faith, which is supernatural in cause and effect. In the view of CUF leadership, the rising generation of younger Catholics, who did not experience the dissent of the 1960s and 1970s, could help regenerate Roman Catholicism in the United States. In order to be a vanguard for renewal, however, these new Catholics need to be the bearers of the deepest and finest in the Catholic heritage. By bringing forward the legacy of Newman, and by reflecting on the sources of Catholic tradition in our publications and books, CUF hopes to play a part in this second spring.

NOTES

1. In many different places, Pope Paul VI reiterated this theme of "inner spiritual renewal" as a key to appropriating the spirit of Vatican II. In the first year of its inception, CUF ordered large quantities of Paul's *Credo of the People of God*. The approach of the apostolate was to Vatican II through the words and enactments of Pope Paul VI.

2. John Paul II notes that a "new state of affairs today both in the Church and in social, economic, political and cultural life, calls with particular urgency for the action of the lay faithful" (*Christifideles Laici*, 3); also Russell Shaw, *To Hunt to Shoot to Entertain: Clericalism and the Catholic Laity* (San Francisco: Ignatius Press, 1993), and Jordan Aumann, O.P., *On the Front Lines: The Lay Person in the Church after Vatican II* (Staten Island, N.Y.: Alba House, 1990).

3. Second Vatican Council, Decree on the Apostolate of the Laity *(Apostolicam Actuositatem)*, declares that the group apostolate is needed because "often, either in ecclesial communities or in various other environments, the apostolate calls for concerted action. Organizations created for group apostolate afford support to their members, form them for the apostolate, carefully assign and direct their apostolic activities; and as a result a much richer harvest can be hoped for from them than if each one were to act on his own" (#18). Commenting on this same document, Pope John Paul II affirmed, "We can speak [in recent days] of a new era of group endeavours of the lay faithful" (*Christifideles Laici*, 29).

4. The magisterium frequently uses the term *activism*. John Paul II: "Each of Christ's followers . . . is incorporated as a living member in the Church and has an active part to play in her mission of salvation" (*Christifideles Laici*, 3). Pius XII spoke of "active participation" *(actuosa participatio)* in *Mediator Dei*, his encyclical on the sacred liturgy. Such an active role would differ from a kind of "activism" of the political order, where human will and striving become the supreme good.

5. "Just as there is an evil zeal of bitterness which separates from God and leads to hell, so there is a good zeal which separates from vices and leads to God and to life everlasting" *(The Rule of St. Benedict)*.

6. Because of the concentration required in the study of the faith, the necessary format of CUF chapter meetings has not appealed to certain people who would prefer the organization to be more task-oriented. While the planning of conferences, even days of recollection, is important, such tasks flow from an inner disposition of prayer and study of the faith. In one respect, CUF sought to take a page from the older "Tuesday Club," where the pastor of the parish would meet in the rectory parlor with certain of the parishioners who wished to deepen themselves on a particular aspect of the faith.

7. To cite only a few examples, CUF chapters in Plandome, New York; Wilmington, Delaware; Phoenix, Arizona; Jacksonville, Florida; and Wichita, Kansas have made pro-life work a keystone of their "active" dimension.

8. Both Bishop Austin Vaughan and Joan Andrews have strong ties to Catholics United for the Faith and to CUF's Long Island chapter, Immaculate Conception. Bishop Vaughan has publicly credited the Long Island chapter with awakening his commitment to the unborn, while Joan has been a long-time member of CUF. Both individuals have been honored locally and nationally by CUF.

9. The problem of liturgical deviations has many repercussions. Certainly before Vatican II there was a hypercritical tendency on the part of some people ("rubricists," they were called). Yet with the flood of unauthorized "additions, deletions and omissions" from the liturgy, following upon the revised Mass of Pope Paul VI, even the most magnanimous and sanguine among the People of God began to look like a rubricist. Pope John Paul I adopted as his own a widely circulated quotation by the French Dominican Yves Congar, to wit: "The greater part of the ideas that are attributed to the Council today are not at all from the Council. For many the Council simply means change. Some things that we had believed or done before, according to them, are now no longer to be done, no longer to be believed. This has become the meaning of the

Council" (originally quoted in *Our Sunday Visitor*, 19 September 1978). Such a distorted view of Vatican II gathered a momentum which carried into many areas of church life. CUF's pre-occupation with some of these distortions has been unfairly linked to prior obsessive strains, such as rubricism. Our concern about liturgical abuses has been for the sake of keeping true concord and unity in the church.

10. There has been a recent upsurge in books on apologetics, including Jeffrey A. Mirus, ed., *Reasons for Hope* (Front Royal, Va.: Christendom Press, 1982); Peter Kreeft, *Fundamentals of the Faith* (San Francisco: Ignatius Press, 1988); Peter Kreeft, *Yes or No: Straight Answers to Tough Questions about Christianity* (San Francisco: Ignatius Press 1991); William G. Most, *Catholic Apologetics Today: Answers to Modern Critics* (Rockford, Ill.: TAN Press, 1986); G. H. Duggan, S.M., *Beyond Reasonable Doubt* (Boston: Daughters of St. Paul, 1987).

11. The author wishes to thank Msgr. Richard J. Schuler, pastor of St. Agnes Church, St. Paul, Minnesota, for providing the minutes of this first organizational meeting, at which he was in attendance.

12. Madeleine F. Stebbins, chairman of the CUF Board of Directors and widow of H. Lyman Stebbins, is preparing the diaries of her late husband, material of which relates to his years as a Yale undergraduate.

13. It was not only in the intellectual realm that Stebbins collaborated with von Hildebrand. The two men were linked by the friendship formed by their wives. Alice Jourdain von Hildebrand and Madeleine Froelicher Stebbins were roommates in New York City before marriage to their distinguished husbands.

14. George A. Kelly, *The Battle for the American Church* (New York: Doubleday, 1979), pp. 129–98.

15. News conference to announce the formation of CUF. Text reprinted in *The Wanderer*, 3 October 1968, p. 1.

16. Philip Trower, *The Revolt of the Scholars* (St. Paul, Minn.: The Wanderer Press Reprint, 1972?). In this pamphlet, Trower gives voice to a generalized perception among conservative Catholics that dissent was first and foremost in the academy. Msgr. George A. Kelly, writing ten years after the publication of *Humanae Vitae*, could remark: "A guerrilla-type warfare is going on inside the Church and its outcome is clearly doubtful. The Pope and the Roman Curia are fending off with mixed success the attacks of their own theologians, who, in the name of scholarship, demand more radical accommodation with Protestant and secular thought." Kelly, *The Battle for the American Church*, p. vii.

17. In *Christifideles Laici*, John Paul II would make explicit this "right" of lay association to form. "First of all, the freedom for lay people to form such groups is to be acknowledged. Such liberty is a true and proper right that is not derived from any kind of 'concession' by authority, but flows from the Sacrament of Baptism which calls the lay faithful to participate actively in the Church's communion and mission" (#29).

18. Marshall Fightlin, "The Kingship of the Laity," *Lay Witness*, October 1992, and H. Lyman Stebbins, *The Priesthood of the Laity in the Domestic Church* (New Rochelle, N.Y.: CUF, 1978).

19. Stebbins did much of his exhorting and encouraging in personal correspondence. The volumes of this correspondence remain at the CUF office, and extracts from letters are printed on a regular basis in the pages of *Lay Witness*, the monthly publication.

20. Patrick M. Arnold, S.J., drew a distinction between conservatism and fundamentalism ("The Rise of Catholic Fundamentalism," *America*, 11 April 1987), but then placed CUF in the fundamentalist category. Fundamentalist Catholics, according to Arnold's perspective, were "frightened and hurt," "voices of fear and anger." Unfortunately, Arnold tries to deal with CUF from a psychological point of view, but he never addresses issues of dissent from an ecclesiological point of view. And when he does, he suggests that we are interested in "subordinate" issues such as "sexual morality" but are unconcerned about "the Creed or Catholic dogma." Preposterous.

21. In the same article (note 22), Arnold indicates that Catholic fundamentalists were "co-opted by Ronald Reagan" in the 1980 and 1984 elections. Catholics and CUF members did

support Reagan on the abortion issue. And most of them did prioritize the killing of the unborn as an issue topping any other concern. Moreover, certain Catholic bishops exited the Democratic Party over the abortion issue by making public statements of the fact (Bishop Austin Vaughan, New York Auxiliary, and Archbishop John Francis Whealon of Hartford). Arnold invokes Cardinal Bernardin's "seamless garment" image to suggest that Catholic votes for Reagan (due to his pro-life stance) were excessively narrow, more an instance of gratifying a latent Republican inclination than a display of Catholic conscience. Still, Cardinal Bernardin himself clarified the "seamless garment," indicating that abortion was an ongoing and ubiquitous evil that elevated it as a moral concern.

22. CUF member Dr. Rupert Ederer, professor of economics, in an address to the Buffalo chapter of CUF, "Reganomics, Economics, and the Church," took issue with supply-side theory, suggesting that the church had a wider conception of the role of government in economic affairs than many political conservatives would allow. He specifically challenged the idea that Catholic social theory and supply-side economics were necessarily equivalent. See also David M. Rooney, "A Commentary on Lamentations—Over Papal Social Teachings," *Lay Witness,* February 1990. Rooney was reacting to an earlier piece, "The Last Socialist" by John Gray, which had appeared in *National Review.* There has been conservative upset with papal social teaching, but such is not the position of Catholics United for the Faith.

23. CUF never adopted a *parti pris* for Spain, or Catholic monarchy, for example, as did the editors at *Triumph,* although L. Brent Bozell and Michael Lawrence, both *Triumph* editors, were original founding members of CUF. Brent Bozell later served as a special ambassador for CUF, while Don McLane was CUF president. For further analysis of *Triumph* and the lure of Spanish Catholicism, see Patrick Allitt, *Catholic Intellectuals and Conservative Politics in America, 1950–1985* (Ithaca: Cornell University Press, 1993), pp. 144–46.

24. John A. Coleman, S.J., "Who Are the Catholic 'Fundamentalists'?" *Commonweal,* 27 January 1989. Coleman regards CUF as "integralist," asserting that our claim to represent the authentic spirit and letter of Vatican II is a case of "tortured rhetoric." Like Patrick Arnold, S.J., Coleman is not above "purple" phraseology. He finds affinity between CUF and European movements such as Schonstadt and Communio e Liberazione, as well as earlier protofascist groups which supported Petain, Salazar, and Franco. CUF is thoroughly apolitical, however. Sympathy for pro-life politicians, certainly, but no grandiose political vision; no cadet corps for some rightist regime. In fact, CUF has never even hinted at the fact that it might be a remnant. We deplore a recent tendency among certain Catholic traditionalists who seem to be resurrecting the Montanist heresy, imagining themselves uniquely deputed to restore health to the church. Nevertheless, a desire to avoid superciliousness need not lead one to cover one's eyes to the fact of dissent. Unity in the church will necessarily be a unity in truth. The "remnant" approach, while having an "enthusiastic Protestant" flavor, was challenged by St. Augustine, who favored the image of the church as a great net into which many fish would swim. Jean Danielou, S.J., appealed to Augustine's metaphor precisely in order to rebut the remnant typology. Jean Danielou, *Prayer as a Political Problem* (New York: Sheed and Ward, 1965), p. 10.

25. Interview with Madeleine F. Stebbins, 1 September 1993.

26. John Henry Cardinal Newman, *Parochial and Plain Sermons,* vol. 3 (New York: Longmans, Green, and Co., 1906), p. 81, quoted in "We Have But One Teacher," CUF pamphlet drawing together catechetical texts from papal, curial, and episcopal documents.

27. John Henry Newman, *An Essay on the Development of Christian Doctrine* (New York: Longmans, Green, 1909), pp. 88, 89, as quoted in M. K. Strolz, ed., *John Henry Cardinal Newman: The Mystery of the Church* (257 Via Aurelia Rome, 1981), pp. 15–16.

28. Newman quoted by H. Lyman Stebbins at a news conference in Washington, D.C., 26 September 1968, *The Wanderer,* 3 October 1968, p. 1.

29. George Weigel references Richard John Neuhaus's *The Catholic Moment,* where Neuhaus argues that present-day preoccupation with church authority by the left and the right "is theologically debased," inasmuch as the debaters are not so much interested in "truth-claims" as they are interested in "contesting for power." Given the ever-recurrent presence of the *libido*

dominandi, we would not contest the view that some in the church seek to instate their own desires rather than the truth of the Gospel. Still, if the truth is communicated, we cannot dispense with an interpreter. For an analysis of how some leading Catholic theologians (eg. Dulles, Brown, and McCormick) have shifted the ground on the relationship between theologians and the magisterium in order to accommodate dissent, see Germain Grisez, *The Way of the Lord Jesus*, vol. 1 (Quincy, Ill.: Franciscan Press, 1983), chaps. 35, 36.

30. Grisez, *The Way of the Lord Jesus*, vol. 1, chap. 3, pp. 840–41.

31. John Henry Newman, *Parochial and Plain Sermons*, vol. 1 (Westminster, Md.: Christian Classics, 1966), pp. 312–13.

32. In part because of the pressure from some members who resisted the revisions in the Roman Missal, CUF began to build up an extensive filing system on liturgical matters, with special emphasis on documentation coming from the Roman discasteries. This was done in the early years so as to focus on the legitimate enactments of the Holy See, which were coming to be opposed by so-called traditionalists. On the other hand, these documents were also telling against the myriad departures from the rubrics, the liturgical anarchy that was taking place. The desacralization of the liturgy is covered in many different volumes, and its present course is charted by Thomas Day, *Where Have You Gone Michelangelo: The Loss of Soul in Catholic Culture* (New York: Seabury Press, 1993).

33. E. William Sockey III, "The Pope, the Council and the Mass," *Lay Witness*, October 1988, pp. 6–7.

34. Bishop Thomas J. Welsh commended the authors of *The Pope, the Council and the Mass* for "showing the consistency of the Church's liturgical reforms since Vatican II and for answering the typical criticisms that have been made of the reformed liturgy." In order to make explicit our link with the hierarchy, as well as the clergy and laity, CUF has recently established a board of advisors, to include bishops, priests, theologians, and laypersons.

35. Likoudis and Whitehead, *The Pope, the Council and the Mass* (W. Hanover, Mass.: Christopher, 1981), p. 26.

36. "Let me sing of your Law," intones the Psalmist. Deference to church authority was practiced by CUF at a time (the late 1960s and 1970s) when antinomianism was a preferred style for many American Catholics.

37. The recent permission given by Pope John Paul II for the use of altar girls is a case in point. In our response in *Lay Witness*, June 1994, we counsel the members "to respect the authority of the Holy See that gave permission and acknowledge that it had the authority to do so."

38. H. Lyman Stebbins, "The Responsibility of the Laity to the Bishops—and Vice Versa," *Lay Witness*, March 1985.

39. We address the need to focus on the episcopacy in a recent article: Milton J. Walsh, "Shepherds in Christ's Church," *Lay Witness*, November 1992. The author details how Bismarck sought to weaken the power of the German episcopate in the aftermath of Vatican I by claiming "that the definition of Papal Primacy meant that the bishops were merely delegates or functionaries of the Pope. Both the German Bishops and Pope Pius IX rejected this interpretation in the strongest terms."

40. The U.S. bishops have given formal approval to classroom education in human sexuality. In a foreword to the USCC document "Human Sexuality: A Catholic Perspective for Education and Lifelong Learning" (NCCB/USCC, 12 December 1990), general secretary Monsignor Robert N. Lynch states that the document is designed "for parents, parishes, and other church-related institutions as they design and implement programs of *formal instruction in human sexuality*" (my emphasis). The vexing prudential issue that faces many parents, however, is whether "formal instruction" does not already collapse the primary/subsidiary model that informs the pope's thinking.

41. At CUF's 25th Anniversary Conference in Philadelphia, 16 October 1993, Monsignor Peter Elliott delivered an address from Cardinal Alfonso Lopez Trujillo, president of the Pontifical Council for the Family, in which the cardinal maintained that "parents' rights must be respected in this area (education in sexuality), because they are the primary educators of their

children, and no one else is entitled to take away this right or to take over the duty inseparable from it." His Eminence allowed that "many children and young people do not receive adequate formation at home." In meeting their needs, "there is no need to surrender in any way to invasive courses and methods of sex education which amount simply to sex initiation." *Lay Witness,* March 1994, pp. 4–5.

42. Interview with James Likoudis, 7 May 1993. The erosion of faith was itself an explosive topic. Some in the church wished to think in terms of "diversity" or a Catholic spectrum, so as to mute the issue of "abandoned faith." Newman was invoked along the lines of development of doctrine, so that what might appear as novelty in doctrine might be entertained as development. Recently, Msgr. George G. Higgins made the case for the spectrum of viewpoints in the church by recommending Richard McBrien's *Catholicism.* "Father McBrien wrote *Catholicism* for you and for me, whether we think of ourselves as conservative, traditional Catholics or progressive, renewed Catholics." George C. Higgins, " *'Catholicism'* Most Important Book since Vatican II," *The Catholic Observer,* 8 July 1994, p. 5. We feel, on the contrary, that this spectrum is bogus. It confounds what may exist in the political or cultural order with what must prevail in the order of faith. Are you a liberal or a conservative on the Creed?

43. Donahue Transcript #2822, "The Lucy Killea Controversy," National Feed Date: 20 November 1989.

44. Diocese of Tyler, Memorandum to Pastors of the Diocese of Tyler from Sister Sara Dwyer on the Faith and Life Series, 25 May 1988. Dwyer went on to call the series "rigid and moralistic," stating that it created a "false sense of security" in the student. "In the light of these basic concerns, this Office will not at this time endorse the selection of this textbook series." The Columbus Diocese evaluation of Faith and Life was unsigned, yet stated on page 3, in conclusion, "This series is not approved for use in the Diocese of Columbus." The Norwich Diocese delivered a scathing critique of Faith and Life, rating it as "poor." Sister Kathleen Kandefer, BVM, urged religious education coordinators, "Of course this office recommends you chose a text rated GOOD overall."

While CUF would agree that certain revisions ought to be undertaken, nevertheless the opprobrium that Faith and Life has fallen under is also a reflection of the lock grip on catechetics that the "experiential school" maintains. Fr. Alfred McBride, O. Praem., a noted expert in catechesis, revealed that a large percentage of teachers of religious education thought that the proposed universal catechism was unnecessary.

45. Whitehead's efforts and those of the CUF chapters were singled out by the secretary of the NCD, Msgr. Wilfrid Paradis, who related that "CUF had more input into the draft process than any other lay group" (Letter from Msgr. Wilfrid Paradis to Kenneth Whitehead, office correspondence file).

6

The Neoconservative Difference
A Proposal for the Renewal of
Church and Society

GEORGE WEIGEL

Prologue

Neoconservative American Catholicism is a distinctive feature of
the contemporary religious scene in the United States. Less a "movement" than an ongoing community of intellectual conversation and
cooperation, it has no precise analogue in American Protestantism or Judaism. This chapter analyzes the phenomenon "from the inside," with
primary reference to the work of Richard John Neuhaus, Michael Novak,
and George Weigel, three figures whose writing has been the focus of
analysis and critique precisely *as* "neoconservative."

Neoconservative American Catholicism has not been essentially a po-
litical-religious movement, a Catholic chaplaincy, so to speak, to the wider
political movement of neoconservatism. Rather, the American Catholic
neoconservative perspective emerged in the late 1970s and early 1980s out
of religious, indeed theological, and specifically ecclesiological concerns. It
is, in that respect, one facet of the American "reception" of Vatican II.

The neoconservatives have argued that the crisis of postconciliar Catholicism is not a crisis of authority but rather a crisis of faith; moreover, the
neocons have insisted (contra the Lefebvrists) that this crisis of faith is
rooted not in "the Council" but in certain inadequate (but institutionally

well-entrenched) interpretations of the Council. Further, the "neocons" believe that these misinterpretations have led to serious pastoral problems, particularly in terms of Catholic identity; that they have been exacerbated by a new "political correctness" in Catholic intellectual and ecclesiastical-bureaucratic circles; and that, unchallenged, this religious "p.c." will eventually lead American Catholicism down the path of demographic collapse and cultural marginalization scouted by mainline/oldline Protestantism.

But the neocons' approach to these problems has not been that of the "Catholic right," strictly defined. Among the more salient characteristics of the "Catholic right" has been its profound nervousness about modernity and, specifically, about the capacity of modern intellectual life to give an adequate account of classic Catholic truth claims. This has not been a defining characteristic of neoconservative American Catholicism. Rather than adopting a strategy of rejection and retrenchment, the neocons have sought to engage modern intellectual life, in which they have discerned openings to the transcendent. Thus they have pioneered new modes of ecumenical and interreligious conversation with evangelical/fundamentalist/pentecostalist Protestants and with leading American Jewish intellectuals. In those conversations they have worked to develop new theological methodologies capable of fostering "dynamic orthodoxy" in a church on the edge of its third millennium.

Neoconservative Catholicism has also steered a distinctive course in American public life. Although regularly (and simplistically) described (and dismissed) as gung-ho promoters of capitalism and perfervid critics of American episcopal interventions on issues of foreign policy and the U.S. economy, the neocons have in fact taken up the more fundamental intellectual challenge laid down by John Courtney Murray, S.J., thirty-five years ago, namely, to devise a religiously grounded moral philosophy for the American experiment in ordered liberty.

Advancing this "Murray Project" has involved several interlocking sets of concerns. It has required challenging the establishment of secularism in American political culture and constitutional jurisprudence. It has meant developing a distinctive understanding of "democratic capitalism" as a multidimensional system in which a vibrant, pluralistic moral culture disciplines a democratic polity and a free economy (a model the neocons have applied to the changing circumstances of North America, Latin America, and east central Europe). In the 1980s, it meant revitalizing the American commitment to the cause of human rights (particularly religious freedom) as the indispensable antidote to the poison of Marxism-Leninism. Since the Communist crack-up, it has meant reconceiving the just war tradition as a moral logic for statecraft in a post–Cold War world. In the early 1990s, and at the most fundamental philosophical level of their "public" agenda, the neocons were prominent in defining the contemporary American "culture war" as a contest between a thin theory of the "autonomous self" and a thicker concept of the "communitarian individual." In all of this, the Catholic neocons have worked to help develop a *public* church that is not a *partisan* church.

Neoconservative American Catholicism is not an attempt to define a self-consciously "centrist" position theologically, ecclesiastically, or politically. And because they do not think of themselves as "centrists," the neocons are not to be understood primarily in terms of any "over-against," to left or right. Rather, the neocon passion has been for a genuinely broadly gauged debate aimed at the renewal and revitalization of both church and society. Still, for purposes of orientation, the neocon "difference" can be sketched as follows.

As distinguished from the Catholic right, the neocons welcomed, and continue to welcome, Vatican II's opening of the windows of the church to the modern world. As distinguished from establishment Catholic liberalism and the Catholic left, the neocons want to complete the exercise by challenging the modern world to open its windows to the worlds of which it is a part, primarily the world of transcendent truth and love. As distinguished from elements on both the Catholic right and Catholic left, the neoconservatives do not regard the United States as an ill-founded experiment. In the contemporary American "culture war" and in the celebration of "autonomy" as the highest of democratic values, however, the neocons see the gravest threat to the integrity of the American experiment since the days before the Civil War.

The neocons have found considerable inspiration in the magisterium of Pope John Paul II. There they find an authentic interpretation of the deepest dynamics of Vatican II in which a retrieval of the early sources of Christian wisdom and self-understanding (*ressourcement*) ground and discipline the church's "updating" (*aggiornamento*). That approach, and the pope's evident interest in the modern quest for freedom, make his teaching a resource of great consequence for the renewal of church and society in America.

Introduction

When did Catholics begin to be classified as "liberals" and "conservatives"—and thereby celebrated or dismissed, according to the respective categorizer's proclivities?

Some might argue that the general pattern formed early, in the debates between Judaizers and Hellenizers in the apostolic and subapostolic church. More to the immediate point, there were rough analogies to today's familiar monikers in recent centuries; the approach taken by different popes to the church's long-running struggle with the legacies of the Enlightenment was one focus of ideological appraisal. Thus Benedict XIV (1740–1758) and Pius VII (1800–1823) were considered, in their own times, "conciliatory" (or, in today's jargon, "open") leaders, while Gregory XVI (1831–1846) was taken to be the very model of a reactionary (or, as they used to say, "absolutist") pontiff. Pius IX changed positions in mid-Tiber, so to speak. Elected in 1846 as a "reformer," perhaps even a political "liberal," by 1864 he had become the "Pio No-No" of the *Syllabus Errorum*. Similar labels were used to identify different camps in the church during the controversies over modernism in the early twentieth century and over the *nouvelle theologie* of the 1940s.

Whatever the historical antecedents, the use of the cribbed political terms *liberal* and *conservative* as all-purpose ecclesiastical identifiers in American Catholicism vastly accelerated under the impact of the "Xavier Rynne" articles and books on the Second Vatican Council.[1] Here, the deliberations of some two thousand bishops, who conducted their business in an arcane ancient language absent the real-time scrutiny of CNN, were rendered intelligible, or at least explicable, to American readers (at first, of the *New Yorker!*) by a brilliantly simple interpretive device: good guys and bad guys, "liberals" and "conservatives," were contesting the future of the world's oldest institution, the Roman Catholic Church.

The "liberals," legatees of the beloved Pope John XXIII, were "open to the modern world" and sought to strip the church of what one of their heroes, Belgian bishop Emile Joseph de Smedt, called its "clericalism, legalism, and triumphalism."[2] The "conservatives" were the party of reaction and the traditional wielders of the anathema. Afraid of modernity and fearful of change, they took their vision of the church, on "Rynne's" reading of things, from the coat of arms of Alfredo Cardinal Ottaviani, pro-prefect of the Holy Office: *Semper Idem* ("Ever the Same"). But "Rynne's" plot line also contained a prescriptive subtext: all right-thinking people were, or ought to be, on the side of the "liberal" good guys—especially right-thinking Americans, citizens of the nation which believed itself to embody (at least in the early 1960s) the inevitability of progress and the benignity of "change." To sympathize with even some of the concerns of the "conservatives" was to confess to a psychological, and perhaps even moral, aberration.

The "Rynne" images quickly became the lingua franca of the post-conciliar American church. They were also readily absorbed by the secular media, and so a feedback loop reinforced the imagery. If *Time,* CBS, and the *New York Times* could speak of "liberals" and "conservatives" in the same tone and with the same meaning as "Xavier Rynne" and the *National Catholic Reporter,* the categories must fit. Thus the American Catholic world bifurcated in the mid- to late 1960s: there were "liberal" and "conservative" bishops, dioceses, parishes, pastors, seminaries, theologians, religious orders, colleges, publishers, newspapers, magazines, and personalities. There were occasional "defections" in either direction (quondam "conservative" Garry Wills celebrated the Berrigan brothers in 1972; quondam "liberal" William W. Baum became the "conservative" archbishop of Washington in 1973 and later a curial cardinal). There were idiosyncratic curmudgeons who refused to fit the pigeonholes (Dorothy Day during one of Dan Berrigan's freestyle liturgies at the Catholic Worker, modestly garbed in a black mantilla according to the injunction in 1 Cor. 11:10). The categories remained more or less intact, however, throughout the pontificate of Pope Paul VI. And at a popular level, they remain more or less intact today, like needles stuck in the grooves of aging records.

Whatever journalistic purpose "Rynne's" imagery served at the time—and careful students of the Council now believe that it distorted at least as much as it clarified about that complex event—recent Catholic history has demonstrated how unsatisfactory these terms are for understanding the dramatis personae in Roman Catholic life thirty years after the opening of Vatican II. For the situation within the church has changed dramatically over the past generation. Radical interpretations of Catholicism, particularly in Marxist and feminist forms, have compelled some who were once considered "liberals" to what is, according to the regnant taxonomy, a more "conservative" position. But why should we consider as "conservative" (in "Rynne's" sense of the term) orthodox Christians who are experimenting with distinctively modern philosophical and theological methodologies in quest of a more adequate contemporary understanding of Christianity's classic truth claims? Nor is there any longer, save on the fringes, a "conservative" rejection of Vatican II; rather, the question is the proper interpretation of the Council, and here mainstream "conservatives" are drawing not on Ottaviani but on the work of such notable "progressive" theologians of the preconciliar and conciliar periods as Henri de Lubac, Hans Urs von Balthasar, and Joseph Ratzinger.

The pontificate of John Paul II has also demonstrated how distorting a lens the "liberal/conservative" dyad has become: for how does one fit into the standard "Rynne" categories a pope who has challenged Küng and Lefebvre, Pinochet and Ortega, Marcos and Jaruzelski? Is *Redemptor Hominis,* his inaugural encyclical and the basic theological statement of the pontificate's incarnational humanism, "liberal" or "conservative"? Or consider *Centesimus Annus,* the most developed of John Paul II's social encyclicals: is it "liberal" or "conservative"? And what does it mean to call the *Catechism of the Catholic Church* "conservative"? Simply asking the question reveals its shallowness, if one has taken the trouble to read these documents seriously.

My purpose here is to sketch the development and perspective of a community of conversation that has self-consciously challenged the "liberal/conservative" hermeneutic of the contemporary Catholic situation. For that is what "neoconservative American Catholicism" has been—a community of conversation and friendship, institutional cooperation and literary endeavor, built around a convergence of ecclesiastical and public interests and concerns.

This "movement," such as it is, has had a lot of serendipity in it—though we who are involved in it like to think that the serendipity has been touched by elements of the providential. There was no founding convention, and there has been no "master plan" (and, in that sense, there is no comprehensive "neoconservative project"). There are no conclaves to determine who is "in" and who is "out." There has been no attempt to define ourselves with methodological rigor as a "school"; indeed, among our intellectual and spiritual mentors we count a Missouri Synod Lutheran systematic theologian, a Jewish sage, philosophers from France and Canada, a Jewish political theorist and activist, and an American Jesuit theologian of the old school. Thus neoconservative American Catholicism is not a "faction" or a "camp" as those terms are usually parsed in ideological politics; it is, to repeat, far more a community of intellectual conversation, gathered around certain of the convictions and experiences noted below. Given the long paper trail the neoconservatives have left behind in the past ten or twelve years, it is understandable that we have come to be regarded as a "movement." But it really is (and has been) much more ad hoc, much less formal, and thus far less "political" than that.

Telling the story of this particular conversation will inevitably involve more autobiographical reflection than is usually the case in essays such as this, for I have been active (at least as a junior subaltern) in the development of the position I shall attempt to describe. This vantage point undoubtedly has its liabilities. But, like Dean Acheson, I have been "present at the creation"—in this instance, of neoconservative Catholicism in America; and perhaps, like the former secretary of state, my seat in the

arena allows me to cast some light on what others, sitting in the mezza-
nine or the bleachers, perceive as mere darkness.

Origins

The term *neoconservative* was first popularized in the 1970s by the
social democrat Michael Harrington to characterize the politics of his
former compatriots on the left who no longer shared Harrington's continuing enthusiasm for socialism, Great Society welfare programs,
"affirmative action," and anti-anticommunism. The neologism was intended to delegitimate at least as much as to describe, for in the circles in
which it was first used, "conservatism" of any form carried connotations
of moral opprobrium. But whatever Harrington's intentions, the term
stuck, and its referents were reasonably clear: "neoconservatives" were
men and women who had once shared the "liberal" political agenda but
who had "broken ranks" over policies that their erstwhile allies understood as the natural working out of "liberalism," but which they perceived
as a "liberalism gone berserk" into radicalism.[3] The origins of political
"neoconservatism," in other words, had far more to do with ideological
developments within the liberal camp than with a natural evolution of
conservative political thought. Indeed, the "neocons" were held suspect
in more establishment conservative quarters for some time, and are still
regarded as Trojan horses threatening the conservative fortress by the
denizens of the paleoconservative fringe.[4]

"Neoconservative" Catholicism in America—of the sort identified with
Richard John Neuhaus, Michael Novak, and me—is often portrayed as a
kind of chaplaincy to this political "neoconservatism." On this interpretation, our energies and passions are primarily focused on the public
policy arena, and our goal is to buttress our political agenda by recruiting
the church and its authority into our ideological camp.[5] That is not, however, how we understand ourselves.[6]

Two related concerns prompted the emergence of American Catholic
neoconservatism as a distinctive body of thought in the early 1980s. The
first concern was ecclesiastical, indeed theological, and specifically ecclesiological. Fifteen years after the completion of a council whose work
we had celebrated, we saw a church in serious disarray. But the disarray
did not have to do, *pace* Archbishop Lefebvre and his epigones, with a
fatal flaw in the Council itself. Rather, it had to do with an interpretation
of the Council that dominated the chief intellectual and organizational
networks of American Catholicism. According to this hermeneutic (itself

influenced by the "Xavier Rynne" stories), there was a direct connection between the "spirit of Vatican II" and the projects being aggressively promoted in the late 1970s and early 1980s by Catholic practitioners of "Marxist analysis" and Catholic feminists, many of which struck us as forms of theological deconstructionism with little discernible linkage to the classic Catholic tradition.[7] As in politics (and in some cases driven by politics), significant currents in theological and ecclesiastical liberalism seemed to have lurched (those in control would have said evolved) into radicalism—and we who declined to make that passage suddenly found ourselves "neoconservatives."[8]

This misinterpretation of the Council (in which, to take symbolic reference points, Karl Rahner was the grandfather of Matthew Fox, Mary Daly, and Leonardo Boff) had led, we believed, to grave pastoral problems. Roman Catholicism in America had become a church with porous boundaries and a severe identity crisis—lacking in self-confidence, beset by bureaucratization, flaccid evangelically, and sterile liturgically.[9] Moreover (and here we touch on our secondary concern), it was a church whose official agencies had become, in our view, increasingly troubling in their address to matters of public policy: insouciant about the threat of communism, inattentive to the travail of the persecuted church behind the Iron Curtain, nervous about its pro-life position on abortion, reflexively statist on questions of social welfare policy, and vulnerable to the siren songs of *Tercermundismo* that had already swept through the mainline Protestant churches and the National and World Councils of Churches.[10]

These developments had resulted in an ecclesial atmosphere which we found not merely unpleasant but really quite noxious. In the name of an "open church," the liberal mainstream seemed to have effectively shut off critical debate within many of the key organizational structures of American Catholicism, imposing its own "correct" positions with a vigor, indeed ruthlessness, that would have been familiar to any gangster-prelate practitioner of the old *Romanità*. This seemed to be the case within many Catholic departments of theology and philosophy; the same rigorous policing of the ideological precincts was also distorting the work of the chief Catholic intellectual organizations (such as the Catholic Theological Society of America), as we saw things.[11] The new liberal establishment was even more firmly in control of the Leadership Conference of Women Religious, the Conference of Major Superiors of Men, and the National Federation of Priests' Councils, and in these quarters, no dissent from the new ecclesiastical correctness was countenanced. Many diocesan structures reflected a similar narrowness of vision, we believed, as did too many of the offices of the National Conference of Catholic Bishops and the United States Catholic Conference. A "new class" of church bureaucrats seemed to be imposing rules of ideological conformity as impervious to real "dialogue" as the old clericalism it allegedly abhorred.

The formulation of our position was also influenced by what we took to be a crucial cautionary tale in modern American religious history: the collapse of the old Protestant mainline denominations. The reasons for this demographic free-fall remain controverted, but the current social science research seems to bear out our intuition of a decade or more ago, that the mainline had become the oldline because its quest for theological and political "relevance"—which in fact constituted a strategy of appeasement toward liberalism-turned-radicalism in the American academy and in politics—was doomed to failure.[12]

That strategy not only did not work (as the demographics proved), it could not work, for it could provide no compelling case for why one *ought* to be a Christian.[13] Moreover, the appeasement or "relevance" strategy was inherently tendentious, for it was in the very nature of the secular left to constantly raise the ante; and as the "cutting edge" issues increasingly revolved around deconstruction in the humanities and the legitimation of the counterculture (and specifically the sexual revolution) in public life, the position of believers committed to classic Jewish and Christian truth claims and morals became simply untenable. Moreover, the strategy of "relevance" was ecclesiastically counterproductive to the point of being self-destructive, for it denied that the church had any agenda that was distinctively and specifically ecclesial. "The world sets the agenda for the church," a maxim of the mainline/oldline, seemed to us both theologically false and pastorally disastrous. It was time for the church to be the church. But what church would it be?

The Renewal of Church and Society

Though we have come to share some of the concerns of those who happily labeled themselves "conservatives" in the immediate postconciliar period, the neoconservative analysis of the church's situation in America today, and our prescription for the revitalization of Catholicism in the United States, has been different from the analysis and prescription of what is usually thought of as the "Catholic right."

Contemporary (i.e., postconciliar) conservative Catholicism in America—the "Catholic right," properly speaking—is a luxuriantly various vineyard planted in the common soil of a profound skepticism about modernity—about contemporary culture, contemporary mores, and the capacity of self-consciously post-Cartesian (and certainly post-Kantian) intellectuals to provide a satisfactory account of classic Christian and Catholic truth claims. That analysis is complemented, among conservative intellectuals, by a strategy of countermodernization. The integrity of the church, indeed the truth claims of Christianity, can be defended only on the basis of a deliberate rejection of the Western intellectual project in its Cartesian/Kantian trajectory. Various alternatives have been proposed, perhaps most prominently the neo-Thomism of Gilson and Maritain. However the alternative is defined, the basic position remains clear: an intellectual retrenchment is the necessary propaedeutic to that restoration of authority within the church that conservatives believe is the besetting problem of Catholicism in the postconciliar period. Absent such a "restoration," the church will be in no credible position to bear witness against the forces of modernity that have defined one line of trenches—those inhabited by the proponents of debonair nihilism—in the American culture war.

American Catholic neoconservatism is not unsympathetic to elements of this analysis and strategy, particularly in terms of the national Kulturkampf. Richard Neuhaus's *America against Itself,* while challenging those conservatives who believe that the American democratic experiment is fundamentally ill-founded, is a sharp critique of what passes for "modern culture" (and especially modern moral culture) in America today.[14] Similar themes may be found in part three of my own book, *Catholicism and the Renewal of American Democracy,* and in many of Michael Novak's works.[15] But the elements of continuity at this level of the debate should not obscure the differences that distinguish the neoconservative position from the traditional "Catholic right," in at least four significant ways.

The Roots of the Crisis

For American Catholic neoconservatives, the current crisis in the church is not, in the first instance, a crisis of authority but rather a crisis of *faith*. The most urgent question we face today is not, "Who's in charge here?" but rather, "When the Son of Man returns, will he find faith on earth?" (Luke 18:8). The crisis of authority in the church is, in fact, an expression of a deeper crisis of faith.

We have found in the pontificate of John Paul II a bold and persistent effort to address this crisis of faith. But the pope's new evangelism does not involve a nostalgia-driven "restoration" in which modernity is rejected root and branch; rather, the new evangelization of John Paul II transcends modernity by engaging and amplifying those elements of modern experience and thought that are, in Peter Berger's fetching phrase, "rumors of angels," or openings to the transcendent. Richard John Neuhaus caught this dimension of the "Wojtyla Project" in these terms:

> This Pope . . . is attempting to chart a Christian course that is not so much against modernity as it is beyond modernity. The only modernity to be discarded is the debased modernity of unbelief that results in a prideful and premature closure of the world against its promised destiny. This Pope is giving voice to the Christian correlate to the opening to the transcendent that in culture, philosophy, and science is the great intellectual and spiritual event of our time. The Christian correlate, of course, is Christ.[16]

To argue that the root of the contemporary Catholic crisis is a crisis of faith—and here we mean "crisis" in the original Greek sense of a decisive moment, a crossroads, in which there is opportunity as well as danger— is to challenge those Catholics who, as Neuhaus put it, "are only now learning to accommodate the faith to a debased modernity that history is fast leaving behind."[17] That accommodation sometimes bespeaks a failure of nerve as well as of intellectual imagination or creativity, for it not infrequently involves (varying degrees of) acquiescence to the fact that the up-market despisers of religion occupy the commanding heights of our cultural institutions, especially the academy and the prestige press.[18] But whereas a more traditional "Catholic right" approach to this problem would be to understand that failure of nerve as the inevitable by-product of any outreach to modernity, the neoconservative approach is to identify, in the interstices of the entrenched (and tenured) redoubts of skepticism and empiricism, openings to a more ample view of human experience and human intellectuality. We believe those openings exist vis-à-vis the hard sciences as well as the social sciences.

Thus in confronting the contemporary intellectual elite, we decline to concede the field at the outset to the modernist quadrilateral of Darwin-Marx-Freud-Nietzsche. We do so not because these thinkers focused on the human to the exclusion of the transcendent, but because their account of the human has no room within it for those aspects of transcendence which other contemporary intellectuals believe to be of the essence of the *humanum*. Where the Catholic right tends to see endless warfare with modern intellectuals, Catholic neoconservatives, who have not been hesitant to critique the foolishness of many contemporary intellectual tastemakers,[19] also discern some possibilities of serious conversation and real debate, not as the result of preemptive tactical concessions on the part of believers, but precisely as the physical and social sciences shed their crude empiricism under the weight of unavoidable evidence. Thus a neo-conservative approach to the crisis of faith is not surprised by, but rather expects, a conclusion like the one with which an eminent American astronomer closed a book on the frontiers of our knowledge of the universe. The scientist, "who has lived by his faith in the power of reason," now finds himself in a curious position—"He has scaled the mountains of ignorance; he is about to conquer the highest peak; as he pulls himself over the final rock, he is greeted by a band of theologians who have been sitting there for centuries."[20]

Put another way, neoconservative American Catholicism welcomes Pope John XXIII's call for the church to open its windows to a dialogue with the modern world, but it wants the dialogue to be that, a dialogue, and not a monologue in which the *ecclesia docens* simply collapses into the *ecclesia discens*. We do not believe that ours is an ineluctably secular city. Rather, with John Paul II, we argue that the church should "enter the modern world to help open the windows of the modern world to the worlds of which it is part"—which include, preeminently, the world of transcendent truth and love.[21] Moreover—and here we touch on the central claim in Neuhaus's *Catholic Moment*—neoconservative American Catholics have (with varying degrees of confidence) seen the Catholic Church as singularly well-positioned for that task of evangelization and re-evangelization in the worlds of secularism and religious indifferentism. We would further argue that the Council, properly understood, was an essential element in the creation of this special "Catholic moment." Whether that moment is being seized is, of course, another question.

Communities of Conversation: Abraham, Martin, and John

The second distinctive feature of the neoconservative Catholic project in America is that its response to the contemporary crisis of faith is determinedly ecumenical and interreligious. These characteristics have not been prominent on the "Catholic right" since the Council (even as they were not prominent in the 1940s and 1950s, the "real Catholic Moment," as some on the right would insist). But here, too, our enterprise has taken the ecumenical and interreligious conversation in a different direction from that characteristic of liberal Catholicism.

The ecumenical dimension of the neoconservative enterprise has several components. It includes a commitment to the pursuit of ecclesial communion according to the classic intention of the ecumenical movement, as that was defined in the early stages of the postconciliar bilateral dialogues between Catholicism and the Lutheran, Reformed, and Anglican-Methodist traditions. The quest for full ecclesial communion—not as a product of bureaucratic negotiation but as a result of a Spirit-led theological and spiritual plumbing of the depths of these traditions—is, in our view, a Gospel imperative, even if its institutional fruition seems farther in the future than might once have been expected or hoped. Moreover, ecumenicity in theological conversation at this "depth" level is crucial in crafting a persuasive Christian response to modernity and its discontents.

But neoconservative American Catholics have also scouted the terrain of a new American ecumenism, in which for perhaps the first time in our national history Roman Catholics are in intense and sustained conversation with evangelical, fundamentalist, and pentecostal Protestants. This new ecumenism reflects several convictions and concerns. The first has to do with the changing demographics of American Christianity. Here, two powerful sets of facts presented themselves in the late 1970s and early 1980s.

The first datum was the striking phenomenon described by a former general secretary of the National Council of Churches as the Protestant mainline's decline into the oldline and possibly the sideline. The meaning of this decline, we believed, should not be understood solely, or even primarily, in demographic terms. For the mainline-oldline-sideline declension also presaged a dramatic circulation of elites among the culture-forming institutions of our national life. The mainline had been, since the days of John Winthrop and his "Citie on a Hill," the chief agency of moral-cultural formation in America. Its demise left a large gap—and created an unprecedented opportunity (and responsibility) for Catholicism in America.[22] The second datum was the emergence of conservative Protestantism from the autoconstructed enclaves which its adherents had inhabited since the 1920s, when, in the aftermath of the Scopes trial and the liberal/fundamentalist split at Princeton Seminary, evangelical, fundamentalist, and pentecostal Protestants retreated (and were not infrequently driven) into the cultural wilderness.[23] Both of these realities seemed to us to deserve a more careful (and, in the case of the resurgent evangelicals, respectful) consideration than they were being given by liberal establishment Catholicism, by their mainline/oldline brethren, and by the media.[24]

The new ecumenism with conservative Protestantism began with coalitional activity on public policy issues in the early 1980s. Here—in the right-to-life movement, in support for religious liberty around the world, in a critique of the moral failures of the welfare state, and in a shared concern for the politicization of Christian social witness as that honorable term was (mis)understood by the mainline/oldline bureaucracies and the National and World Councils of Churches—conservative Protestants and Roman Catholics began to get used to each other, so to speak.[25] One important institutional expression of that rapprochement was the ecumenical Institute on Religion and Democracy, founded in 1981.

But the new ecumenism did not remain stuck at the level of politics. For while that public expression of these new alliances continued, a serious theological conversation also began to evolve, facilitated by the founding of the quarterly journal *This World* in 1982, and accelerated by its monthly successor, *First Things,* established in 1990. Throughout the 1980s and into the 1990s, the programs of institutions such as the Center on Religion and Society (led by Richard John Neuhaus), the Institute on Religion and Public Life (also led by Neuhaus), the American Enterprise Institute (in its religion and society programs led by Michael Novak), the Institute for the Study of Economic Culture at Boston University (led by Peter L. Berger), and the Ethics and Public Policy Center (led by Ernest Lefever and subsequently by George Weigel) regularly featured evangelical/Catholic conferences, seminars, and conversation, which, in addition to some useful cadre-building, also provided a steady flow of material for the journals noted above. The dialogue had advanced sufficiently in the early 1990s that a Catholic/evangelical-fundamentalist-pentecostal task force could come together, independent of ecclesiastical structures, to consider a common theological and missiological statement on the "rules of engagement" for Catholic/evangelical interaction in the United States, in Latin America, and in postcommunist eastern Europe.

Christian-Jewish dialogue has also been a central concern of neoconservative American Catholicism. Here, too, new ground has been broken, far transcending the political conversation between Jews and Catholics that has been a chief dynamic of political neoconservatism. The lead on this front has been taken by the Institute on Religion and Public Life, whose quarterly theological colloquium has become, in the words of one of its senior Jewish participants, an arena in which Jews and Christians are in conversation as they "haven't been for two thousand years." That dialogue has focused on key theological and moral issues, such as the notions of "election" and "covenant" in Judaism; the quest for an adequate "postmodern" theological method; and abortion, euthanasia, and homosexuality. It has also engaged the role of biblical religion and religiously based moral values in American public life. This Jewish-Christian conversation, like the conversation with conservative Protestantism, was brought to the wider public through *This World* and, later, *First Things;* it has also shaped some influential Jewish theological scholarship over the past half-decade.[26]

Finally, and in terms of a somewhat different form of "ecumenism," neoconservative American Catholicism, operating through the institutions and publications noted above, has made a deliberate effort to engage its critics, from both right and left, in serious theological and political conversation about the renewal of both church and society.[27] In our scholarly and publishing activities we have tried to resist the temptation to sectarianism, reaching beyond our community of conversation to invite others to challenge our views and/or to provide rather dramatically different appraisals of the religious and political imperatives of the time. It is a continuing disappointment to us that many of our critics, in their conferencing and publishing, seem studiously indifferent to following suit.

Dynamic Orthodoxy and Theological Method

The third distinctive characteristic of neoconservative Catholicism in America is its quest for a theological method adequate to the transmission of the *traditio* in the intellectual circumstances—debased, but also suggestively challenging—in which we find ourselves.

A pro-active Catholicism, capable of being salt and light in an America characterized by a vibrantly religious population and a thoroughly secularized cultural elite, must be a Catholicism capable of giving a persuasive account of "the hope that is within [us]" (1 Peter 3:15). This means doing theology seriously, and in ways that challenge both "progressives" and "restorationists" in the church. The kind of theology we envision would not accept the radical epistemological skepticism of the contemporary academy as the starting point for serious intellectual activity today. Nor would it lie doggo before the claims of race/class/gender political correctness. But neither would it seek to revive the style of the preconciliar theological manuals.

Recognizing that it is difficult, if not impossible, to talk about the supernatural and the transcendent today as was done in the days before Schleiermacher, neoconservative American Catholics would nonetheless insist that it is still possible (indeed imperative) to talk about the supernatural and the transcendent, and to do so without replicating the errors of some forms of Protestant theological liberalism by collapsing those categories into the naturalistic and the immanent. The issue, in short, is to develop a theological grammar and vocabulary that can confront secularism and satisfy the (often latent) religious hungers of the contemporary world, without requiring our contemporaries to become medievals in their *Weltanschauung* and without dissolving Christian truth claims into expressions of a wholly subjective "religious experience."

That grammar and vocabulary would take seriously, even as it would decline to absolutize, the distinctive modern experience of relativity, that is, our awareness of the historical and social contingencies that shape our beliefs. Rather than holding beliefs as givens (the distinctive characteristic of traditionalism), we recognize that our beliefs are choices. Yet we insist that those beliefs, even as choices, disclose the truth of things.[28] Various labels—"postmodern," "transmodern," "postliberal"—have been tried in an attempt to capture the distinctive character of this approach; none of them seems very satisfactory. But while no sensible neoconservative Catholic would suggest that such a theology, however labeled, has been developed, we do believe that any such theology would exhibit the following characteristics.

It would be thoroughly ecclesial, a theology developed in and for the church. It would assume that the corporate and communal aspects of Christian faith are not optional, and would, with Karl Rahner, regard the patronizing question "Why I stay in the church" as "abominable."[29] While accepting at the descriptive level David Tracy's identification of the three audiences of theology as the church, the academy, and the world,[30] it would insist that theology begins *in* the church, and must attend first and foremost *to* the church as its originating community of discourse—a community in which the sacramental and evangelical rhythms of the life of faith give birth to systematic reflection on the content of faith.

This would not, however, be a theology for the catacombs. Rather, a distinctive quality of this ecclesial theology would be its intensely evangelical focus, in terms of the re-evangelization of an increasingly illiterate Catholic population and the evangelization of the secularized sectors of our society. And it is precisely in this context of re-evangelization and evangelization, rather than as the disciplinary tool feared by "progressives" and applauded by "restorationists," that neoconservative American Catholicism warmly welcomed the new *Catechism of the Catholic Church*. A church incapable of explaining to itself its own creed, liturgy, and practice will be a church utterly stymied in its mission *ad gentes*. Thus the new catechism is an essential aspect of the re-evangelization that is the prologue to evangelization. But the catechism is also a bold assertion, *ad gentes* (and especially *ad viros eruditos*), that the Catholic Church, at the end of the twentieth century and on the edge of the third Christian millennium, is still confident that it can give a coherent account of its faith, its hope, and its love.

The theological approach we seek to advance would, we believe, shift the debate from the question beloved of both left and right—"Who has authority in the church?"—to the more evangelical (and far less narcissistic) question, "What is *authoritative* for the church?" Neuhaus put the issue sharply in *The Catholic Moment:*

> The present Roman Catholic preoccupation with church authority is
> theologically debased . . . because it fixes attention not upon the truth
> claims derived from God's self-revelation but upon who is authorized
> to set the rules for addressing such truths, if indeed they are truths.
> This tends to confirm the cynic's view that theology is not a deliber-
> ation about truths but a contestation over power.[31]

The defense of the truth of those truth claims is a project whose
methodology will never be finally settled prior to the final coming of the
Kingdom, precisely because the truth to which we are witnessing is a truth
that transcends our capacity to understand and articulate it. Thus the theological conversation in which we are engaged is a multidimensional affair,
engaging such mentors in contemporary theological method as George
Lindbeck, Wolfhart Pannenberg, Avery Dulles, and Robert Jenson.[32] We
do not pretend that these conversations will achieve some kind of grand
ecumenical synthesis; indeed, between the critical foundationalism of Pannenberg and Dulles and the moderate postmodernist "cultural-linguistic"
approach of Lindbeck, there are significant differences indeed (as there are,
of course, between Pannenberg's Hegelian/Lutheran synthesis and
Dulles's creative extension of Thomism). Rather, our task is to engage
those differences within the bond of a common concern for dynamic
Christian orthodoxy, to conduct the kind of frank exchange that is often
difficult in more formal or ecclesiastically sanctioned ecumenical and/or
interreligious settings, to bring the results of those conversations to the
church and the wider society through our publications and books, and to
facilitate theologically informed common action on some of the public
matters described immediately below.

The Renewal of American Democracy

The fourth distinctive characteristic of neoconservative Catholicism in
America is the approach we have forged to questions of social, cultural,
and political transformation. As noted above, our concern with public
policy issues is, in virtually all cases, an expression of our interest in and
concern for the crisis of faith in modern society. For the fevered debates
over how we should, as a nation, order our life together reflect, in no small
part, the division between those Americans who affirm transcendent (and
most often religious) moral reference points for that discussion, and those
who deny the reality of any such norms (or our capacity to know them).

Neoconservative Catholicism in America has never sought to construct
an undifferentiated apologia for the American experiment in ordered
liberty. Rather, we have sought a critical engagement with the experiment,

historically as well as in terms of contemporary controversies. But unlike some of our colleagues to port and starboard, we have tended not to think of the American experiment as fundamentally ill-founded. We reject the progressives' critique of the American Founding in both its vulgar-Marxist and race/gender-deconstructionist forms; but we also reject the notion that the Founding was the triumph of a radical Lockean individualism and voluntarism, of which today's attempts to create the Imperial Republic of the Autonomous Self are but the logical consequence.[33] In our view, there has always been a covenantal, not merely contractual, character to the American experiment.[34] Moreover, we believe that that covenantal experience of America has been sustained over time, even as it was first formed, by biblical religion. And further, we believe that it is still possible to discern, amid the abundant plurality of American life, the outlines of a genuine pluralism sustained by a covenantal commitment to the pursuit of the common good.

But something is clearly missing. And that something is what John Courtney Murray identified as the American lacuna more than thirty years ago. What America lacks today, in our view as in Murray's, is a religiously grounded public philosophy capable of informing and disciplining the public moral argument that is the lifeblood of democracy.[35] That is, to be sure, a sharp criticism—and thus the charge of "apologist" has seemed to us, frankly, absurd. But in any case, that is the premise on which we have been working in the public sphere—and we would like to think that, in our sundry commentaries on issues political, social, economic, and cultural, we are contributing to the formation of just such a public philosophy.

It is because of this analysis of the current American situation that neoconservative Catholics in America were so enthusiastic about *Centesimus Annus*, Pope John Paul II's pathbreaking 1991 encyclical. The pope's bold proposal for the revitalization of the free society in all its component parts, and his emphasis on the moral-cultural arena as the crucial battleground in both established and new democracies, struck us as precisely right. We were also enthusiastic about the encyclical's empirical sensitivity to the data on economic development, which led to the abandonment (for good, one expects) of the old quest for a "Catholic third way" that was neither socialist nor capitalist. But while we welcomed the Holy Father's endorsement of the "free economy" as the form of economic activity most congruent with the "truth about man," we were just as pleased by his insistence in *Centesimus Annus* that the free economy had to be tempered and disciplined by a democratic polity and a vital moral culture. These were not only points we had been urging for some time; the encyclical's description of the virtues necessary to make freedom work (economically or politically) seemed to us both true and timely, given both the American circumstance and the situation in central and eastern Europe postcommunism.[36]

The development of a religiously informed public philosophy for the renewal of American democracy in the 1990s will require sustained attention to a host of "life issues," of which abortion and euthanasia are the most urgent in terms of moral gravity and public impact. The ecumenical and interreligious conversation in which neoconservative American Catholics have been engaged for more than a decade now has recently borne fruit on these fronts in three major manifestos: "Always to Care, Never to Kill," on the euthanasia controversy; "A New American Compact: Caring about Women, Caring for the Unborn," on abortion; and "The Inhuman Use of Human Beings," on embryo research.[37] In addition to whatever impact they may have had on the public policy debate, these three statements were (in part) examples of the neoconservative Catholic effort to "translate" classic Catholic moral understandings into a moral vocabulary and grammar accessible to the American public. That these statements also drew the endorsement of chastened liberals and more traditional conservatives may indicate something about the role that the neoconservatives are playing at the intersection of religion and public life in America today, as the collapse of communism and the American culture war lead to a series of realignments on basic questions of how Americans should order our life together and our responsibilities in the world.

The "culture war" will be a major focus of our attention in the 1990s, for what is at stake here, it seems to us, is nothing less than the moral legitimacy of the American constitutional order. The trajectory of church-state jurisprudence in the Supreme Court since *Everson* in 1947 has been pointing inexorably toward the legal enforcement of a "naked public square" in American public life; we flatly deny that this establishment of secularism is congruent with the Framers' intention to foster the free exercise of religion through the means of disestablishment.[38] The moral philosophy lurking just beneath the surface of the Court's recent abortion decisions suggests that the "liberty" referred to by the Fourteenth Amendment is now to be understood as the liberty of the autonomous, unencumbered self to do whatever he or she deems necessary to the "satisfaction" of his or her "needs" (for so long as nobody in whom the state declares a "compelling interest" gets hurt). We flatly deny that the Imperial Self was, has been, or plausibly can be the *telos* of the American experiment.[39] Were the Court and our elected officials to continue to press constitutional law and public policy in these directions, we believe that the most serious questions would thereby be raised about the moral continuity of the present constitutional order with the constitutional order ratified in 1788–89. And in that case, the "renewal of American democracy" would involve a major work of fundamental reconstruction indeed.

Concluding Unscientific Postscript

Taken together, these distinctive elements of the neoconservative enterprise in American Catholicism suggest that we have been less interested in "restoration" than in renewal and revitalization, in both church and society. That "neoconservative difference" is in part a function of the fact that we do not share the view that American Catholicism in the immediate preconciliar generations had achieved the kind of Golden Age fondly remembered in some precincts of the Catholic right.[40] But the larger issue, of course, is the question of whether the maxim *ecclesia semper reformanda* has any status in a dynamically orthodox Catholic conception of the church. We believe it does.

What has been the impact of neoconservative American Catholicism? That is a judgment for the future, and for others, to make. At the present moment, we can say only what we have tried to do.

Neoconservative American Catholicism has worked hard to create a new conversation on the evolution of Catholic social teaching between the United States and the Holy See. It has tried to develop the new ecumenism and the new forms of interreligious dialogue cited above. It has worked to create arenas for theological conversation and public policy debate that are free of the distractions of current campus political correctness. It has attempted fresh interpretations of Catholic thought on the just-war tradition, on the pursuit of peace, on political economy, on social welfare policy, and on the "life issues." It has tried to extend the work of John Courtney Murray in the development of a religiously informed American public philosophy, even as it has had to confront both the lacunae in Murray's own work and a far more corrupt moral-cultural environment. It has provided reference points, neither "traditionalist" nor "liberal," for central and eastern European and Latin American Catholic thinkers and activists working to build democratic societies. It has established journals that have been intellectually fruitful and "successful" (in that their circulation figures suggest that a considerable audience is being nurtured by them). It has fostered the scholarship and writing of a cadre of younger Catholic intellectuals who are just now coming to the forefront of the discussion.

Whether this effort has had a significant impact on the life and thought of the church in the United States is, as I say, for others to judge. The tendency to follow Lyndon Johnson's advice—to "hunker down like a Pedernales jackrabbit in a windstorm"—still seems widespread in an American Catholic establishment trying very hard to ignore (and thus wait out) the current pontificate.[41] The neoconservative interpretation of John Paul II and of such distinctive initiatives as the 1985 Extraordinary Synod, *Centesimus Annus*, and the *Catechism* does not seem to have made a significant impression on the official national structures of the church in the United States. This is a failure perhaps presaged in the lack of sustained discussion (much less success) the neoconservatives have achieved with many NCCB/USCC agencies on issues of the church and public policy (the NCCB Secretariat for Pro-Life Activities being a notable exception to the rule).[42] Nor does it seem to us that our work, especially in terms of its attempt to mediate the thought of John Paul II into the American debate, has very successfully challenged the hegemony of the liberal establishment in the American Catholic intellectual elite.

This strikes us, frankly, as a great tragedy for the life of the church here in America, but also for the American contribution to the church universal. For as *Centesimus Annus* ought to have made clear, there has been no pope in modern history more interested in the American experiment, and in the American experience of a vibrant Catholicism amid democratic pluralism.[43] A great opportunity may have been missed. Again, only time will tell.

But it must not be thought, at the end of these reflections, that neoconservative American Catholics sit around brooding over scorecards. Having never tried to create a formal "movement," we can be a bit more relaxed about relative "successes" and "failures." And then there is that providential serendipity alluded to at the outset: given the fact that, twenty years ago, no one expected (much less planned) the evolution of the community of conversation described above, it would seem the height of ingratitude (much less hubris) to expect the future to be any more predictable.

That the "neoconservative difference" in American Catholicism has been deeply influenced by John Paul II should be plain. For we have seen in the Holy Father's ministry and teaching a model of the Catholicism to whose development we would wish to contribute our best intellectual energies. God willing, there will be many more years of direct inspiration from John Paul II. But the mark that this pope has left on the church seems likely to be an enduring one. And thus the effort to develop the distinctive neoconservative approach to the renewal of church and society will continue, quite possibly along the trajectories sketched above, for some time to come.

NOTES

1. Xavier Rynne, *Letters from Vatican City—Vatican Council II: The First Session* (New York: Farrar, Straus and Giroux, 1963); *The Second Session* (New York: Farrar, Straus and Giroux, 1964); *The Third Session* (New York: Farrar, Straus and Giroux, 1965); and *The Fourth Session* (New York: Farrar, Straus and Giroux, 1966). "Xavier Rynne" was the pseudonym employed by the Reverend Francis X. Murphy, C.SS.R.

2. Henri Fesquet, *The Drama of Vatican II* (New York: Random House, 1967), p. 88.

3. Brigitte Berger and Peter L. Berger, "Our Conservatism and Theirs," *Commentary* 82, no. 4 (October 1986): 62. See also Norman Podhoretz, *Breaking Ranks: A Political Memoir* (New York: Harper and Row, 1979).

4. As any issue of *Chronicles*, the flagship paleocon journal, will readily demonstrate.

5. This interpretation of the "Catholic neoconservatives" has been propounded from both port and starboard. For representative examples of the former, see David Hollenbach, "War and Peace in American Catholic Thought: A Heritage Abandoned?" *Theological Studies* 48, no. 4 (December 1987); the reviews of George Weigel's *Catholicism and the Renewal of American Democracy* by Dennis McCann in *Commonweal* 19 (May 1989): 312–16 and by J. Leon Hooper, S.J., in *America,* 19 August 1989, pp. 88–90; and the review of Neuhaus's *Doing Well and Doing Good: The Challenge to the Christian Capitalist* by Paul McNelis, S.J., in *America,* 13 March 1993. From a different direction, see David L. Schindler, "Is America Bourgeois?" *Communio* 14 (Fall 1987): 262–90; Glenn Olsen, "The Catholic Moment?" *Communio* 15 (Winter 1988): 474–87; David L. Schindler, "The Church's 'Worldly' Mission: Neoconservatives and American Culture," *Communio* 18 (Fall 1991): 365–97; David L. Schindler, "Christology and the Church's 'Worldly Mission,'" *Communio* 19 (Spring 1992): 164–78; and Kenneth L. Schmitz, "Catholicism in America," *Communio* 19 (Fall 1992): 474-77. There have also been (increasingly bizarre) attacks from abroad on "the three theologians of the American way of life," e.g., "Teologici USA Contra Il Vaticano II," *30 Giorni,* June 1992, and Lucio Brunelli, "La Trinità a Stelle e Strisce," *Il Sabato,* 13 June 1992; the somewhat fevered Brunelli had some fun with "Il Padre" (Novak), "Il Figlio" (Weigel), and "Lo Spirito Santo" (Neuhaus, not altogether displeased by being described as "il più religioso del terzetto").

6. The "neoconservative" conversation among American theologians, moral philosophers, and political theorists is, of course, carried on by many distinguished people: it is a thoroughly ecumenical and interreligious grouping, including Orthodox, Conservative, and Reform Jews, mainline and evangelical Protestants, Eastern Orthodox, and Roman Catholics. To dwell here on Neuhaus, Novak, and myself is not to suggest that we occupy some defining leadership position in this large and complex cadre. It is simply that our work has been more the focus of comment and attack, precisely as "neoconservative," from both "left" and "right" in the Catholic Church; and that suggests that it may not be inappropriate to clarify just what it is that we, at least, think we are doing.

7. Key texts include Gustavo Gutierrez, S.J., *A Theology of Liberation* (Maryknoll: Orbis Books, 1973); Juan Luis Segundo, *A Theology for Artisans of a New Humanity,* 5 vols. (Maryknoll: Orbis Books, 1974); Jon Sobrino, S.J., *Christology at the Crossroads* (Maryknoll: Orbis Books, 1978); Rosemary Radford Ruether, *New Woman—New Earth: Sexist Ideologies and Human Liberation* (San Francisco: Harper and Row, 1982); Rosemary Radford Ruether, *Sexism and God-Talk: Toward a Feminist Theology* (Boston: Beacon Press, 1984); and Elisabeth Schüssler-Fiorenza, *In Memory of Her: A Feminist Theological Reconstruction of Christian Origins* (New York: Crossroad, 1983).

8. In this sense, the 1975 "Hartford Appeal for Theological Affirmation"—which challenged many of the methodological and substantive preoccupations of postconciliar theological "liberals"—was an early effort to define an ecclesial and theological position that was neither "traditionalist"/"conservative" nor "liberal," as those terms had been defined in the "Rynne" imagery and as they had played themselves out in the immediate postconciliar debates. See Peter L. Berger and Richard John Neuhaus, eds., *Against the World for the World: The Hartford Appeal and the Future of American Religion* (New York: Seabury Press, 1976).

9. This view was neither ours alone nor confined to the worlds of the intellectuals. See Nancy Yos, "Teach Me: A Catholic *Cri de Coeur,*" *First Things* 22 (April 1992): 23-28. For more detailed analyses of these problems, see also Michael Novak, *Confession of a Catholic* (San Francisco: Harper and Row, 1983), and Richard John Neuhaus, *The Catholic Moment: The Paradox of the Church in the Postmodern World* (San Francisco: Harper and Row, 1989).

10. See Michael Novak, *The Spirit of Democratic Capitalism* (New York: Simon and Schuster, 1983) and *Will It Liberate?* (New York: Paulist Press, 1987); and George Weigel, *Tranquillitas Ordinis: The Present Failure and Future Promise of American Catholic Thought on War and Peace* (New York: Oxford University Press, 1987).

11. A distinguished Lutheran theologian once told me of his shock on attending the annual meeting of the CTSA and hearing any invocation of the pope's name met with a mixture of titters and the occasional hiss; the theologian in question said that he wondered for a moment whether he had blundered into a conference sponsored by the Southern Baptist Convention.

12. See Wade Clark Roof and William McKinney, *American Mainline Religion: Its Changing Shape and Future* (New Brunswick, N.J.: Rutgers University Press, 1987).

13. See Benton Johnson, Dean R. Hoge, and Donald A. Luidens, "Mainline Churches: The Real Reason for Decline," *First Things* 31 (March 1993): 13–18.

14. See Richard John Neuhaus, *America against Itself: Moral Vision and the Public Order* (Notre Dame, Ind.: University of Notre Dame Press, 1992).

15. George Weigel, *Catholicism and the Renewal of American Democracy* (New York: Paulist Press, 1989), and, among many others of Novak's occasional pieces, his editorial "The Coming Cultural Crisis," *Crisis* 10, no. 9 (October 1992): 2–3.

16. Neuhaus, *The Catholic Moment,* p. 284.

17. Ibid.

18. See George Weigel, "The New Anti-Catholicism," *Commentary* 93, no. 6 (June 1992): 25–31. The lack of sustained attention to (and agitation about) the "new anti-Catholicism" by American Catholic intellectuals is a striking phenomenon of our times, and in some cases is rooted, I believe, in a sense of embarrassment about the magisterium's politically incorrect views on abortion and homosexuality, especially as those issues, construed in their most libertine form, have emerged as litmus tests of "sensitivity" and "tolerance" in the academy.

19. Among many possible examples, see Richard John Neuhaus, "Joshing Richard Rorty," *First Things* 8 (December 1990): 14–24.

20. Robert Jastrow, *God and the Astronomers* (New York: W. W. Norton and Co., 1978), p. 116.

21. See George Weigel, "The Catholic Moment: Blocked, Botched, or Transformed?" *First Things* 1 (March 1990): 16.

22. John Courtney Murray believed this to be the case as recently as 1948; see his (very) posthumously published essay, "A Common Enemy, a Common Cause," *First Things* 26 (October 1992): 29–37.

23. For a wide-ranging discussion of these developments and their impact on American public life, see Michael Cromartie, ed., *No Longer Exiles: The Religious New Right in American Politics* (Washington: Ethics and Public Policy Center, 1992), and Michael Cromartie, ed., *Disciples and Democracy: Religious Conservatives and the Future of American Politics* (Grand Rapids: EPPC/Eerdmans, 1994), especially chap. 3. See also George Weigel, "Evangelicals and Catholics: A New Ecumenism," in Richard John Neuhaus and Michael Cromartie, eds., *Piety and Politics: Evangelicals and Fundamentalists Confront the World* (Washington: Ethics and Public Policy Center, 1987).

24. Richard John Neuhaus, in *The Naked Public Square: Religion and Democracy in America* (Grand Rapids: Wm. B. Eerdmans Publishing Co., 1984), offered the first sustained critical appreciation of the evangelical resurgence from outside the worlds of evangelicaldom.

25. A notable intellectual expression of the new evangelical interest in Roman Catholic thought was the publication of Dean C. Curry, ed., *Evangelicals and the Bishops' Pastoral Letter* (Grand Rapids: Wm. B. Eerdmans Publishing Co., 1984), in which fourteen evangelical Protestant scholars analyzed the biblical, theological, political, and strategic claims advanced by the National Conference of Catholic Bishops in their 1983 statement "The Challenge of Peace" with a seriousness of purpose as least as impressive as that found in the many Catholic commentaries on the pastoral letter.

As younger evangelical intellectuals have confronted the lacunae in their own traditions' patterns of social-ethical reflection (which gaps are themselves a by-product of the evangelical "exile" of midcentury), a new interest in Catholic social teaching, particularly in its use of natural law categories of moral reasoning, has emerged in evangelical circles. Fostering the development of this reflection has been one leitmotif of American Catholic neoconservative activity and publishing.

26. See David G. Dalin, ed., *American Jews and the Separationist Faith: The New Debate on Religion in Public Life* (Washington: Ethics and Public Policy Center, 1992); David Novak, *Jewish-Christian Dialogue: A Jewish Justification* (New York: Oxford University Press, 1989); and David Novak, *Jewish Social Ethics* (New York: Oxford University Press, 1993).

27. For examples of this intention at work, see the fifteen volumes of the Encounter Series, edited by Richard John Neuhaus (Grand Rapids: Wm. B. Eerdmans Publishing Co., 1986–92), and Richard John Neuhaus and George Weigel, eds., *Being Christian Today: An American Conversation* (Washington: Ethics and Public Policy Center, 1992).

28. On this, see Berger and Berger, "Our Conservatism and Theirs," p. 63.

29. Paul Imhof and Hubert Biallowons, eds., *Karl Rahner in Dialogue: Conversations and Interviews, 1965–1982* (New York: Crossroad, 1986), p. 332. Rahner believed that in a Christian's criticism of the church, one should be able to detect—and precisely from the way in which the criticism was formulated—that the critic "comprehends the Church as an unconditional reality at the heart and center of . . . Christian existence and of one's relationship to God, who is eternal salvation."

30. David Tracy, *The Analogical Imagination: Chrsitian Theology and the Culture of Pluralism* (New York: Crossroad, 1981), pp. 3–46.

31. Neuhaus, *The Catholic Moment*, p. 89.

32. See George A. Lindbeck, *The Nature of Doctrine: Religion and Theology in a Postliberal Age* (Philadelphia: Westminster Press, 1984); Wolfhart Pannenberg, *Systematic Theology*, vol. 1 (Grand Rapids: Wm. B. Eerdmans Publishing Co., 1991); Avery Dulles, S.J., *The Craft of Theology* (New York: Crossroad, 1992); Avery Dulles, S.J., "From Symbol to System: A Proposal for Theological Method," *Pro Ecclesia* 1, no. 1 (Fall 1992): 42–52; George Lindbeck, "Dulles on Method," ibid., pp. 53–62; and Robert W. Jenson, *Unbaptized God: The Basic Flaw in Ecumenical Theology* (Minneapolis: Fortress Press, 1992). (Each of these books was discussed in the Institute on Religion and Public Life's quarterly theological colloquium in 1991–93.) For an interesting discussion of the foundationalist/moderate postmodernist debate, see Thomas Guarino, "Between Foundationalism and Nihilism," *Theological Studies* 54 (Spring 1993): 37–54.

33. See William Lee Miller, *The First Liberty: Religion and the American Republic* (New York: Alfred A. Knopf, 1986). This question of the "ill-founded Republic" is one root of the dispute between the neoconservatives, on the one hand, and David Schindler and others of the *Communio* circle, on the other. This argument, in which one may hear echoes of the dispute between John Courtney Murray and his adversaries in the 1950s, also engages the status of *Dignitatis Humanae* and the queston of a legitimate Catholic development of doctrine on matters of church and state. See my "Response to Mark Lowery," *Communio* 18 (Fall 1991): 439–49.

34. Richard John Neuhaus made an early probe in this direction in his *Time toward Home: The American Experiment as Revelation* (New York: Seabury Press, 1975); see especially chap. 7, "The Covenant and the Salvation for Which We Hope."

35. See John Courtney Murray, *We Hold These Truths: Catholic Reflections on the American Proposition* (New York: Doubleday Image Books, 1964).

36. Neuhaus, Novak, and I were frequently charged with hijacking *Centesimus Annus,* presumably in the direction of an unabashed, even libertarian, celebration of the free market. (See, *inter alia,* Richard P. McBrien, "Encyclical Is Not Pope's Imprimatur on Capitalism," *The Progress* [Seattle], 20 June 1991.) But an examination of the brief op-ed analyses we wrote immediately after the encyclical was released, as well as a review of our longer reflections on this remarkable document, demonstrates that, from the very beginning, we stressed that *Centesimus Annus* was first and foremost a religious and moral reflection on human freedom in all its dimensions (an emphasis that was not always made clear, alas, by the editors who write headlines for op-ed pages). See Richard John Neuhaus, "The Pope Affirms the 'New Capitalism,'" *Wall Street Journal,* 2 May 1991; George Weigel, "Blessings on Capitalism at Its Best," *Los Angeles Times,* 3 May 1991; Michael Novak, "Wisdom from the Pope," *Washington Post,* 7 May 1991; George Weigel, "The New 'New Things,'" in George Weigel, ed., *A New Worldly Order: John Paul II on Human Freedom—A "Centesimus Annus" Reader* (Washington: Ethics and Public Policy Center, 1992); Neuhaus, *Doing Well and Doing Good;* and Michael Novak, *The Catholic Ethic and the Spirit of Capitalism* (New York: Free Press, 1993).

37. See "Always to Care, Never to Kill," *First Things* 20 (February 1992): 45–47; "A New American Compact," *First Things* 27 (November 1992): 43–46; and "The Inhuman Use of Human Beings," *First Things* 49 (January 1995): 17–21. On a related issue, see "The Homosexual Moment: A Response by the Ramsey Colloquium," *First Things* 41 (March 1994): 15–20.

38. See Mary Ann Glendon and Raul F. Yanas, "Structural Free Exercise," *Michigan Law Review* 90, no. 3 (December 1991): 477–550; see also Richard John Neuhaus, "Genuine Pluralism and the Pfefferian Inversion," *This World* 24 (Winter 1989): 71–86, and George Weigel, "Achieving Disagreement: From Indifference to Pluralism," ibid., pp. 54–63.

39. See "Abortion and a Nation at War," *First Things* 26 (October 1992): 9–13.

40. On the other hand, neoconservative American Catholics have not adopted the deprecatory view of American Catholicism in the 1930s, 1940s, and 1950s that characterizes works such as Jay P. Dolan's *The American Catholic Experience* (Garden City, N.Y.: Doubleday, 1985) and William M. Halsey's *The Survival of American Innocence: Catholicism in an Era of Disillusionment, 1920–1940* (Notre Dame, Ind.: University of Notre Dame Press, 1980). Rather than focus on the alleged inanities or glories of "ghetto Catholicism," we would tend to concentrate on figures such as Msgr. Martin Hellriegel and Msgr. Reynold Hillenbrand as heralds of the kind of Catholic renewal in America that ought to have taken place through the mediation of the Second Vatican Council. See the essay "Capturing the Storyline: The New Historiography of American Catholicism," in my *Freedom and Its Discontents: Catholicism Confronts Modernity* (Washington: Ethics and Public Policy Center, 1991).

41. See William M. Shea, "The Pope, Our Brother," *Commonweal* 7 (November 1987): 587–90.

42. The neoconservative critique of the NCCB/USCC complex is, at bottom, a matter of theology rather than of politics. See my essay "When Shepherds Are Sheep," *First Things* 30 (February 1993): 34–40, which discusses the ecclesiological problem posed by the "denominationalization" of American Catholicism, i.e., the transformation of the charism of religious leadership into bureaucratic managership.

43. See Rocco Buttiglione, "The Free Economy and the Free Man," in Weigel, ed., *A New Worldly Order,* pp. 65–70.

7

Women for Faith and Family
Catholic Women Affirming Catholic Teaching

HELEN HULL HITCHCOCK

Prologue

In September 1984, six St. Louis women gathered around a dining room table to discuss responding to the American bishops who were planning to write a pastoral letter on "women's issues." The bishops said they wanted to hear the concerns of Catholic women, and had initiated a process of gathering this information through "listening sessions" to be held in all dioceses of the United States. We were concerned that these sessions would not give the bishops an accurate picture of Catholic women. First of all, only a small minority of Catholic women would be able to attend them, and secondly, the sessions seemed designed to elicit maximum expression of disaffection and complaints from women who did attend and to discourage participation from those who supported church teaching or who were critical of any aspect of feminism.

The result of our discussion was the circulation of the *Affirmation for Catholic Women* (see Appendix A.1), an eight-point statement of fidelity to church teachings, including abortion, ordination, and related issues. We wanted to make it possible for Catholic women who accept the teachings of the Catholic Church to give concrete testimony of their faith to the bishops.

Although in the beginning Women for Faith and Family was envisioned simply as an ad hoc effort to provide a means whereby the voices of women faithful to the church could be heard, the response to the *Affirmation* statement was so immediate and so strong that we soon realized that many women were depending on us for much more than this, and our work began to expand rapidly. It seemed clear that Women for Faith and Family had appeared at a propitious time. In the years following the Second Vatican Council, two events—the issuance of Paul VI's encyclical *Humanae Vitae,* which reaffirmed the Catholic Church's opposition to artificial birth control, and the U.S. Supreme Court's 1973 *Roe v. Wade* decision permitting abortion—caused a great deal of attention to be focused on Catholics who rejected the church's teaching. Both secular and Catholic media publicized the "dissent" of influential Catholic theologians and academics from these and other church teachings which had always been regarded as essential to Catholicism. A notable example of this was the confrontation of Pope John Paul II on the matter of ordination by Sr. Theresa Kane, the official representative of the Leadership Conference of Women Religious, during the pope's 1979 visit to the United States.

Catholic women theologians and journalists and feminist activists who were at odds with the church over a wide spectrum of issues they regarded as oppressive of women dominated the Catholic press. Church-sponsored workshops resembling feminist consciousness-raising sessions proliferated, and many women's religious orders suffered radical identity crises and a heavy loss of membership. That many of the most vocal women espousing these views held positions of influence within the church's official structure and on university and seminary faculties lent credibility to their claim that half of the church—the female half—was bitterly angry at the "patriarchal" church, deeply resentful of "oppressive" Catholic teachings, and in open rebellion. Women who did not subscribe to this view of the church were commonly stereotyped as ignorant collaborators in their own victimization, against equality for women, and "antifeminists."

With few exceptions, Catholic women who described themselves as "feminist" held opinions on social issues, including abortion, indistinguishable from those of secular feminists. This was made dramatically clear in October 1984, when an advertisement appeared in the *New York Times* stating that the church's condemnation of the "direct termination of pre-natal life [is not] the only legitimate Catholic position," that "a large number of Catholic theologians hold that even direct abortion, though tragic, can sometimes be a moral choice," and that public dissent from the church's "hierarchal statements," even by priests and religious, "should not be penalized by . . . religious superiors, church employers or bishops." The ad was signed by ninety-six individuals, a majority of whom were women, including nuns and prominent theologians who described themselves as feminists.

The *New York Times* statement made it clear that there was a fundamental and probably irreconcilable cleavage between Catholic belief and contemporary feminism's advocacy of abortion "rights" for women. Since it was well known that thousands of Catholic women were leaders and activists in the anti-abortion movement, the opposition of most Catholic women to an essential tenet of feminism should also have been clear. Yet feminist Catholic women continued to present their views as those of Catholic women collectively. Several factors may have made their claim believable, among them (1) the success of Protestant feminists in achieving their goals (e.g., the Episcopal Church had approved both ordination of women and "choice" on abortion in 1976); (2) the strong influence of feminists on the programs and policies of the Canadian Catholic Conference of Bishops; and (3) the public support given by a few American bishops to feminist critics of the Catholic Church who demanded ordination and more "decision-making power" in the church as a matter of justice to women.

It was apparent to many Catholic women that a new definition of feminism had emerged, one that was no longer compatible with their most deeply held beliefs. At the time that the U.S. bishops began their work on a pastoral letter on women's concerns, there had been no effective critique either of feminists' charges against the "oppressive, patriarchal" church or of their claim to speak for all Catholic women. Indeed, the bishops' decision to write a pastoral on women was said to be the result of consultations of several bishops with feminist activists and theologians. The appearance of the *New York Times* ad probably had the effect of galvanizing many pro-life Catholic women into action in defense of their faith.

Women for Faith and Family thus came into being within a climate of cultural opposition to religious beliefs in general, but also within the particular aura of highly publicized dissent within the church—among the professional class, the educated elite, and especially women's religious orders—from even the most essential Catholic teachings. This situation remains unchanged. Because the conflict within the church so often revolves around so-called women's issues (from social issues such as "reproductive rights" to church issues, including liturgical roles for women and so-called inclusive language) and because it is women, especially religious professionals and sisters, who are often the church's most severe and vocal critics, Women for Faith and Family has continued its efforts to amplify the voices of women who affirm the truth of Catholic teaching and accept the church's authority, in the hope that this may support and encourage bishops and clergy. We also hope to assist and encourage Catholic women to accept their responsibility—as *women* and as *Catholics*—for the transmission of the faith.

In less confused and conflicted times, an organized effort such as this would have seemed puzzling. Affirmation and acceptance of Catholic teaching would seem to be implicit in the very word *Catholic;* but we can no longer assume that Catholic women *do* affirm Catholic teaching. People now employ modifiers such as *conservative* or *liberal* before the word *Catholic,* even though these are politically loaded terms which cannot accurately be applied to religious belief. Still, most Catholic "conservatives" would agree that there is much to conserve in the Catholic faith, that active conservation of even the most essential elements of Catholic belief and practice has become necessary in an atmosphere of hostility to any religion which claims to be objectively true—and to Catholic religious truth in particular.

Only very recently in the history of the church would an organization of Catholic women whose principal purpose is to affirm publicly and to defend Catholic teaching have been thought necessary. Only within the context of opposition to many essential beliefs of Catholicism—opposition not only coming from sources external to the Catholic Church, but often arising from within its own official structures and by people in positions of leadership who openly reject not only Catholic dogmas and discipline but also, most fundamentally, the church's claim to authority and truth—only in such anomalous circumstances is the existence of organizations such as Women for Faith and Family comprehensible.

Beginnings: "Affirmation for Catholic Women"

Women for Faith and Family was established for the following purposes: (1) to assist orthodox Catholic women in their effort to provide witness to their faith, both to their families and to the world; (2) to aid women in their efforts continually to deepen their understanding of the Catholic faith; (3) to aid faithful Catholic women in their desire for fellowship with others who share their faith and commitment; and (4) to serve as a channel through which questions from Catholic women seeking guidance or information can be directed. The organization fulfills its purposes mainly through its publications, conferences, and other meetings, through participation in coalition efforts, and through personal communication (e.g., mail, telephone).

Although its outreach is primarily to Catholic women, both lay and religious, it also encourages participation by men in its conferences and other activities. It addresses both religious and social issues involving women and the family. Its concerns extend to the application of Catholic teaching in contemporary life, and thus to all aspects of the Catholic faith, including religious life, liturgy, and doctrine.

The first project of Women for Faith and Family was the *Affirmation for Catholic Women,* intended to provide a means for Catholic women to make their fidelity to the church and its magisterium visible and effective. Many women did not believe that their views would be adequately represented to the bishops, and their experience with the "listening sessions" would later confirm their apprehension.

We wrote the *Affirmation* statement and began to circulate it among friends and colleagues, hoping to gather several hundred signatures which could be sent to the bishops. We invited people to reproduce the *Affirmation* and send it to others, and asked that the signatures be returned to us, where they would be recorded. We were unprepared for the actual response, however. The outpouring of support for the church from women in all walks of life was nearly overwhelming. Within a few months (March 1985), four thousand signatures had been received, and we sent a copy of the *Affirmation* with a list of its signers to the bishops' committee on the pastoral letter on women. In June 1985, a list of ten thousand names of *Affirmation* signers was presented to Pope John Paul II. By August, a list of about seventeen thousand signatures was given to the bishops' Pastoral Committee when, at their invitation, testimony from Women for Faith and Family was presented to them.

By late 1985, the *Affirmation* project was extended by the spontaneous efforts of women in Canada, Australia, and Holland, where allied groups were soon formed (Women for Faith and Family—Canada, Women for Faith and Family—Australia, Vrowen in de R. K. Kerk). Affiliated groups were also formed in New Zealand (WFF—New Zealand) in 1987, and in the United Kingdom (Association for Catholic Women) in 1988.

By October 1987, we had received approximately ten thousand letters from women expressing their personal concerns about their faith and problems within the church, so we decided to prepare testimony based on the letters for bishop delegates to the Synod on the Laity. This testimony, along with a list of names of *Affirmation* signers (then about thirty thousand from the U.S., but including some from other countries, such as Mother Teresa of Calcutta), was presented in Rome and received by Cardinal Edouard Gagnon on behalf of Pope John Paul II. Lists of signers from Holland, Australia, New Zealand, England, and Canada were also presented to the Holy See by WFF affiliates and/or allied organizations in these countries.

The *Affirmation* has been translated into at least seven languages in addition to English (French, Spanish, Italian, Polish, German, Dutch, and Chinese) through the spontaneous efforts of its supporters. About 10 percent of the signers are women religious, many from "troubled" orders. Signers represent all ages, all states in life (single, married, mothers, religious), and all educational and economic levels. They include home-makers, professional women (doctors, nurses, lawyers, university pro-fessors, writers, teachers, etc.), women whose work is in their homes, and women with full- or part-time employment outside the home. New signa-tures continue to be received regularly. To date, approximately fifty thousand Catholic women in the United States have expressed their fidelity to the church in this way, and an estimated twenty thousand from other countries.

Updated lists of signers have been transmitted to the U.S. bishops and/or to the Holy See at least twice in the past five years. An updated list was presented to Pope John Paul II in 1994, the International Year of the Family.

The response to the *Affirmation for Catholic Women* is evidently with-out precedent. No petition of dissent in the postconciliar era, including the highly publicized statement of dissent from *Humanae Vitae* in 1968, has attracted comparable response. This phenomenon becomes particu-larly significant in the light of the explicit nature of the *Affirmation* and the grassroots means of its circulation.

The Expansion of WFF and the Broadening of Its Apostolic Work

What began as a way to show support by Catholic women for church teachings about women and family quickly grew beyond this relatively limited goal; response to the needs of women led to a continually expand-ing set of initiatives. It soon became apparent to Women for Faith and Family's organizers that its original aim—to communicate information from Catholic women to the bishops—was only one means of serving the church and women. Along with signatures to the *Affirmation,* which we continue to gather, Women for Faith and Family receives many letters and telephone calls from women requesting assistance and information of vari-ous kinds, as well as advice and encouragement.[1] These communications typically ask for help in addressing problems with religious and/or moral education affecting their children in Catholic schools, or raise questions about church doctrine and discipline which affect the life and worship of every Catholic; but there are also many requests for help on matters such as family, marriage, or spiritual problems.[2] Increasingly, these requests come from men as well.

The volunteer staff responds to these requests. In 1994, at this writing, three volunteers spend one day a week in the "mailroom" in one woman's home, answering letters and fulfilling routine requests for WFF publications. More involved inquiries are referred to other staff members for response. Occasionally a request may involve research and/or consultation with or referral to other individuals or organizations with appropriate expertise. Most research, when necessary, can be done in the office library or nearby university libraries, or via computer-accessible resources.[3]

Women for Faith and Family often collaborates with other groups, both within the Catholic orbit and outside it. For example, we were involved in the formation of the nondenominational National Women's Coalition for Life and the Catholic group Women Affirming Life, and we have worked closely with the International Anti-Euthanasia Task Force, the Value of Life Committee, the Missouri Catholic Conference, Missouri Nurses for Life, and other organizations for the handicapped in efforts to save the lives of Nancy Cruzan and Christine Busalacchi. WFF has also filed amicus curiae briefs in court cases involving religious education and pro-life issues.[4]

In order to respond to the needs of our members for support and conversation, as well as to increase their knowledge of Catholic teachings, annual national conferences have been held each year since 1985, and have featured distinguished orthodox speakers from the U.S., Canada, England, and Ireland. Among those who have addressed us are cardinals, bishops, and clergy, as well as university professors, theologians, and writers. A particular effort has been made to provide a forum for outstanding Catholic women such as theologian Joyce Little; Birthright founder Louise Summerhill; the pro-life representative of the United States Catholic Conference, Helen Alvare; Mother Angelica, abbess and founder of the Eternal Word Television Network; and philosopher and *Humanae Vitae* expert Janet Smith, among many others.[5] Cardinal Lopez Trujillo, prefect of the Pontifical Council on the Family, addressed the 1994 conference. Pope John Paul II has sent a message and has given his apostolic blessing to each of these conferences.

Conference addresses on topics of current and perennial importance have included women's roles in the evangelical mission of the church, the recovery of the sacred, critiques of feminism, euthanasia and abortion, the issues of language and worship, the role of Mary, education for the

Catholic family, and the revival of Catholic culture, among others. The *Catechism of the Catholic Church* was the conference theme in 1993, and the International Year of the Family provided the theme for 1994. As part of our continued outreach efforts, audio tapes of conference sessions are made available at low cost to those who could not attend.

For several years, these annual conferences were held jointly with the Consortium Perfectae Caritatis, in the belief that closer ties between women religious and lay women would be mutually encouraging and helpful. Although the Consortium effectively dissolved in 1992 at the time of the organization of the Conference of Major Superiors of Women Religious, religious women continue to meet with us.

Besides the conferences, Women for Faith and Family publishes a quarterly newsletter, *VOICES,* the organization's primary means of communicating with *Affirmation* signers, other organizations, and individuals, including clergy, religious, and bishops. The first issue in 1994 had a print run of fifteen thousand copies, an increase of nearly four thousand from the previous issue, and a sixfold increase over five years ago.[6] At present *VOICES* is supported only by voluntary donations, because some interested families are on fixed incomes, and the board of directors views this conduit for information and encouragement as apostolic work. *VOICES* covers a wide range of subjects affecting Catholic women, families, and others, including interviews, editorials, and articles on pro-church, pro-life, and pro-family activities, excerpts and summaries of papal encyclicals and apostolic letters, prayers and devotional material, book reviews, letters and news of orthodox Catholic organizations and individuals in the United States and elsewhere in the world. For the past several years, reports on the meetings of the National Council of Catholic Bishops and its counterpart, the United States Catholic Conference, have been featured in the publication. A special "Supplement" edition in April 1994 contained a complete transcript of the bishops' discussion of liturgical revisions from the 1993 NCCB meeting.

WFF receives many letters from women asking for reliable information and concrete suggestions, both in the area of deepening understanding of church teachings and in practical matters. Because so many women ask how to increase their effectiveness in teaching the faith to their children, we have produced family sourcebooks which suggest ways of observing the church's liturgical year in the home, the "domestic church." In 1989, the first in a planned series of these books for families was published. The "Family Sourcebook for Advent and Christmas" contains Advent and Christmas prayers, activities, background on traditions and customs, and craft projects. A similar book, "Family Sourcebook for Lent and Easter," followed, and research for a third, on Marian feasts and holidays, is underway. These books were researched, written, edited, and illustrated by WFF staff members, and are available from the WFF office and a few Catholic bookstores.

Because classroom sex education has become a great concern to many Catholic parents, we also published *Sex Education: The Catholic Scene,* written by WFF associate Margaret Whitehead, cofounder of the Educational Guidance Institute. Another WFF publication which responded to a current concern is a monograph, "On Female 'Altar Servers.'" WFF also produces an assortment of brochures and leaflets which are sent in information packets, distributed at meetings and lectures, etc.[7]

In addition to its publications, Women for Faith and Family has issued public statements and responses on matters of importance in the church and in society. Such statements provide a useful means of communicating the concerns of women, but in addition serve an educative function vis-à-vis the media. One example is the *Statement on Feminism, Language and Liturgy* (see Appendix B), issued in 1989 jointly with two other women's groups (both religious: the Forum of Major Superiors of the Institute on Religious Life, and the Consortium Perfectae Caritatis). Also, detailed critiques of the various drafts of the "women's pastoral" were sent to the U.S. bishops. To help disseminate Catholic teaching on issues affecting women and their families, especially those contained in recent papal writings, and to increase the outreach of Women for Faith and Family, staff members and associates also write articles for other publications, lecture widely, and appear on radio and television on issues concerning the faith and family life.

Although the need for a national presence to support the teaching efforts of our bishops continues, in order to respond to the needs of women on practical issues, Women for Faith and Family is also committed to working effectively on the local level and encouraging other women to do so. During the past two or three years, chapters of Women for Faith and Family have been formed through the initiative of local women in various parts of the country,[8] and others are in the process of formation.[9] From the beginning, however, we have assisted in the formation of independent groups of women and/or family associations around the U.S., by providing contacts, guidance, and planning suggestions. While we are conscious of the burden of administrative duties and problems local chapters often entail, and have hesitated to promote "satellite" chapters of WFF largely for this reason, we are sensitive to the deep desire on the part of many Catholic women for a doctrinally reliable and spiritually nourishing source of companionship and mutual support, which such local groups might provide; accordingly, we have developed a structure which will permit prudent formation of local chapters. WFF's St. Louis staff also sponsors area meetings from time to time, such as days of recollection, holy hours, lectures, and family holiday festivals, and frequently participates with other Catholic groups in local efforts.

VOICES Reader Survey

All these local and national efforts have been pursued to give Catholic women a genuine sense of solidarity among themselves and increased spiritual energy, which we hope will extend to their families and their communities. At the same time, we thought it might be useful to learn more about the women affiliated with WFF, and what they think about some of the issues that are now dividing Catholics in America. In 1992 we invited VOICES readers to respond to a survey in order to obtain a demographic profile, as well as information related to church participation and opinions on ecclesial and related matters (see Appendix C). The survey includes a personal profile and questions about participation in worship (section D); religious education and moral formation (section E); general areas of concern (section F); and liturgy, doctrine, and church structure (section G). Although only a small space was allotted for comments, many respondents filled every available space on the form with details of their personal religious history, education, and concerns about the church. Several wrote separate letters, some of them very lengthy. The impression is unavoidable that most of the respondents were extremely eager for the opportunity to communicate their concerns and opinions to someone; and their remarks indicate that they believe they have been ignored by church officials at almost every level.

About 500 responses were received, and objective data from 476 of these survey forms were compiled. Some questions on the survey elicited detailed handwritten responses. Processing information from these often anecdotal and personal reflections required a rather complex categorization in order to tabulate responses and give them some objective form. The areas of investigation of the survey included a personal profile, a self-description of Catholic belief, and general areas of concern. (See Appendix C, VOICES Reader Survey: A Preliminary Report.)

Of the 476 respondents recorded, 437 were women and 32 were men. Most respondents gave their ages. Sixty-eight responses were entered from individuals in the 20–39 age group, 171 from those between ages 40 and 59, and 217 from ages over 60.

Respondents were asked to choose a description approximating their own views. Six choices were given: "mainstream," "conservative," "liberal," "progressive," "traditionalist," and "orthodox." An overwhelming majority of respondents chose "orthodox" (296), followed by "traditionalist" (76), "conservative" (58), and "mainstream" (14). Eleven respondents described themselves as "liberal" or "progressive." Two of those in these last groups were in the 40–59 age group; the remainder were over 60. Of the 68 respondents recorded from the 20–39 age group, 51 described themselves as "orthodox," 6 as "traditionalist," and 12 as "conservative." None in this age group described themselves as "liberal" or "progressive." Fewer than 10 respondents gave combined answers, e.g., "orthodox/conservative." One woman described herself as "liberal/traditionalist." Although most who chose "traditionalist" indicated a preference for the Tridentine rite Mass, it was clear from other answers that few or none understood the term to denominate exclusively Catholics who are "Tridentinists" or schismatic followers of Archbishop Lefebvre.

Not unexpectedly, the widest divergences within these categories are evidenced in responses to the survey's section G, "Liturgy, Doctrine and Church Structure." Although very few respondents to the survey (11) described themselves as "liberal" or "progressive," it is not surprising that their responses to so-called "neuralgic questions"—for example, whether the church's doctrine on ordination can be changed, the use of "altar girls" and liturgical language—were exactly opposite to the responses of those who describe themselves as "orthodox," "conservative," "traditionalist," or "mainstream." However, in the survey's section F, "General Areas of Concern," all respondents gave high priority to religious instruction of children ("mainstream" and "progressives" both ranked this 10; the "liberal" category was lowest, with a ranking of 8). All except "liberal" gave a high ranking to seminary formation.

The results from this study tend to confirm the view that there are, in effect, "two churches" within American Catholicism. How, whether, or when this situation might be resolved and the church effectively reunified remains to be seen.

Organizational Structure of WFF

Women for Faith and Family, incorporated in the state of Missouri as an IRS 501(c)(3) tax-exempt corporation, operates, like many similar organizations, with a board of directors and a basic list of officers (president, vice-president, secretary, and treasurer).[10] Its volunteer staff (at present, all are laywomen) meet weekly for planning sessions. Decisions concerning the work of the organization are made by consensus of the board members and staff. An unusual feature of operation is the decentralized "office."

Staff members carry on the vast majority of WFF work by telephone, facsimile machines, computers, and modems. This allows maximum flexibility of time scheduling, as well as making it possible for the staff members, all of whom have family responsibilities and some of whom have other jobs, to do the work of the organization primarily from home. Mailroom operations (sorting and routine response to requests for information) are handled by three women volunteers working in one home, while the weekly staff meetings are held in another woman's home. Files, the reference library and archives, and WFF's principal office are maintained in the home where staff meetings are held. Other staff members may do office work there a few hours a week, as their own schedules permit. Financial records, bookkeeping, and related work are maintained in still another home office. Staff members generally take their work home with them after each staff meeting. Questions which may arise over any aspect of the organization's work between weekly staff meetings are handled through electronic conferences, that is, by phone, fax, or computer modem.

This innovative structure affords family women, including those who have very young children, the opportunity to continue active work with the organization. Since there is no overhead for either office space or salaried workers, this structure also has the advantage of maximizing the use of funds, the overwhelming majority of which are from small donations from individuals. To date no financial suppport comes from foundations or dioceses, although a few bishops have contributed financially to Women for Faith and Family's efforts and/or have sent representatives to the annual conferences.

One obvious disadvantage of such a structure is that the location of the "offices" may change. When a staff member moves or goes on pregnancy leave, or if there are changes in membership of the staff, there may be temporary confusion. For this reason, the mailing address of Women for Faith and Family is a post office box. For several years the complete list of all *Affirmation* signers and the complete active mailing list have been maintained by a professional computer company. These records are now also maintained on WFF's own computers, and the updating and maintenance of the lists is gradually being transferred to WFF staff.

Conclusion

It has been ten years since that first meeting of Women for Faith and Family, where we considered how to respond to the bishops who proposed to write a "women's pastoral." What we then thought would be a short-term effort has expanded into an international movement of Catholic women with a multifaceted program and growing responsibilities. Many things have changed. The nine-year process surrounding the women's pastoral ended, more or less, in a whimper, and excessively optimistic predictions a decade ago by some members of the Women's Ordination Conference that women would certainly be ordained as Catholic priests "by the end of the decade" are conveniently forgotten. Yet much remains monotonously the same. Dissent from *Humanae Vitae* and other magisterial teachings of the church persists, despite repeated and frequent statements from the Vatican reaffirming them. And if some of the media's favorite "maverick Catholics" of a decade ago—such as the Franciscan liberation theologian Leonardo Boff and the Dominican feminist "panentheist" Matthew Fox—have since left the priesthood and forsworn the Catholic Church, others, including Father Charles Curran, Rosemary Ruether, and Elizabeth Schussler-Fiorenza, remain as persistently vocal in their unchanged views as ever.

One thing that has changed is that we are all ten years older. The luster has worn off the "renewal" promoted by the still-youthful dissenters and liturgical reformers of a decade or two ago, although the new wave of Scripture and liturgical translations incorporating feminist language and ideological cleansing may be an attempt to revive it. Fr. Richard McBrien boasted a few years ago that the dissenters have now become the establishment. His claim is not far from the truth: the former Young Turks are now the Graying Middle Management—salaried, tenured, comfortably ensconced in well-appointed offices within venerable institutions, and, as often as not, their latest projects enriched by commodious foundation grants. Orthodox Catholic movements, on the other hand, long undernourished, ignored, and on the margins, have proliferated as the poor often do, even though they grow ever leaner and remain as far as ever from positions of influence. Still, their expectations are low, and they have learned to survive for long periods of time on the refreshment of the apostolic exhortations and encyclicals with which Pope John Paul II has continued to nourish them—including the recent *Veritatis Splendor* and the long-delayed English translation of the *Catechism of the Catholic Church*. They still look with shining, hungry, hopeful eyes toward their courageously orthodox priests and bishops.

What has Women for Faith and Family achieved in nearly ten years? Were we successful even in our initial modest goal? Yes and no. The controversial "women's pastoral" (somewhat ironically called *One in Christ Jesus*) was never issued as a pastoral letter of the bishops. But, despite what some may think, it is not dead. In a compromise proposed by Chicago

Cardinal Joseph Bernardin, the document was issued only as a report of the pastoral's writing committee to the bishop's executive committee. However, its recommendations, such as advocating "nonsexist" language, training seminarians to be sensitive to women, and establishing "women's commissions" in the dioceses, are quietly being implemented by officials of the United States Catholic Conference. Even though feminists who initially supported the pastoral were not entirely pleased with its final draft, many of their goals are being achieved. But many feminist women had long since declared the Catholic Church "beyond patching,"[11] although most continue to remain Catholics in good standing, and their jobs, whether as seminary professors or as church bureaucrats, remain secure.

One modest achievement with which Women for Faith and Family might be credited is that it is now impossible for dissenting feminists to claim convincingly to speak for all Catholic women. Too many voices contradict this. However, a greater long-term gain may come from our daily, unglamorous labor of helping a few Catholics to understand their faith better, in praying for them and encouraging them in prayer and study in order that they might equip themselves for the arduous job of transmitting their precious (and, especially for younger Catholics, unexpected) gift of faith to others—to their children and to their children's children. Ours will certainly continue to be difficult, exhausting, unpopular work, as "women's work" so often is. Nevertheless, as with many other things mothers do out of love, it is through this work that we may hope to contribute things of irreplaceable value. Furthermore, we must continue. Because we believe the liberating truth of Christ is embodied in the Catholic Church, it is our simple, basic duty as Catholics to transmit it. We are unlikely to hear ourselves praised for our labors. But of this much we may be certain: our share in Christ's splendor is to be found nowhere but in His truth.

Affirmation for Catholic Women

By signing this affirmation women pledge their loyalty to the teaching of the Catholic Church. The names will be forwarded to the Pope.

Because of the assaults against the Christian Faith and the family by elements within contemporary society which have led to pervasive moral confusion, to damage and destruction of families and to the men, women and children which comprise them;

Because we adhere to the Catholic Christian faith as expressed in Holy Scripture, the Nicene, Apostolic and Athanasian Creeds, in the early ecumenical Councils of the Church, and in the continued deepening of the understanding of the revelations of Sacred Truth to the Church by the Holy Spirit through the teaching authority of the Church and of the Successors of Peter, Apostle;

Because we wish to affirm our desire to realize our vocations and our duty as Christians and as women in accordance with these authentic teachings, following the example and instruction of Our Savior Jesus Christ, and the example of Mary, His mother;

Because we are cognizant of our obligations as Christian women to witness to our faith, being mindful that this witness is important to the formation of the moral conscience of our families and of humanity, we wish to make this affirmation:

1. We believe that through God's grace our female nature affords us distinct physical and spiritual capabilities with which to participate in the Divine Plan for creation. Specifically, our natural function of childbearing endows us with the spiritual capacity for nurture, instruction, compassion and selflessness, which qualities are necessary to the establishment of families, the basic and Divinely ordained unit of society, and to the establishment of a Christian social order.

2. We believe that to attempt to subvert or deny our distinct nature and role as women subverts and denies God's plan for humanity, and leads to both personal disintegration and ultimately to the disintegration of society. Accordingly, we reject all ideologies which seek to eradicate the natural and essential distinction between the sexes, which debase and devalue womanhood, family life and the nurturing role of women in society.

3. We affirm the intrinsic sacredness of all human life, and we reject the notion that abortion, the deliberate killing of unborn children, is the "right" of any human being, male or female, or of any government. Such a distorted and corrosive notion of individual freedom is, in fact, inimical to authentic Christianity and to the establishment and maintenance of a just social order.

4. We accept and affirm the teaching of the Catholic Church on all matters dealing with human reproduction, marriage, family life and roles for

men and women in the Church and in society.

5. We therefore also reject as an aberrant innovation peculiar to our times and our society the notion that priesthood is the "right" of any human being, male or female. Furthermore, we recognize that the specific role of ordained priesthood is intrinsically connected with and representative of the begetting creativity of God in which only human males can participate. Human females, who by nature share in the creativity of God by their capacity to bring forth new life, and, reflective of this essential distinction, have a different and distinct role within the Church and in society from that accorded to men, can no more be priests than men can be mothers.

6. We recognize and affirm the vocations of women who subordinate their human role of motherhood and family life in order to consecrate their lives to the service of God, His Church and humanity. Such women's authentic response of consecrated service to the physical, spiritual and/or intellectual needs of the community in no way diminishes or compromises their essential female nature, or the exercise of inherent attributes, insights and gifts peculiar to women. Rather, it extends the applications of these gifts beyond the individual human family.

7. We stand with the Second Vatican Council which took for granted the distinct roles for men and women in the family and in society and affirmed that Christian education must impart knowledge of this distinction: "In the entire educational program [Catholic school teachers] should, together with the parents, make full allowance for the difference of sex and for the particular role which Providence has appointed to each each sex in the family and in society. (*Declaration on Education*, Sec. 8, paragraph 3, from Vatican II Documents, ed. Austin Flannery, 1981)

8. We pledge our wholehearted support to Pope John Paul II. We adhere to his apostolic teaching concerning all aspects of family life and roles for men and women in the Church and in society, especially as contained in the Apostolic Exhortation, *Familiaris Consortio;* and we resolve to apply the principles contained therein to our own lives, our families and our communities, God being our aid.

- -

Please Print Clearly

NAME:_____

STREET:_____ CITY:_____ STATE:_____ ZIP: _____

☐ Enclosed is my donation of $5_____ $10_____ $25_____Other $ _____

☐ Please send information about Women for Faith & Family

☐ I will help collect signatures. (*NOTE: You are free to reproduce this Affirmation.*)

Send to: **Women for Faith & Family** • PO Box 8326 • St. Louis, MO 63132
• Ph./Fax 314-863-8385 •

Women for Faith and Family Purposes

1. To assist orthodox Catholic women in their effort to provide witness to their faith, both to their families and to the world.

2. To aid women in their efforts to continually deepen their understanding of the Catholic Faith.

3. To aid faithful Catholic women in their desire for fellowship with others who share their faith and commitment.

4. To serve as a channel through which questions from Catholic women seeking guidance or information can be directed.

Additional AFFIRMATION Signers

Please Print Clearly

Name——————————— Name ———————————
Address——————————— Address ———————————
City, State——————————— City, State ———————————
Zip——————————— Zip ———————————

Name——————————— Name ———————————
Address——————————— Address ———————————
City, State——————————— City, State ———————————
Zip——————————— Zip ———————————

Name——————————— Name ———————————
Address——————————— Address ———————————
City, State——————————— City, State ———————————
Zip——————————— Zip ———————————

Name——————————— Name ———————————
Address——————————— Address ———————————
City, State——————————— City, State ———————————
Zip——————————— Zip ———————————

WOMEN FOR FAITH & FAMILY — P.O. BOX 8326, ST. LOUIS, MO 63132
PH / FAX (314) 863–8385

Statement on Feminism, Language and Liturgy

Women for Faith & Family, Forum of Major Superiors,
Consortium Perfectae Caritatis
April 18, 1989

Because we are Catholic women who accept and affirm all the teachings of the Catholic Church, not only as true propositions but as the norms of our thought and life;

Because we are aware of the influence within the Church and in society of alien ideologies which attack the fundamental assumptions of Christianity about human life and of the relationship of human beings with their Creator, and which effectively undermine the Catholic Church;

Because we understand our responsibility as Catholics and as women to witness to the truth which the Catholic Church teaches and our willing and free acceptance of her just and true authority vested in the Magisterium of the Church, particularly in Christ's vicar, the Pope, and Bishops in union with him, we believe it our duty to make the following statement:

1. In our time and culture, ideological feminism, which denies the fundamental and psychic and spiritual distinctiveness of the sexes and which devalues motherhood and the nurturing role of women in the family and in society, is often misrepresented as expressing the collective belief of women. As women, we are particularly concerned about the pervasive influence and the destructive effects on the Church, on families and on society of this "feminism."

2. As Catholics who have been formed, inspired and sustained by the Sacraments of the Church through participation in the liturgy, the Church's central action and principal means of transmission of the Catholic faith, we are strongly aware of the power of symbol in human consciousness. We therefore deplore attempts to distort and transform language and liturgy, both of which make such potent symbolic impressions on the human mind, to conform to a particular contemporary ideological agenda at odds with Catholic belief and practice.

3. We reaffirm our belief in the divine origin of the Church and that the hierarchy of the Catholic Church, which is often criticized in our time as insufficiently egalitarian, was intentionally established by Christ, and that He selected the Apostles and Peter, among them, as head, giving them and their legitimate successors magisterial authority to guide His Church until He comes again.

4. We believe that Jesus Christ, the Word of God made man, was limited and restricted by His culture only in that which, apart from sin, limits man. But we also believe that He came in a time and to a people chosen by God. Thus, all that Jesus took up from His culture by His teaching or action is normative for every culture of every time and place. We reject the notion that Jesus Christ,

God Incarnate, was limited or restricted in the fulfillment of the Mission entrusted to Him by the Father by the cultural context of His presence on Earth, His life as a Jew of the first third of the first century, or by any other factor.

5. Accordingly, we also reaffirm the constant teaching of the Catholic Church that ordained priesthood is not a "right" accorded to any member of the Church, but a state of life and a service to which, by Christ's will, only men, not women, may be called.

6. Following the teachings and example of Christ and the constant tradition of the Catholic Church, and mindful of its full significance, we consider it a privilege to call God 'Our Father,' a name which reflects not only the relationship between human beings and their Creator, but which also provides a powerful symbolic model for men of the steadfast love, faithfulness, justice, mercy, wisdom and objectivity which are ideal components of human fatherhood vital to women, to families and to the social order. Contemporary efforts to impute a 'feminine' aspect to the Godhead, by retrojection of alien and anachronistic notions into the body of Sacred Scripture, by forcibly changing the language used to refer to God, by deliberate reversion to pagan notions of deity, or by any other means, we regard as dangerously misguided and perverse.

7. Therefore we reject all attempts to impose ideologically motivated innovations on the liturgy of the Church or changes in official lectionaries or sacramentaries or catechisms in the name of 'justice' to women. We deplore the deliberate manipulation of liturgical actions, signs and symbols and politicization of both liturgy and language which ef-

fectively impede both receiving and transmitting the Catholic faith and harm the unity of the Church.

8. For these reasons, we oppose the systematic elimination from Scripture translations, liturgical texts, hymns, homilies and general usage of 'man' as a generic. The claim that the language is "sexist" and that such changes are required as a sensitive pastoral response to women collectively is false. We believe that the symbolic effect of mandating such changes in the language and practice of the Catholic Church is negative and confusing, effectively undermining the authority of the Church and her hierarchy.

9. We also oppose changing the constant practice of the Church in such liturgical matters as acolytes or 'altar servers' and homilists, and repudiate the increasingly frequent practice of women saying parts of the Eucharistic Prayer with the priest or in his place or performing other liturgical functions reserved to ordained men.

10. We are grateful for the profound contribution of Pope John Paul II to our understanding of the meaning of human life and of the fundamental relationship of human beings with one another and with God through the many theological works he has given the Church during his pontificate, including his Apostolic Letter, *Mulieris Dignitatem*, which help to deepen our understanding of the centrality of the role of Christian women to the Church's evangelical mission. Constantly seeking the aid of the Holy Spirit, and in solidarity with the Pope, the Bishops in union with him, and with the universal Church, we pledge to respond to our Christian vocation with wisdom, with love and responsibility.

APPENDIX C

VOICES Reader Survey
A Preliminary Report

WE ARE MOST GRATEFUL to all those who took the time and trouble to respond to the Reader Survey contained in the Fall-Winter, 1992 issue of VOICES. A total of **476 completed surveys** were received (about 4% of approximately 8,000 copies of VOICES mailed—considered a very good rate of response). Many surveys contained extensive additional comments or appended detailed letters. Processing the information from the Survey is nearing completion. Information from **Section D** (Participation in Worship and Church Related Activities) and **Section E** (Education, Religious Education and Moral Formation) and the final comments are not included in this preliminary report. Further results will be published in future issues of VOICES.

Survey respondents were predominantly women (although 32 were men) ranging in age from 21 to 87, and representing **123 U.S. Latin Rite dioceses** as well as one US Ukrainian Rite diocese and one diocese in England. Respondents have **1,633 children** and **1,933 grandchildren** (probably more by the time these results are published, as many respondents mentioned children or grandchildren "on the way" in their lists). Results from the first three sections of the survey, which dealt with personal, family, and religious profiles are tabulated below. (The totals do not always add up to 476 because some respondents left some questions blank.)

A. Personal Profile
Men: 32 Women: 437
Affirmation for Catholic Women Signers—Yes: 320 **No or don't know:** 156
Age: 20–29: 13 **30–39:** 55 **40–49:** 71 **50–59:** 100 **60–69:** 118 **>70:** 99

B. Family Profile
Clergy/Religious: 24 **Married:** 322 **Single:** 50
Widowed: 51 **Divorced:** 18 **Separated:** 4

C. Religious Profile
Cradle Catholic: 416 **Convert:** 60
Preference among terms often used to describe Catholics.
Mainstream: 14 **Conservative:** 58 **Liberal:** 5 **Progressive:** 6
Traditionalist: 76 **Orthodox:** 296

F. General Areas of Concern
In this section respondents were asked to rate each issue on its importance on a numerical scale of 1 to 10 with 10 representing the highest importance. Numerical responses were averaged and statements are listed below ranked from highest to lowest in average ranking of importance.

Importance	Area of Concern
9.8	Religious and moral instruction of children.
9.7	Seminary formation of priests based on orthodox Catholic teaching.
9.7	Clear presentation of Catholic teachings by pastors.
9.5	Sense of sacredness, reverence, at Mass.
9.5	Religious and moral instruction of new Catholics.
9.2	Preparation of *parents* for moral, ethical, religious training of children.
9.1	Increase in vocations to priesthood, religious life.
8.6	Need for spiritual directors, models of spiritual life, spiritual formation.
8.3	Adequate preparation for "lay ministries" in the liturgy (e.g., lectors, CCD teachers, altar work, altar boy training).
8.3	Opportunities for para-liturgical devotions (e.g., Holy Hours, Benediction of the Blessed Sacrament).
8.2	Accessible, doctrinally sound resources for advanced academic study and/or professional "adult education."
8.1	Opportunities for adults to deepen understanding of Church teachings in *non*-professional "adult education."

PRELIMINARY ANALYSIS of the responses revealed no significant differences in responses from different age groups or between opinions of lay people and religious, either in Section F (above) or Section G (below). However, in **Section G** (on liturgy, doctrine and Church structure) striking differences appeared if the answers were compared with the *descriptive terms* in **Section C** (e.g., 'orthodox,' 'liberal,' etc.) There was general agreement in responses among those who called themselves orthodox, traditionalist, conservative, or mainstream; and those who considered themselves liberal or progressive tended to give responses similar to each other—but very different from those in the other four groups. The number of the liberals and progressives responding to the reader survey was, as expected, very small (only 11 of the 476), but the difference of opinion seems significant. On many questions the responses of the two sets of groups are not just noticeably different, but almost opposite—note, for example, the responses to #4, on girls and women as altar servers, #12, on kneeling during the Consecration at Mass, #7, on ordination. All groups responded negatively, however, to #24, on changing unpopular Church doctrines to attract more people.

The numerical responses for each statement were averaged separately for each group and the averages shown in the table **Section G**. (Some of the survey statements in this section appear in abridged form here.) Respondents were asked to rank their views on each statement on a numerical scale ranging from 5 (strongly agree) to 1 (strongly disagree). The column headings represent the descriptive terms in **Section C**, with M standing for mainstream, C for conservative, etc.

G. Liturgy, Doctrine and Church Structure

	M	C	L	P	T	O
1. Pastors do not do enough to explain Church teaching on moral issues.	4.3	4.2	2.8	3.3	4.5	4.6
2. Pastors do not do enough to explain Church teaching on doctrine.	3.9	3.9	3.0	3.5	4.2	4.4
3. Pastors and bishops are too sensitive to feminist concerns.	4.2	4.1	2.2	2.7	4.4	4.6

4. It is unfair that girls or women are not allowed to serve at the altar.	2.6	1.3	4.4	3.5	1.3	1.2
5. Religious sisters should wear habits as sign of consecration.	4.5	4.5	1.6	2.7	4.6	4.6
6. Liturgy should change continually to conform to current social ideas.	1.4	1.3	3.8	2.6	1.2	1.1
7. That only men may be ordained is a central, unchangeable teaching.	4.1	4.6	1.8	2.5	4.5	4.7
8. Scripture and Mass prayers should be changed to use feminist language.	1.2	1.4	4.2	3.7	1.2	1.1
9. Translations for Catholic worship should be faithful to original text.	4.9	4.8	2.8	4.0	4.8	4.9
10. Latin Masses (Novus Ordo, Tridentine) should be more available.	3.5	3.9	1.6	2.0	4.3	4.2
11. There are too many Masses where the liturgy is poorly done.	3.4	3.8	3.5	2.8	3.9	4.1
12. People should kneel during the Consecration at Mass.	4.8	4.7	1.8	3.5	4.9	4.8
13. Greater use of traditional music would aid Catholic worship.	4.1	4.1	2.5	2.5	4.5	4.7
14. A sense of sacredness is missing from most Masses.	3.7	3.8	1.6	2.3	4.4	4.2
15. The "Tridentine Mass" is personally important to me.	2.4	3.1	2.0	1.8	4.1	3.3
16. The US bishops generally teach clearly with the Church.	2.5	2.2	3.0	3.5	1.9	2.0
17. Most bishops are aware of problems in dioceses and try to correct them.	2.1	2.3	3.0	4.0	2.0	1.9
18. The Church is served well by its national and diocesan bureaucracies.	2.2	2.0	2.3	3.3	1.8	1.7
19. Catholic schools are doing a good job of educating in secular subjects.	3.7	3.6	3.4	4.7	3.6	3.6
20. Catholic schools are doing a good job of educating in faith & morals.	2.8	2.3	3.0	4.3	2.1	1.8
21. Dissent by Catholics in leadership positions is a serious problem today.	4.6	4.7	2.6	3.0	4.6	4.7
22. My bishop sets a courageous example of defense of Catholic teaching.	3.5	2.9	3.6	4.0	2.7	2.5
23. Catholics who reject Church teaching should look for another Church.	3.3	3.8	2.0	3.2	4.0	4.1
24. Unpopular doctrines can & should be changed to attract more people.	1.4	1.3	2.6	1.8	1.3	1.2

There is an interesting footnote on this survey, although no attempt will be made to tabulate it. We had asked that the form be returned by April 1. The first wave of responses were overwhelmingly from people over age 50. Responses from younger people, especially those with children at home, came in much later, and the overall totals were smaller. This should not be surprising, since completing a detailed survey, finding an envelope and stamp—and then remembering to put it in the mail—is not usually high on the list of busy young mothers, as we know only too well. So a special note of gratitude goes to those among our younger readers who actually managed to get it done.

NOTES

1. Between April 1992 and March 1993, 4,371 pieces of mail were handled by the mailroom staff; 772 letters were received in September 1992, the most for any month that year.

2. Although we keep no statistics on this, we estimate that about half of all requests for help involve problems with catechetics or sex education. A typical letter or call would be from a parent concerned that a child being prepared for First Communion is being taught that confession is unnecessary and that the Eucharist is "created" by the gathered community; or that explicit information about birth control methods is being given to adolescents in sex education classes in a Catholic school. A large percentage of requests for advice relate liturgical concerns, such as female "altar servers," church renovations, improvised Eucharistic Prayers, feminist language, etc.

Typically, people contact us after they have had an intimidating encounter with a parish priest or nun and do not know what to do next. We may recommend resources and suggest approaches to aid in resolving the problem.

3. There are eight staff members, plus two regular "mailroom" workers. Two staff members are academics, with Ph.D.s in English and physics; one is a nurse, one a professional artist; two are writers; two are former teachers. Two are single, the rest are married, and all married members but one are mothers. They range in age from thirty to sixty. Regular consultants of the staff include physicians, theologians, Scripture scholars, canon lawyers, and academics of various disciplines—both clergy and lay, both men and women.

4. E.g., WFF filed a brief jointly with the Catholic League for Religious and Civil Rights: *Dayton School* case, 1986, involving the right of a religious school to require a faculty member to accept and abide by the tenets of its religion. We agreed to file as an amicus curiae in the Busalacchi case, involving withdrawal of food and water from a disabled patient. We have also agreed to file jointly in *J.M. v. V.C.*, currently being appealed to the U.S. Supreme Court, which involves the rights of the father of an unborn child.

5. A partial list of past speakers includes John Joseph Cardinal Carberry, James Cardinal Hickey, Anthony Cardinal Bevilacqua, Archbishop John May, Bishops Austin Vaughan, Glennon Flavin, John Myers, Charles Koester, Thomas Welsh, Fabian Bruskewitz, James Keleher, Charles Chaput, and Jeremiah Newman (Ireland), Helen Alvare (USCC), Ronda Chervin, Joyce Little, Suzanne Scorsone (Canada), Ellen Wilson Fielding, Louise Summerhill, Janet Smith, Mother Angelica, Rev. Joseph Fessio, S.J., Rev. Paul Mankowski, S.J., Donna Steichen, Juli Loesch Wiley, James Hitchcock, Helen Hull Hitchcock, Sr. Assumpta Long, O.P., Anne Roche Muggeridge (Canada), Msgr. George A. Kelly, Mary Ellen Bork, Joanna Bogle (England), Dolores Grier, Sr. Joan Gormley, Sr. Vincent Marie Finnegan, Karl Keating, Rev. James A. Viall, Rev. George Rutler, Donald DeMarco (Canada), Germaine Murray, Rev. Mitchell Pacwa, S.J., Msgr. Michael Wrenn, Kenneth Whitehead, and Margaret Whitehead.

6. Since the acquisition of computer equipment in 1989, all phases of production of *VOICES* except printing and bulk mailing have been handled by WFF's volunteer staff, including editing, typesetting, layout, illustration, and most writing.

7. E.g., "Changing the Way We Talk about Euthanasia," "Ten Things People Can Do," "Abortion: Myth and Reality," and several prayer leaflets, including a "Novena for the Unborn."

8. WFF—Cleveland; WFF—Toledo; WFF—Kansas City, Mo.

9. Rapid City, Scranton.

10. Officers at the time of this writing are: president, Helen Hull Hitchcock; vice-president, Sherry Tyree; secretary, Jocelyn Johnson; treasurer, Susan J. Benofy.

11. *Beyond Patching* is the title of a 1991 book by Sr. Sandra Schneiders, who teaches Jesuit seminarians at the Jesuit School of Theology in Berkeley. She finds that the Catholic Church and Holy Scripture are so intrinsically infested with oppressive patriarchalism as to be hopelessly beyond repair; only complete "reweaving" according to feminist designs can make them acceptable. Her views are now standard fare in many Catholic institutions of higher learning.

The Fellowship of Catholic Scholars
Bowing Out of the New Class

JAMES HITCHCOCK

Prologue

Most "conservative" Catholics are probably unhappy with the term,
both because they do not recognize alternative "brands" of Catholicism,
preferring to speak merely of authentic and inauthentic kinds, and because
the political connotations of the word can be misleading. But against their
wills they have been drawn into debates where the label seems unavoidable.
Many of us who have ended up under the "conservative" umbrella once regarded ourselves as ecclesiastical "liberals," a term with similar inherent
problems. Before the Council, for example, I was interested in liturgical
reform which promised greater lay participation and a pruning away of
what seemed like dubious and extravagant popular devotions, and I welcomed the initial liturgical changes, including the use of the vernacular.

Lay American Catholics around 1960 had difficulty discovering what
theological alternatives to Thomism might exist, but I tried to learn something about the more "personalistic" approach being taken in Europe by
people such as Gabriel Marcel, Dietrich von Hildebrand, Hans Urs von
Balthasar, Romano Guardini, Henri de Lubac, and Jean Danielou. Ecclesiastical authorities seemed to me often short-sighted and arbitrary, fixed
on rules which sometimes obscured the deeper reality of the faith. Politically I judged that authentic Catholic social thought, as found especially
in papal encyclicals, came close to endorsing the New Deal tradition in the

United States. The nexus of such ideas was conveniently dubbed "*Commonweal* Catholicism," after the lay-edited magazine, and while the term may have been intended originally as a jibe, it became a badge of honor to many of us.

The preconciliar liberal position was in effect that it was indeed possible to put new wine in old skins, that the Catholic faith could be rethought and re-expressed in categories more suitable to the late twentieth century, without losing any of its essential truths. In some ways our agenda was deeply conservative. For example, we favored a return to patristic forms of theology and liturgy.

Liberal Catholics at the beginning of the Council worried that recalcitrant clergy would thwart its reforms, and we assumed that it would take decades for the Council's promises to be realized. Instead, the seemingly solid wall of ecclesiastical resistance proved to be made of paper, and things over which we thought we might spend the rest of our lives contending were implemented almost instantaneously, in virtually every area of Catholic life.

Most of those who later became active in the Fellowship of Catholic Scholars were, if not "liberals" at the time of the Council, at least undisturbed by its proposed changes. In those days a principled resistance to such change was offered in the pages of the short-lived magazine *Triumph,* for example, but that enterprise involved almost no one later prominent in the Fellowship. Until 1968, most of us who later became "conservatives" probably wished to separate ourselves as far as possible from those who were raising questions about the conciliar agenda.

My earliest writings were either attempts to promote reform or criticisms of that reform from the inside, arguing that in certain ways reformers were being unfaithful to their own principles. With what I now see as absurd naiveté, I thought that if a few seeming contradictions were pointed out, reformers would quickly remedy the problems. Until 1968, few of us self-defined liberals understood what an enormous intellectual chasm was opening through the middle of the church, a split that absolutely no one would be able to straddle.

The papal birth-control encyclical *Humanae Vitae* in 1968 probably revealed the dividing line for most people. I had not paid a great deal of attention to the subject and had assumed that in time the church would make some kind of adjustment on the issue. But I soon realized that the reaction to that document involved far-reaching questions indeed and that acceptance of the liberal position was incompatible with any determination to preserve the substance of the faith unchanged. Beyond the issue of birth control itself was the blunt assertion by its critics that Catholic doctrine was radically historically conditioned and could thus be radically revised. It seemed to me that a reform which had sought to deepen the faith was instead making it a pale copy of liberal Protestantism, which itself seemed to me a religious cul-de-sac.

The imprecision of the term *conservative* allows it to cover what are sometimes rather disparate people and movements. The kind of conservatism represented by the *National Review,* for example, has always attracted more than its share of Catholics. Theologically conservative Catholics are not necessarily devotees of the "free market," however, and William F. Buckley has sometimes been regarded as a less than fully committed ally on issues involving sexuality. The leading Catholic "neo-conservative" of the 1980s was Michael Novak, who remained a religious liberal considerably beyond 1968 and was suspected by some theological conservatives of using religion to promote a primarily political agenda.

What brought political and religious conservatives into a working alliance was the conservative movement's adoption of an anti-abortion position during the late 1970s, and the prevalent conservative belief that under liberal administrations, government power was being used to promote an objectionable social agenda. *Crisis* magazine, cofounded by Novak and the Notre Dame philosophy professor Ralph McInerny, was in a sense an attempt to bridge the gap between religious and political conservatives. *First Things,* edited by the convert priest Richard John Neuhaus, has done the same, albeit in a generally ecumenical context. Under the editorship of David Schindler, the American edition of the international journal *Communio* has engaged in sharp debate with some of the Catholics clustered around *First Things,* generally identified with the Washington conservative establishment, with *Communio* expressing serious reservations about the entire American experiment and arguing that some conservative Catholics have lost touch with their intellectual roots.

Both as a group and in terms of most of its individual members, the Fellowship of Catholic Scholars has remained somewhat aloof from these debates, tending to concentrate on questions where matters of Catholic doctrine and practice are obviously at stake, in effect conceding a legitimate divergence of opinion on wider cultural issues. (Novak, Neuhaus, and Schindler have not been active in the Fellowship.)

Introduction

As late as 1965, Catholic intellectual life in the United States was still dominated by scholastic theology and philosophy, but this situation changed swiftly and dramatically. Within five years, not only was there remarkable diversity in American Catholic thought, but scholasticism was no longer even the first among equals.[1] From the time of the controversy over *Humanae Vitae*, Catholic intellectuals were claiming a right of dissent from official teaching, on the grounds that Catholics had an obligation to follow their consciences wherever those might lead, and that the church itself would ultimately benefit from an open discussion of all questions.

As a result of some of the unsettling events which followed the Council, by the mid-1970s some Catholic scholars were beginning to feel isolated in their dioceses, their religious communities, or their educational institutions. It seemed to them that proponents of dissent were dominant not only in colleges, universities, professional societies, and publishing houses, but even in those educational institutions which might have been thought of as bastions of orthodoxy, namely, seminaries. At first these isolated feelings of discontent resulted in little more than the private exchange of laments among old friends.[2] Eventually, however, it began to seem desirable that there should be an organized group for Catholic scholars who were alarmed by dissent and eager to support what they regarded as the authoritative interpretation of the conciliar documents.

"Conservatives" in relation to the Second Vatican Council (1962–65) were like "strict constructionists" or proponents of "original intent" in interpreting the American Constitution, accepting the authority of the documents but insisting that they did not constitute a charter for sweeping change.[3] Fundamentally, the various issues—dogmatic, moral, liturgical, ecclesiastical—were really only one issue, namely, the authentic interpretation of the Second Vatican Council. Vatican II had issued decrees on all aspects of Catholic life, and various groups within the church almost immediately began contending over the meaning of those documents. The Fellowship of Catholic Scholars was founded, therefore, to invite likeminded Catholic intellectuals to join forces against those who they thought were betraying the Council by interpreting it in radical ways.

Early in 1976, Msgr. George A. Kelly, then a professor at St. John's University in New York City and director of a catechetical institute there, made a journey across the country specifically in order to confer with scholars who were dissatisfied with the prevailing situation. Besides Kelly, the original organizers included the Jesuits Joseph Mangan and Earl Weis of Loyola University, Chicago; Capuchin father Ronald Lawler of the Josephinum Seminary; Joseph Fessio, S.J., of the University of San Francisco; Redemptorist father Henry Sattler of the University of Scranton; the Canadian philosopher Germain Grisez; the theologian William May of the Catholic University of America; and James Hitchcock of St. Louis

University. Over the next year there were several small meetings held to discuss formation of a group, and in 1977 the Fellowship of Catholic Scholars was founded in response to what was perceived as a dangerous general trend within American Catholicism.

Certain specific occurrences, while not precisely the occasion for the organization's founding, nonetheless contributed to the sense of urgency which propelled its founders. One instance was the Catholic Theological Society of America's 1977 report *On Human Sexuality*,[4] which seemed to open the door to a variety of sexual activities theretofore forbidden by Catholic teaching. The report was "received" by the CTSA rather than endorsed, but probably motivated a number of Fellowship members to sever their ties with the older organization. The "sex report" seemed to many conservative scholars graphic proof that established Catholic institutions, beginning with the universities themselves, had fallen into alien hands.

Statement of Purpose

Prospective members are required to subscribe to a "Statement of Purpose" (see Appendix B), which includes an affirmation of personal faith as well as scholarly competence, including phrases such as "serve Jesus Christ," "service that they owe to God," "thanks for our Catholic faith," and "personal assent to the mystery of Christ as made manifest through the lived faith of the Church." Perhaps the key passage is the following:

> We accept as the rule of our life and thought the entire faith of the Catholic Church. This we see not merely in solemn definitions but in the ordinary teachings of the Pope and those bishops in union with him, and also embodied in those modes of worship and ways of Christian life and practice, of the present as of the past, which have been in harmony with the teachings of St. Peter's successors in the see of Rome.

While theologians in the group might distinguish varying degrees of official teaching authority, most members probably regard John Paul II as practically a reliable guide to authentic Catholic doctrine and regard his "ordinary magisterium" as deserving of assent.

The issues Fellowship members regard as important are often chosen for them by their opponents. If the doctrine of the Trinity were under attack, they would turn their interests to rarefied and abstract metaphysical ideas. As it is, however, the influence of feminism, the sexual revolution, and academic historicism, to cite three major movements, lies behind most of the issues in which the Fellowship becomes involved.

Perhaps because of the bluntness of the "Statement of Purpose," there has never been a "heresy" case, or any suggestion that a particular member is not in harmony with the spirit of the organization. There is no formal provision for dealing with internal dissent, and any case would probably be dealt with ad hoc by the board, but it has never been tested. At the same time, over the years a number of people have joined and then failed to renew their membership, some of whom, it may be supposed, did not find the group to their theological tastes.

The "Statement of Purpose" broadly suggests three functions of the organization: the study and clarification of "challenges" to the credibility of the faith, the sharing of members' work with one another, and the dissemination of that work to others in the church who might profit from it. Probably most members think that the last function has been only imperfectly fulfilled. At the time the organization was founded, organizers believed that theological dissenters achieved public prominence in part because no one was available to speak on the other side. Over the years, however, there has been a growing sense that support of disputed teachings is not considered "newsworthy" and that the organization does not have the visibility it would like to have.

Membership and Character

Because most postconciliar controversies finally turn on theological issues, the Fellowship began with a heavily theological focus. From the beginning, however, it also included philosophers, historians, literary critics, and at least a smattering of people from the social sciences, the natural sciences, and the professions, the common thread being a public commitment to the Catholic faith and the assumption that a religious perspective was relevant even to secular disciplines (see Appendix A). Thus for some years there was an active literary caucus, in which members met to discuss literature influenced by a religious spirit, such as the works of the Metaphysical Poets, Walker Percy, or Flannery O'Connor.

Regular members are required to hold a terminal degree in their field or to have demonstrated professional competence through publication. The group also has associate members who are interested in its activities but without the right to vote for officers. Each convention attracts a significant number of people with a serious but nonprofessional interest in Catholic issues.[5] Many members of the Fellowship continue to maintain membership in other scholarly organizations, tending to find Catholic organizations devoted to primarily secular disciplines—the Catholic Philosophical Association and the Catholic Historical Association, for example—more congenial than those which are explicitly ecclesiastical. Groups such as the Catholic Theological Society of America and the Canon Law Society appear to Fellowship members as dominantly liberal in their orientation. Members of FCS almost never publish in *Theological Studies* but do sometimes appear in the *Modern Schoolman,* the *New Scholasticism,* or the *Catholic Historical Review.* Although the theological journal *Communio* has no official connection with the Fellowship, theologians in the organization have sometimes found it a hospitable place to publish, and its first American editor, James Hitchcock, was one of the organizers of the Fellowship. Some members also belong to secular scholarly groups, such as the American Historical Association or the Modern Language Association.

Probably most members of the Fellowship feel themselves to be on the margins of their academic disciplines and their institutions, whether secular or Catholic. In a sense the Fellowship would not need to exist if members judged that other organizations were functioning as they ought. A sense of alienation from the intellectual mainstream of the church and of society is therefore a pervasive theme in many of the writings of Fellowship members. The Fellowship is not an umbrella for all conservative Catholic intellectuals in the United States, for some who would be prominently classified as such either do not belong or maintain a merely nominal membership. At the same time, the organization is at the center of a loose network of conservative Catholic intellectuals which includes some faculty and administrators from the "neo-Catholic" colleges, especially the Franciscan University of Steubenville; Ignatius Press, whose Jesuit director, Joseph Fessio, has served on the Fellowship board and has received the Cardinal Wright Award; and *Crisis* magazine, whose copublisher and cofounder, Ralph McInerny of the University of Notre Dame, became president of the organization in 1991. FCS meetings are usually also attended by representatives of a number of other Catholic groups, such as the John Paul II Institute for Studies on Marriage and the Family, the Pope John Center for Medical Ethics, the Couple to Couple League, the Institute for Religious Life, and Women for Faith and Family.

Fellowship members are distinguished from other conservative Catholic scholars by a certain sense of urgency, a judgment that time is running short and great things are at stake. Debate is often carried on with passion, and sometimes even with acrimony. Fellowship members thus tend to distinguish themselves fairly sharply from "moderates" on the Catholic academic scene, such as the Scripture scholar Father Raymond Brown and the Jesuit theologian Avery Dulles, on the grounds that these men espouse unstable compromises which in the end also undermine Catholic belief.[6]

But just as the debate over "liberal versus conservative" interpretations of the Second Vatican Council has its secular counterpart in debates over the American Constitution, the alienation that conservative Catholics feel from the mainstream of American Catholic intellectual life is not due wholly to their religious beliefs. Many "conservative" scholars at one time considered themselves liberals, and their sense of marginalization is comparable to that which "neoconservative" intellectuals have experienced in secular academia in the age of feminism, multiculturalism, and deconstruction. Thus they would see themselves not as deficient in scholarly attainments but as victims of the degradation of scholarship itself.[7]

The influence of individual members is sometimes difficult to measure, in part because it is often exerted under circumstances of confidentiality, as when particular scholars are asked by particular bishops to provide critiques of disputed documents within the church. FCS members were consulted about the bishops' now-abandoned pastoral letter on women and about the *Universal Catechism,* but only a small number of prelates seem to request this kind of assistance, and the effect of these confidential critiques is not always evident. Fellowship members are almost never appointed to boards and committees of the National Council of Catholic Bishops or the United States Catholic Conference, and many have come to believe that they are systematically shut out of the deliberations of those official bodies.[8]

From the beginning the group has attempted to maintain strong ties with the Vatican, and many of its members see the major division in American Catholicism as being over the authority of the Holy See. Individual members, although not the organization as such, have maintained ties to particular Vatican officials, and two members, William May and John Finnis, have served on the International Theological Commission. Theologians are the single largest category of scholars belonging to the organization, but probably all of its members, in whatever discipline, have strong theological interests which they see as affecting their own scholarly work. Those who do not see such a connection presumably do not become active, and an occasional scholar has resigned with the complaint that the tenor of the organization is too theological.

Although no members would describe themselves as reactionary, of necessity they often find themselves responding to initiatives mounted by others with whom they disagree. Over a period of years, for example, both the *Newsletter* and the annual convention have presented studies on subjects already being widely discussed, sometimes because the National Council of Catholic Bishops or some other church agency has proposed a document for public consideration. Thus when a universal catechism was suggested in 1986, Fellowship members strongly supported it as necessary to ensure minimum doctrinal unity among Catholics, and in order to correct serious deficiencies in existing religious education. As both the idea of the catechism and some of its specific parts came under strong criticism, Fellowship members defended it while suggesting revisions, meanwhile acting as advisors to particular bishops on specific sections. In particular, two members—Fessio and Msgr. Michael Wrenn, a New York City catechetical specialist—while strongly supporting the idea of the catechism, became equally strong critics of the first English translation. The first version, which featured gender-inclusive language, they deemed to be seriously unfaithful to the French original, and they were successful in having it replaced by an English-language version that retained traditional language.[9]

On other contested issues, the Fellowship has formulated positions it considered orthodox and yet at odds with prevailing opinion in American Catholic scholarly circles. For example, Fellowship members have strong opinions on the religious character of Catholic colleges and universities,[10] the forms of liturgical worship,[11] the annulment of marriages,[12] the ordination of women to the priesthood,[13] and the morality of homosexuality.[14] The reactive character of much of the Fellowship's work is determined mainly by a sense of urgency, an estimate that dissenters control much of the machinery of public discourse. Thus priority is almost always given to immediate questions with obvious practical implications, and Fellowship members often find themselves fighting rear-guard actions. At the same time, some of them—Robert George, Germain Grisez, Donald Keefe, Paul Vitz, and others—are engaged in ambitious intellectual projects aimed at altering the terms of the discussion itself.

Governance and Finance

By 1993 the Fellowship had about a thousand members, almost equally divided between regular and associate membership. It had thus grown about tenfold since its founding in 1977, when it had barely a hundred members. Official membership is calculated on the basis of those who have been accepted and who pay their dues.

Governance is in the hands of a board of twelve who are nominated by a committee and proposed to the regular membership in a mail ballot.

The president, who serves a two-year term, is similarly elected (for the presidents see Appendix C), as are the other officers. Until 1992, Msgr. Kelly served as executive secretary of the group, handling most of its administrative work from his office at St. John's University. In that year he began relinquishing his various duties to other members.

Excluding the costs and revenues of the annual convention, the group has an income of approximately $30,000 a year, of which about 60 percent is provided by membership dues. Other monies come from some bishops and foundations. For example, during the fiscal year 1992–93, bishops gave the organization a total of $8,235, or 29 percent of its overall budget. From time to time the organization has received relatively modest grants from a few foundations—DeRance and Wethersfield primarily—for specific ventures such as publications.

Excluding the annual convention, the chief expenditure is the quarterly *Newsletter* and the proceedings of the annual convention, which together constitute about two-thirds of the annual costs. The convention is by far the largest annual expenditure, costing about $20,000, funded by registration fees but also subsidized in part by the Franciscan University of Steubenville, through the donated services of its Conference Office.

The Fellowship has maintained fairly close relations with some American bishops, choosing the site of its annual convention in part on the basis of the apparent interest of the local ordinary. Recent meetings have been held in New York, Boston, Philadelphia, Atlanta, Los Angeles, Denver, Pittsburgh, Orange (California), and Corpus Christi. Several bishops, notably Cardinal Anthony Bevilacqua of Philadelphia, Cardinal Adam Maida of Detroit, and Bishop Donald Wuerl of Pittsburgh, were members of the Fellowship before being elevated to the episcopacy. (After becoming bishops, most members do not remain active in the organization.) At various times the organization has received contributions from most of the leading members of the American hierarchy—Cardinals John J. O'Connor of New York, Bernard Law of Boston, Bevilacqua, and Roger Mahony of Los Angeles, for example—and occasionally even from some "liberal" bishops, such as Francis Quinn of Sacramento and John Cummins of Oakland.[15]

The organization annually bestows the John Cardinal Wright Award on an individual deemed to have given outstanding service to the church in intellectual matters. The award is named for an American prelate who was an official of the Papal Curia, and the recipient is chosen by the Fellowship Board (See Appendix D).

The Fellowship has usually been represented at meetings of the Joint Committee of Catholic Learned Societies, a group that meets periodically for discussion of subjects of mutual interest. Often, however, the Fellowship representative has considered himself a minority of one on controversial issues (for example, the criteria for bishops' granting an "imprimatur" to books), and the organization's long-time representative once complained that the Joint Committee "desired the bishops to accept the 'consensus' of theologians on critical issues facing the Church."[16]

Operational Activities

The Fellowship has several ways of maintaining contact among members, addressing significant issues within the church, and generally promoting its agenda. The quarterly *Newsletter* is the organization's principal organ, offering brief items of information as well as longer analyses of current Catholic issues. The *Newsletter* for fifteen years bore Kelly's strong personal stamp until Ralph McInerny became its second editor in 1992. Besides going to all members, it is sent to all bishops and to all Catholic institutions of higher learning. The group also publishes annually the proceedings of its convention.

Perhaps the most important means of networking and mutual support is the annual meeting. The first convention was held in 1977 in Kansas City, Missouri, chosen mainly for its central location. Each subsequent annual convention has been organized around a particular theme, addressed from a variety of disciplines.[17] "Historicisms and Faith" (1979), for example, focused on what is perhaps the most basic philosophical issue in contemporary religious thought—the degree to which supposedly eternal truths are conditioned by their historical milieu. A Jesuit biblical scholar proposed a deeper understanding of symbol and its relation to history, while a historian argued that history yields meaning only insofar as human beings know God as its author and fulfillment. A literary scholar found hints of transcendence in the work of T. S. Eliot and Saul Bellow, and a philosopher argued that there is a defined human nature discernible amid the flux of history.

"Christian Faith and Freedom" (1982) saw a historian, a philosopher, a political theorist, and several theologians argue for the traditional Christian notion of freedom which transcends its modern understanding as mere self-determination. The latter idea was dismissed as unfaithful to the best humanist traditions as well as to Christianity. "Faith and the Sources of Faith" (1983) concentrated mainly on faith's reality in the lives of people of faith, including Flannery O'Connor, Simone Weil, and the Welsh poet David Jones.

"Catholic Higher Education" (1989) included efforts to apply the criticisms of Allan Bloom to the situation of the Catholic universities, and ranged over such topics as the implications of public aid for religious schools, the status of particular disciplines on Catholic campuses, practical suggestions for "recatholicizing" an institution by Franciscan father Michael Scanlan of the University of Steubenville, campus ministries, the legal and juridical status of Catholic universities, the real meaning of academic freedom, and the necessary place of theology. Virtually all speakers agreed that Catholic higher education is on an unhindered path to secularization which might have been avoidable.

"The Church in the Service of the Family" (1993) concentrated on the secular institution which many Fellowship members see as most beleaguered next to the church itself, the two crises closely related. Male and female scholars attempted to harmonize the legitimate needs of women for social fulfillment with the necessities of family life, reaffirmed the family's principal function as the transmitter of life, discussed social pressures bearing on the family, and explored the family's identity as a "domestic church." As in most Fellowship activities, there was much attention to papal statements, especially John Paul II's encyclical letter *Familiaris Consortio,* and there was an address on the family as an organ of evangelization by the president of the Vatican's Council on the Family, Cardinal Alfonso Lopez Trujillo.

Thus most convention programs are planned around a subject that has practical applications in the church and the world and is the focus of controversy. Scholars address the issue from a theoretical standpoint, attempting to connect it with the deepest springs of the Catholic tradition, but with an eye to practical prescriptions.

Conclusion

Fellowship members disagree with many of what they perceive to be the dominant liberal positions in American Catholic intellectual life, and their disagreement is linked to their sense of alienation from the institutions of that life. Fellowship members oppose the directions in which Catholic higher education has gone since 1965,[18] but are in no position to change it. Fellowship members believe that Catholic higher education ought to be different from secular institutions of higher learning. Thus Kelly argued that academic freedom "assures institutional autonomy far more than it protects the speech of either teacher or student," and urged that Catholic colleges withstand both internal opposition and external criticism in order to protect the integrity of Catholic teaching and practice.[19] Like other Fellowship members, he defended the dismissal of the moral theologian Charles Curran from the faculty of Catholic University of America, on the grounds that the university belied its name and its character by tolerating theological dissent.[20] In this regard the Fellowship looks to the original statement on academic freedom by the American Association of University Professors, which allowed dismissal of faculty by church-affiliated institutions for doctrinal reasons, provided that the institution offered a clear statement of its rules.[21] Some members also regard the rhetoric of academic freedom as suspect, and believe that some of their own members have suffered professionally for dissenting from academic orthodoxy.[22]

In addition to their general concerns about higher education, Fellowship members assume that they must address precisely those issues that are most contested in the church, including those that have in effect been dismissed as no longer worth discussing. Thus several members—May, Grisez, Janet Smith—have been prominent defenders of *Humanae Vitae* years after it ceased to be discussed by most American Catholic moral theologians. This strong sense of fighting unpopular causes unlikely to bring rewards was expressed in a special commendation given by the organization to the Jesuit moralist John Ford in 1988, shortly before he died. Ford had publicly defended *Humanae Vitae* in 1968, had advised Cardinal Patrick O'Boyle of Washington on how to deal with dissent, and as a result, the commendation stated, "he experienced others' hostility and lived with their alienation. Truly, the experience has been a slow martyrdom, and one not yet ended."[23]

The Fellowship takes no political positions as such, although a large number of members supported the Reagan-Bush administrations over the question of abortion. Members' interventions on public issues have been confined mainly to questions in which some principle of Catholic moral teaching seems to be at stake. Thus when the American bishops proposed a pastoral letter on the economy in 1986, the *Newsletter*, rather than defending the workings of the free market, as did some other conservative Catholics, criticized the letter for accepting the premise of a worldwide "population crisis," which it said was alarmist and empirically unproven,[24] while Kelly argued that the letter was essentially faithful to traditional Catholic social teaching and that its criticisms of the capitalist system should be heeded.[25] In giving its special award to Ford, the Fellowship cited his moral opposition to American saturation bombing during World War II as a courageous practical application of an absolute moral principle.[26] Grisez and Finnis, two prominent Fellowship members, have argued for an absolute prohibition on nuclear weaponry.[27]

If the collapse of the Thomistic ascendancy in American Catholic intellectual life helped stimulate the establishment of the organization, not all members necessarily regard themselves as Thomists. Probably a majority of the theologians and philosophers do, but there are also people working in the Anglo-Saxon analytical tradition, in phenomenology, and in other philosophical schools, even as many in secular disciplines do not have a consciously formulated philosophical position of their own. All are united by what they understand to be the authentic doctrines of the church.

Thus the Fellowship's approach to every subject is likely to be on three levels: (1) restatement and defense of traditional Catholic doctrine, especially when under attack; (2) philosophical arguments showing the reasonableness of those doctrines; and (3) empirical arguments demonstrating that, where Catholic doctrine has practical applications (for example, on family life), disregarding it results in social disasters. Thus the overall intellectual picture that the organization espouses is in effect the traditional Thomistic idea that the universe is an intelligible whole, faith rests on rational foundations, and the law of God expresses itself through both divine revelation and nature. Faith does not force a rejection of the natural order; rather, the abandonment of faith itself disturbs the natural order. The errors of modernity are considered to be at least as much the forsaking of "right reason" as of religious faith.

Perhaps mainly because of their strong sense of being a cognitive minority, there are relatively few public disagreements among Fellowship members, and practically no continuing debates. One of the very few such splits was in response to the attempts by Grisez to create an ambitious new formulation of Catholic moral theology, *The Way of the Lord Jesus.* While the work inspired high praise from some members, it also brought forth claims that it departed from classical Thomism in significant and damaging ways and was intellectually unsound.[28]

The Fellowship would not need to exist if the world were as its members believe it should be. In 1960 they would have been content with existing Catholic intellectual institutions, including professional societies, and probably would have found the idea of a comprehensive, interdisciplinary group of this kind both impractical and unnecessary. By the late 1970s, however, its growing membership harbored a strong sense that the world, and especially the Catholic world, was not as it should be. Regarding themselves unabashedly as "Roman Catholics," they detected a growing estrangement between the Vatican and some of the leadership of American Catholicism.[29] Often looking to Cardinal Joseph Ratzinger for intellectual bearings, they tended to agree with his pessimistic view of the state of the church.[30]

When the leftist Catholic philosopher Thomas Sheehan asserted that there are no valid historical claims to be made on behalf of Christianity, he was refuted by some liberal Catholics. However, some Fellowship members almost welcomed his remarks as showing the inevitable end of liberal Christianity and as stating candidly what others had only implied. The *Newsletter* endorsed Sheehan's claim that much of the Catholic educational machinery was under the sway of people who shared his assumptions, and it hinted that those liberals who denied Sheehan's claims were being disingenuous.[31]

Given this view of the Catholic intellectual situation, the Fellowship predicates its existence on a gamble whose stakes are very high indeed, not merely the survival of more or less traditional kinds of Catholicism, or alternative ways of theologizing, but the very possibility of making claims of truth which support historical Christianity. This estimate of the present historical situation of the church has thus spawned an organization whose members believe that they have been entrusted with a task of importance and urgency, but who also doubt that they will see that task successfully completed in their lifetimes.

Prominent Fellowship Members and the Nature of Their Work

• Elizabeth Anscombe (philosophy), Cambridge University. Wittgenstein scholar, exponent of Catholic sexual morality, including *Humanae Vitae*.[32]

• Kenneth Baker, S.J. (theology), editor of the *Homiletic and Pastoral Review*, a magazine for priests. Former president of the University of Seattle.

• William Bentley Ball (law—private practice). Perhaps the leading "conservative" lawyer in church-state cases, with numerous pleadings before the United States Supreme Court.[33]

• J. Brian Benestad (theology), University of Scranton. Specialist in Catholic social teachings, especially of the papacy.[34]

• Gerald Bradley (law), University of Notre Dame. Scholar of church-state issues.[35]

• Francis Canavan, S.J. (political theory), Fordham University. Relation of morality and law, church and state.[36]

• Warren Carroll (history), Christendom College. Founder of Christendom, one of the "neo-Catholic" colleges. Author of a number of historical works.[37]

• Joseph Fessio, S.J. (theology), Ignatius Press. Founder of the St. Ignatius Institute at the University of San Francisco, an attempt to organize a "neo-Catholic" program within a larger institution. Founder of Ignatius Press, the principal conservative Catholic publishing house in the United States.

• John Finnis (philosophy), Oxford University. An exponent of traditional Catholic moral doctrine within the general framework of the British analytical philosophical tradition.[38]

• Robert George (politics), Princeton University. Relationship of law and morality within the framework of both traditional natural-law theory and analytic philosophy.[39]

• Germain Grisez (philosophy), St. Mary's College (Md.). Outspoken defender of *Humanae Vitae*. Author of a systematic attempt to rethink all of Catholic moral theology.[40]

• James Hitchcock (history), St. Louis University. Author of a number of books on the contemporary religious situation.[41] First editor of the American edition of *Communio*.

• F. Russell Hittinger (philosophy), Catholic University of America. Natural-law theorist.[42]

• Donald J. Keefe, S.J. (theology), St. Joseph's Seminary, Archdiocese of New York. Author of a systematic effort at rethinking Catholic sacramental theology.[43]

•George A. Kelly (sociology), St. John's University (N.Y.) (emeritus). Author of a number of works on the contemporary church.[44] Founder and long-time executive secretary of the Fellowship.

•Assumpta Long, O.P. (theology), Dominican Sisters of Nashville. Theologian, leading figure in attempts to strengthen traditional forms of religious life in America.

•Ralph McInerny (philosophy), University of Notre Dame. Thomistic scholar, author of popular detective stories ("Father Dowling"), cofounder of *Crisis* magazine.[45]

•William E. May (theology), John Paul II Center for Marriage and the Family (Washington, D.C.). Defender of *Humanae Vitae* and other controverted moral teachings, former professor at Catholic University of America.[46]

•Marvin O'Connell (history), University of Notre Dame. Has written on a wide variety of historical subjects.[47]

•Glenn Olsen (history), University of Utah. Medievalist who has also written extensively on contemporary religious and educational issues.[48]

•Janet Smith (theology), University of Dallas. Author of a comprehensive work on *Humanae Vitae*.[49]

•William B. Smith (theology), St. Joseph's Seminary, Archdiocese of New York. Moral theologian who has lectured widely on controversial issues.

•Joseph A. Varacalli (sociology), Nassau Community College (N.Y.). Relationship of society and moral values.[50]

•Paul Vitz (psychology), New York University. Contemporary moral education, relationship of modern psychology to religion.[51]

•Michael J. Wrenn (catechetics), Archdiocese of New York. Leading advocate of strong doctrinal content in catechetical works.[52]

Fellowship of Catholic Scholars

Statement of Purpose—Application for Membership

Applicants for membership should first study the purposes of the fellowship.

These purposes may be stated as follows:

1. We Catholic scholars in various disciplines join in fellowship in order to serve Jesus Christ better by helping one another in our work and by putting our abilities more fully at the service of the Catholic faith.

2. We wish to form a fellowship of scholars who see their intellectual work as an expression of the service that they owe to God. To Him we give thanks for our Catholic faith and for every opportunity He gives us to serve that faith.

3. We wish to form a fellowship of Catholic scholars open to the work of the Holy Spirit within the church. Thus we wholeheartedly accept and support the renewal of the Church of Christ undertaken by Pope John XXIII, shaped by Vatican II, and carried on by succeeding pontiffs.

4. We accept as the rule of our life and thought the entire faith of the Catholic Church. This we see not merely in solemn definitions but in the ordinary teaching of the Pope and those bishops in union with him, and also embodied in those modes of worship and ways of Christian life and practice, of the present as of the past, which have been in harmony with the teaching of St. Peter's successors in the see of Rome.

5. The questions raised by contemporary thought must be considered with courage and dealt with in honesty. We will seek to do this, faithful to the truth always guarded in the Church by the Holy Spirit and sensitive to the needs of the family of faith. We wish to accept a responsibility which a Catholic scholar may not evade: to assist everyone, so far as we are able, to personal assent to the mystery of Christ as made manifest through the lived faith of the Church, His Body, and through the active charity without which faith is dead.

6. To contribute to this sacred work, our fellowship will strive to
   • come to know and welcome all who share our purpose;
   • make known to one another our various competencies and interests;
   • share our abilities with one another unstintingly in our efforts directed to our common purpose;
   • cooperate in clarifying the challenges which must be met;
   • help one another to evaluate critically the variety of responses which are proposed to these challenges;
   • communicate our suggestions and evaluation to members of the Church who might find them helpful;

• respond to requests to help the Church in its task of guarding the faith as inviolable and defending it with fidelity;

• help one another to work through, in scholarly and prayerful fashion and without public dissent, any problems which may arise from magisterial teaching.

7. With the grace of God for which we pray, we hope to assist the whole Church to understand its own identity more clearly, to proclaim the joyous Gospel of Jesus more confidently, and to carry out its redemptive mission of all human-kind more effectively.

APPENDIX C

Presidents of the Fellowship of Catholic Scholars

Ronald Lawler, O.F.M.Cap.	Josephinum Seminary	1977–79
James Hitchcock	St. Louis University	1979–81
(Rev.) William B. Smith	St. Joseph's Seminary (N.Y.)	1981–83
Earl Weis, S.J.	Loyola University (Ill.)	1983–85
(Msgr.) George A. Kelly	St. John's University (N.Y.)	1985–87
William E. May	Catholic University of America	1987–89
Kenneth Baker, S.J.	*Homiletic and Pastoral Review*	1989–91
Ralph McInerny	University of Notre Dame	1991–

APPENDIX D

John Cardinal Wright Award

1979	(Msgr.) George A. Kelly	St. John's University (N.Y.)
1980	William E. May	Catholic University of America
1981	James Hitchcock	St. Louis University
1982	John Connery, S.J.	Loyola University (Ill.)
1983	Germain Grisez	St. Mary's College (Md.)
1984	John A. Hardon, S.J.	Institute for Religious Life
1985	Herbert Ratner	Oak Park, Ill.
1986	Joseph Scottino	Gannon University
1987	Joseph Fessio, S.J.	Ignatius Press
	Joseph Farraher, S.J.	San Francisco
1988	John F. Harvey, O.S.F.S.	Courage (New York City)
1989	John Finnis	Oxford University
1990	Ronald Lawler, O.F.M.Cap.	Diocese of Pittsburgh
1991	Francis Canavan, S.J.	Fordham University
1992	Donald J. Keefe, S.J.	Archdiocese of Denver
1993	Janet Smith	University of Dallas
1994	Jude Dougherty	Catholic University of America

568 Regular Members, Fellowship of Catholic Scholars

Age		Gender		Status	
21–30:	.002%	Male:	88.9%	Priest:	38.5%
31–40:	9.7	Female:	11.1	Religious:	5.4
41–50:	23.2			Lay:	56.2
51–60:	24.8				
61+:	41.5				

Highest Degree		Institution of Highest Degree		Subjects	
Ph.D.:	70.1%	Secular:	42.3%	Theology:	24.5%
S.T.D.:	11.8	Catholic:	57.7	Humanities:	12.0
M.D.:	6.0			Philosophy:	20.5
J.D.:	5.4			Social Sciences:	6.9
M.A.:	3.2			Health:	7.6
Other:	3.4			Law:	6.4
				Other:	21.8

Occupations		Teaching Positions	
Academic:	67.9%	Catholic Colleges:	68.8%
Church:	14.8	Seminaries	5.0
Other:	21.8	Non-Catholic	26.3

NOTES

1. For a discussion of this, see Hitchcock, *The Decline and Fall of Radical Catholicism* (New York: Herder and Herder, 1971).

2. Since the author has been actively involved in the Fellowship from its beginning, some of the information in this article is based on personal experience.

3. For a summary of this debate, see Hitchcock, "Catholic Activist Conservatism in the United States," in Martin E. Marty and R. Scott Appleby, eds., *Fundamentalisms Observed* (Chicago: University of Chicago Press, 1991), pp. 102–104.

4. Anthony Kosnik, ed., *Human Sexuality: New Directions in American Catholic Thought* (New York: Paulist Press, 1977).

5. Unless otherwise indicated, information about Fellowship procedures and governance is taken from unpublished documents in possession of the author.

6. See, for example, George A. Kelly's comments on Dulles in *Inside My Father's House* (New York: Doubleday, 1989), pp. 274–76, and his book *The New Biblical Theorists: Raymond E. Brown and Beyond* (Ann Arbor, Mich.: Servant Books, 1983).

7. For a discussion of the overall subject, see Patrick Allitt, *Catholic Intellectuals and Conservative Politics in America, 1950–1985* (Ithaca, N.Y.: Cornell University Press, 1993).

8. See the discussion in Kelly, *Inside My Father's House*, pp. 324–35. On one occasion, at which the author of this study was present, the president of the American bishops, Archbishop John R. Quinn of San Francisco, directly rebuffed a delegation of Fellowship officers who traveled to an appointment with him in Washington.

9. The proposed catechism was discussed in issues of the *Newsletter* for March 1986, September and December 1990, December 1991, and September 1992.

10. Committee report, "Concerning Catholic Higher Education," *Newsletter* 9, no. 1 (December 1985): 5–7, 12.

11. Eugene V. Clark, "Exposition of the Blessed Sacrament and Rules for Interpreting Liturgical Regulations," *Newsletter* 10, no. 1 (June 1987): 6–8.

12. Edward M. Egan, "The Nullity of Marriage," *Newsletter* 10, no. 1 (December 1986): 9–11, 20. Bishop Egan was a former judge of the Sacred Roman Rota, the highest marriage tribunal in Rome.

13. "Is a Female Priesthood Possible?" *Newsletter* 13, no. 1 (December 1989): 3–5.

14. Joseph Nicolosi, "Repetitive Theory and Therapy of Male Homosexuality," *Newsletter* 15, no. 4 (September 1992): 19–20; John F. Harvey, O.S.F.S., "Sexual Abstinence for Homosexual Persons," ibid., pp. 20–22.

15. Bishops' donations are periodically acknowledged in the *Newsletter.*

16. William May, "Meeting of the Learned Societies," *Newsletter* 8, no. 1 (November 1984): 5.

17. Papers presented at the convention are published in the annual *Proceedings of the Fellowship of Catholic Scholars.*

18. See the essay by Mary Jo Weaver in this volume.

19. "Academic Freedom and the Catholic College," *Newsletter* 10, no. 4 (September 1987): 11–12.

20. "Charles Curran and the ACCU," *Newsletter* 9, no. 3 (June 1986): 1, 3–4.

21. The statement in question was used by the AAUP from 1940 until sometime in the 1960s.

22. For a summary of earlier cases, see Kelly, *Inside My Father's House*, p. 299. In 1990, Janet Smith, author of a book defending *Humanae Vitae*, was denied tenure at the University of Notre Dame, a decision regarded by many Fellowship members as punitive, and the Jesuit theologian Donald Keefe was required by his religious superiors to resign his professorship at Marquette University.

23. Text of the presentation is in the *Newsletter* 12, no. 1 (December 1988): 13–14.

24. "The Economic Pastoral: Draft Three," *Newsletter* 9, no. 4 (September 1986): 3–4.

25. "'The Bishops' Economic Pastoral," *Newsletter* 10, no. 2 (March 1987): 9–10.

26. *Newsletter* 12, no. 1 (December 1988): 14.

27. With Joseph Boyle, *Nuclear Deterrence, Morality, and Realism* (Oxford: Clarendon Press, 1987).

28. Besides Grisez the disputants included F. Russell Hittinger, May, and Joseph Koterski, S.J. Exchanges were published in the *Newsletter* for June 1984, March and June 1989.

29. Michael Schwartz, "Causa Finita Est," *Newsletter* 12, no. 1 (December 1988): 3–7.

30. *The Ratzinger Report* (San Francisco: Ignatius Press, 1987) was a widely read interview with the head of the Congregation of the Doctrine of the Faith in Rome, in which he expressed pessimistic opinions about the progress of postconciliar renewal.

31. Sheehan's comments were published in the *New York Review of Books,* 14 June 1984. For the Fellowship reaction see "Where Is the Truth?" *Newsletter* 7, no. 4 (September 1984), and "The Liberal Consensus," ibid. 8, no. 1 (November 1984): 1–3.

32. Elizabeth Anscombe, *Ethics, Religion, and Politics* (Minneapolis: University of Minnesota Press, 1981); *From Parmenides to Wittgenstein* (Minneapolis: University of Minnesota Press, 1981); *An Introduction to Wittgenstein's Tractatus* (New York: Harper and Row, 1965).

33. William Bentley Ball, ed., *In Search of a National Morality* (San Francisco: Ignatius Press, and Grand Rapids, Mich.: Baker Book House, 1992).

34. J. Brian Benestad, *Quest for Justice* (Washington, D.C.: National Council of Catholic Bishops, 1981).

35. Gerald Bradley, *Church-State Relationships in America* (New York: Greenwood Press, 1987); (with Robert Barry, O.P.) *Set No Limits: A Rebuttal to Daniel Callahan's Proposal to Limit Health Care for the Elderly* (Urbana: University of Illinois Press, 1991).

36. Francis Canavan, S.J., *Freedom of Expression: Purpose as Limit* (Durham: North Carolina Academic Press, 1984).

37. Warren Carroll is engaged in writing a multivolume history of the Christian West (Front Royale, Va.: Christendom College Press), among other projects.

38. John Finnis, *Moral Absolutes* (Washington, D.C.: Catholic University of America Press, 1991); *Natural Law and Natural Rights* (Oxford: Clarendon Press, 1980).

39. Robert George, *Natural Law Theory* (Oxford: Clarendon Press, 1992).

40. Germain Grisez, *The Way of the Lord Jesus,* 2 vols. (San Francisco: Ignatius Press, 1987).

41. James Hitchcock, *Decline and Fall: Catholicism and Modernity* (New York: Crossroad, 1978); *What Is Secular Humanism?* (Ann Arbor, Mich.: Servant Books, 1984).

42. F. Russell Hittinger, *A Critique of the New Natural Law Theory* (Notre Dame, Ind.: University of Notre Dame Press, 1987).

43. Donald J. Keefe, S.J., *Thomism and the Ontological Theology of Paul Tillich* (Leiden, the Netherlands: Brill, 1971); *Covenantal Theology,* 2 vols. (Lanham, Md.: University Press of America, 1991).

44. George A. Kelly, *The Crisis of Authority* (Chicago: Regnery Gateway, 1982); *Birth Control and Catholics* (Garden City, N.Y.: Doubleday, 1963); *The New Biblical Theorists* (Ann Arbor, Mich: Servant Books, 1983).

45. Ralph McInerny, *Being and Predication* (Washington, D.C.: Catholic University of America Press, 1986); *Boethius and Aquinas* (Washington, D.C.: Catholic University of America Press, 1990); *St. Thomas Aquinas* (Boston: Twayne Publishers, 1977).

46. William E. May, *An Introduction to Moral Theology* (Huntington, Ind.: Our Sunday Visitor Press, 1991); *Moral Absolutes* (Milwaukee: Marquette University Press, 1989).

47. Marvin O'Connell, *John Ireland* (Minneapolis: Minnesota Historical Society, 1989); *The Counter-Reformation* (New York: Harper and Row, 1974); *The Oxford Conspirators* (New York: Macmillan, 1969).

48. Glenn Olsen has published widely in journals such as *Speculum, Traditio,* and *Thought.*

49. Janet Smith, *On Humanae Vitae: A Generation Later* (Washington, D.C.: Catholic University of America Press, 1991).

50. Joseph A. Varacalli, *Towards the Establishment of Liberal Catholicism in America* (Washington, D.C.: University Press of America, 1983).

51. Paul Vitz, *Censorship: Evidence of Bias in Our Children's Textbooks* (Ann Arbor, Mich.: Servant Books, 1986); *Psychology as Religion* (Grand Rapids, Mich.: Eerdmans, 1977); *Sigmund Freud's Christian Unconscious* (New York: Guilford Press, 1988).

52. Michael J. Wrenn, *Catechisms and Controversies* (San Francisco: Ignatius Press, 1991).

PART III
Outsider Perspectives

9

The Marian Revival in American Catholicism
Focal Points and Features of the New Marian Enthusiasm

SANDRA L. ZIMDARS-SWARTZ

Prologue

Roman Catholic Marian devotion in the United States today is a complex phenomenon with a complicated history. Various ethnic traditions of Marian piety from Eastern and Western Europe and Latin America have been established and have interacted here for many years, sometimes solidifying ethnic identities, sometimes succumbing to pressures of acculturation and disappearing, and sometimes coalescing with other forces and movements in ways that we have barely begun to understand.

Among the traditional expressions of Marian devotion that have been the object of some scholarly attention are parish-based devotions of various kinds, private prayers and novenas, popular devotional images and artifacts, pilgrimages to Marian shrines, Marian hymns and liturgies. The proliferation of official and unofficial pronouncements by church authorities to inform and guide this piety of the laity is also an important factor in Marian devotionalism and has often been the focus of scholarly attention. Much less studied are those expressions of Marian piety presumed to be less well established or peripheral. These include lay organizations dedicated to particular Marian devotions or missions, the hundreds of publicly and privately printed books and pamphlets, traveling statues and images, Marian centers and their newsletters, Marian conferences and the persons who speak at them, and the visits, whether ad hoc or well-organized, of many thousands of American Catholics to the sites of alleged Marian apparitions.

It is not my intention here to attempt a comprehensive history of American Catholic Marian devotion or even a comprehensive survey of its present-day manifestations. This chapter, rather, focuses on some phenomena surrounding recent alleged Marian apparitions that have been focal points for both personal and cultural anxieties and, for many American Catholics, a context for the construction of a renewed Catholic identity through a personal appropriation of Marian imagery.

The study of Marian devotion around recent Marian apparitions raises some important issues that are not easily resolved, the first of which concerns the number of such apparitions. Many devotees are convinced that in the past ten or fifteen years, there has been a proliferation of appearances of the Blessed Virgin. All that the scholar can say, however, is that, perhaps as a result of the publicity accorded to Medjugorje, a great deal of public attention has been given in recent years to what might otherwise have been private or semiprivate Marian visions and locutions. Conversations with many people who participate in apparition-related devotions suggest that such phenomena are not uncommon experiences among American Catholics, but that few of these are shared in ways or in circumstances that would lead to their being treated as apparitions. It would seem that even now, only a small percentage of these experiences are coming to public attention. Those in the public eye are receiving more attention than in the past and are generating more interest on the part of the local and national media.

A second important issue raised by the study of recent apparition-related Marian devotion concerns the institutional affiliations or influences that may affect or be affected by these phenomena. Some of the Catholics who visit the sites of recent apparitions or who participate in the networks that circulate information about them are explicit about their affiliation with the charismatic movement, but others say nothing to suggest any charismatic influence or even to specifically disavow such influence. Some of this devotion has been shaped directly or indirectly by members of religious orders, for example, Medjugorje-related piety by the Franciscans, and devotion at Conyers, Georgia, by some nearby Cistercians; but some of it shows no such influence. Some apparition-related piety, such as that at Lubbock, Texas, and Scottsdale, Arizona, has been incorporated into the life of particular parishes, but some, of course, has not. Finally, a considerable amount of recent apparition-related devotion has been linked with conservative social movements, particularly the anti-abortion movement; but there are also devotees of recent apparitions who reject these linkages.

While there are a few studies that focus on and shed some light on some of these issues in a European or a worldwide context,[1] a study has yet to be done that would sort out and clarify the institutional affiliations and influences that have been important for recent apparition-related Marian devotion in the United States. In the meantime, it will be instructive to focus attention on two rather new institutions whose ties to recent Marian apparitions are especially apparent: Marian centers and Marian conferences.

The phenomena we will look at must be seen in the context of what most new Marian devotees see as a great revival of Marian devotion today, after about two decades of decline or lukewarmness in the wake of the Second Vatican Council. Indeed, the perception of such a revival has become so widespread that the scholar has good reason now simply to treat this revival as a fact. To understand the memories and the mindset of the American Catholics who are at the forefront of this movement, it will be useful to begin with some comments about the treatment of the Virgin Mary in the documents of the Second Vatican Council, a "profile" of Marian devotion published in 1968, several years after the end of the Council, and a sketch of some of the events of the 1980s that are seen as having launched this revival.

From Vatican II to Medjugorje:
The Background of the Marian Revival

After much debate, the theologians gathered at the Second Vatican Council decided to put their discussion of the Virgin Mary, which might have been treated as an independent topic, into *Lumen Gentium*, which is a discussion of the nature of the church. This decision seemed to many to mark a significant shift in Catholic Marian theology, for here Mary was being presented as a person closely identified with and indeed as one of the pilgrim people of God. Many of those who welcomed the Council's ecumenical overtures and irenic spirit understood Mary's portrayal as a model of the faithful Christian to be an important step forward, both in the ecumenical dialogue and in Catholic Mariology.

Whatever position the Council took on Mary was likely to cause some controversy. It was widely held that the Council's pronouncements would dampen enthusiasm for "popular" forms of Marian devotion, but there was little agreement about whether this outcome was desirable. There were many Catholics at that time who believed that popular devotions had gotten quite out of hand and that Marian apparitions, in particular, were little more than superstition. There were many other Catholics, however, whose personal piety had been very much influenced by apparitions such as Lourdes and Fatima, which the church had declared worthy of "the assent of human faith" and which before the Council had been an important touchstone of Catholic identity in many Catholic schools.

The popular perception was correct: devotion to Mary did change after the Council. Fewer people said the rosary, attended evening novenas, and showed enthusiasm for pilgrimages to apparition sites. While this slackening of Marian devotion was perceived as a step forward in some quarters, it was viewed as a serious cause for alarm in others. Within a few years after the close of the Council, there arose a lament among some parish priests and theologians that in its wake there had been a general and regrettable decline in matters of Marian devotion. A cry of alarm can be clearly heard, for example, in the Reverend Joseph E. Manton's paper "Profile of Marian Devotion on the Parochial Level" in the 1968 issue of *Marian Studies*. Manton described himself as "an ordinary ecclesiastical GI," who for six months had been trying "dutifully and sometimes deviously" to ascertain from his fellow clergy the state of Marian devotion in their parishes. He had, in addition, haphazardly monitored the entire spectrum represented in the Catholic press. He stated as his overall impression that "public devotion to Our Lady, if measured by perpetual novenas, October Devotions, May Processions and the like, has definitely deteriorated."[2]

Manton did not believe that this deterioration was directly due to the documents of Vatican II, since few laypersons had read them. Rather, he suggested, it was the result of an impression built on secondhand information from commentators and from the occasional religious article in the secular press. Manton argued that the average layperson had a vague idea that since the Council the Virgin Mary had been downgraded in importance, and he provided examples of this alleged downgrading. He cited the view, reportedly taught in a catechism class, that the Annunciation didn't happen but was just a literary form. He related a story about a priest announcing at a West Coast workshop, "We have affection for Mary but no cult."[3] Finally, he pointed to the attempt by liberal Catholics, in the interest of ecumenism, to remove statues of Mary from churches.

Manton believed that this downgrading of Mary was based on a misreading of Council documents and a misinterpretation of its intentions. Because the Council affirmed that Mary was the Mother of God, he said, she was clearly above all creatures and worthy of devotion, and he pointed to some clear expressions of this devotion in the ceremonies of the Council itself. For example, on the final day of the Council's third session, Pope Paul VI concelebrated Mass with the bishops of dioceses having major Marian shrines, and Manton noted that this Mass was preceded by half an hour of Marian hymns sung by the Sistine Choir at the pope's express direction.

Manton conceded, nonetheless, that there were connections between the Council and the recent noticeable decline in Marian devotion. Clearly, he said, fewer people were now saying the rosary, and he saw this as an indirect and unintended result of one of the basic changes sanctioned by the Council. Before the Council, the Mass had been the private preserve of the priest, and laypersons had naturally turned to their rosaries for a sense of active participation. But with the changes in the Mass approved at the Council, in "this brave new day of dialogue and participation,"[4] the rosary, Manton was sad to say, has been relegated to the inferior status of a private devotion.

Manton also commented on a decline in novenas, and associated it both with characteristics of the postconciliar church and with changes and trends in American culture. When Mass had been offered only in the early morning, he observed, public novenas in the afternoon or the evening probably seemed to many to be an attractive alternative. Now that Masses were offered several times during the day, however, and now that a more active participation was possible in the liturgy, people who had previously gone to novenas were instead attending Masses. Manton pointed also to the general social malaise of the 1960s and to the decline in morals in a postconciliar church that had made people "spiritually flabby and anemic"[5] and less willing to make sacrifices. There was also, now, the problem of crime-ridden neighborhoods around many churches, as well as the attraction of television.

While Manton's article gives us a picture of the frustrations of many Catholic Marian devotees in the years following the Council, a feature article on Mary and Marian devotion by Richard Ostling in the December 1991 issue of *Time* magazine well summarizes much of what has led in more recent years to their excitement. As evidence of a revival of Marian devotion in the 1980s and early 1990s, Ostling cited the increased numbers of pilgrims, including young people, flocking to Marian shrines around the world. For example, he noted that in 1989 and 1990, annual attendance at Lourdes increased 10 percent, to 5.5 million, with some of this increase coming from a new influx of pilgrims from Eastern Europe. In the wake of a visit from Pope John Paul II in 1979, attendance at the Marian shrine at Knock, Ireland, doubled to 1.5 million pilgrims. Before travel to Yugoslavia became difficult, the reported apparition at Medjugorje drew some 10 million pilgrims annually.[6] And at Emittsburg, Maryland, yearly attendance at the National Shrine Grotto of Our Lady of Lourdes has doubled to half a million people.

As further evidence of a Marian revival, Ostling cited the increasing number of reported Marian apparitions. Reports of appearances of the Blessed Virgin, he noted, have been coming in recent years from all corners of the world, including Nicaragua, Ukraine, Japan, Rwanda, and the United States. The most important of these apparitions, of course, has been that reported by six young people beginning in June 1981 in Medjugorje, now in the republic of Bosnia-Herzegovina. Those who believe in the authenticity of this apparition, Ostling observed, have formed some extensive networks, whose members cooperate in disseminating information, organizing pilgrimages, sponsoring prayer groups, and promoting Marian devotion in general.

It would be a mistake to say that the apparition at Medjugorje has been the cause of the recent resurgence of some traditional forms of Marian devotion. But in the United States, Medjugorje has clearly been related to and has provided a context for such a resurgence. It has been associated with demands for a return to traditional understandings of Catholic doctrine, with a renewed campaign for papal statements declaring Mary to be Coredemptrix and Mediatrix of All Graces, and with some strident calls for public protests and other forms of political action on issues such as abortion, artificial birth control, and homosexuality. The American Catholic Marian revival which has been associated with Medjugorje, however, involves much more than a resurgence of "traditional" Catholic devotions and values, as we will see in the following discussion of some of its key focal points and features.

Marian Centers and Their Proliferation in the Wake of Medjugorje

Although the alleged apparition at Medjugorje began drawing Catholic pilgrims from the United States as early as 1983 and 1984, René Laurentin, a well-known Marian scholar who has recently become an enthusiast for a number of contemporary apparitions, noted that when he began to speak in the United States about Medjugorje in those years, his talks were received with restraint and reservation. In 1985, however, he was interviewed at length on Medjugorje, and that year, he believes, marked a kind of turning point in this country for interest in the subject. It was two years after that, he says, that the rush really began and Americans were suddenly interested in apparition sites.[7] Indeed, if one peruses the Catholic Periodical Index, one finds that it was in 1987 and 1988 that articles about Medjugorje began to proliferate in the Catholic media.

Especially important for spreading the word about Medjugorje have been the Marian centers and prayer groups formed by people who have been on one or more pilgrimages to this apparition site. There have been several motivations for establishing these institutions. Although the initial impulse seems to have been the felt need of the founders to repay the Virgin for a grace they believe they received at the site, a second, perhaps more important reason was a concern for the Virgin's messages about the need for prayer groups. She is reported to have said at Medjugorje, "Yes, there is a need for a prayer group, not only in this parish, but in all parishes. A spiritual renewal is necessary for the entire church."[8] A third impetus which appears in some of the responses is the apocalyptic end-time scenario in terms of which many devotees of the Medjugorje apparition have understood the Medjugorje messages. Important here are the ten secrets that each of the visionaries is said to receive from the Virgin, some of which are thought to pertain to imminent, historic events of global importance. Since it is believed that there will be only a short time between the announcement of the content of these secrets and the events to which they refer, some respondents have seen a need for a nationwide network of centers to be in place to distribute this important information just as soon as it should be announced. Recent issues of *Mary's People* (a supplement to the *National Catholic Register*) list 175 Marian centers.

In the spring of 1993 I sent a survey to the directors of these centers. In addition to a question about the motivation for establishing the centers, there were questions about when they were founded and by whom, how they were organized, what services they offered (bookstore, prayer groups, speakers' bureau, newsletter), whether they had a mailing or membership list and how extensive it was, what information they distributed, whether any charisms were reported among those with whom they were associated, and what they believed to be the main issues relating to Marian devotion in the wake of the Second Vatican Council. About one-third of the directors or contact persons for these 175 centers replied, some sending examples of the newsletters, brochures, books, and videotapes they have available. The following is a summary of some of the information gathered from the responses to this survey.

There were a few centers founded in 1984, 1985, and 1986, but the peak years of establishment were 1987, 1988, and 1989, coinciding with the extensive reporting on Medjugorje in the Catholic press and with the increased pilgrimage activity. A few centers have been founded in subsequent years. Interestingly, only a handful of these were founded by priests. Indeed, most of the centers were established by laypersons, that is, individuals, couples, or small groups of people who had been on a pilgrimage to Medjugorje. Most of the founders were moved by a desire to express their gratitude to the Virgin for graces received during their pilgrimages, and believed they could best do this by making information available on Medjugorje. Although several people expressed concern over the proliferation of centers, only one (whose center was founded in 1992) listed as a primary motivation the desire to bring all Marian centers into unity because there was too much conflict and competition among them.

The services that these centers offer vary widely. Some dispense only information, usually through brochures or newsletters, while others support prayer groups, bookstores, a speakers' bureau, and pilgrimages. Many of the books made available by the centers are published by the Riehle Foundation, which has recently changed its name to Faith Publications of Milford, Ohio. This center claims some of the most popular and significant publications within the movement, including Michael Brown's *The Final Hour*, Laurentin's *Our Lord and Our Lady in Scottsdale*, and four volumes of messages from the Scottsdale visionaries entitled *I Am Your Jesus of Mercy* and *Apostolate of Holy Motherhood* (messages to an anonymous visionary designated "Mariamente"). Some of the centers distribute information only on Medjugorje, while others also dispense information on apparitions approved by the Roman Catholic Church, or on all reported apparitions.

The membership and mailing lists of these centers also show considerable variation. The Pittsburgh Center for Peace (McKees Rocks, Pennsylvania) claims to have a list of about 150,000 names, and its newsletter, *Our Lady, Queen of Peace*, is widely distributed, both by other centers and at conferences and apparition sites. Two centers reported lists of about 30,000 names, but the majority claim direct contact with no more than a few thousand or a few hundred people. Most of the centers are in informal contact with other centers and founders. About half of the centers reported that charisms (visions, locutions, healings) have been experienced either by members of the center or in groups sponsored by it, but only a few provided any details about these charisms.

Virtually all of those responding to the question of the issues pertaining to Marian devotion in the wake of the Second Vatican Council believed that the documents of the Council had been widely misunderstood or misinterpreted. Priests, they said, had misunderstood the intent of Vatican II with regard to Mary, and one person said that the Council has been used "to promote whatever priests, nuns, etc. want to promote." Another wrote with passion about the decline of Marian devotion in the church after the Council and the reception of those who try to keep it alive:

> Marian devotion has practically disappeared in the Catholic Church. The rosary, First Saturdays, her images, novenas, etc. are viewed as unnecessary relics from a past age that merely clutter up our "enlightened" and "renewed" church. Her virtues are ridiculed and her crucial role in salvation history is ignored, distorted, derided, or outright rejected by many priests and a majority of Catholics. In this area, except for those priests who have been to Medjugorje, Marian devotion cannot even be talked about let alone put into practice. We who persist in Marian prayer and devotion are seen as fanatics out of step with the modern church. Mary and Marian devotion have been relegated to an insignificant and unimportant role in the Post Vatican II church. It is primarily the lay people and priests in the Marian movement who keep Mary's role alive.

Others, however, were not so pessimistic. They began by noting that Mary's cult was acknowledged in the documents of Vatican II, they argued that Marian devotion was becoming stronger than ever, and they commented on what they saw today as a great deal of interest in Marian prayer such as the rosary.

Several people put this renewed interest in Marian devotion in the context of a perceived "age of Mary." Many claim that a renewed awareness of Mary corresponds with a revival of interest in St. Louis-Marie Grignion de Montfort's *True Devotion to Mary,* which, in turn, coincides with some of the statements of recent popes, and with an increasing number of reported apparitions. One person wrote,

> Pope John Paul II stated, "This *is* the Age of Mary." And it is through Mary that Our Lord will be coming to us again, as she is recognized not only as the Mother of God (Council of Ephesus) but also the Coredemptrix and the Mediatrix of all God's graces. She is here now, at the pleasure of Our Heavenly Father, to prepare her children for the glorious event which is to take place in the near future, the Second Advent of her Son, Jesus.

A number of people said that along with renewed devotion to Mary in this final age, they expected a recognition of Mary's special privileges through an affirmation of titles such as Coredemptrix and Mediatrix of All Graces.

The 1993 Cleveland Marian Conference

One of the activities of the Marian centers has been to sponsor conferences around the United States. Many of the nation's major cities are now host to such a conference annually, most of which are organized to provide a context for revivifying Catholic faith through a renewal of Marian devotion. These gatherings are usually held in the city's convention center and provide a program that balances speakers with religious musical entertainment.

All conferences, it seems, invite and try to enlist as speakers either some of the Medjugorje visionaries or the clergy who have been associated with them. For example, some advance publicity for the Third Annual Chicago Marian Conference (October 1–3, 1993) noted that one (unnamed) Medjugorje visionary was expected to attend, and that Fr. Jozo Zovko, formerly a priest at Medjugorje, had been invited but had not yet confirmed his attendance.[9] Because of the difficulty in obtaining these visionaries or their associates, however, most conferences feature only speakers prominently associated with spreading the Medjugorje message or with promoting conservative Catholic causes.

The 1993 Cleveland Marian Conference that I attended was a midsized conference with a typical program and typical speakers. Held at the Cleveland Convention Center from Friday evening, August 27, through Sunday afternoon, August 29, it was sponsored by "Medjugorje in America," a "Marian-Eucharistic Centered Organization whose mission is the promotion of the Messages of Our Lady."[10] About five thousand people, most of them apparently preregistered, attended some or all of the sessions of the conference, the majority of whom, judging from visual observation, were over the age of fifty. A significant minority of adults, however, appeared to be under thirty-five, many of them accompanied by small children.

The organizers of Marian conferences are clearly very adept at transforming the physical setting of a large secular auditorium into a religious and devotional environment conducive to religious thought and devotion. One of the most striking features of the Cleveland Marian Conference was the skillful and well-planned use of modern media and modern staging techniques. A large video projection screen was mounted above each side of the platform to give those in the balcony and near the rear of the main floor a better view of speakers and performers; there were strategically placed video cameras and a large video production desk. Colored lights and a series of slides of religious symbols were projected onto the backdrop behind the main platform to accent the themes of the program, and just below this, behind and above the main platform, was a prominent bishop's chair and chairs for other major participants in the daily Masses.

The program, which was professionally arranged and executed, consisted of worship, speeches or personal testimonials, and religious music. While not all conference participants were seated in the auditorium for all parts of the program, there were not very many people in the halls or in the exhibit rooms downstairs during the worship services or the presentations of the major speakers. The speakers were allotted about forty-five minutes each. The program listed the participants in traditional order: clergy participating as either speakers or liturgical celebrants were listed first, followed by lay speakers and musical performers. Many of the priests who participated in the conference—George Tracy, Stephen Barham, Kenneth Roberts, and Robert Faricy—have been popular speakers at other Marian conferences and in other conservative Catholic forums, and the same can be said of most of the lay speakers.

Laymen and -women featured at this conference were described in the program in terms of their traditional Catholic family lives (spouses, number of children, upholding of family values) and public accomplishments (books, workshops, lectures). The lay speakers included Jan Connell, Louis Kacmarek, Jerry Coniker, Michael Brown, Daniel Lynch, Molly Kelly, Andy Parisi, Rita Klaus, Char Vance, Bob and Penny Lord, Maureen Digan, and Ray Burke. Featured musical performers included Dana, an Irish singer now living in Birmingham, Alabama, who has a television series on Mother Angelica's Eternal Word Television Network, and Joseph Morin, a recording artist and founder of Marian Productions. Most of the speeches were followed by a period of religious music in a contemporary, popular vein.

It must be noted that there were no apparition-seers speaking at this conference. The presence of one or more of these seers, and indeed sometimes their reception of apparitions or locutions in the course of the program, has been a significant feature of some recent American Marian conferences, and in some cases, as at Wichita, Kansas, early in the summer of 1993, this has been accompanied by reports of miraculous signs from some of the persons in attendance.

The tone of the Cleveland Marian Conference was set by the major speakers. The Saturday morning speaker, for example, was Michael Brown, whose recently published and already popular book, *The Final*

Hour,[11] gives an apocalyptic interpretation of the messages of many contemporary apparitions. Because his story is so dramatic, Brown would be a fascinating figure in any number of settings. A former reporter who worked for some prominent journals and newspapers, including the *New York Times Magazine,* he was a lapsed Catholic whose return to the church began with an eschatological dream. According to his account, Brown was writing a book on the Mafia in 1984 when a dream, which he understood as a prophetic sign, led him to confront evil with the aid of the Archangel Michael and to return to the practice of Catholicism.

Brown's talk, like his book, focused on an apocalyptic scenario of warnings and coming chastisement. Invoking a story in *Life* magazine on recent unusual weather, Brown argued that the natural disasters of the past few years—Hurricane Andrew, the great blizzard which struck the East, and the flooding of the Midwest—were forebodings of God's judgment. He also identified some of the evils of modern American culture—sexual immorality, rampant homosexuality, abortion, and an increase in violent crime—as signs of the times and of approaching judgment. Many in the audience applauded enthusiastically as he spoke of heavy metal music as demonic and as he characterized the entertainer Madonna as a satanic ploy sent to blaspheme the Virgin Mary. We are veering toward societal chaos, Brown said, as a result of our self-indulgence. He also lamented the situation of a church in which a priest, in the interest of ecumenism, may hire and work with a practicing witch—a reference to Matthew Fox's controversial association with Starhawk. Brown also criticized the "far right" for calling the pope a heretic, and he drew another round of applause when he declared that whatever might happen, he would be loyal to John Paul II.

Although Brown said that some of the recently reported apparitions are satanic dupes designed to cause confusion, he added that others, which are calling for urgent responses, are authentic and important. Furthermore, Brown himself, it must be said, left some room for confusion by not specifically identifying the apparitions he believed to be authentic. He simply stated that most recent apparitions contain a consistent theme about coming chastisements, which is a sign of God's mercy, because one of the most merciful things God can do is assert His justice to save our souls. Brown was critical of his former colleagues in the media, most of whom he said were atheists, because they do not want people to see these events in a spiritual context. The apparitions are occurring to break down evil and to bring people back to the "religion of the ancients." Brown finally exhorted the audience "to come away with fire for war, fire for love of God," because "love with faith gets us to heaven."

Two themes in Brown's talk were echoed by other speakers through-out the day. Several speakers said that they had been lukewarm at best in the practice of their faith when, at the behest of Mary or, as in the case of Brown, some other heavenly figure, they were recalled to a fervent Catholic devotion. The literature circulated by the Marian centers, from monthly newsletters and magazines to privately printed books, is rich in anecdotes about miraculous interventions, in many of which an unfaith-ful son or daughter is brought back to the faith. One of the most dramatic of these stories is Thomas Rutkoski's account of his conversion, *Apostles of the Last Days: The Fruits of Medjugorje*. Rutkoski has printed and dis-tributed this book through his nonprofit foundation, Gospa Missions, which also supports some other activities common to Marian centers. As its title suggests, Rutkoski and the devotees with whom he associates con-sider themselves to be the apostles of the last times spoken of by St. Louis-Marie Grignion de Montfort.

Other speakers shared the apocalyptic framework of Brown's talk. Daniel Lynch, for example, also cited the article in *Life* magazine men-tioned by Brown and repeated Brown's suggestion that the events noted here were warnings of coming judgment. Lynch, who is a lawyer for the Marian Movement of Priests and, as the program noted, the "husband of Sue and father of nine children," represents persons active in the pro-life movement and Operation Rescue. He is also the "National Guardian of the Missionary Image of Our Lady of Guadalupe," which was promi-nently displayed at the convention just to the right of the platform.

In his book *Our Lady of Guadalupe and Her Missionary Image,* Lynch argues that the contemporary world re-creates the cultural situation of sixteenth-century Aztec Mexico, which he vividly describes as the context for the appearances to Juan Diego of Our Lady of Guadalupe.[12] The "bloodthirsty Aztec priests offering human sacrifices to the god Quet-zalcoatl," according to Lynch, have their contemporary counterpart in doctors willing to perform abortions. As Our Lady of Guadalupe completed the Christianization of the Indians, ending the religion of the Aztecs with its human sacrifice, so her missionary image, Lynch says, will end the contemporary human sacrifice of abortion.[13]

The traveling image of which Lynch is the guardian is said to be an exact photographic reproduction of the original image of Our Lady of Guadalupe, Protectress of the Unborn, which Lynch accompanies to vari-ous parishes, Marian conferences, and abortion clinics. Lynch said that his vocation as the national guardian of this image has been confirmed by visionaries, whom he does not name. His talk was replete with miracle stories associated with the image (e.g., conversions, healings, and sun miracles), many of these taking place at abortion clinic protests.

It should be noted that while messages opposing abortion have been reported at several recent apparitions in the United States, for example, at Conyers (Georgia) and Cold Spring (Kentucky), which have no particular tie to Our Lady of Guadalupe, this image has been the predominant devotional image of Mary among recent Catholic opponents of abortion. This may be due in part to the idea of a pregnant Mary which it suggests. A section of the Winter 1993 issue of *Our Lady, Queen of Peace* newsletter, published by the Pittsburgh Center for Peace, devoted two pages to "The Modern Day Miracle of Guadalupe: The Blessed Virgin Mary Promises God Will End All Abortion." Another page was dedicated to "The Apostolate of Holy Motherhood."[14]

This newsletter, along with a variety of brochures, flyers, cassette tapes, and small paperback books, was available in a large basement room of the convention center which had been designated "the free room." Staffed by representatives of Marian centers, conferences, and other Catholic institutions and open throughout all but the worship segments of the convention program, this room contained all of the free materials that had been approved by the conference organizers. (The distribution of literature was not permitted anywhere else in or on the grounds of the convention center during the conference.)

Besides the *Our Lady, Queen of Peace* newsletter, which is the most visible of the free publications distributed at Marian conferences and which is a good source of information about current apparitions, there were flyers about forthcoming Marian conferences in Chicago, Pittsburgh, and San Antonio. There was a free audiotape distributed by the Mary Foundation of Lakewood, Ohio, entitled "Marian Apparitions Explained," which was a lecture delivered by a layperson at a parish in New Jersey about Mary's appearances throughout history and their rationale. There were also free copies of St. Louis-Marie Grignion de Montfort's *The Secret of the Rosary*.[15] Other groups with displays or literature here were the Franciscan University of Steubenville, which is an important center of Medjugorje-related devotion, and the Legionnaires of Christ.

In an even larger room in the convention center basement, space had been leased to about fifteen Catholic business establishments, including several major bookstores, a distributor of religious T-shirts, and an anti-abortion center. The books, videotapes, and cassettes of the major speakers and performers at the conference were especially prominent here and appeared to be very much in demand. A number of the books on display were conservative offerings from such publishers as TAN and Ignatius Press, but there were many of general Catholic interest as well, including some volumes of the Paulist Press Classics in Spirituality series.

Marian centers and the conferences that they sponsor may be the most important institutional expressions of the Marian revival in modern American Catholicism. The focal points of this revival, however, are the experiences that many modern Catholics, reflecting the influence of the charismatic movement, are calling charisms, and the very public events that have crystalized around some of these.

Two Important Ongoing Apparitions:
Conyers and South Phoenix

It would probably be hard to find a Catholic diocese in the United States today in which there is no one, typically in a Medjugorje prayer group, who admits to the reception of a healing, a vision, or a locution which he or she understands as a special spiritual gift or charism. Most of those who responded positively to the question about charisms in the survey were very circumspect, and some cautioned that the recipients of these charisms wished to remain anonymous. But a few respondents, whose experiences are already common knowledge on the Marian grapevine, were not so cautious. An increasing number of American Catholics believe they are receiving, or are being more open about their receiving, charisms, which until recently most Catholics would have seen as extremely rare.

One of the most striking of these charisms is the Marian apparition. In the past few years, the number of American Catholics publicly claiming or admitting to visions of the Virgin Mary has sharply increased, and in many of these cases these visions have become focal points for public gatherings of hundreds or even thousands of people. The prototypical American Marian visionary today is an adult, usually a woman, who has returned from a pilgrimage to Medjugorje.[16] We will turn now to an examination of the stories and experiences of two of these American visionaries, which have come to public attention in rather different ways and which have led to two rather different types of ongoing apparitions.

The visions of the Virgin Mary that have been drawing the largest crowds in recent years are those of Nancy Fowler of Conyers, Georgia. Little has been written about Fowler's background, but her speech suggests that she is not a native Georgian. Published devotional literature does give us some information about some events in her life just preceding her "public visions" which may, in fact, shed some crucial light on these visions.

Fowler began having peculiar experiences in 1983, at which time she was married, had a three-year-old son, and was working as a registered nurse. Fowler accepted another nursing job that brought with it more prestige and pay but required her to work on weekends, taking her away from her family and her customary religious devotions. She began to be assailed by demons, she said, and she tried several avenues of help, including seeking out a priest. It was only when she gave up her new job, went to confession, and began to attend Mass that she found relief. Not long thereafter, however, in February 1987, she found herself in a severe depression, "full of despair and not wanting to live, feeling like there was no hope."[17] But this depression ended, apparently, when the Lord appeared to her in a silent apparition.

In October of that year Fowler made a pilgrimage to Medjugorje, and there she said she received a call to become a prophet. Her visions of Mary began shortly after her return, sometime in 1988, and two years after that, Fowler was told by the Virgin to make her experiences public. At that time she was evidently living in the Atlanta suburb of Norcross, but a connection with the Cistercian brothers in the monastery near Conyers apparently led to her purchase of a home a few miles from that town, and it was there that her visions became "public." Soon large crowds began to gather around her home, creating problems which led supportive devotees to purchase some adjacent property, which they call "The Farm," which was much better suited to accommodate the visitors. Since then, Fowler's experiences have taken place there regularly on the thirteenth of each month. After the apparition, Fowler speaks to those who have gathered, delivering what both she and they understand as the Virgin's public messages to "her children of America." It should be noted that Fowler has had and continues to have visionary experiences in addition to these monthly "public apparitions."

According to Fowler, Mary wishes to be known at Conyers as "Our Loving Mother." The messages she reports to receive from the Virgin are decidedly apocalyptic, with warnings directed to America that chastisements will come unless people amend their personal and religious lives. Emphasized in these messages are the need for a veneration of mothers, a return to traditional gender roles, and an end to abortion, which is explicitly defined as murder. America is being given notice that unless it heeds the warnings of Our Lord and Our Loving Mother, it will feel the judgment of God.

In the summer of 1993, the largest of the public gatherings at Conyers drew an estimated eighty thousand people. On August 13, 1993, which coincided with the visit of Pope John Paul II to Denver, about fifty thousand people gathered at the Conyers farm, and the comments that follow are based in part on my observations there on that day.

The majority of the pilgrims who come to Conyers are from the Miami area, and many of these are Cuban immigrants who come on chartered buses. Often included on these bus tours is a visit to the nearby Cistercian Monastery of Our Lady of the Holy Spirit, some of whose members are said to be supportive of the events at Conyers. Fowler specifically appeals, it seems, to a Spanish-speaking audience: all messages are distributed in both Spanish and English, and all public announcements, including the reported messages of the Virgin, are made in both languages.[18]

The apparitions themselves take place in a room in a house, behind which special provision has been made for the ill, the elderly, and the physically challenged. One may, at certain times, visit this "Apparition Room," but late in the morning of August 13, a visit to the room would have required waiting in line for about an hour. Near the front of this line a table filled with anti-abortion literature had been set up, and people were encouraged to take this literature and to sign anti-abortion petitions.

About forty-five minutes before the apparition, which takes place about noon, there is a public recitation of the rosary. Then, after her brief vision, Fowler, with the aid of a public address system, reports the Virgin's message to the crowd in English, pausing after every sentence for a Spanish translation. She then answers questions asked by persons in the crowd, and these questions and answers are also then translated into Spanish. On August 13, Fowler reported, among other things, that America had again been warned to mend its ways or face frightful chastisements. She said that the Virgin was pleased that the pope was in America and that the Virgin was with him. Mary reportedly told Fowler that she would soon have a new mission for her. In response to questions from the crowd, Fowler affirmed that reception of communion in the hand was appropriate, she spoke in favor of chastity, and she said again that Jesus and Mary consider abortion to be murder.

During the morning and especially around noon when the apparition was in progress, many people in the crowd took pictures with their Polaroid cameras, especially pictures of the sun, and some people circulated through the crowd, displaying their "miracle pictures" of clouds or of streaks of light in the shape of various religious symbols or figures. A makeshift bookstore in one of the farm buildings was distributing, without charge, the two volumes of messages delivered at Conyers, published by "Our Loving Mother's Children." Water was available at various places, and Polaroid film and sunscreen were on sale at the site. Sanitary facilities were also available. Before and after the organized midday events, many people walked the half-mile path that connects The Farm with Fowler's suburban home, where she has erected a backyard shrine called the "Holy Hill" and where "holy water" can be obtained from a well. Several commercial religious bookstores and souvenir shops have sprung up several miles from these sites, on the road to Conyers, selling religious paraphernalia of various kinds—books on Conyers, on other apparitions, and on saints, mostly from conservative publishers, as well as T-shirts, coffee mugs, statues, rosaries, religious medals and pictures, and videotapes.

The Archdiocese of Atlanta has taken a cautious approach to the events at Conyers. On September 10, 1991, the diocesan office issued a statement that the events did not warrant an investigation but that the archbishop would monitor them. Catholics drawn to the apparitions were asked to remember that their worship ought to be centered in the sacramental life of the parish, and the people visiting the Cistercian Monastery were reminded that this is a place of contemplation and that they must not disrupt the monks' lives. The monks had been asked not to be involved in the events. On January 17, 1992, the diocesan office issued another statement asking the priests of the archdiocese not to initiate or lead pilgrimages to Conyers, not to celebrate Mass on the site, and not to give any impression of endorsing the events. Finally, on March 6, 1992, Archbishop Lyke addressed a letter to all bishops of the United States asking them to admonish priests not to lead pilgrimages to Conyers and not to celebrate Mass at the site.[19]

The Diocese of Phoenix, Arizona, has been the site of two significant apparitions in recent years. The first, in the parish of St. Maria Goretti, located in the affluent suburb of Scottsdale, involves the experiences of nine young adults of the parish and their priest, Fr. Jack Spaulding. The second, in the Mexican-American barrio of South Phoenix, focuses on the experiences of Estela Ruiz. While the Scottsdale apparition is probably better-known to Anglo-American Catholics and is an interesting example of how an apparition can be integrated into the life and worship of a parish, the apparition in South Phoenix may ultimately be the more significant.

Estela Ruiz is a mature Mexican-American woman whose prayer group meets in the backyard of her very modest home, which borders a South Phoenix trailer park. Ruiz traces the beginning of her devotion to Mary to the time when she and her husband, Reyes, were involved in the Cursillo movement while they were raising their children. When the children left home, Ruiz decided to return to school to finish her education: she became a teacher's aide, got a teaching degree, and, in her own words, began to focus on her career and to grow away from God. In 1988, however, on a trip to Mexico, Reyes, who had for some time been interested in the Virgin Mary, picked up a newspaper published by Wayne Weible, a Lutheran who had converted to Catholicism after a trip to Medjugorje. As a result of this, Reyes's interest in and devotion to the Virgin sharply increased, and soon he was talking about going to Medjugorje. Estela, who was then finishing a master's degree, did not want to go and urged Reyes to go without her, which he did. While he was gone, Estela passed by a painting of Our Lady of Guadalupe which Reyes had painted in 1981, and she heard a woman's voice say, "Good morning, daughter." Her visions of the Virgin Mary, with accompanying locutions, began in December 1988.[20]

Ruiz's experiences are perhaps best understood as an expression of an integration of Hispanic devotion to Our Lady of Guadalupe with the transcultural devotion that surrounds most contemporary Marian apparitions. This is suggested by her report that on the diocesan feast of Our Lady of Guadalupe, at the Immaculate Heart Church in Phoenix, Mary appeared to her and told her, "I am the Immaculate Heart of Mary. This is my reign—this is the time of my reign. I am here to bring my children back to my Son. The one who sent me is God, Our Father." Mary then directed Ruiz to look around the church at the different forms in which she had appeared. She said that Mary told her, "I am the Mother of God and I have appeared in different places. There is only one and that is me and I am all of these. But I come today, at this time, as the Immaculate Heart of Mary as this is the reign of my Immaculate Heart. And I've come to call my children back to God."[21]

The messages reported by Ruiz have an apocalyptic tone like that of the messages reported at Conyers. For example, Mary told Ruiz on July 17, 1993, that "men continue to move at a fast pace towards destruction, and the heavens cry and the earth trembles as man ignores God's love and peace. My voice cries out over all the earth, that men may open their ears and their hearts to the words I bring, that humanity may listen to the voice of its heavenly mother."[22]

The Ruizes have created a shrine to "Our Lady of the Americas" in their backyard, and a sign near the street indicates that persons are welcome to visit and pray at this shrine at any time. There, in a wall that separates their property from the adjoining trailer park, Reyes has created a statue of Our Lady of Guadalupe, and nearby, in a patio-like area, he has built a freestanding altar. There are a number of images and statues on and around this altar, most of which have been painted or constructed by Reyes himself, some of the most impressive of which are a statue of the Sacred Heart, a portrait of Mary as Queen of Peace as in the famous

Medjugorje painting, and several collages of photographs in the shape of a cross and the Immaculate Heart. These collages, which are constructed mostly of pictures of visitors and their loved ones, but at the center of which are pictures of Estela and Reyes, illustrate how both the Ruizes and their visitors understand the offering of their personal prayers and concerns here and their integration into the events and symbols that they believe have made this a holy place. Prayer meetings are held here on Tuesday and Saturday nights, at which time Estela receives the Virgin's messages and may then speak with visitors, and flyers with texts of the latest messages, in both English and Spanish, are available at the shrine throughout the week. A fax machine in the Ruiz home, whose number is noted in these flyers, facilitates communication with what is probably a rather large network of acquaintances and friends.

The bishop of Phoenix established a commission to investigate both the Scottsdale and the South Phoenix apparitions. With regard to the latter, the commission conducted a four-month investigation that included personal interviews, the observation of several prayer services, and a study of the messages. The report of the commission praised Ruiz as a sincere and faithful Catholic, but said that her experiences were the result not of supernatural intervention but probably of "exceptional faith" and concluded that these experiences were not extraordinary or miraculous. The commission added, however, that "no harm is presently being done to either the church as an institution or to the faithful by the devotions." Thus, it was decided that prayer meetings and public devotions could continue, for the spiritual welfare of both the Ruiz family and those who were coming for these devotions. An ongoing committee would monitor the prayer services and messages, and a spiritual director was selected for the family.[23]

There are some interesting similarities in the personal histories and situations of Fowler and Ruiz. Both are women who had embarked on secular careers and who, when at a point of achieving a measure of success in those careers, seem to have experienced an acute conflict between the active enjoyment of this success and traditional religious and family values. This conflict seems to have been resolved when these women were called by their visions to assume a prophetic role, and this in turn brought them a level of involvement with the public and a level of recognition equal to or exceeding what they might have achieved in their secular careers. I have spoken with several other female visionaries and locutionists whose lives fit this pattern. As yet, too little is known about the lives of these adult visionaries, male and female, to speak of an emerging prototype of a seer of either gender. But it does seem safe to say that the literature of the Marian centers which surrounds and supports these visionaries stresses the rejection of materialism and worldliness and a return to family-centeredness, and that this is reinforced both by the lives of most of these visionaries and by the messages of their apparitions.

Ethnic Tradition and Imagery in the Marian Revival

The largely Hispanic following of Fowler and Ruiz and the prominence of the image of Our Lady of Guadalupe at the Cleveland Marian Conference recall our opening observation that Marian devotion in the United States has been shaped by various ethnic traditions and their interaction with American culture. It would seem that some Hispanic devotional traditions are assuming some importance in the current Marian revival, and while a thorough study of this would go far beyond the scope of this essay, a few well-focused observations may shed some light on this matter and suggest some directions for further research. It will be helpful, I think, to focus first of all on a specific tradition of Hispanic Marian devotion at a popular shrine in the Rio Grande Valley, and then on a symbolic trip to Moscow in 1992 by a group of people prominent in the modern Marian revival, several of whom we have already encountered in this study.

The shrine of the Virgen de San Juan del Valle in San Juan, Texas, is the most important shrine in the overwhelmingly Hispanic Rio Grande Valley. Devotion to Our Lady of San Juan was encouraged in the late 1940s by Fr. Jose M. Azpiazu to offer an alternative devotion to that which was growing up around an alleged vision of Our Lady of Guadalupe in the area. A shrine to Our Lady of San Juan was soon established and became a major focal point both for annual group pilgrimages and for ad hoc pilgrimages of persons with special needs. In 1980, the original shrine was replaced by a mammoth new structure, clearly visible from the freeway, and in the summer of 1993, the shrine literature indicated that much work still remained to be done in the construction of suitable permanent housing for the statue that is the shrine's focal point. The ex-voto room below this statue and behind the main altar is eloquent testimony to the continuation among the Hispanic population of "the Valley" of the centuries-old understanding of Mary, particularly in a time of crisis, as an intermediary with her Son. Several large tables are covered with votive offerings and letters in both Spanish and English with requests made of the Virgin, either fulfilled or awaiting fulfillment, and a dozen large bulletin boards which swing out from the wall are covered front and back with some thirty to forty thousand pictures left behind by devotees.

These pictures and letters reveal the sorts of concerns which the Hispanic visitors to this shrine have been bringing before the "Virgencita." Foremost among these concerns, it seems, is high-school graduation, for not only do many of the letters ask Mary for assistance in graduating, but the tables contain some of the actual diplomas received, and the bulletin boards are full of graduation pictures. A second concern is for conceiving children, and a third, rather mixed group focuses on legal and social problems relating to assimilation in a sometimes hostile culture. A large number of recent pictures of young men and women in military uniform testify to the impact here of the 1992 conflict in the Persian Gulf.

It was before this visit, in conversations with some priests who had spent a number of years in Mexican-American parishes in "the Valley," that I began to realize the importance of such shrines for Mexican-American Catholics, and how the shrine-based devotion of Hispanic Catholics in general may be affecting the modern Marian revival. Several of these priests told me that they themselves had been awakened to a childlike faith in the Virgin by following the advice of their Mexican-American parishioners that they visit the basilica of Our Lady of Guadalupe in Mexico City, where they experienced conversions. Their conversions had occurred when they were drawn into the "sacred space" of a major shrine that was the focal point not just of an ethnic but of a regional devotional tradition, and as they surrendered, as it were, to the authority of this tradition. Many if not most of the conversion narratives of modern Marian devotees are really pilgrimage narratives and can be understood in terms of this structure.

Today, of course, there are various kinds of pilgrimages. The traditional pilgrimage to an apparition site such as Lourdes, Fatima, and Guadalupe has begun to give way in recent years, for American Catholics, to pilgrimages to "active" apparitions such as Medjugorje, Conyers, and South Phoenix, where pilgrims may encounter and even speak with apparition-seers—and one scarcely knows what to say here about the phenomenon of the Marian conference, where a traveling seer may have an apparition or a locution before tens of thousands of people in a major convention center, or where a photograph of an image representing an apparition may be treated with much of the reverence and celebrated with much of the rhetoric that might once have been accorded to a relic of the Holy Cross.

Sometimes ethnic tradition and imagery are subsumed in transcultural devotions with particular religio-political agendas—in ways even more striking than those we have noted at the Cleveland Marian Conference. Estela Ruiz, the visionary of South Phoenix, participated in a trip to Russia in the fall of 1992 sponsored by the 101 Foundation, a Marian center in Asbury, New Jersey. This, it should be noted, was a year after the defeat of the coup that seemed to pose the last serious threat to the leadership and to the wide-ranging political and economic reforms of Boris Yeltsin. Another Hispanic visionary from Texas, Jane Garza, was also on this trip, along with Vassula Ryden from Switzerland, Dorothy Romano of Levittown, Pennsylvania, and Christina Gallagher from the Republic of Ireland, all of whom have reported apparitions of the Virgin. They were accompanied by Father Ken Roberts, who spoke at the Cleveland Marian Conference, by a number of other priests and bishops, and, reportedly, by about a thousand other pilgrims. The messages received by each of the visionaries while on this pilgrimage, which included stops at Fatima and other religious sites and which commemorated the seventy-fifth anniversary of the Fatima apparition, have been printed and distributed by the 101 Foundation. Designated the "Victorious Queen of the World Peace Flight," this international group of visionaries and other pilgrims presented Fatima materials to the Russian Orthodox archbishop/metropolitan of Moscow and held a ceremony in Red Square celebrating the demise of communism and the triumph of the Fatima message.

Daniel Lynch, who has been discussed in connection with the Cleveland Marian Conference, participated in this flight accompanied by the Missionary Image of Our Lady of Guadalupe. Lynch has provided a very dramatic account of the march that he and his fellow pilgrims on this flight made into Red Square. As the pilgrims approached the square, he said, they processed together to the edge of it carrying the Missionary Image, an image of Jesus King of All Nations, and a large cross, and singing "Onward Christian Soldiers." There they broke through police barricades and entered the square, moving toward St. Basil's Cathedral. Lynch said that he then saw a circular platform with nine concrete steps, which he surmounted, urging his fellow pilgrims to follow him and to surround him and the images so that they would not be arrested. He said that he then "planted the cross at the top of the platform in a manner reminiscent of the Marines planting the flag on the top of Mt. Surabachi on Iwo Jima."[24] Lynch then proclaimed Our Lady as Queen of Russia and All Nations and Jesus as King of Russia and All Nations. A small statue of Our Lady of Fatima, carried by one of the pilgrims, was spontaneously crowned by John Haffert, founder of the Blue Army. Lynch said that visionary Jane Garza told him that at that moment she had a vision in which Red Square "lit up like the Fourth of July" and Our Lady appeared to her and told her she was pleased.[25]

Final Reflections

The Marian revival has not yet had much effect on the majority of American Catholics. Because of the dedication and zeal of many of the persons involved in this movement, however, and their often considerable skills and resources—and because most Catholics, in the wake of Medjugorje, are more willing to ascribe some importance to visions or locutions—it is certainly a force to be reckoned with.

In their epilogue to *Under the Heel of Mary*, Nicholas Perry and Loreto Echeverría observe that today "Our Lady is going through the acutest identity crisis, but whatever new guises she may assume, her cult is likely to remain rooted in apparitions and at the service of manipulative powers."[26] My observations and studies suggest that this is basically correct. Marian apparitions have been the focal point of the recent Marian revival in the United States, but as the pilgrimages to the apparition site that launched this revival have, as a result of the turmoil in the former Yugoslavia, sharply declined in the past few years, some of the attention that had been focused on this site has shifted to apparition sites and apparitions in the United States. The messages featured in the literature and emphasized at the conferences of this modern Marian movement have increasingly been coming from American seers and speaking to some distinctly American anxieties.

Mary's messages, as reported by these seers, reflect quite a bit of generic American Catholic piety: there are calls for prayer, sacrifice, the rejection of materialism, and "conversion." The messages of most apparitions, however, put special weight on "family values," and, as we have seen at Conyers, this is the starting point in many cases for the proclamation of conservative social agendas. The "conversions" that have occurred in conjunction with these messages have usually given their subjects a strong sense of a renewed Catholic identity, typically manifested by scrupulous participation in the sacraments and dedication to traditional Catholic devotions. In many cases, however, they have been understood as conversions to one or more of these particular agendas.

In most of the recent American apparitions, and especially at Conyers, Mary is presented by her seers as a loving mother. But when her messages advocate a particular social or political cause, such as the abolition of abortion or the reintroduction of prayer in public schools, they may also be accompanied by a warning about the punishments that await those who oppose her agenda and the persons who speak for it. Many of the more popular publications of the Marian movement, and many of the speakers at Marian conferences, are quite forthright about these anticipated punishments.

The modern American Marian revival purports to be a movement of lay Catholics, and certainly the majority of its official leaders and organizers, as well as the seers whose experiences and messages are at its focal point, are laity. But at the level of the Marian conferences, it is clear that some conservative priests—many of whom, like Fr. Ken Roberts, are not American—have been involved in shaping its agendas and emphases. And the more one looks behind the scenes at the apparitions that feed this revival, the more one suspects that the messages coming from these sites have, in many cases, been influenced by spiritual advisors, who may live in religious communities hundreds of miles away from the seers with whom they are in communication.

One of the most important features of this revival is its association with, and one might even say grounding in, pilgrimages. It is not very likely that one would be converted to this movement simply by reading its literature, by watching Mother Angelica's Eternal Word Television Network, or even by talking with converted friends or attending a Marian conference. These things are important as support structures for a distinctly religious understanding of an experience which typically takes place on a visit to an apparition site or an apparition-related shrine. This religious understanding may have crystalized during the actual course of such a journey, but it may also be shaped by contacts, conversations, and other influences encountered in its aftermath. The weeks and months surrounding these experiences are crucial for shaping how these experiences are understood, and thus, what is communicated in the various Marian support structures is crucial as well.

It is the stories told in these support structures that supply the larger social meanings for these persons' otherwise only "personal" experiences and that usually give rise to charges of manipulation. A case in point might be Lynch's dramatic account of the storming of Red Square seventy-five years after the apparition of Fatima by the pilgrims of the "Victorious Queen of the World Peace Flight."

This triumphalistic account may or may not correspond very closely to the memories of onlookers or even of Lynch's fellow pilgrims, but what matters is not so much its factual accuracy as its symbolism. Lynch is building here, of course, on the well-known Fatima prophecy about the fall of communism and the conversion of Russia, and while persons who do not share his political orientation or agenda may find his tale somewhat ludicrous, they cannot deny that he is attempting something very important in terms of religious symbolism. The Fatima prophecy contained in Sister Lucia's memoirs made an immense impression on many American Catholics in the years after the Second World War. Many of these people have now lived to see the collapse of the Soviet Union and of communism. And in the years to come, some version of this pilgrimage story may very well be attached to these prophecies as a way of helping to complete, for these persons and for many others who need to make sense out of such things, the great saga of Fatima.

Manipulation, however, seems too harsh a word to describe what Lynch has done here with the imagery of Guadalupe and Fatima, or indeed what any believer dedicated to a particular cause may do with such imagery in his or her stories. It seems to deprive the persons who hear or read and might appropriate these stories of any ability to assess their religious adequacy or to modify them in memory or in their retelling. Moreover, visionaries, priests, bishops, spiritual advisors, friends, the religious media, ethnic communities, and even the pope may all be involved in the negotiation of the meaning that a Catholic may attach, finally, to his or her religious experiences, or those of someone else. And rather than suggesting that any of these parties, in the context of the modern Marian revival, is engaged in anything illegitimate, it would be better for the student of Marian devotion simply to seek a better understanding of their operations.

NOTES

1. The most recent and important of these studies are M. Bax, "The Madonna of Medjugorje: Religious Rivalry and the Formation of a Devotional Movement in Yugoslavia," *Anthropological Quarterly* 63, no. 2 (1990): 63–75; and N. Perry and L. Echeverría, *Under the Heel of Mary* (London: Routledge, 1968).

2. Joseph E. Manton, "Profile of Marian Devotion on the Parochial Level," *Marian Studies* 19 (1968): 41–42.

3. Ibid., p. 42.

4. Ibid., p. 44.

5. Ibid., p. 46.

6. Richard N. Ostling, "Handmaid or Feminist?" *Time,* 20 December 1991, p. 62.

7. René Laurentin, *Our Lord and Our Lady in Scottsdale: Faithful Charisms in a Traditional American Parish* (Milford, Ohio: Faith Publishing Company, 1992), pp. x, xiii.

8. Tomislav Vlašić, *Our Lady, Queen of Peace,* November 1985, p. 6.

9. Confirmed speakers for the Third Annual Chicago Marian Conference included Lisa Weible Addison, Fr. Tim Deeter, Wayne Weible, Fr. Larry Gesy, Fr. Mitchell Pacwa, S.J., Fr. Ken Roberts, Fr. Michael McDonough, and Bishop Thad Jakubowski, representing the Archdiocese of Chicago. Music and testimony were to be provided by Dana, Brian Fife, Mark Forrest, Fr. Joe Hirsch, Jerry and Regina Morin, and Joe Morin.

A circular promoting the St. Paul/Minneapolis Marian Conference (8–10 October 1993), sponsored by Covenant Ministries, listed as featured speakers Fr. Ralph DiOrio, known for his healing ministry; Wayne Weible; Fr. Robert Faricy; Sr. Lucy Rooney; Rita Klaus; Fr. Richard

Foley; Fr. Michael Joncas; Jerry and Regina Morin; Fr. Robert Altier; Fr. Mark Stang; Fr. Jeff Bayhi; Sister Jean Thuerauf; Larry and Mary Sue Eck; Donna Lee; Shar Gill; Bishop Robert Carlson; Archbishop John Roach; and Daniel Lynch with the Missionary Image of Our Lady of Guadalupe. Music was to be provided by Robert Wills, Michael O'Brien, and John Michael Talbot; Lola Falana was to be master of ceremonies.

A circular for the Steel City Medjugorje Conference (10–12 September 1993) at the David Lawrence Convention Center of Pittsburgh featured the following speakers: Rev. Ken Roberts, Fr. Robert Faricy, Fr. Svetozar Kraljević, Fr. Immanuel Iweh, Joseph Morin, Mathew Swizdor, Fr. Al Winshman, R. Rev. Fr. Barham, Jan Connell, Jim Jennings, Wayne Weible, Char Vance, Jill Jensen, Larry and Mary Sue Eck, Fr. John Hampsch, Fr. Shamon, and Gerry Matatics. Music was to be provided by Jerry and Regina Morin and Michael O'Brien, as well as St. Paul's 60 Member Cathedral Choir and the Dalmatian 20 Member Choir of Mostar (Herzegovina), David Parkes, Antonio Aguilar, Mark Forrest, Marian Cornetti, and the "Sound Castle." Two Medjugorje visionaries, Vicka and Jacob, were listed as having confirmed their attendance.

10. "Behold My Son/Behold Your Mother," program of the 1993 Cleveland Marian Conference, 17–19 August 1993, the Cleveland Convention Center, p. 31.

11. Michael H. Brown, *The Final Hour* (Milford, Ohio: Faith Publishing Company, 1992).

12. Daniel J. Lynch, *Our Lady of Guadalupe and Her Missionary Image* (St. Albans, Vt.: The Missionary Image of Our Lady of Guadalupe, 1993).

13. It should be noted that not all devotees of Our Lady of Guadalupe, especially those who are Mexican American, would agree with Lynch's presentation of the Spanish conquest of Mexico or his depiction of the bloodthirsty Aztec priests. For other perspectives on the complex history of this image and its significance for contemporary Marian devotion, see Jacques Lafaye, *Quetzalcoatl and Guadalupe: The Formation of Mexican National Consciousness, 1531–1813,* trans. Benjamin Keen (Chicago: University of Chicago Press, 1976); Donald V. Kurtz, "The Virgin of Guadalupe and the Politics of Becoming Human," *Journal of Anthropological Research* 38 (1982): 194–210; William B. Taylor, "The Virgin of Guadalupe in New Spain: An Inquiry into the Social History of Marian Devotion," *American Ethnologist* 14 (1987): 9–33; Ena Campbell, "The Virgin of Guadalupe and the Female-Self Image: A Mexican Case History," in James Preston, ed., *Mother Worship* (Chapel Hill: University of North Carolina Press, 1982), pp. 5–21; I. Gebara and M. Bingemer, *Mary: Mother of God, Mother of the Poor,* trans. P. Perryman (Maryknoll: Orbis Books, 1989); Jeanette Rodriquez, *Our Lady of Guadalupe: Faith and Empowerment among Mexican-American Women* (Austin: University of Texas Press, 1994).

14. Pittsburgh Center for Peace, *Our Lady, Queen of Peace,* Special Edition II (Winter 1993): 16–17, 18.

15. St. Louis-Marie Grignion de Montfort, *The Secret of the Rosary,* trans. Mary Barbour (Bay Shore, N.Y.: Montfort Publications, 1954).

16. As noted in the prologue, it is impossible to ascertain how many visionaries there are at any particular time. Among the visionaries in the United States who have come to public attention in the wake of Medjugorje are the following:

Male visionaries: Joe Rineholtz, Hillside, Illinois; Tony Fernwalt, Barberton, Ohio; Alfredo Raimondo, Tickfaw, Lousiana; Joseph Januszkiewicz, Marlboro Township, New Jersey.

Female visionaries: Estela Ruiz, Phoenix, Arizona; Carol Nole, Santa Maria, California; Theresa Lopez, Denver, Colorado; anonymous female visionary, Cold Spring, Kentucky; Elizabeth Weaver, Kansas City, Missouri; Jane Garza, Austin, Texas; Ruth Ann Wade, Bloomington, Indiana; Nancy Fowler, Conyers, Georgia.

17. Judith Child, "The Conyers Story Part II," in *To Bear Witness That I Am the Living Son of God,* vol. 2 (Newington, Va.: Our Loving Mother's Children, 1992), pp. vii–viii.

18. The pilgrimage of Miami Catholics to the Conyers apparitions may be based on a longstanding "Cuban" connection between Atlanta and Miami. The Cursillo movement played an important role in the 1970s and 1980s in establishing this link. Included in the Spanish-speaking audience of the Conyers apparition may be an older generation of Cuban immigrants as well as other non-Cuban Latinos. I am grateful to Orlando Espín for these insights.

19. The correspondence concerning the Conyers apparition issued by the Archdiocese of Atlanta has been printed in Ann Marie Hancock, *Wake Up America!* (Norfolk, Va.: Hampton Roads Publishing Company, 1993), pp. 195–99.

20. "Our Lady of the Americas: An Interview with Visionary Estela Ruiz," *Our Lady, Queen of Peace,* Spring 1992, p. 8.

21. Ibid., p. 9.

22. "Message from Our Lady of the Americas, Sat., July 17, 1993," flyer distributed by Mr. Reyes Maria Ruiz.

23. John Conway, "S. Phoenix 'Apparitions' Not Miraculous—Report," *The Catholic Sun,* 3 May 1990, pp. 1, 12.

24. Lynch, *Our Lady of Guadalupe and Her Missionary Image,* p. 83.

25. Ibid., p. 84.

26. Perry and Echeverría, *Under the Heel of Mary,* p. 313.

10

"We Are What You Were"
Roman Catholic Traditionalism in America

WILLIAM D. DINGES

Prologue

For nearly three decades, an international movement of self-proclaimed "Roman Catholic Traditionalists" has carried on a campaign of resistance to the reform initiatives of the Second Vatican Council. Labeled "divisive" by their coreligionists, derided by the Vatican for their "fanaticism of the chosen" mentality,[1] tainted with the specter of schism, and handicapped by internal division, the "remnant faithful" have nevertheless seen their campaign to preserve preconciliar forms of Catholic doctrinal and disciplinary life both endure and grow.

In previous work I have discussed the origins of the traditionalist movement, the history of its organizational initiatives, the nature of its ideology, and other issues surrounding traditionalism's evolution among American Catholics.[2] This study focuses on the course of the movement in the United States over the last decade.

As a social movement phenomenon, Catholic traditionalism consists of a segmented network of associations, organizations, publishing initiatives, home schooling programs, priories, religious orders and foundations, and chapel and Mass location sites. Until his death at age eighty-six in 1991, French archbishop Marcel Lefebvre (and his clerical Society of St. Pius X [SSPX], founded in 1970 in Econe, Switzerland) was the most media-visible symbol of traditionalist dissent both here and abroad. To date, the SSPX remains the largest and best-known traditionalist initiative.[3]

Traditionalist Catholics have raised many concerns regarding church doctrine, discipline, and liturgical practice that have surfaced in other Catholic quarters in the wake of the Second Vatican Council. There are many affinities between traditionalist Catholic critiques of *aggiornamento* and those associated with conservative Catholic groups and organizations discussed in this volume. There are, however, important distinctions that differentiate these groups. Although conservative Catholics have espoused certain anticonciliar motifs, they have generally endorsed the legitimacy of the Council (albeit in strict constructionist terms) while (often begrudgingly) maintaining that the new liturgy is the true and immemorial Mass of all time and "here to stay."[4] Nor have conservative Catholics set up counterchurch institutional structures or allied themselves with a reactionary and antidemocratic political ideology that extols the virtues of the ancient regime.[5] Catholic traditionalism, by contrast, is a much more sectarian-like response to the problem of change in the church rooted in a value-oriented repudiation of the Council. As such, traditionalism is the most radicalized segment on the Catholic right and the most representative Catholic analogue to Protestant fundamentalism.

At present, there are slightly more than 375 traditionalist Mass sites and/or chapel locations in the United States, accommodating between 15,000 and 20,000 Catholics. Approximately 104 of these locations are served by priests of the SSPX, 30 by priests of the Society of St. Pius V (SSPV). Another 60 are led by priests, some of whom serve more than one chapel location, who consider themselves in union with Rome but who operate without permission of the local bishop. Another 29 traditionalist chapels are served by "sedevacantist" (coined after the Latin ecclesiastical expression *sede vacante* ["vacant chair"]) priests. The remaining chapels operate under the provisions of the 1984 Indult and are attended by Catholics who are not necessarily "traditionalists" as the term is used here. The formation of traditionalist Mass and chapel locations has leveled off since the mid-1980s. Internationally, Vatican estimates currently place the size of the traditionalist movement at more than 1 million.[6]

The Emergence of Traditionalist Dissent

As an evolving social movement, Catholic traditionalism has passed through three phases. The first ran from the beginning of the Second

Vatican Council in 1962 to the mandatory implementation of the new liturgy in 1971. The second extended from 1971 to 1984, the year of the papal indult "reinstating" the Tridentine Mass. During the third phase, traditionalism has acquired a de jure schismatic status.

Phase I: 1962–1971

The reaction among American Catholics to the Second Vatican Council included a combination of enthusiasm and confusion that rapidly transformed into dramatically polarized positions pitting liberal and progressive "New Breed" Catholics against their conservative coreligionists. The "traditionalist" aspect of this discontent with *aggiornamento* was not organizationally distinct at first, nor did it represent an ideologically self-conscious repudiation of Vatican II. Self-professed "traditionalists" such as Fr. Gommar De Pauw, a professor of theology and academic dean at Mt. Saint Mary's Major Seminary in Emmitsburg, Maryland, who launched the Catholic Traditionalist Movement, Inc. (CTM), in 1965, echoed other conservative voices at the time in calling for a renewal of familiar Catholic customs and devotions while admonishing church leadership against the purported dangers *aggiornamento* posed to Catholic identity and the church's sense of the sacred.

By the late 1960s, however, dissent on the Catholic right had became more differentiated and ideologically rigid. With the introduction of the *Novus Ordo Missae* in 1967, the critique of liturgical *aggiornamento* intensified. Those who were most alienated by the changes began charging that the New Mass was the symbol of resurgent "modernism" in the church and the key instrumentality for establishing the Council's "revolutionary errors" at the parish level. In addition, allegations arose that the new liturgy contained "heresy" and was "invalid" because the canon of the Mass had been "mistranslated."[7] The traditionalist attack on the doctrinal integrity of the new liturgy, reinforced by similar allegations emerging from the highest sources within the church itself,[8] rapidly shifted the focus of dissent on the Catholic right from the question of errant discipline to one of errant doctrine. Increasingly strident and conspiracy-laden attacks on the Council and on Pope Paul VI accompanied this shift.[9]

Throughout this formative period, the traditionalist movement remained dependent on crusading individuals and on localized efforts of individual Catholics. The financial resources of the movement were drawn primarily from voluntary donations. Aside from Fr. De Pauw's efforts, traditionalist dissent had no national organizational infrastructure; nor had any traditionalist coalitions emerged. By the time of the mandatory implementation of the *Novus Ordo* Mass in 1971, however, the repudiation of Vatican II had become inextricably linked in traditionalist circles with the campaign to "save the true Mass." In addition, attacks by American traditionalists that had previously been leveled at liberal European theologians now centered increasingly on American bishops, Catholic educators, and others who ran the church's administrative infrastructure.

Phase II: 1971–1984

During the second period of expansion following the mandatory implementation of the *Novus Ordo* Mass, the traditionalist movement evolved from individual localized efforts into more nationally organized ones. The two most notable efforts in this regard were the Orthodox Roman Catholic Movement, Inc. (ORCM), founded in 1973 by Fr. Francis Fenton, a priest/pastor in Bridgeport, Connecticut, and the establishment that same year of the first traditionalist chapels in the United States by American priests of Archbishop Lefebvre's SSPX.

Although the particulars varied, the pattern in which traditionalist chapels formed typically involved small groups of dissident Catholics gathering in homes, motels, VFW halls, or rented facilities for discussion and devotional practices. In some instances, individuals allied themselves with a local priest or long-time pastor resisting Vatican II reforms. In others, Catholics contacted priests of the SSPX or the ORCM. As the number of traditionalists increased in a particular area, larger and more permanent chapel locations were often secured.

As the traditionalist movement slowly expanded, tensions increased on several fronts. In Europe, escalating conflict between the Vatican and Archbishop Lefebvre led to the latter's suspension on July 22, 1976, for disobeying a direct Vatican order not to ordain seminarians. Internally, the movement began to fragment over support for the archbishop and over issues related to the status of the papacy, the question of the "validity" of the new Mass, and the mobilization of resources among competing groups. Traditionalist Catholics also found themselves in an increasingly contentious relationship with more moderate Catholic conservatives.

Phase III: 1984 to the Present

By the time the Vatican promulgated the Mass Indult *(Quattuor abhinc annos)* of October 3, 1984, traditionalist opposition to the Council and the new Mass had the markings of a full-fledged counterchurch movement. The Indult initiative reflected this fact, as did the more conciliatory position taken by Pope John Paul II toward conservative interpretations of *aggiornamento* in general. While ostensibly issued as a "pastoral consideration" in light of the opposition to the new Mass, the 1984 Indult also represented a Vatican reaction to Archbishop Lefebvre's threat, first publicly voiced in 1983, to consecrate a successor without papal permission.[10] The purpose of the 1984 Indult was to allow Catholics to return to the use of the old Mass, but only under strictly controlled conditions; those desiring the old liturgy had to secure permission of the local bishop and make it "publicly clear beyond all ambiguity" that they were in no way connected with any group that impugned the lawfulness and doctrinal integrity of the new Mass.[11]

While conservative Catholics generally welcomed the Indult as an acceptable solution to the problem of the liturgy,[12] traditionalists were guarded and skeptical. For some, the Indult signaled a change in the "disastrous policies" of Vatican II, thereby giving sustenance to the traditionalist cause. Apologists such as Michael Davies encouraged traditionalists to send their bishops as many requests for the old Mass as possible.[13] Others were less sanguine: the effort was a gesture of "crumbs," a "separate but equal" approach that levied unfair conditions on traditionalists and that would not be supported by the bishops.[14] The SSPX took the position of "tolerant skepticism" toward the Indult: tolerant because of the old liturgy's spiritual edification, and skeptical because the official structures of the "modernist" church were behind the effort.[15] The society made it clear, however, that the overall conditions of the Indult were "unacceptable."[16] The fact that those petitioning for the old Mass were to indicate that they had no doubts about its "doctrinal soundness" missed a central axiom of traditionalist dissent: there would not be a crisis in the church if there were not something wrong with the *Novus Ordo*. Archbishop Lefebvre warned his supporters to avoid traditional Masses celebrated by "progressive priests"; he did not want them to "benefit in a regular manner" from the Indult because of the "compromises" into which petitioners risked being led.[17] Emboldened by the Vatican initiative, however, the society launched a petition drive calling not only for permission for any priest to say the old Mass without the "discriminatory and inhibiting conditions," but also for recovery of its juridical status and for the creation of a "personal prelature" conferring upon the society's superior general "ordinary jurisdiction" over its scattered faithful.[18]

Although the Indult initiative met with skepticism in most traditionalist circles, talks between Archbishop Lefebvre and the Vatican continued. These discussions intensified dramatically after Lefebvre's threat, posed again in 1987, to consecrate a successor. After protracted negotiations, the archbishop signed a protocol on May 5, 1988, granting much of the substance of his previous demands, including official recognition of the society, semi-independence from diocesan bishops, and permission to continue use of the Tridentine liturgy and to consecrate a successor.[19]

The long-sought solution to the "Econe problem" proved short-lived, however. The archbishop withdrew his assent to the protocol the following day. Insisting that the Vatican was stalling and had not collaborated effectively, he demanded a June 30 date for consecrations and a papal mandate allowing him to consecrate more than one episcopal successor. Above all, the "rebel" prelate made it clear that he had no intention of compromising nearly two decades of struggle and persecution on behalf of the traditionalist cause by now relinquishing control of his fraternity to agents of "modernist Rome."[20] On July 1, 1988, Lefebvre consecrated four of his priests to the episcopacy and was summarily excommunicated.

In the wake of the breakdown of the Econe negotiations, the Vatican extended another olive branch to traditionalist Catholics, this time in the form of the *Motu Proprio, Ecclesia Dei* of July 2, 1988. This initiative, like the 1984 Indult, was an attempt to integrate traditionalists back into the church while mollifying conservative Catholics still disillusioned with liturgical reform.

In *Ecclesia Dei,* Pope John Paul II insisted that the root of the Lefebvre schism lay in "an incomplete and contradictory notion of tradition." However, where attachment to the old liturgy had been a "problem" in 1984, it now attained the status of a "rightful aspiration."[21] The pope maintained that reconciliation of Catholics who did not wish to follow Archbishop Lefebvre into schism necessitated a new awareness of the diversity of the church's spirituality and apostolates. Respect was now to be shown for the feelings of all those, whether supporters of Lefebvre or not, who were attached to the Latin liturgy "by a wide and generous application of the 1984 Indult." The *Ecclesia Dei* Pontifical Commission, headed by West German cardinal Augustin Mayer, was set up to facilitate this effort.[22]

Traditionalist Catholics in the United States lost little time in rejecting *Ecclesia Dei.* Archbishop Lefebvre and his supporters denounced the effort as another Vatican attempt to co-opt traditionalists and draw them away from SSPX chapels "so as to make them swallow the conciliar pill."[23] Traditionalists were warned that not all priests saying the Indult Mass were "honest or sincere traditionalists" and that the initiative was another "confusing" and "hypocritical" effort.[24] Others derided *Ecclesia Dei* for permitting the "mixing" of liturgical texts, thereby implicitly equating the Tridentine liturgy with the "false" conciliar Mass and "religious errors" of Vatican II. Traditionalists also attacked the Society of St. Peter as a "stooge" organization and a Vatican ploy to "steal" priests and seminarians from the SSPX.[25] The controversy over the SSPX schism and the

Indult initiatives continued throughout the late 1980s. In May 1989, Pope John Paul II met with leading members of the Curia and several European bishops to discuss a plan to remove all restrictions on the use of the Tridentine Mass. After intense deliberation, the pope decided not to sign the document.[26] Since then, the *Ecclesia Dei* commission has continued exhorting episcopal authorities to facilitate use of the old liturgy. In April of 1991, shortly before leaving the commission, Cardinal Mayer again wrote the American bishops, suggesting that they make use of the old Mass in parish churches, at convenient locations and times, on a "trial basis" for those who had "lapsed into schismatic worship." The mixing of missals was now permitted, and bishops were to assume that the fact that people came to celebrate an authorized Mass was a sign of "good will and desire for full communion." In response to episcopal protests over the initial practice of granting "celebrets" (a document issued from Rome giving an individual priest permission to say the old Mass), Mayer indicated that the commission now preferred that such faculties be granted by the ordinary himself.[27]

Current Status of Traditionalist Organizations

Since they were first established, most of the early traditionalist organizations have been transformed in some fashion or another. In addition, several new organizational efforts have arisen, both among those whose opposition to the establishment church has intensified, and among those desiring to find a solution to the traditionalist cause within it.

The historical forerunners include:

The Catholic Traditionalist Movement

On June 23, 1968, in a former Ukrainian Orthodox church, Fr. Gommar De Pauw and his supporters opened Ave Maria Chapel, CTM's headquarters in Westbury, Long Island. De Pauw has maintained his headquarters there, serving a congregation of local traditionalist Catholics along with visitors, many of whom come from the tri-state area for Mass and devotions. Although widely recognized for his pioneer role in the traditionalist cause, Fr. De Pauw has refused involvement with other traditionalist groups or organizations. He continues to broadcast a worldwide Traditionalist Radio Mass, to produce Tridentine Mass videocassettes, and to edit his own publications. In 1990, Fr. De Pauw celebrated twenty-five years as leader of the Catholic Traditionalist Movement and American progenitor of the campaign to "save the true Mass."

The Orthodox Roman Catholic Movement

The ORCM was founded by Fr. Francis Fenton in Monroe, Connecticut, in 1973. For the next five years, the organization established traditionalist chapels throughout the United States while publishing numerous anticonciliar pamphlets blending right-wing political themes with denunciations of the Council and the church hierarchy.

By 1979 the ORCM was in the midst of internal turmoil over issues of authority and control and various financial problems. Fr. Fenton and half of the ten ORCM priests subsequently left. Fenton formed the Traditional Catholics of America (TCA) in Colorado Springs, Colorado, an organization which he still heads. The remaining ORCM priests continued operations from Monroe, but eventually disbanded when the lay board of directors "interfered" with their spiritual guidance of the organization, accusing them of schism in their support of the bishops ordained in 1982 by the late Archbishop Ngo-Dhin-Thuc.

Following the departure of Fr. Fenton, Fr. Robert McKenna, O.P., continued his traditionalist work at Our Lady of the Rosary Chapel in Monroe. In 1986, McKenna was ordained a bishop by a French Dominican, Guerard des Lauriers, who had been consecrated in 1982 by Archbishop Thuc. In 1989, McKenna and John Hesson (another Thuc bishop) of Philadelphia formed the "Catholic Alliance" on behalf of the traditionalist cause.[28]

The Tridentine Latin Rite Church

The Tridentine Latin Rite Church (also known as the Congregation of Mary Immaculate Queen or the Mt. St. Michael's group) is one of the most controversial of all traditionalist organizations in the United States. The TLRC was started by Francis Schuckardt, a layman and one-time head of the Blue Army of Mary. Schuckardt's early anticonciliar thinking attracted tradition-minded Catholics who had worked with him in promoting Marian piety; his conflict with local episcopal authorities over his public repudiation of Vatican II eventually led to his founding the TLRC and the CMRI Order in Coeur d' Alene, Idaho, in 1967. Schuckardt was ordained and consecrated bishop in Chicago in 1971 by Bishop Daniel Q. Brown of the Old Catholic Church. Schuckardt later acquired property in Washington State, including Mt. St. Michael's, a former Jesuit seminary northeast of Spokane. He moved his center of operations to that location in 1977.

In 1984, following several years of internal turmoil, allegations of sexual abuse, gross mismanagement, and "bizarre" and "extreme" penitential and devotional practices, Schuckardt and a small group of supporters were

ousted from Mt. St. Michael's. In an effort to shore up their episcopal credentials, several of the priests whom Schuckardt had previously ordained
at Mt. St. Michael's were re-ordained by George J. Musey, a traditionalist
priest from Friendswood, Texas, who had been consecrated in 1981 by a
Mexican traditionalist bishop associated with Archbishop Thuc.

Since the ouster of Schuckardt in 1984, the Mt. St. Michael's group
has reorganized itself and tried to establish a new identity and legitimacy
in traditionalist circles as the Congregation of Mary Immaculate Queen.
The organization currently operates a ten-state network of Mass centers,
a convent, and a publishing facility and seminary serving several thousand
traditionalist Catholics in the United States.[29]

Priestly groups include the following:

The Society of St. Pius X

On August 28, 1972, Archbishop Lefebvre ordained Fr. Gregory Post,
an American and one of his first Econe seminarians, at the Shrine of Our
Lady of the Prairies, a traditionalist enclave in Powers Lake, North
Dakota. Several of Lefebvre's priests began their work among American
Catholics the following year, establishing the first SSPX priory outside of
Switzerland in Armada, Michigan, in October 1973, along with other
chapel locations in Texas, California, and New York.[30] Within a decade,
the society had its own national network of publishing enterprises,
chapels, schools, and priories in the United States, including a seminary,
first located in Ridgefield, Connecticut, and moved in 1988 to Winona,
Minnesota. National headquarters were established in Oyster Bay, New
York, in the former Long Island estate of millionaire William Woodward,
Jr. In 1979 the society purchased an abandoned Jesuit College at St.
Mary's, Kansas, where they established a school and college. By the late
1980s, the St. Mary's complex had become the society's largest center in
the United States, attracting several hundred traditionalist families to the
area. In 1991 the National Headquarters of the District of the USA of the
SSPX was moved to Kansas City, Missouri, along with the organization's
Angelus Press.

While generally viewed as the foremost organizational initiative among
American traditionalists, the society's endeavors in the United States have
not been without difficulties—as will be discussed later. However, in spite
of internal schism and ongoing turmoil, the SSPX has continued to
expand its network of schools, chapels, and Mass locations among American Catholics. In the wake of the excommunication of Archbishop
Lefebvre in 1988, relatively few American supporters were lost. According to Fr. Peter Scott, district superior for the United States, the society

has been increasing its support base among American Catholics by between 10 and 20 percent annually.[31]

The Society of St. Pius V

The internal conflict within the SSPX during its first decade in the United States came to a dramatic head in April 1983, when nine American priests of the Eastern District rebelled against Archbishop Lefebvre. The immediate cause of the rebellion centered around acceptance of the Mass of John XXIII and the question of whether John Paul II was a "true pope."

Archbishop Lefebvre, who feared at the time that the controversy over the liturgy would split the society in two, had taken the position that the Mass of John XXIII was acceptable. Lefebvre also rejected the view that the *Novus Ordo* liturgy was intrinsically invalid—although professing that no "true" Catholic would assist at it. On the question of the papacy, Lefebvre declared that he would not tolerate anyone in the society who refused to "pray for the Pope."[32] These positions were rejected by most of the American priests of the North East District. Conflict escalated when it became known that several of them sought to gain hold of the legal and financial matters of the SSPX in the United States by placing society property under their own control.[33]

On April 28, 1983, Archbishop Lefebvre ousted nine of these American priests from the society.[34] Several years of lengthy litigation ensued, after which the deposed priests were forced to relinquish some of the property they controlled. Following their expulsion, the ex-society priests, led by Fr. Clarence Kelly, founded the Society of St. Pius V (SSPV) at the SSPX headquarters in Oyster Bay, New York, which they retained.

The SSPV is currently composed of a small group of priests. The organization has no official canonical or juridical status and is presented simply as an association of "like-minded" clerics who subscribe to "A Statement of Principles in a Time of Crisis" condemning Vatican II, the hierarchy of the establishment church, and the new "conciliar religion." Three of the original priest members have now dissociated themselves from the SSPV and developed closer ties with the CMRI. The SSPV currently operates a convent in Round Top, New York, along with several traditionalist schools, in addition to publishing material promoting traditional Catholic teachings and sponsoring annual Roman Catholic forums.

The Society of St. Peter

Shortly after the SSPX schism, several French and German priests and seminarians of the SSPX who had broken with Archbishop Lefebvre over the consecrations met with Vatican officials. They were encouraged to es-

tablish a priestly fraternity as a means for keeping the "traditions of spirituality and apostolate" to which traditionalist Catholics were committed.[35] As a result, the Society of St. Peter was founded at the Cistercian
Abbey of Houterive (Canton of Fribourg, Switzerland) on July 18, 1988.
Members of the new fraternity were given the same terms that Archbishop Lefebvre had rejected in the May 5 protocol: the full use of the
liturgical books in force in 1962, status as a congregation of pontifical
rights, with the possibility of founding seminaries and other foundations
as needed. The fraternity, in turn, accepted the documents of Vatican II
"in the light of Tradition" and pledged fidelity to the pope. The fraternity's special mission was to reconcile Catholics who were lapsed or who
had joined a schismatic group because of their attachment to the Tridentine Mass. A seminary for the SSP opened in Wigratzbad (Germany) in
October 1988, with thirty candidates.[36]

The SSP initiatives in the United States began the following January,
when two of its priest representatives toured the country to meet with
several bishops and gather students for the fraternity's seminary. In 1991,
a fraternity priest was invited into the diocese of Dallas. In July of the
following year, the SSP national headquarters was moved to Scranton,
Pennsylvania.

Although the SSP has worked since 1989 to open more parishes
among American Catholics, only three members of the American hierarchy have responded positively. SSP priests have labored under a cloud of
suspicion as potential "troublemakers" and "foreigners," while the alleged
"backward nature" of their commitment to Catholic belief and practice
has also remained suspect.[37]

Pan-traditionalist initiatives include the following:

The Tridentine Rite Conference

The Tridentine Rite Conference is a relatively new traditionalist organization founded in 1986 in Chicago, largely under the initiative of
Fr. Francis Le Blanc, a traditionalist priest activist and pastor of Our
Lady of the Sun International Shrine in El Mirage, Arizona, and Fr. Paul
Wickens of Orange, New Jersey. The TRC seeks to unite isolated traditionalist Catholics, to provide "networking" for those unaffiliated with
other traditionalist organizations around the United States, and to address
issues confronting traditional-minded Catholics.

In September of 1987, the first convention of the TRC met in
Phoenix, Arizona (paralleling the pope's visit there at the time). About
120 clergy and laity attended, including non-Catholic "observers." As organizational goals, the TRC officially committed itself to pursuing the

establishment of a separate apostolic vicariate for the Tridentine rite under a cardinal protector sympathetic to traditionalists, and secondarily to providing a course of study and spiritual encouragement for traditionalist Catholics.[38] Since that time, the TRC has continued to hold annual national meetings that draw several hundred participants in support of the traditionalist cause.

The Society of Traditional Roman Catholics

The Society of Traditionalist Roman Catholics is another recent traditionalist initiative, founded in Charlotte, North Carolina, in 1985, largely in response to the 1984 Indult. Unlike most other traditionalist organizations, the STRC is a lay initiative, striving to unite all traditionalist Catholics in common cause, especially for the restoration of the Tridentine Mass. The STRC has no priests per se, nor does the organization hold conventions. The STRC produces a quarterly newsletter *(The Catholic Voice)* with a readership that society officials estimate at more than ten thousand.[39] No dues are charged. Support for the organization comes entirely from individual donations. The STRC also helps traditionalists set up separate Mass chapels when the local ordinary refuses permission for the Tridentine Mass.

Motifs in Contemporary Traditionalist Ideology

For three decades, traditionalist apologists have produced popular and semischolarly literature denigrating virtually all aspects of *aggiornamento* while repudiating the conservative position that the crisis in the postconciliar church is merely a normative one related to abuses and distortions. In its most sectarian mode, the traditionalist rejection of the Council is unequivocal: Vatican II was a "false" and "heretical" deliberation, the work of a satanic-driven conspiracy of humanistic, Protestant, liberal, socialist, and Masonic forces that have been working since the French Revolution to "de-Christianize" the West and destroy "Catholic civilization."[40] In less categorical language, traditionalists malign Vatican II as a "flawed" Council laden with ambiguities and doctrinal "time bombs," or they reduce it to a misguided "pastoral" undertaking with the status of a debatable option in the church.[41] By either account, the Council was a "betrayal" of Catholicism's Sacred Deposit by those who had been divinely commissioned to preserve and protect it. By embracing *aggiornamento*, the conciliar bishops and their theological *periti* "sold out" the faith. As a result, the Roman Catholic Church now faces an unprecedented crisis of contradiction and apostasy. Vatican II and its destructive "fruits" are therefore to be rejected by all true Catholics.[42]

The traditionalist attack on liturgical reform (paralleling the critique of the Council) continues to follow a twofold stratagem of asserting the "right" to maintain the traditional liturgy[43] while casting aspersions on the doctrinal integrity of the new Mass.[44] The *Novus Ordo* is not a proper development of the Roman rite but an entirely new liturgy that breaks with the true Mass in form, structure, and theology. Traditionalists who do not explicitly hold that the new Mass is intrinsically invalid assert that it is an inferior exposition of Catholic doctrine or a "Protestant" rite. Those who concede the possible validity of the new Mass nullify that affirmation by holding that the "Catholic intention" necessary for such validity is no longer true of today's priests who have been formed by "Protestant" theology.[45] In spite of the Vatican overtures to accommodate traditionalist liturgical needs by way of the Indult initiative, the goal of the movement remains "the total extirpation of the *Novus Ordo Missae* and related sacramental rites from every Catholic Church in the World."[46]

In addition to the repudiation of the Council and the new Mass, traditionalist ideology continues to be animated by conspiracy theories coupled with apocalyptic imagery of the Great Apostasy. Contradiction motifs show how postconciliar doctrine and discipline oppose what was taught in the past as "unchanging" truth, while exposés highlight "abuse" and organizational dysfunction in the establishment church.

While the main currents of the traditionalist rejection of the Council and the Mass have remained essentially unchanged over the last three decades, several interrelated ideological themes have become more prominent since the mid-1980s. The first centers on renewed efforts to legitimate dissent in the wake of formal schism; the second involves escalating denunciations of Pope John Paul II and his initiatives on behalf of ecumenism and religious liberty. Collaterally, a growing critique of American political institutions and democratic ideology has also emerged within the movement. A third theme revolves around the question of sedevacantism.

Legitimation themes among traditionalist Catholics have assumed added significance since the 1988 excommunications, especially the question of whether the priests and bishops of the society are in actual schism.[47]

In response to Vatican censure, the society has continually pressed the case that the archbishop and his bishops were not excommunicated and that the SSPX is not in schism. Echoing Lefebvre's oft-quoted phrase "Satan's Masterstroke is to have succeeded in sowing disobedience to all Tradition through obedience," society apologists insist that the consecrations do not violate canon law because they were necessitated by the current crisis in the church and legitimated by a "higher law." Preserving the "true faith" in the present situation is a greater imperative than that of obedience to corrupt authority.[48] The society and its supporters cannot be excommunicated for maintaining the faith in a church under a "foreign occupation" by a pope who is a prisoner of "modern philosophy and modernist theology" and a determined conspiracy of "Illuminati and the Freemasons" allied with "Marxist infiltrators."[49] Furthermore, SSPX apologists assert that because the consecrations did not involve power of "jurisdiction" but only that of "orders" (to ensure a future supply of priests), the SSPX is not in schism. Accordingly, only "territorial jurisdiction" is the true hallmark of schism.[50] The traditionalist attack on the "spirit of Vatican II" and the quest for legitimation in the wake of formal schism have also been accompanied by heightened invective toward Pope John Paul II. This antipapal recrimination stems in part from a sense of betrayal by a pontiff who was initially perceived as a conservative who would respond positively to traditionalist concerns but who has, in fact, continued to endorse the "false" Council. In addition, the pope's failure to produce a document shortly after his accession that would have allowed freer use of the old Mass—as was rumored at the time—further exacerbated traditionalist disillusionment with him.[51]

The most vivid evidence from the traditionalist perspective of John Paul II's collusion with the "errors" of the Council can be found in his ecumenical initiatives, espousal of religious liberty, and irenic overtures toward non-Christian religions. Ecumenical work such as that of the Anglican Roman Catholic International Commission discussions, along with the pope's praying with Jews in their synagogue in Rome, praise for Martin Luther, and trips abroad during which he has acknowledged the spiritual truths of non-Christian religions, has been soundly denounced by traditionalists as "blasphemy" and "scandal" that give credence to "pagan" and "heretical" religions, "relativize" the faith, and are tantamount to an "absolute denial of Truth."[52] In particular, John Paul II's meetings at Assisi in October 1986 and January 1993 in which he publicly prayed with religious leaders in celebration of a World Day of Peace have evoked bitter condemnation as prima facie evidence of his "errors" and misguided leadership.[53]

A related ideological motif paralleling the traditionalist attack on the pope is a heightened critique of American constitutional principles and democratic political ideals. This reactionary theme has arisen within the movement primarily, but not exclusively, through several priests who occupy leadership positions within the SSPX in the United States. The thrust of the criticism accentuates the incompatibility of "true" Catholicism with American constitutionalism. According to Bishop Richard Williamson of the society, the American republic was built on "Freemasonic principles profoundly harmful to religion."[54] Other traditionalists have asserted that America was "founded by Protestants" and has a "moral defect" in its polity because of the presumption that all authority proceeds from the people.[55] Traditionalists have also linked the American Revolution with "Masonic" influences in the republic and with a "coup d'etat directed against Christ the King,"[56] while attacking the First Amendment for promoting religious indifferentism. Central to this traditionalist criticism of the American democratic experiment is a rejection of John Courtney Murray's thinking on Catholic acceptance of the separation of church and state.[57] From a traditionalist perspective, the doctrine of separation is an idea inherently "fixed against Catholic Truth."[58]

Although traditionalist "anti-Americanism" ironically resurrects one of the informing assumptions of anti-Catholic prejudice in American society, it is also a position that illustrates the movement's rejection of the legitimacy of a "secular" sphere of thought and culture while promoting a full "restoration of Christendom" modeled on a highly idealized Catholic medieval world.[59]

Issues of Internal Conflict

Traditionalism has been characterized by internal divisions and conflict in spite of the fact that expansion of the movement has increased pressure for cooperation and for a central organization that could coordinate traditionalist initiatives. Conflict has revolved around questions of doctrine, priestly credentials, disputes over property, the proper mode of dissent, whether or not to respond to blandishments of the official church, organizational competition, and the questions of sedevacantism and episcopal succession. While traditionalist Catholics have gathered together for expressions of ritualized solidarity in the form of conventions or forums combining nostalgia, public ritual display, and belligerent denunciations of the "scourge of modernism" in the church, none of these efforts have led to unity or arrested the movement's penchant for internal turmoil.

Following a failed attempt in 1967 to circumvent the American hierarchy by affiliating with what subsequently proved to be a bogus religious order, Fr. De Pauw vowed not to align himself with any other traditionalist group. He has remained independent since. Early traditionalist organizations such as the CTM and the ORCM attacked SSPX priests for "taking over" traditionalist chapel locations in the United States. The TLRC, because of its dubious episcopal credentials, has had a pariah status among many traditionalists since its formation, as have "Feeneyities" and Old Catholic groups linked with the traditionalist cause. Over the years, traditionalist publications have refused to carry notices and advertisements of one group or another, while other organizations have refused to support petition drives for the Tridentine Mass. More recent "pantraditionalist" efforts such as those of the TRC and the STRC to promote cooperation and create coalitions have met with little success because of hard-liner opposition to the embrace of anyone saying the Latin Mass as an ally.[60] The most sectarian traditionalists refuse cooperation with groups that do not take specific ("doctrinal") positions on issues. They also denounce any organizations (such as the SSPX) that show a willingness to "bargain" with Rome. More moderate elements, in turn, eschew any cooperation with "schismatic" sedevacantist groups. Accusations of "schism" and "sect" have been traded repeatedly among partisans within the movement.[61]

Given its current size and organizational resources, the status of the SSPX vis-à-vis the question of unity and cooperating with other traditionalist initiatives is highly significant. However, the society's leadership role in the movement has been impaired by the need to maintain independence and autonomy as a religious order and, more important, by conflict within its own ranks. While the SSPX has been criticized because of the "brash" or "immature" nature of its youthful priest leaders in the United States, more significant disputes have centered on issues ranging from divisions between priest leadership to priests with bogus credentials saying Mass at society-sponsored chapels.[62] Although the SSPX works with some independent traditionalist priests in the United States, provided that they share its "doctrinal" position, refuse to say the new Mass, and are not sedevacantists, the society has refused other cooperative efforts. Fr. Peter Scott, district superior in America, would not permit a listing of SSPX chapels in Fr. Le Blanc's (TRC) *Directory of Tridentine Latin Masses* because the directory was based upon "the principle of Religious Liberty and Ecumenism among traditionalists" and included "strange traditional groups."[63] In 1992 an SSPX priest was dismissed from the society in a dispute over participation in a TRC conference in New Jersey where Bishop Williamson was to accept an award on behalf of Archbishop Lefebvre.[64] In the last several years, controversies have arisen within the society over the improper use of mission funds, alleged "Gestapo tactics" in SSPX schools, and the "anti-American" perspective discussed earlier.[65] These latter attacks on American political values and institutions by society priests have been a source of demoralization that has divided supporters in several

SSPX chapels.[66] The charges have also been condemned by other traditionalist leaders as seriously detrimental to the movement's credibility.[67] In addition to the controversy over reactionary political views within the society, the alleged sedevacantist convictions among some of its leadership have also been a source of dispute impairing the organization's leadership role.

The question of sedevacantism is one of the most divisive issues within the traditionalist movement. Sedevacantist traditionalists hold that the See of Peter is vacant because the current pope and his conciliar predecessors have advanced doctrines ("heresies") and established laws from the Chair of Peter that are "plainly contrary" to the church's solemn teachings (which he could not do were he a valid pope, since the charisma of the office preserves its occupant from promulgating error). The logic of the sedevacantist position is that one cannot repudiate the *Novus Ordo* as a false Mass, and the postconciliar church as a false church, without also concluding that the pope is a false pope.[68] In the United States, the Traditional Catholics of America, the Mt. St. Michael's group, and traditionalists connected with the Thuc episcopal lineage have been the primary promoters of sedevacantism, attacking both conservatives and other traditionalists for "concealing or evading" the truth on this issue.[69] Other groups such as the SSPV hold that while there is "certain and sufficient evidence" that those who profess the "conciliar religion" (i.e., the present hierarchy) do not legitimately hold any position of authority, the issue involves "theological questions" that cannot be resolved conclusively or be made binding on the consciences of the traditionalist faithful (SSPV, "A Statement of Principles"). Because of the "divisive" character of the issue, and out of concern not to alienate Catholics new to traditionalist chapels with such an extreme position, other traditionalist priests who privately adhere to sedevacantism have simply remained silent on the question.

Closely aligned with the sedevacantist issue is the question of episcopal succession. This concern highlights the problem of legitimation faced by traditionalist Catholics; as self-proclaimed heirs to the "true church," traditionalists need a hierarchical and sacramental structure constituent of Catholic identity. There can be no "true church" without the "true Mass," no "true Mass" without "true priests." There cannot be "true priests," however, without seminaries and bishops to ordain them. Traditionalist groups such as the CTM, the ORCM, and the SSPV or those chapels served by individual clerics without an episcopal means of succession are, therefore, necessarily self-limiting endeavors.

Archbishop Lefebvre has been the most prominent expression of hierarchical legitimation in the traditionalist movement. The French archbishop and his SSPX episcopal successors have produced validly ordained (although illicit after 1976) priests who invest the SSPX with ecclesial status and authority. These priests, in turn, enhance the society's claims that it is both restoring and perpetuating the "true church," and that, institutionally, it is the only "realistic hope" for the future of the traditionalist cause.[70]

Two other episcopal initiatives among traditionalists are noteworthy. The first was Francis Schuckardt's "consecration" in 1971 by an American Old Catholic bishop. This consecration was the first attempt in American traditionalist circles to ensure episcopal credentials outside establishment church channels.[71] A later but equally controversial attempt came through the actions of Pierre Martin Ngo-Dhin-Thuc, former archbishop of Hue.

Archbishop Thuc attended the Second Vatican Council. He remained in Rome after its conclusion because of the political situation in South Vietnam. On Christmas in 1975, Thuc went to Palmar de Troya, a small village south of Seville, Spain, where he ordained five laymen to the priesthood, subsequently consecrating three of them as bishops and incurring excommunication for so doing. The following September, Thuc made peace with Rome and repudiated his earlier actions. However, in 1979 he again consecrated bishops, this time in France. Two years later he consecrated two Mexican priests, Fr. Moises Carmona Rivera and Fr. Adolfo Zamora Hernandez. The following year, two traditionalist priests in the United States, Frs. George J. Musey of Friendswood, Texas, and Louis Vezelis, head of the "Order of St. Francis" in Rochester, New York, were consecrated by Thuc bishops who, in turn, consecrated other bishops. Musey subsequently became connected with the Mt. St. Michael's group when in 1985 he "re-ordained" several CMRI priests in the wake of Schuckardt's ouster. Since then, other Thuc bishops have also ordained CMRI priests.[72]

Controversy among American traditionalists over the Thuc bishops, their dubious canonical credentials, and the sedevacantism they promote has been protracted. The Mt. St. Michael's group, in particular, has been the subject of criticism because of its connections with the Thuc bishops. Organizations such as the SSPV and the SSPX advise all traditionalist Catholics to "shun" groups or individuals with which this "schismatic sect" is connected and not to assist at any of their masses.[73]

As previously noted, the most recent attempt to endow traditionalism with episcopal credentials—and thus legitimate and incorporate the movement into the church—has come in the call for a separate apostolic vicariate. This initiative, however, is not considered a viable option by most traditionalists.[74]

Opposition to the Traditionalist Movement

While liberal and progressive Catholics have discounted traditionalists as a fringe element of recalcitrant individuals clinging to a mythic past, the primary opposition to the movement continues to come from conservative Catholic quarters and from the church's official hierarchy. By the mid-1970s, the battle lines between these groups over the pope, the Council, and the Mass had been drawn. Since then, charges and counter-charges have flourished on all sides.

As noted in the prologue, conservative Catholics have generally supported the legitimacy and validity of the Council and the New Mass and repudiated the more value-oriented traditionalist rejection of *aggiornamento*. In addition, conservatives have consistently opposed the traditionalist challenge to hierarchical (notably papal) authority as a manifestation of a "Protestant principle."[75] Following Archbishop Lefebvre's excommunication, publications such as *The Wanderer* and the *Homiletic and Pastoral Review* took the position that traditionalism was a "sect" that had left the church. Catholics were admonished not to participate in the movement's "schismatic services."[76]

Aside from the issues of authority and schism, conservative Catholic opposition to traditionalism also reflects concern that the latter's radicalism damages the conservatives' own campaign against modernist influence in the postconciliar church along with any conservative-inspired efforts to preserve preconciliar modes of Catholic piety and devotionalism in line with the Indult initiatives. Conservatives have been especially concerned that traditionalist sectarianism will harm legitimate efforts to preserve the Latin liturgy. This concern has been forcefully and repeatedly stated by Dr. Anthony Lo Bello, past president of the Latin Liturgical Association. Dr. Lo Bello does not want to see the Latin liturgy disappear from the mainstream of Catholic culture or be relegated to marginalized groups linked with a reactionary anticonciliar campaign against religious liberty or ecumenism. Lo Bello has warned that the Latin liturgy movement, inspired by aesthetic and cultural considerations and the desire to implement *Sacrosanctum Concilium*'s charge not to impose "unnecessary uniformity in matters of worship," is vulnerable to "contamination" and "ruin" if it becomes associated with the schismatic and confrontational tactics of traditionalist Catholics.[77]

The position of the American hierarchy toward traditionalist Catholics has varied since the 1960s but has generally reflected a desire to blunt the movement through a policy of firmness, enticement, and circumvention. Bishops have avoided public debates with traditionalist apologists and have disciplined traditionalist priests under their authority by imposing early "retirement," withdrawing their pensions, or denying them canonical faculties to celebrate Mass publicly or to administer other sacraments in their diocese. Since the mid-1970s, local episcopal authorities have also advised Catholics that they are not "fulfilling their Sunday obligations" by attending traditionalist-sponsored liturgies.

While the American hierarchy has adopted various stratagems in response to the traditionalist challenge, the 1984 Indult and *Ecclesia Dei* have mitigated these efforts. The episcopal reaction to these initiatives, however, has been less than enthusiastic, in part because of the perception that the Tridentine Mass is a "divisive" issue provoked by a small but vocal group of alienated Catholics. Episcopal policy has also reflected uncertainty as to whether the 1984 Indult was strictly a concession to Catholics who grew up with this liturgy, or for more general use irrespective of age. And, as noted earlier, objections were also raised to the *Ecclesia Dei* Commission's practice of issuing "celebrets" to individual priests who had not gone through local episcopal authorities.

Following the 1984 Indult, the majority of American bishops took the position that the action was not designed to foster perpetuation of the officially suppressed form, but was to be used merely as a means of demonstrating the church's "pastoral concern" for Catholics experiencing difficulties adjusting to the new liturgy.[78] In July of 1989, one year after Archbishop Lefebvre's excommunication, the bishops approved various norms regarding the Indult during a meeting at Seton Hall University. According to published reports, agreement was reached to interpret the document as narrowly as possible. Use of the Tridentine Mass among American Catholics would be approached as a privilege rather than a "right," as traditionalists had been contending.[79]

Some American bishops subsequently allowed the Indult Mass only on an "experimental basis," with a minimum attendance requirement, or with the understanding that it was for "elderly" Catholics. In other instances, diocesan newspapers were not permitted to announce the time and place of the Mass. In a few dioceses, permission was refused or was made applicable only with regard to the traditional Mass; all other sacraments had to be obtained at regular parishes. In a move that was anathema to most traditionalists, several bishops granted use of the Indult Mass, provided that the readings and calendar of the *Novus Ordo* were incorporated into the liturgy along with instruction on the spirit and theology of Vatican II.

To date, the American hierarchy continues to approach the Indult initiative as a temporary arrangement rather than a permanent one. The policy is to try and remain "pastorally" sensitive without giving aid and comfort to "extremist elements" in the church. The majority of bishops clearly do not want to see a viable traditionalist community or parish develop around a symbol of dissent that has led to the sidestepping or undermining of their own authority.[80]

Traditionalism in Contemporary Culture

Catholic traditionalism in the United States has had only limited media visibility, in part because of the size and diffusion of the movement and its character as an introversionist sect. Although sharing some attitudes with members of the new religious right—e.g., condemnations of homosexuality, feminism, and New Age religion—traditionalists have generally avoided public connections with politicized evangelical or fundamentalist Christian groups. This avoidance stems in part from the fact that traditionalism is a vehemently anti-ecumenical phenomenon composed of ideological purists resistant to making common cause with Protestant "heretics." Whether the current round of culture wars and escalating debate over abortion and homosexuality will alter this situation remains to be seen.[81] To date, however, the focus of Catholic traditionalism is primarily on *internal* ecclesial conflict. Traditionalists seek to clarify religious boundaries, to offset perceived secular trends *within* the fold, and to gather together "the remnant" to hold fast to the true faith while launching a counterrevolution against those who have purportedly subverted it. As one traditionalist interviewee put it: "We do battle in the sanctuary, not in the street."

Catholic traditionalism has also been marginal on the American religious landscape because it has not been perceived as part of the "cult milieu" that has attracted scholarly and media attention over the last several decades. Although allegations of brainwashing and improprieties have been directed toward the movement—especially Schuckardt's TLRC and the Mt. St. Michael's group, and more recently against the SSPX and SSPV[82]—these charges have not been linked with traditionalism as a whole, nor have they carried the sensationalism of similar charges against the Unification Church or Hare Krishna groups. Because the beliefs and practices of traditionalist Catholics are not deviant enough to provoke widespread public fear or hostility, the movement has not attracted much media attention.

Whether traditionalism will be able to grow into a more viable movement in the next decade is not clear. One can see that traditionalist dissent

262   WILLIAM D. DINGES

is becoming a second-generation phenomenon at the same time that the charismatic leaders who first mobilized that dissent are passing. Furthermore, although followers of Lefebvre and Thuc bishops have provided the ecclesial and sacramental infrastructure needed for the future, other groups have not. Paradoxically, the parts of the movement in the best position to move into the future are the ones that are most identifiably schismatic. The SSPX, for example, has a centralized authoritarian leadership, standardized dogmas, a clearly delineated boundary differentiating insiders and outsiders, and a means of episcopal succession.

In comparison to the social composition of traditionalism two decades ago, the movement now attracts an increasing number of young Catholic families. While traditionalist chapels headed by independent priests serve an aging constituency, those run by organizations such as the SSPX attract a significantly younger one. Many of these families are drawn to SSPX enclaves not only because of a desire for spiritual edification in a community of like-minded people, or for a more "integral" Catholic environment with the "true Mass" and "orthodox" Catholic schools, but because of their concern to save their children from what is perceived as the moral chaos and cultural degeneracy of society at large. Thus the broader societal breakdown that has stimulated the rise of other expressions of religious totalism, militant traditionalism, and fundamentalist apocalypticism also stands to benefit the Catholic traditionalist cause. Traditionalist schools in particular provide both a refuge from this breakdown and a spiritual and cultural antidote to it. In addition, these institutions are relevant to the generation of priestly vocations, a human resource crucial to the future of the movement.

While traditionalism has been institutionalized in an array of organizations and infrastructures, it is not clear at this point that the sectarian protest embodied in the movement is moving in a more routinized and churchlike pattern of adaptive accommodation (denominationalism) traditionally associated with sect development. The doctrinal rigidity of the movement has hardened, not softened, in the wake of Archbishop Lefebvre's excommunication. Additionally, and as several critics have noted, the more typical pattern has been a sect-to-sect dynamic marked by continued division and fragmentation in which individuals follow local (charismatic) traditionalist leaders into another independent initiative claiming to represent the true church.[83]

In spite of the traditionalist call for faithful Catholics in the United States to quit the "modernist" church in the name of "truth and tradition," few have done so. The movement's world-rejecting ethos places traditionalists at a disadvantage in drawing participants from a population of better-educated and more affluent American Catholics who are tied to conventional commitments and networks and who currently give little indication of favoring a high-tension faith over a low-tension one. Growth of the traditionalist movement is also limited by the lack of access to the establishment church's vast administrative and communicative infrastructure, as, for instance, charismatic Catholics have had. Nor, with the exception of Archbishop Lefebvre, have traditionalists had enough social resources or anything but a symbolic means of bargaining with those in positions of power. Nor, as already indicated, have traditionalists resolved the internal conflicts that have divided them and dissipated their organizational resources.

Traditionalist ideological underpinnings are also relevant to the future of the movement because they are so vulnerable. The idea that the See of Peter is vacant or occupied by the "Antichrist" is inherently limited as a rationale for Catholic dissent. In addition, the traditionalist penchant to consider *all* church leadership, even conservative elements within the hierarchy, as "infected" with modernism strains the movement's credibility.[84] The reactionary "anti-American" motifs equating patriotism with sin, along with bizarre theories ranging from anti-Semitic Holocaust denial[85] to the denigration of women, are also unlikely to enhance the credibility of traditionalism among mainstream American Catholics. Furthermore, the traditionalist penchant to make ideology the primary datum of religion is also problematic. The leadership of the SSPX has repeatedly asserted that the society's problems with the Vatican are "doctrinal," not juridical or disciplinary, and that this "doctrinal" level is the *only* one at which negotiations must continue.[86] Given the consistency of the society's position on matters of doctrine, reconciliation with Rome would ipso facto necessitate the repudiation of the Second Vatican Council, the new Mass, the new code of canon law, and the new catechism.

With the waning of the more exaggerated excesses surrounding the initial implementation of Vatican II and the reform of the liturgy, the recruitment base for traditionalism has also contracted. In addition, and as traditionalists themselves have noted, the spread of the Indult Mass and of parishes of the Society of St. Peter may work in a limited fashion to "lure away" Catholics who might otherwise affiliate with SSPX chapels.

Several contemporary issues may facilitate the growth of the movement: a church more responsive to the feminist agenda, more engaged in liturgical renewal, and less dogmatic about doctrinal and pastoral questions contributes to a desire for the church of Pius X. Narrative accounts of converts to Catholicism who have taken up the traditionalist cause often underscore the need for old-fashioned certitude and the beauties of the old liturgy.[87]

Traditionalism stands to make at least minor membership gains as a result of disputes involving Catholics in conflict with a local bishop. Traditionalist organizations such as the SSPX have also embraced more sophisticated use of computers and communications technology in support of their cause. These adaptations will enhance the movement's networking and public visibility and thereby prove conducive to its growth. The increase in the number of younger traditionalist families—who eschew artificial birth control and who tend to have large numbers of children—is also a factor relevant to the future of the movement. In addition, traditionalism has "strong"[88] church characteristics and has thus far maintained sufficient tension with society without inviting undue opposition. These are structural dynamics associated with successful religious movements.[89]

In the American context, traditionalism is unlikely to become a major religio-cultural force, although the movement has assumed a distinctive place in America's dynamic sect and cult milieu while itself exemplifying a diffuse collection of religious subcultures. Traditionalism points to the increased ideological and organizational diversification among American Catholics. In so doing, the movement illustrates one element of Catholicism's "restructuring" along liberal and conservative lines following the pattern of mainline Protestantism.[90]

In the broader context of global Catholicism, traditionalism's symbolic significance extends beyond its sociological status as a sectarian indictment of a perceived tame and worldly faith. As a schismatic movement, traditionalism strikes at the image of the church's unity. It points to the failure of church leadership to deal with the postconciliar crisis of faith and authority by bureaucratic and disciplinary methods,[91] while highlighting the shortcomings of the institutional concern with the appearance of unity over the reality of conflict and dissent. Traditionalism also points to the depth of the discord currently dividing Catholics; the public challenge to hierarchical authority is not confined to liberal or progressive elements or to "dissenting" theologians but can also be found among those holding positions of hierarchical leadership and claiming the high ground of orthodoxy.

While traditionalists, such as those establishment church Catholics with whom they contest, have a coherent system of belief, it is increasingly obvious that the two sides no longer share key theological or cultural assumptions. In this situation, discourse is confined to nearly totally discrete argumentative fields, thereby seriously narrowing the possibility of meaningful reconciliation.

NOTES

1. Joseph Cardinal Ratzinger, remarks in the *National Catholic Register,* 13 August 1989.

2. William D. Dinges, "In Defense of Truth and Tradition: Catholic Traditionalism in America, 1964–1974," *Working Paper Series* 17, no. 2 (Notre Dame, Ind.: Cushwa Center for the Study of American Catholicism, 1986); William D. Dinges, "The Quandary of Dissent on the Catholic Right," in Roger O'Toole, ed., *Sociological Studies in Roman Catholicism: Historical and Contemporary Persepctives* (Lewiston, N.Y.: Edwin Mellen Press, 1989), pp. 107–27; and William D. Dinges, "Roman Catholic Traditionalism," in Martin E. Marty and R. Scott Appleby, eds., *Fundamentalisms Observed* (Chicago: University of Chicago Press, 1991), pp. 66–101.

3. The society currently has 320 priests and 200 seminarians worldwide. Since 1988 there have been an average of eighteen ordinations per year (Robert Moynihan, "The Curia's Dilemma," *Inside the Vatican,* August–September 1993, pp. 8, 12–22).

4. James Likoudis, "CUF and the Liturgy," *Lay Witness,* March 1991; James Likoudis and Kenneth Whitehead, *The Pope, the Council and the Mass: Answers to the Questions "Traditionalists" Are Asking* (West Hanover, Mass.: The Christopher Publishing House, 1981); and Jane Grer, "New Mass, Old Truths: Time for Traditionalists to Stop Bickering," *Crisis,* December 1990.

5. Traditionalists counter that conservative Catholics lack courage in acknowledging that a "definite break" with the church occurred at Vatican II while charging them with a "false sense of obedience" in the face of grave crisis. Accordingly, conservative accommodation to papal authority has undercut resistance to *aggiornamento,* given "aid and comfort to the enemy," and further contributed to the church's "auto-destruction" ("The Remnant Speaks," *The Remnant,* 31 May 1993; Editorial, *The Angelus* 14 [October 1991]; John S. Weiskittel, "Still No Pope in Rome: Answering Our Critics," *The Athanasian* 14 [1 March 1993]: 2–7).

6. *National Catholic Reporter,* 30 July 1993.

7. Patrick Henry Omlor, *Questioning the Validity* (Reno, Nev.: Athanasius, 1969); William Strojie, *The New Mass Invalid Because of Defect of Intention* (Sheridan, Oregon, 1972).

8. Six months after Pope Paul VI promulgated the *Novus Ordo* rite, Cardinal Alfredo Ottaviani, pro-prefect of the Congregation of the Faith, sent a personal letter to the pontiff (25 September 1969) accompanied by a "theological study" of the New Mass. This study (the "Ottaviani Intervention") was a highly critical indictment of the new liturgy as a "grave break" with the liturgical tradition of the church. It first appeared in the United States in *Triumph,* December 1969.

9. James Wathen, *The Great Sacrilege* (Rockford, Ill.: TAN Books, 1971); Lawrence Brey, "The Final Test of Orthodoxy, Pro Multis" (author's file, n.d.); and Strojie, *The New Mass Invalid Because of Defect of Intention.*

10. On the occasion of the ordination of several society priests in October 1983, Lefebvre intimated that in order to "safeguard the Catholic priesthood which perpetuates the Catholic Church," he would consecrate a successor with or without Vatican permission (Archbishop Marcel Lefebvre, "A Public Statement on the Occasion of the Episcopal Consecration of Several Priests of the Society of St. Pius X," 19 October 1993; in "The Episcopal Consecrations: A Decision and Explanatory Documents," SSPX, St. Thomas Aquinas Seminary, Ridgefield, Conn., pp. 2–3).

11. In addition, such celebrations could take place only for those requesting them, not in a parish church, and only under conditions laid down by the local bishop. Masses were to be in accordance with the 1962 missal, in Latin, and with no "interchanging" of liturgical texts.

12. A. J. Matt, "Give the Tridentine Mass a Chance," *The Wanderer,* 18 January 1985.

13. Michael Davies, "Random Thoughts," *The Angelus* 7 (December 1984): 18–22, 27.

14. See *The Wanderer,* 10 January 1985.

15. Richard Williamson, "An Interview with the Bishop," *The Angelus* 12 (May 1989): 11.

16. *The Angelus* 7 (December 1984).

17. *The Angelus* 8 (January 1985): 7.

18. *The Angelus* 8 (January 1985). In addition to the issues raised by traditionalist Catholics, the impracticality of the Indult was also confirmed by the conclusion of an ad hoc commission of cardinals in 1986 that its conditions were too restrictive and should be relaxed. See comments of Augustine Cardinal Mayer, former prefect of the Congregation of Divine Worship, in *30 Days,* October 1988.

19. Francois Laisney, *Archbishop Lefebvre and the Vatican, 1987–1988* (Dickinson, Tex.: The Angelus Press, 1989).

20. Ibid., pp. 114–15.

21. James Scheer, "*Ecclesia Dei:* Summary and Analysis," *The Remnant,* 31 July 1989, p. 6.

22. The *Ecclesia Dei* text and further documentation surrounding the Lefebvre controversy can be found in Laisney, *Archbishop Lefebvre and the Vatican, 1987–1988.*

23. *The Angelus* 14 (November 1991): 2–9; and 15 (April 1992): 2–5.

24. Michael Matt, "ICEL and the Indult Mass," *The Remnant,* 31 January 1993, p. 12.

25. *The Angelus* 13 (August 1990).

26. The deliberations of this "secret meeting" were described in a report in the London *Spectator,* 15 July 1989. Accordingly, the most forceful opposition to the plan came from Cardinal Hume of Great Britain and Cardinal Martinez-Somalo, prefect of the Sacred Congregation for Divine Worship (cf. "A Near Miss for the Old Mass," *The Remnant,* 31 July 1989, pp. 9–10).

27. Letter to the American bishops from Augustine Cardinal Mayer, O.S.B., president of Pontificia Commissio *"Ecclesia Dei,"* author's file. On 2 February 1990, the *Homiletic and Pastoral Review* reported that the *Ecclesia Dei* Commission would not grant "celebrets" to priests unless the local bishop approved. See also Eric Maria de Saventhem, "Red Light for Celebrets?" *The Remnant,* 28 February 1990, pp. 1–5, 7.

28. Catholic Alliance bishops included Robert McKenna, O.P., Monroe, Conn.; J. Vida Elmer, Albany, N.Y.; Oliver Oravec, London, Ontario; and Richard Bedigfeld, South Africa.

29. Anthony Cekada, *The First Stone* (Milwaukee, Wis., 1991); Peregrinus, "Two Bishops in Every Garage," *The Roman Catholic* 12 (Fall–Winter 1992): 16–32; Tarcisius Pivarunas, "Just for the Record" (author's file); Tim Hanson, "A Bishop's Life on the Run," *The Spokesman-Review,* 26 August 1984.

30. *The Angelus* 15 (November 1992): 22–23.

31. Michael Davies, *An Open Letter to Thomas W. Case* (Kansas City, Mo.: Angelus Press, 1993), p. 1.

32. See Lefebvre, "The New Mass and the Pope" (author's file) and "Clarification of Misinformation," *The Angelus* 6 (July 1983): 2–8.

33. For SSPX accounts of the dispute, see Lefebvre, "Clarification of Misinformation"; also Terence Finnegan, "To Refute Their Errors," *The Angelus* 7 (July 1983): 8–12; Richard Williamson, "The Archbishop and the Nine," ibid., pp. 2–7.

34. Lefebvre, "Clarification of Misinformation."

35. The group was headed by Fr. Joseph Bisig and three other priests; sixteen priests and twenty seminarians withdrew from SSPX and went over to the Holy See (*Latin Liturgy Association Newsletter,* 31 December 1988, p. 6).

36. The fraternity, which currently has about forty priests, serves Catholics in France, Germany, Austria, Italy, Switzerland, and the United States (*The Catholic Register* 11 [January 1993]: 8; the Scranton, Pennsylvania *Sunday Times,* 7 February 1993, p. A-24).

37. Interview with Fr. Arnaud Devillers, U.S. regional superior, 23 July 1993, Scranton, Pennsylvania. (See also "Untangling the Latin Mass Controversy," *Our Sunday Visitor* 7 [March 1993]: 12–13; Paul Likoudis, "Fraternity of St. Peter," *Challenge,* March 1993, pp. 21–22.)

38. See letter from Msgr. Raymond Ruscitto, TRC director, to American bishops, 2 June 1989, author's file.

39. Letter to the author from Robert D. De Piante, director, STRC, 10 April 1993.

40. Conde McGinley, *The Enemy within the Church* (n.p., n.d.).

41. Michael Davies, *Liturgical Renewal: Pope John's Council* (New Rochelle, N.Y.: Arlington House, 1977).

42. Francis Fenton, *Holding Fast* (Monroe, Conn.: ORCM, Inc., 1977); Christopher Hunter, "Vatican II: The Council of Contradiction," *The Roman Catholic*, November 1980, pp. 7–11; Ursula Oxford, "The Hidden Enemy of the Church," *The Voice* 13 (November 1972).

43. James Wathen, *The Great Sacrilege* (Rockford, Ill.: TAN Books, 1971); Michael Davies, *The Legal Status of the Tridentine Mass* (Dickinson, Tex.: Angelus Press, 1982); Jacques J. Belderok, "Just How Much Are We Obliged to Attend the New Mass?" *The Catholic Voice* 8 (1 April 1992): 4–5.

44. Omlor, *Questioning the Validity;* Wathen, *The Great Sacrilege;* Michael Davies, *Pope Paul's New Mass* (Dickinson, Tex.: Angelus Press, 1980).

45. *The Angelus* 15 (April 1992); Marc van Es, "The Attendance at Today's Sunday Masses," *The Angelus* 16 (June 1993): 28–31.

46. Anthony Mazzone, "Words to the Wise," *The Remnant,* 15 April 1993.

47. This issue was publicly debated by Michael Davies (negative) and Michael Jones (affirmative) in a forum in Montvale, New Jersey, on 22 August 1993.

48. Tissier de Mallerais, "Supplied Jurisdiction and Traditional Priests," *The Angelus* 16 (February 1993); Frank Denke, "To Rebel . . . or to Preserve?" *Remnant* reprint, 9 August 1988; Davies, *An Open Letter to Thomas W. Case;* Wayne Nichols, "An Apologia Pro Marcel Lefebvre," *The Angelus* 11 (June 1988): 21–23, 26.

49. Franz Schmidberger, "Letter to Friends and Benefactors," 12 February 1989.

50. Richard Williamson, "An Interview with the Bishop," *The Angelus* 12 (May 1989).

51. According to Michael Davies, Cardinal Seper, prefect of the Sacred Congregation for the Doctrine of the Faith, had been indicating to Archbishop Lefebvre since 1979 that such a document would be forthcoming. Davies, *The Legal Status of the Tridentine Mass,* p. 38.

52. Franz Schmidberger, "Assisi II: The Position of the Society of St. Pius X," press release, 6 January 1993.

53. Letter to Father Nicholas Gruner (10 August 1992) from Dennis Tucholski, reprinted in *The Athanasian* 14 (15 January 1993): 4; Schmidberger, "Letter to Friends and Benefactors," 19 October 1992.

54. Richard Williamson, "Friends and Benefactors" letter, 4 February 1993; also Mary Buckalew, "Catholic Principles, Freemasonry and the Republic," *The Angelus* 10 (September 1987): 10–11, 27.

55. *The Remnant,* 15 January 1993, pp. 7–9.

56. Solange Hertz, *The Star-Spangled Heresy: Americanism* (Santa Monica: Veritas Press, 1992); Solange Hertz, "Nowhere Now Here," *The Remnant,* 15 April 1993, p. 11.

57. John K. Weiskittel, "More about the New Age in the Conciliar Church," *The Athanasian* 13 (1 March 1992); Davies, *An Open Letter to Thomas W. Case.*

58. *The Angelus* 15 (May 1992): 21–22.

59. Michael Davies, "Archbishop Lefebvre and the Reign of Christ the King," *The Angelus* 15 (June 1992): 5–11.

60. John K. Weiskittel, "The 'Secret' Sedevacantist Priests," *The Athanasian* 14 (15 April 1993).

61. See, for example, the SSPV attack on the Mt. St. Michael's group, *The Bulletin,* January 1991.

62. Frank Morris, "Dissension in the Ranks of Archbishop Lefebvre's American Followers," *The Wanderer,* 4 October 1979.

63. See Fr. Scott's letter to Rev. Francis Le Blanc, 29 July 1991, published in the *Directory,* along with the reply by Rama P. Coomeraswamy, a former apologist for the society.

64. Thomas W. Case, "The Society of St. Pius Gets Sick," *Fidelity* 11 (October 1992): 28–43.

65. Ibid. For a society rebuttal to these charges, see Peter Scott, "Comments on 'The Society of St. Pius X Gets Sick'" (Kansas City, Mo.: Regina Coeli House, 15 October 1992), and Davies, *An Open Letter to Thomas W. Case;* see also Joe Taschler, "Tensions Rise, Church Rumors Run Rampant in St. Mary's," *The Topeka Capital Journal,* 26 March 1993.

66. One of the key sites in the battle over "Americanism" in the society is the Post Falls, Idaho, complex. Fr. John Rizzo, pastor of Post Falls, was expelled from the society in circumstances relating to the "Americanism" conflict. His associate pastor, Fr. Hunter, wrote a book defending the origin of the U.S. government and denying assertions that it was part of a Masonic plot. Society superiors refused to allow the book to be published. Interview with Fr. Rizzo, St. Mary's, Kansas, 31 July 1993.

67. Clarence Kelly, "America-Bashing by 'Traditionalists,'" *The Bulletin,* August 1993.

68. Donald Sandborn, "Una Cum," *Catholic Restoration,* January–February 1993; Weiskittel, "Still No Pope in Rome."

69. Francis Fenton, "Capsule Comments," *The Athanasian* 14, no. 1 (15 January 1993).

70. *For You and for Many* (January 1978).

71. Throughout his early conflict with the American hierarchy, Fr. De Pauw had the episcopal endorsement of Bishop Blaize Kurz, a German-born Franciscan missionary bishop living in retirement in New York. Kurz was a friend of the De Pauw family and moderator of De Pauw's CTM. Kurz did not, however, ordain any traditionalist priests on behalf of the CTM. Bishop Kurz died in 1973 (Gommar De Pauw, "In Memoriam," in *Sounds of Truth and Tradition* [New York, 1973]).

72. See Cekada, *The First Stone,* for a defense of the Mt. St. Michael's group and discussion of the Thuc connection.

73. Kelly, "America-Bashing by 'Traditionalists'"; Michael Davies, "The Sedevacantists," *The Angelus* 2 (February 1983): 10–12; Cornelio Byman, "Who Is Msgr. Pierre Martin Ngo-Dhin-Thuc?" *The Angelus* 6 (April 1983): 11–12.

74. See *Our Catholic Tradition,* newsletter of the Traditional Mass Society. The apostolic vicariate issue has been pressed by conservative groups such as the Coalition in Support of *Ecclesia Dei* and the Traditional Mass Society. The latter organization initiated a petition drive for such a vicariate. The effort was not driven primarily by accusations of doctrinal deficiency in the new liturgy, but emphasized instead the lost "sense of the sacred" in contemporary Catholic liturgy. The vicariate initiative has also been promoted because of the perception that although some American bishops allowed a "token number" of Latin Masses, most have remained "unalterably opposed to granting full liturgical freedom to the Catholic people" (cf. *Our Catholic Tradition* 11 [4 December 1992]). According to W. R. Opelle, president of the Traditional Mass Society, the vicariate effort has the approval of Cardinal Joseph Ratzinger, who sees it as a solution to fulfilling *Ecclesia Dei.* According to *The Wanderer,* 6 December 1990, Cardinal Ratzinger indicated that the pope would set up a "traditional ordinariate" if presented with a petition with 100,000 signatures.

75. Likoudis and Whitehead, *The Pope, the Council and the Mass.* For a recent conservative attack on the integrity of traditionalism in connection with loyalty to Rome, see *The Wanderer,* 5 August 1993.

76. William B. Smith, "Questions Answered," *Homiletic and Pastoral Review,* November 1992; *The Wanderer,* 26 November 1992; *The Wanderer,* 5 August 1993.

77. *LLA Newsletter* 22 (September 1986); 25 (June 1987); 46 (September 1992).

78. See, for example, "Guidelines for Celebration of Tridentine Mass" in the Diocese of Buffalo, New York, (*LLA Newsletter* 26 [September 1987]: 12–13).

79. *The Wanderer,* 29 June 1989; 20 July 1989.

80. See Cardinal Bernardin's comments on the discussion with Rome regarding the Indult (*LLA Newsletter* 35 [1989]: 12); also comments from Bishop Matthew Clark in a letter to Mr. Dominic A. Qauila listing reasons for not allowing the Tridentine liturgy in his diocese (*LLA Newsletter* 42 [September 1991]).

81. On the abortion issue, traditionalists are "automatically" pro-life. However, they have not been embraced by the pro-life movement within their own church because they are typically not in "good standing" with the local bishop. Interview with Fr. Paul Wickens, Livingston, New Jersey, 19 August 1993.

82. For an account of lawsuits against Schuckardt's TLRC and "cult-like" practices, see Tim Hanson, "A Bishop's Life on the Run," *The Spokesman-Review,* 26 August 1984. In August 1983, a district court judge in Coeur d'Alene awarded $1 million to a Montana man who had sued the TLRC claiming that the church had caused the breakup of his eight-year marriage and caused irreparable damage to the couple's children. The verdict was subsequently overturned. On the SSPX, see Case, "The Society of St. Pius X Gets Sick." For allegations of "cult practices" at the SSPX's St. Mary's complex, see Taschler, "Tensions Rise, Church Rumors Run Rampant in St. Mary's." See also the *Washington Post,* 23 July 1988, for the story of a woman abducted from St. Joseph Novitiate Convent in Round Top, New York, run by the Society of St. Pius V, who was purportedly "brainwashed" by the group.

83. Case, "The Society of St. Pius X Gets Sick."

84. Moynihan, "The Curia's Dilemma."

85. *The Angelus* 15 (September 1992).

86. For an exposition on some of these issues, see the interviews with Bishop Williamson (*The Angelus* 12 [May 1989]: 9–11) and Fr. Franz Schmidberger (*The Angelus* 15 [April 1992]: 2–5).

87. See, for example, the account in "Ambrose Speaks," *The Angelus* 14 (July 1991): 22–23.

88. Dean M. Kelly, *Why Conservative Churches Are Growing* (New York: Harper and Row, 1972).

89. David G. Bromley and Phillip E. Hammond, *The Future of New Religious Movements* (Macon, Ga.: Mercer University Press, 1987).

90. Robert Wuthnow, *The Restructuring of American Religion: Society and Faith since World War II* (Princeton: Princeton University Press, 1988).

91. For a treatment of this issue and a theological reflection on traditionalism, see Hermann J. Pottmeyer, "The Traditionalist Temptation of the Contemporary Church," *America* 168 (5 September 1992): 100–104.

11

Life Battles
The Rise of Catholic Militancy within the American Pro-Life Movement

MICHAEL W. CUNEO

Foreword

Like most other broad-based social movements in contemporary America, the pro-life (or anti-abortion) movement defies easy characterization. Indeed, it is somewhat misleading (although, of course, unavoidable) even to speak of the pro-life movement in the singular: there are, more accurately, several different movements, or movement factions, with different and sometimes competing strategies, ideologies, and personalities.

Upon its emergence in the early 1970s, most of the movement's leading activists—including the American Catholic bishops—advocated what might be described as a pragmatic and reformist approach to the abortion issue. While their ultimate goal was an abortion-free society, the pragmatists claimed, pro-lifers were required to do everything possible, within the limits of civility and legality, to protect fetal life in the interim. Among other things, they held, this meant cultivating popular support for the pro-life position, lobbying legislatures for more restrictive abortion codes, and offering concrete assistance to women facing unplanned and (perhaps) unwanted pregnancies. Moreover, the pragmatists claimed, success in reducing abortion was contingent upon presenting the case for the fetus in terms suitably commensurate with the predominantly secular and liberal disposition of American culture. And this could best be done, they claimed, by invoking scientific evidence and the logic of civil rights, while keeping religion, insofar as possible, out of the bargain.

This reformist strategy succeeded in carrying the anti-abortion movement for a decade or so, but in the early 1980s it began to show evidence of severe leakage. By this time an increasing number of pro-life activists had tired of playing a waiting game, and some of them, desperate for some sudden and tangible victory, wound up abandoning reformism for a much more militant and confrontational approach. There was, according to the militants, something self-evidently evil—and quite possibly demonic—about a society that condoned the daily extinction of unborn life in abortion clinics; and it was foolish to think that such evil could be countered by negotiation and persuasion alone. The time for direct action, in their view, had clearly arrived; and, beginning a new chapter in anti-abortion protest, they took to the streets—blockading clinics, engaging in civil disobedience, and sometimes suffering arrest for their efforts.

Underlying this turn to militancy was a powerful religious motivation. At the start, most militant pro-lifers were Roman Catholic of a highly particular stripe. Deeply conservative on almost all cultural and religious counts, they tended on the whole to be greatly disturbed by the rapid liberalization of Catholicism in the United States after the Second Vatican Council. As their church became more and more attuned to the secular chorus of modern life, it seemed to them at risk of losing its transcendent purpose and salvific reach. American Catholicism, they feared, was becoming an afterthought, not much more than an occasional diversion; and religious commitment, of the sort that in previous ages inspired conversion and sometimes even martyrdom, seemed all but lost.

In the view of such Catholics, however, there was one place where exemplary commitment might still be demonstrated. This was on the doorsteps of abortion clinics: protesting, marching, and praying. Fighting abortion was for them (as it still largely is) as much a sacred crusade as a political enterprise. It was a vehicle for the creation of a heroic and contracultural piety, and a protest simultaneously against the killing of unborn life and the secularization of faith in American Catholicism.

The radicalization of certain of its Catholic participants must be counted as one of the pro-life movement's most fascinating stories, and this chapter dissects the dynamics by which this occurred. This is not to say that other stories are not also worth telling. The pro-life movement is a phenomenon of enormous and sometimes bewildering complexity, and chronicling it exhaustively would require several full-length volumes. One story which certainly deserves telling, and to which only brief reference is made below, concerns the joining together of Roman Catholics and evangelical Protestants in street protest against abortion. Although Catholics were the first to engage in civil disobedience and direct action on the anti-abortion front, it was not long before evangelicals also made their presence felt, and by the late 1980s the two groups constituted one of the most unlikely (and abidingly controversial) ecumenical alliances on the American religious scene.

Indeed, the ecumenical character of the pro-life movement as a whole is another theme worthy of more systematic attention. For some time now, the movement has had three major functional divisions, dedicated respectively to protest, service, and more intellectually based endeavors such as political lobbying and public relations. Not only in protest but also in the other two areas, Catholics and evangelicals (and sometimes others as well) have worked closely and intensely, and, considering their inherited theological and cultural differences, this relationship has usually gone remarkably well.

A brief word or two is spoken in this essay about the service dimension of the anti-abortion movement, which includes crisis pregnancy centers and the like, but almost nothing at all about the movement's self-appointed intellectual elite. In addition to the Catholic bishops, a number of individuals over the past two decades have undertaken substantial critiques of America's permissive abortion policy, and also of the political, legal, and cultural factors underlying it. Some of these critiques—most notably Mary Ann Glendon's *Divorce and Abortion in Western Law* (Cambridge: Harvard University Press, 1988) and John T. Noonan's *A Private Choice* (New York: Free Press, 1979)—have made lively and original contributions to the public debate on abortion, and the work of pro-life intellectuals in general is certainly worthy of more extended discussion. Once again, however, and undoubtedly much to the chagrin of at least some intellectuals, the primary concern here is with the rise of street activism among certain Catholic pro-lifers, a topic which is easily as important and about which much less is reliably known.

In terms of street activism, one could focus on Operation Rescue, a "direct action" organization whose support has historically been more heavily evangelical than Catholic, or on such currently newsworthy Catholic activist groups as Mary's Lambs for Jesus and Catholics United for Life. A longer paper almost certainly would have found room to analyze in greater detail the fluctuating political fortunes of the pro-life movement. And a fuller discussion of the ways in which people (Catholic or otherwise) are actually recruited into pro-life activism would have shed additional, and valuable, light on the movement's varied ideological complexion.

Life Battles

The pro-life movement in the United States has never been the preserve exclusively of Roman Catholics. Since its inception more than twenty years ago, the movement has included people of diverse religious allegiance as well as some of no religious allegiance whatsoever. Nevertheless, it has been Catholics, more than anyone else, who have infused the movement with strength and personality. Indeed, without Catholics the movement might never have gotten started.

For all practical purposes, the movement began in July 1970 when Father James McHugh of the Catholic Family Life Bureau called a meeting in Chicago that was attended by about seventy prominent anti-abortion activists. Throughout the 1960s, anti-abortion (or pro-life) groups had been cropping up across the country to battle abortion liberalization at the state level. Most of these groups were heavily Catholic in composition, and they generally held meetings at their local parish church or school. For the most part, however, there was very little contact between groups, and very little sense of shared purpose. In 1967 Fr. McHugh sought to remedy this situation by creating a national network of pro-life leaders which he called the National Right to Life Committee (NRLC). It was not until three years later in Chicago, however, that the NRLC actually met formally for the first time.[1]

Over the next several years, the NRLC evolved into a fully national organization, with chapters in virtually every state and a rapidly expanded grassroots membership. Such growth would clearly not have been possible apart from the institutional support of the American church. In addition to modest funding, the church provided local chapters with meeting facilities, office equipment, and, most important of all, a seemingly endless supply of recruits. Moreover, with their access to both the diocesan press and the Sunday pulpit, local chapters were almost guaranteed a constant flow of free publicity.

Whatever momentum the fledgling movement might have gained during these years was brought suddenly to a halt in January 1973, when the epochal *Roe v. Wade* decision of the American Supreme Court abolished state laws restricting abortion and effectively opened the door in the United States to abortion on demand. Not in their wildest dreams had pro-lifers expected the Court to declare abortion a constitutional right, and it took them several months simply to recover from the shock.[2] But recover they did. In June 1973, at its national convention in Detroit, the NRLC served notice that the battle over abortion had only just begun. Far from resigning themselves to the Court's decision, the organization proclaimed, pro-lifers were prepared to do everything possible to win protection for fetal life.

It was also in Detroit that the NRLC elected to sever formal connections with the church. Prior to 1973, Fr. McHugh had supervised the organization on behalf of the National Conference of Catholic Bishops (NCCB). Not all activists, however, felt comfortable with this arrangement. Some worried that the bishops held too much control, and others questioned the advisability of any formal link to the church whatsoever. In the face of persistent accusations in the media and elsewhere that opposition to abortion was a peculiarly Catholic preoccupation, the last thing the NRLC needed was to be perceived as a mere surrogate of the church hierarchy. Not only, therefore, did the organization declare its autonomy in Detroit, but it also elected a Protestant woman named Marjorie Mecklenburg as its first president and appointed four other Protestant women to its inaugural board of directors.[3]

Although now formally independent of the church, the NRLC remained in many ways inextricably Catholic. Probably upward of 75 percent of its grassroots activists had been raised in the church, and many of these strongly disapproved of artificial contraception as well as abortion. This in particular posed an immediate difficulty for the NRLC leadership. They could hardly denounce artificial contraception without incurring public opprobrium, but neither could they recommend it as a preventive to abortion without offending their largely Catholic constituency. The solution they adopted—which was to declare the NRLC scrupulously neutral on the subject—wound up satisfying virtually no one.[4]

In any event, pro-lifers had far more urgent matters to attend to than internal disagreements over birth control. Their ultimate objective after 1973 was to win support in Congress and state legislatures for a constitutional amendment which, once passed, would nullify *Roe* by guaranteeing protection of fetal life from the moment of conception onward. In the meantime, however, they were determined to cause as much trouble for *Roe* as possible. Beginning in 1973—and continuously thereafter for the next two decades—the NRLC lobbied at both the state and federal levels for laws that would prohibit the use of public funds for abortion services, and also for laws that would require waiting periods (or, in the case of minors, parental consent) before abortions could be performed. And as might be expected, considering the tremendous regional diversity of the United States, the results of all this political activity were notoriously mixed. In some states with heavy Catholic populations, such as Florida and Louisiana, and in Utah, with its Mormon majority, pro-lifers scored notable success in restricting abortion, but in many other areas their efforts went largely unrewarded. (At the federal level, they eventually did reap modest political success, but not for the most part until the 1980s and the Republican administrations of Ronald Reagan and George Bush.)[5]

In addition to exerting intensive political pressure during this period, pro-lifers fought hard to win the battle for public opinion. And for this they counted primarily upon the power of science. Liberalized abortion, in the view of many movement leaders, was a colossal mistake, a tragedy of ignorance. If Americans could only learn more of the fetus—if they could come to terms with its essential humanity—support for abortion would almost certainly evaporate. It was unnecessary and quite likely counter-productive, they reasoned, to bring religion and morality into the equation. Simply advertise the relevant scientific facts, and eventually Americans would recognize the fetus as human and hence worthy of legal protection.

Not all pro-lifers, to be sure, were happy with this approach. Some suspected that much more was involved with the trend toward abortion liberalization than just ignorance of biology. Nevertheless, movement leaders were anxious to prove that a compelling case for the fetus could be made on strictly secular grounds, without reference to either confessional morality or religious dogma. As much as anything else, they wanted to dispel charges (which had become rampant in the news media during the late 1960s and early 1970s) that pro-lifers were mere stooges of the Catholic bishops dedicated to imposing their own straitjacketed morality upon the entire nation. In the wake of *Roe*, then, references to religion were conspicuously absent from movement literature, and pro-life educational materials consisted almost entirely of descriptions of fetal development and graphic depictions of aborted fetuses.[6]

In their efforts during the late 1970s to break the Catholic stigma of their movement, pro-lifers found an unexpected—and immensely important—ally in the person of Bernard Nathanson. Nathanson was an obstetrician-gynecologist in New York City when in 1969 he helped to found the National Association for Repeal of Abortion Laws (NARAL), an organization dedicated to the elimination of restrictive abortion laws in New York and elsewhere. Moreover, from February 1971 through September 1972, he served as director of the Center for Reproductive and Sexual Health in New York City, which was then the world's busiest abortion clinic. In November 1974, however, Nathanson confessed his misgivings in the *New England Journal of Medicine:* "I am deeply troubled by my own increasing certainty that I had in fact presided over 60,000 deaths. . . . We are taking life, and the deliberate taking of life, even of a special order and under special circumstances, is an inexpressibly serious matter."[7]

Dr. Nathanson's change of heart would involve far more than a mere act of literary contrition. In subsequent years the former apostle of abortion freedom would become one of America's foremost champions of the fetus, tirelessly touring the country to dispute pro-choice arguments he himself had once helped to formulate. Nathanson's defection from the enemy was an inspirational boon for the pro-life movement. Although some pro-lifers likened it to Paul's revelation of light on the road to Damascus, the real political value of Nathanson's conversion was precisely its lack of religious motive. An avowed atheist of Jewish background, he credited his changed evaluation of abortion entirely to the scientific testimony of fetology. Only the invincibly obtuse, he claimed, could fail to recognize the humanity of the fetus as it was shown through new diagnostic procedures such as fetoscopy.[8]

Besides invoking the testimony of science, pro-lifers sought during the 1970s to enhance their movement's appeal by comparing it with the movement to abolish slavery in the United States more than a century earlier. Like the abolitionists, they claimed, pro-lifers were committed to defending an entire class of humanity that had been consigned to legal oblivion. Indeed, some activists drew an explicit parallel between the 1857 *Dred Scott* decision, when the Supreme Court decreed that a slave or a slave's child was not an American citizen, and the *Roe* decision, when Justice Blackmun ruled that "meaningful humanhood" did not begin until birth.[9] No less than slavery, they argued, liberalized abortion affronted America's best instincts for justice and betrayed its founding ideals. "When you think about it," Dave Andrusko, a leading pro-life journalist, wrote in 1983, "there is a fundamental irony at the heart of the battle to save the children. For it is the pro-life movement, scorned and ridiculed by the media as a 'reactionary' force, that is the principal defender of the most revolutionary idea of the American experiment—the idea that all men and all women and all children, born and unborn, are created equal."[10]

Rather more controversial was the analogy that some pro-lifers in the late 1970s attempted to draw between post-*Roe* America and Nazi Germany. The ease and rapidity with which abortions were performed after *Roe,* they claimed, was cruelly reminiscent of the systematic annihilation of European Jews under Hitler. In both cases the victims were subjected to a process of thoroughgoing depersonalization, and in both cases as well their killing was justified by a massive campaign of Orwellian propaganda. By the early 1980s, the Holocaust analogy had attained considerable currency within pro-life ranks, and in 1983 it was provocatively fleshed out by William Brennan in his book *The Abortion Holocaust*. More than anything else, as James Burtchaell has pointed out, it vividly captured the sense of rage and helplessness that many anti-abortion activists felt a decade after *Roe*.[11]

The Role of the American Catholic Bishops

Despite having lost control of the NRLC in 1973, the American Catholic bishops were by no means inactive on the abortion front in the years after *Roe*. Almost immediately after the decision was handed down, the bishops declared their intention to fight for a constitutional amendment banning abortion; and they also attempted to sidetrack accusations that their involvement with the issue amounted to theocratic meddling. In testimony before a Senate Judiciary Committee subcommittee that was holding hearings on the subject of abortion in 1974, Philadelphia's Archbishop John Cardinal Krol denied that the bishops wanted "to impose [their] morality on others."

> [First of all], the right to life is not an invention of the Catholic Church or any other church. It is a basic human right which must undergird any civilized society. Second, either we all have the same right to speak out on public policy or no one does. We do not have to check our consciences at the door before we argue for what we think is best for society. We speak as American citizens who are free to express our views and whose freedom, under our system of government, carries with it a corresponding obligation to advocate positions which we believe will best serve the good of our nation. Third, in our free country, decisions concerning issues such as the one before this subcommittee are made by legislators who themselves are free to act according to their own best judgment. We dare not forget, however, that to separate political judgment from moral judgment leads to disorder and disaster.[12]

With these brief remarks, Cardinal Krol established a framework of discourse to which the American bishops would return time and again over the next twenty years: Abortion was by no means a uniquely Catholic concern, but Catholics (and Catholic bishops) had a constitutional right and a moral obligation to inform public policy on the matter. There were limits, of course, to how far they could go in this regard. The doctrine of church-state separation prevented the bishops from dictating abortion policy to legislators, but it most certainly did not exempt legislators (and especially Catholic legislators, one presumes the cardinal to mean) from taking seriously the church's teaching on abortion. Just how seriously Catholic legislators were obliged to take such teaching, and just how far the bishops could go in persuading them to take it seriously, were matters that the cardinal left open to question.

What seemed beyond question, however, was the bishops' own resolve on the issue. Indeed, it is doubtful that the Catholic leadership of any country in the Western world (with the possible exception of Ireland) has been more outspoken on abortion, or more actively engaged in fighting it, than the American bishops.[13] In addition to denouncing *Roe* in the media and testifying against it in Congress, they wasted little time in adding their own specialized structures to the pro-life movement. These included the bishops' Committee for Pro-Life Activities, which has sponsored pro-life educational material for the past twenty years, and the separately incorporated National Committee for a Human Life Amendment, which has vigorously lobbied in support of various pro-life legislation.[14] Moreover, in November 1975, the bishops released their exceedingly ambitious *Pastoral Plan for Pro-life Activities,* which called for, among other things, the creation of action committees in each congressional district to build support for pro-life political initiatives.

The Contraceptive Mentality

These episcopal initiatives were not, of course, meant to detract from the efforts of the wider pro-life movement, and the bishops continued throughout the 1970s and 1980s to lend moral, logistical, and, more rarely, financial support to the National Right to Life Committee, which remained the movement's dominant organization. In addition to battling abortion during this period, however, the NRLC was hard-pressed simply to keep its own house in order. Practically from the beginning, most of the organization's leading activists had advocated a pragmatic and reformist approach to the abortion issue. If progress was to be made, they believed, it was essential that pro-lifers learn to communicate in measured tones with the ambivalent, unconverted sectors of American society. As opinion polls consistently revealed, most Americans (or at least a healthy majority of them) occupied the middle ground on abortion, favoring neither its total availability nor its total prohibition.[15] It would take sustained and reasoned discourse, not diatribes against birth control and other real or imaginary evils, the pragmatists believed, for this ambivalent majority to be converted to the pro-life position.

Moreover, the pragmatists in the NRLC believed as well that political success on the abortion front required a certain measure of strategic flexibility. Although pro-lifers hoped eventually to eliminate virtually all abortions, they were obliged for the moment to operate within the realm of political feasibility. This might mean supporting legislative proposals or other initiatives which would not curtail abortion completely but which held promise nevertheless of reducing its frequency. Any advance (however modest) on the issue, in the pragmatists' view, was preferable to none at all.

Not all pro-lifers agreed with this approach, however, and by the late 1970s the NRLC was rife with dissension. One of the principal causes of dissension was the organization's position on birth control. To begin with, some activists (almost all of whom were Catholic) found it indefensible that the NRLC was tacitly tolerant of so-called abortifacients, such as the IUD and some birth control pills, which worked not by preventing conception but by preventing a newly fertilized ovum from implanting in the wall of the uterus. If human life truly began at conception, the dissenters claimed, pro-lifers were morally compelled to condemn abortifacients just as strongly as abortion itself. The NRLC's failure to do so, in their view, was an unforgivable concession to popular taste.

In any event, the controversy over birth control within pro-life ranks extended well beyond the subject of abortifacients. Throughout the 1970s, pro-lifers had sought desperately to understand the cultural sources of changed attitudes toward abortion. How did something that to past generations seemed self-evidently wrong suddenly achieve the status of a right and even at times a moral good? By the turn of the decade, many Catholic activists were convinced that the evidence pointed to one inescapable conclusion. The primary engine behind increased public acceptance of abortion, they claimed, was the "contraceptive mentality" which had taken thoroughgoing hold of Western culture since the 1960s. With the contraceptive mentality, says Donald DeMarco, a Canadian whose writings on the subject are well known to Catholic pro-lifers in the United States, "the separation of intercourse from procreation is taken for granted and the contracepting partners feel that in employing contraception, they have severed themselves from all responsibility for a conception that might take place as a result of contraceptive failure. . . . At any rate, the 'contraceptive mentality' implies that a couple has not only the means to separate intercourse from procreation, but the right or *responsibility* as well" (emphasis in original). Or, as Father Paul Marx, the most famous American proponent of the "contraceptive mentality" thesis, puts it, once sexual pleasure is divorced from procreation, the "resolve to prevent a child from coming to be is often sufficiently strong that one will eliminate the child whose conception was not prevented."[16]

Quite clearly, then, says DeMarco, the conventional wisdom on the subject could not be more skewed. Far from reducing abortion, contraception leads almost inevitably to its dramatic increase. "Using the contraceptive mentality to fight the abortion mentality confuses cause and effect. It is like trying to put out a fire with matches." If pro-lifers were truly serious about stopping abortion, says DeMarco, they would have to dedicate themselves first of all to defeating the contraceptive mentality and the distorted conception of sexuality of which it was simultaneously symptom and cause. To think otherwise was to engage in mere evasion. "Since abortion thrives on the contraceptive mentality, we fight abortion realistically not by doubling our efforts to intensify the contraceptive mentality, but by working to eliminate it."[17]

The contraceptive mentality thesis would encounter considerable resistance within the anti-abortion movement. Many activists, including quite a few Catholics, were unconvinced of the causal connection it implied between contraception and abortion, and some of these people themselves practiced artificial birth control. Others who found it persuasive in varying degrees were opposed to its public transmission on the ground that an attack against contraception would almost certainly nullify whatever credibility the movement possessed. A public seemingly reluctant to consider biological evidence for the humanity of the fetus could not be expected to swallow an argument of such decidedly Catholic flavor. Nevertheless, the thesis would assume a privileged place in the ideology of several pro-life organizations which arose during the late 1970s and early 1980s in conscious opposition to the National Right to Life Committee.

The first of these, the American Life League (ALL), was founded in 1979 by Judie Brown with her husband, Paul Brown. For several years in the mid-1970s, Judie Brown was a high-ranking administrator with the NRLC, but mounting disaffection with the organization forced her resignation. "I had a number of problems with the NRLC—some personal and some political," she informed me in an interview, "but my main objection was their position on contraception. The NRLC refused to admit that the pill and IUD are abortifacients. And more than that, their entire stance on contraception has been a monumental lie. Ninety-nine percent of the time, contraception results in abortion. How could they claim to be dealing with abortion when they refused to deal with this basic reality?" Significantly, Brown was not pleased either with the NRLC's scrupulously secular approach to the abortion issue. "Even before I left the organization," she told me, "I believed their nondenominational and nonreligious emphasis to be totally ineffective. The practice of religion belongs in the public arena. It is so wrong to suppress this. We should be able to say that abortion is a sin against God and God's law. The NRLC wouldn't stand for this."[18]

With the American Life League, then, the Browns attempted to place pro-life activism in the United States on an entirely new footing. Not only was their organization unabashedly religious in orientation, but it was also fully committed to taking a public stand against artificial contraception. And on this score, the Browns would receive invaluable support from an organization called Human Life International (HLI). Founded in 1981 by Fr. Paul Marx, a Benedictine monk and one-time sociology professor at St. John's University in Minnesota, HLI advertises itself as "a non-profit organization devoted to educating people about the evils of abortion, sterilization, infanticide, euthanasia, contraception and other modern threats to life and family." With an annual budget of almost $5 million, HLI publishes eight periodicals, sponsors pro-life educational conferences and seminars on natural family planning, and maintains twenty-one chapters in the United States and forty-nine worldwide. Moreover, in its promotional literature, HLI boasts that its attacks against "anti-family and anti-life" policies throughout the world have caused Planned Parenthood to label it "Public Enemy No. 1."[19]

As might be expected, HLI's major area of concern over the past fifteen years or so has been contraception and the associated ills to which it has allegedly given rise. "Contraception," an HLI position paper asserts, "poses numerous medical dangers to women. It introduces an artificial barrier between husband and wife. Acceptance of contraception has led to widespread sexual promiscuity and an ever-increasing explosion of crippling and deadly venereal diseases, including AIDS. Contraception does not prevent abortion; rather, contraception always leads to abortion, and to increased abortion rates." According to Fr. Marx, it is simply mind-boggling that contraception has not been universally condemned by pro-lifers in the United States. "When I first started Human Life International," he told me during an interview at the organization's headquarters in Gaithersburg, Maryland, "there was great confusion within the pro-life movement over birth control. The NRLC seemed almost willfully blind to the fact that contraception always—and I mean always—causes abortion. They wouldn't take a stand against it then, and they still won't. It's ridiculous to think we can stop abortion without first doing something about the contraceptive mentality that produces it."[20]

It is difficult to know exactly how many Catholic pro-lifers subscribed to the contraceptive mentality thesis in the late 1970s. What is certain is that the thesis held its greatest appeal among Catholics who were personally attached to *Humanae Vitae,* Pope Paul VI's 1968 encyclical condemning artificial contraception. Pro-life activism had always been attractive to such Catholics (almost all of whom were deeply conservative in both a theological and a cultural sense), and the thesis gained currency as they emerged in the l980s as the movement's most militant force.

Controversies within the Pro-Life Ranks

Contraception was by no means the only source of contention within pro-life ranks during the 1980s. In December 1981, in keeping with its generally pragmatic and reformist tendencies, the NRLC decided to lend its official support to a proposed constitutional amendment sponsored by Senator Orrin Hatch of Utah. Although the so-called Hatch Amendment would not have actually banned abortion, its passage would have permitted individual states to legislate restrictions. While certainly not a perfect solution, according to the NRLC, the Hatch Amendment at least offered a realistic promise of reducing the nation's abortion rate. Moreover, it stood a far better chance of surviving the ratification process than a more radical measure proposed by Senator Jesse Helms which called for explicit constitutional acknowledgment that human life begins at conception.[21] For the moment, anyway, the NRLC believed, the Hatch Amendment was probably the most pro-lifers could reasonably hope for.

In the view of at least some pro-lifers, however, the NRLC could not have been more wrong. Endorsing something such as the Hatch Amendment, they claimed, was equivocation and compromise of the worst kind—a sort of bargaining with the lives of unborn children. If fetal life was truly sacred, pro-lifers were compelled to protect it absolutely and without exception, not settle for halfway measures whereby abortion—at the discretion of state legislatures—would be permitted in some cases and disallowed in others. If there previously had been any doubt, the dissenters claimed, it was now perfectly clear that the NRLC was unprepared to take an unequivocal stand on behalf of unborn life.

Not surprisingly, some of the most vociferous opposition to the Hatch Amendment and the NRLC endorsement of it came from more militant groups such as the American Life League and Human Life International.

What the NRLC utterly failed to appreciate, claims ALL president Judie Brown, was that abortion is an issue that transcends ordinary political solutions. "With the Hatch Amendment and with contraception, the NRLC was always too anxious to compromise. But abortion isn't like other issues where compromise might make sense. We're talking life and death here. In accepting compromise, they've forgotten the baby in the womb, and they've forgotten that only God can finally stop abortion. With compromises like the Hatch Amendment, we limit God—God's out of the picture. We have to take the high moral road and count on God's power for victory." Fr. Paul Marx of HLI is no less emphatic on the question of political compromise. "The Hatch Amendment was totally disastrous," he says, "and it was shameful—but almost to be expected—that the NRLC supported it. Even if it had passed, the best we could have hoped for is that some states would have prohibited most abortions but allowed abortion for the so-called hard cases—rape, incest, some fetal deformity, and so forth. But this is totally unacceptable. The NRLC dislikes me because of my emphasis on contraception, and also because I refuse to support any measure that would eliminate even 99 percent of abortions. I'm an absolutist, and Catholics such as myself say, 'No Killing.'"

Perhaps the most deeply upsetting aspect of the Hatch affair for activists such as Fr. Marx and Judie Brown was the performance of the American Catholic hierarchy. After considerable internal debate, the National Conference of Catholic Bishops decided in late 1981 to throw its support behind the Hatch Amendment instead of the more radical measure sponsored by Senator Helms. In the view of more than a few Catholic activists, this was conclusive proof that the bishops as a group were governed more by considerations of political expediency than by genuine compassion for fetal life. It was bad enough that the NRLC was prepared to settle for a compromise solution, claims Fr. Marx, but the decision of the bishops to do likewise was nothing short of a national disgrace. "Of course the bishops should have known better," he says. "We already knew they were weak on contraception, and with their support of Hatch they proved they were weak on abortion too. Their actions were a scandal to the entire American church. At least now we realized what we were up against—it was up to ordinary Catholics to fight the good fight in spite of their religious leaders."

In the end, both the Hatch and Helms measures failed to pass for lack of congressional support, but the controversy surrounding them brought to full boil an ideological conflict that had been simmering within the pro-life movement almost since its inception. On one side were the pragmatists, who favored an incremental and ostensibly secular approach to the abortion issue; and on the other side were the purists, who were contemptuous of political compromise and who believed that abortion could not finally be eliminated without transcendent intervention. Indeed, by the early 1980s the campaign against abortion had ceased for many pro-life purists to be a political campaign in the ordinary sense. For reasons that were not as yet fully apparent, it had instead become for them a sacred crusade.

Expansion of the Movement

Despite such internal difficulties, the pro-life movement was considerably enlarged in the late 1970s and early 1980s by an influx of Protestant evangelicals.[22] After decades of political quiescence, evangelicalism re-emerged during this period as a major force on the American political landscape, and abortion was one of the issues that immediately engaged it. In the view of most evangelicals, liberalized abortion constituted evidence that American society had become spiritually unhinged and morally destitute. Since the 1960s especially, they claimed, the nation as a whole had shifted its allegiance from Christianity to an ethically bankrupt secular humanism, and abortion, sexual permissiveness, and family breakdown were just some of the more obvious consequences. In order to avoid falling into irrevocable decline, they claimed, America would have to return to the Christian beliefs and values that had once made it great.

With the resurgence of evangelicalism, in fact, there developed within the pro-life movement a rather remarkable ecumenical alliance. Increasingly throughout the 1980s, and sometimes to their mutual astonishment, militant Catholic activists and evangelicals discovered that they inhabited strikingly similar worlds. Both regarded liberalized abortion as a sordid triumph of secular humanism, and both conceived pro-life activism as primarily a religious (rather than a political) undertaking. Moreover, evangelicals were generally delighted to learn that many Catholic activists shared their commitment to traditional biblical teaching as well as their disdain for theological modernism. Though evangelicals sometimes cringed at the ardent Marian piety and anti-contraceptive views of their Catholic colleagues, they were willing to tolerate certain excesses when so much else seemed right. Militant Catholic activists, for their part, were greatly impressed both by the moral zeal of evangelicals and by the strength and apparent sincerity of their religious convictions. Indeed, as evangelicals grew increasingly prominent in the movement throughout the 1980s, pro-life discourse began to take on a more explicitly religious content. Scriptural passages appeared alongside civil rights slogans on pro-life placards and broadsheets, and public prayer, which was exceptional in the movement's earlier years, became a regular feature of pro-life rallies and demonstrations.

An equally important development in the early 1980s was the strategic alliance that certain sectors of the anti-abortion movement, including the National Right to Life Committee, fashioned with the Republican Party. Throughout the 1970s, the anti-abortion movement had prided itself on its political diversity. Far from being uniformly right-wing in political disposition, the movement included a fair number of political liberals and even a smattering of self-described radicals. In 1971, for example, Juli Loesch, who had previously worked as an organizer with the United Farm Workers, founded a radically pacifist organization called Prolifers for Survival. For the next fifteen years, until its disbandment in March 1987, Prolifers for Survival attempted to combine opposition to abortion with opposition as well to capital punishment and the nuclear arms race. Liberalized abortion, according to Juli Loesch and her organization's approximately two thousand adherents, was symptomatic of a deep-seated cultural violence that threatened the very survival of the Western world.[23] Another organization on the pro-life left which also emerged during the 1970s was Feminists for Life. By aligning itself so unequivocally with a pro-choice orthodoxy, the organization claimed, mainstream feminism in the United States had betrayed the egalitarian ideals that were its original inspiration. "Modern feminism has been bewitched by abortion," wrote Rosemary Bottcher on behalf of Feminists for Life in a 1983 article. "Mesmerized by its own evil spell, many feminists have been tricked into advocating the Orwellian notion (everyone is equal, but some are more equal than others) that has been the excuse for all discrimination. Their insistence that the lives of unborn children have no significance poisons the roots of feminism by betraying the very essence of the concept of equality."[24]

It is quite true, of course, that groups such as these were not representative of the broader pro-life movement. Probably a majority of pro-lifers in the 1970s voted Republican, and relatively few had any formal connection with either the peace or the feminist movements. Nevertheless, many of those who voted Republican did so primarily because the Democratic Party subscribed to a pro-choice position on abortion, not because they felt any particular affinity for economic or political conservatism. In the 1970s, in other words, the Republican Party was the party of the anti-abortion movement principally by default.

At the turn of the decade, however, the Republican Party and leading segments of the pro-life movement decided that it was in their mutual interest to join forces more formally. In the view of Republican strategists such as Richard Viguerie and Paul Weyrich, the Republican Party stood to benefit electorally from an alliance with the anti-abortion movement. And in the view of leading pro-lifers such as John Willke of the NRLC and Judie Brown of ALL, the Republican Party under newly elected president Ronald Reagan seemed genuinely committed to winning full legal protection for fetal life. This tactical alliance, or marriage of convenience, between movement and party survived for almost a decade, but in the end it faltered badly.[25] As sociologist James R. Kelly has pointed out, the interests of fiscal conservatives within the Republican Party were never wholly compatible with the interests of the anti-abortion movement.[26] Whereas pro-lifers were committed to eliminating abortion entirely, regardless of the public cost this might entail in terms of expanded welfare and child-support payments, Republicans as a rule were primarily concerned instead with reducing government expenditures. As long as *Roe* remained safely intact, of course, Republicans were free to protest abortion as loudly as they wanted without fear of practical economic consequence. In July of 1989, however, the party's resolve on the issue was put to a critical test when the Supreme Court, in *Webster v. Reproductive Health Services,* upheld as constitutional a Missouri statute that prohibited the use of public funds and facilities for abortion services and stipulated that doctors not abort fetuses of twenty weeks' gestation or more without first testing for viability.

Although the *Webster* decision did not overrule *Roe,* it was, as Lawrence Tribe suggests, an "open invitation" to state legislatures to see how far they could actually go in restricting abortion.[27] Now that restricting abortion was a real possibility, the Republican Party was forced to show exactly how committed it was to the cause of fetal life. The truth was not long in coming. Shortly after *Webster* was handed down, Lee Atwater, then chairman of the National Republican Committee, announced that the party was open to a wide range of positions on abortion. And later the same year, three new Republican political action committees were formed for the express purpose of raising funds for pro-choice candidates. In the view of James R. Kelly, this turn of events was hardly surprising. "When *Webster* moved the question of abortion restrictions from the Court to the state legislatures," he writes, "the Republican Party simply followed the worldwide pattern [whereby] fiscal conservatives quickly come to support abortion as a way of controlling the births of what they take to be the 'unproductive' classes."[28]

Judie Brown speaks for more than a few pro-lifers when she claims that the alliance between movement and Republican Party was exceedingly shortsighted. "It is absolutely correct that we made a huge mistake in aligning ourselves with the Republicans. Our issue is nonpartisan and transcends political parties. Ronald Reagan is the person mainly responsible for the alliance. I and other leaders in the movement met with him at the White House in 1981, and we were tremendously impressed. He seemed very dedicated to our cause, and I still think he was sincere. He made a human life amendment part of the party platform. The problem is that Ronald Reagan is not the Republican Party. We have to stick to our principles and fight all abortions. Too many people in the Republican Party, as we learned too late, don't want to put their money where their mouth is. This hurt us, and we should have known better—I certainly should have."

While the movement leadership was busy negotiating its ill-fated accord with the Republican Party, many grassroots activists in the early 1980s were concerned with the far more practical business of providing counseling and material support to women facing crisis pregnancies. "Crisis pregnancy ministry," which is how pro-lifers often refer to this sort of work, actually got its start back in the late 1960s when Louise Summerhill of Toronto opened her first Birthright pregnancy centers in the United States.[29] "I started Birthright," Mrs. Summerhill told me in an interview several years ago, "because something had to be done for the women whose lives are turned upside down by pregnancies they didn't plan on and they might not be able to afford. We're here to help mothers in concrete ways—to give them someone to talk with, to find them a place to live and maybe help with the rent, to provide maternity clothing and baby clothes and furniture, even to give them someone to hold their hand in the delivery room. We don't lecture anyone, and we stay completely clean of political lobbying. And we're faithful to Rome, so we have nothing to do with contraception." As Birthright centers proliferated across the country throughout the 1970s, the organization as a whole managed to stay faithful to the ideals of its founder. Its volunteer counselors were instructed to do everything possible to ease the sting of unplanned pregnancy but were forbidden to discuss contraceptive practice with clients or to share office space with more politically inclined right-to-life groups.

From the mid-seventies onward, hundreds of additional crisis pregnancy centers were opened across the country by evangelicals and other conservative Protestants, and sometimes also by Catholics and Protestants in collaboration. Almost all of these centers (and almost all of Birthright's, too, for that matter) were run on a volunteer basis by married women with families. And almost all of them as well were forthright about their connection to the anti-abortion movement. By the mid-eighties, however, an increasing number of centers were resorting to deceptive advertising in an attempt to reach women who might be considering abortion. In 1983 Conrad Wojnar, a Catholic committed to fighting contraception as well as abortion, opened several so-called "women's centers" in the Chicago area that were prominently advertised in the Yellow Pages as offering "free pregnancy testing" and "abortion-related services." There was no mention in the advertisements that the centers were actually opposed to abortions, and that their primary purpose was to dissuade women from having them. Insofar as Wojnar was concerned, such subterfuge was fully justified. In matters of life and death, he claimed, aggressive (and perhaps even illegal) action was sometimes the only moral recourse.[30]

Wojnar was hardly alone during the mid-eighties in calling for more aggressive action on the abortion front. By this time, many pro-lifers—and particularly those of a more purist bent—were thoroughly frustrated with the gradualist approach favored by the NRLC and the mainstream movement in general. Educational efforts, political lobbying, and crisis pregnancy services, they insisted, constituted an inadequate response to the daily destruction of fetal life in abortion clinics across the country. One of the earliest, and most articulate, advocates of a more militant approach was John Cavanaugh-O'Keefe, a Maryland native and product of a staunchly devout Catholic upbringing. In his *No Cheap Solutions,* a 1984 booklet which immediately caught the attention of many Catholic activists, Cavanaugh-O'Keefe called upon pro-lifers to take their convictions directly to the street:

> Offering alternatives to abortion is prochoice—*truly* prochoice, but *only* prochoice. Education, while urgently necessary, is extremely dangerous when it is not accompanied by action to clarify the urgency of the message. Legislation may shape the future, but children are dying now. . . . What is missing in the Right-to-Life Movement is the simple statement, fleshed out in action, that the unborn are our brothers and sisters. The heart of the movement is loving action to protect our unborn brothers and sisters. The future of the movement is direct action.[31]

Juli Loesch of Prolifers for Survival was in total agreement. It was imperative, she argued, that pro-lifers graduate beyond merely symbolic protest, such as picketing or leafleting outside abortion clinics. The whole point of direct action, she claimed, was to disrupt the operation of clinics and possibly shut them down altogether. "Symbolic action is very limited. . . . The analogy is if you had a fire and you called the fire department and they came and they picketed the fire and started chanting, 'No more fire, no more fire.' That's protesting fire. So we don't do [direct action] to express our inner feelings. . . . We do it to stop abortions in that clinic on that day."[32]

This call for direct action immediately engaged the imagination of activists who were already disturbed by the conciliatory approach of the NRLC and the NCCB. Most of these activists were Catholics, intensely religious, and adherents of the contraceptive mentality thesis. They were, by and large, the militant purists of the pro-life movement, and by late 1984, thousands of them across the country had committed themselves to veritable careers of civil disobedience—blocking access to abortion clinics, vandalizing clinic property, and staging sit-ins and demonstrations. Indeed, for many activists, participation in civil disobedience carried with it a certain cachet—it was a badge of pro-life heroism—and they were more than willing to suffer arrest and even imprisonment in the process.[33]

The National Right to Life Committee, for its part, looked upon this latest development with considerable alarm. If progress was to be made, its leaders insisted, it was essential that pro-lifers limit themselves to legal and institutionalized avenues of protest. Public defiance of the law through civil disobedience, they claimed, would almost certainly cost the movement popular support and would likely damage its relations with the Republican Party as well. For the most part, however, militant pro-lifers were unimpressed with this line of reasoning. Many of them, as young Irish-American Catholics with socialist leanings, had little stake in the existing order and very little affection for the Republican Party, and they were prepared to demonstrate their commitment to the anti-abortion cause regardless of expense to themselves personally or to the movement's public reputation.

The NRLC's appeal for calm took on heightened urgency in early 1986 in the wake of a dozen or so bombings at abortion clinics across the country. Movement radicals such as Cavanaugh-O'Keefe were quick to disavow any connection with these bombings (claiming that they were the responsibility of individuals not formally associated with any pro-life group) but refused to condemn as immoral any action, if merely destructive of private property, that was intended to save unborn life. Joseph Scheidler of the Pro-Life Action League, a militant group based in the Chicago area, told the news media that he "personally disapproved" of what the bombers had done but was hardly in a position "to impose [his] own morality upon them."[34] In the view of the NRLC leadership, such comments cast the entire movement in a negative light and further jeopardized its chances for cultural respectability.

The conflict within pro-life ranks between radicals (or purists) and moderates (or pragmatists) reached a climax of sorts in May 1986, at the NRLC's national convention in Denver. NRLC president John Willke and his staff saw the Denver convention as an ideal opportunity for the anti-abortion movement to put on its most respectable face. In an open letter published in *National Right to Life News* two weeks prior to the convention, Willke called on all pro-lifers to abstain from acts of civil disobedience while in Denver and to limit themselves instead to peaceful picketing. Any illegal or particularly dramatic acts of protest, he warned, would only play into the hands of a national news media eager to vilify the movement as a clearinghouse for social misfits and religious fanatics. Lest anyone still not grasp the point, Willke stipulated in a convention handout that the distribution of radical or politically subversive literature at the convention site was strictly prohibited.[35] Not in the least deterred by such warnings, radical activists from around the country descended upon the convention site and immediately set up literature booths and began broadcasting plans for "rescues" (or campaigns of civil disobedience) that they intended to carry out at Denver abortion clinics. After about a day and a half of this, the NRLC leadership stepped in and had the radicals forcibly evicted from the site. Among those evicted were John Cavanaugh-O'Keefe and other members of his newly founded Prolife Nonviolent Action Project, representatives from Human Life International and Prolifers for Survival, and about a dozen activists apiece from the St. Louis–based Pro-Life Direct Action League and Joseph Scheidler's Pro-Life Action League. If previously there had been any doubt, this episode made vividly clear just how deeply anti-abortionists were divided by the mid-eighties over questions of strategy, ideology, and, perhaps most important of all, spirituality.[36]

Divisions among the Bishops

By the mid-eighties there was mounting evidence that the American Catholic bishops themselves were divided over some of these same questions. While some bishops remained staunchly loyal to the anti-abortion movement, others believed it important that the institutional church create strategic distance between itself and the movement. Many of these liberal bishops were disturbed by the right-wing alliance that the movement had fashioned with the Republican Party, and some worried as well that the confrontational tactics employed by pro-life radicals might escalate into full-blown violence. Moreover, liberal bishops in general were concerned that the church had placed so great an emphasis on abortion since the *Roe* decision that it had neglected other issues of equal pastoral importance.

The leader of the liberal camp was Cardinal Joseph Bernardin of Chicago. In 1983, during a speech at Fordham University in New York City, Bernardin unveiled what he called the "seamless garment" or "consistent ethic" approach to Catholic social action. It was not enough, he claimed, for Catholics to fight abortion without also fighting for a better economic deal for women and their children. And it was perilously short-sighted, he claimed, to condemn abortion without also condemning militarism, racism, sexism, and poverty. All of these issues were interrelated, they all had bearing upon the "sanctity of life," and *together* they constituted a proper focus for Catholic social engagement.[37]

The seamless garment ethic did not wear at all well within most quarters of the pro-life movement. To many activists, it seemed that the cardinal was merely beating a strategic retreat from the anti-abortion position. To treat abortion as the moral equivalent of poverty or health care was to dilute its significance. Moreover, they claimed, the seamless garment or consistent ethic approach gave Catholic politicians in the United States a convenient excuse to disregard abortion and focus instead on trendier issues such as unemployment and the nuclear arms race.

As the seamless garment ethic became increasingly popular within episcopal ranks during the late 1980s and early 1990s, many Catholic pro-lifers became increasingly convinced that the bishops as a group were not seriously committed to stopping abortion. "I'm very hesitant to criticize my church," Monica Migliorino Miller told me just two weeks before she was scheduled to begin serving a nine-month jail sentence for acts of civil disobedience she had carried out at Milwaukee abortion clinics, "but the bishops simply have not done their job. Our bishop [Rembert Weakland] here in Milwaukee is a prime case in point. He talks about the seamless garment, but this just gives everyone, including himself, an easy out on abortion. The seamless garment ethic has submerged and weakened the abortion issue. The bishops refuse to condemn the United States as a society of death. They've allowed the Gospel to be judged by secularism."[38]

Mary Anne Hackett and Richard O'Connor, both executive officers of Illinois Right-to-Life, agree. "The seamless garment ethic has diluted the abortion issue," they informed me during a recent interview at their Chicago office. "It has allowed Catholic politicians to declare themselves pro-life for being against poverty and capital punishment, or whatever.

And it's given most of our bishops something to hide behind while nothing is done about abortion."[39] Mary Anne Hackett has decided not to suffer such grievances in silence. In early February 1993, she and five other Chicago-based activists formed an ad hoc group called the Committee of Pro-Life Catholics, and on February 17 they wrote their local bishop, Cardinal Bernardin, to complain about "the failure of the Church to respond to the defining moral issue of our time." Since 1973 and the *Roe* decision, they told the cardinal, "we [have] waited as the Bishops squandered years writing pastorals on peace, the economy, and women, but [have] heard no voice raised for the defenseless unborn." And at the parish level, they went on, "homilies on abortion are rare or non-existent. Many, if not most, parishioners have never heard one word on abortion from the pulpit in 20 years of legal abortion. Pro-lifers who have tried to educate the Catholic population are driven away by the pastors, even vilified from the pulpit and in person and threatened with arrest."

In a personal letter of response dated March 4, Cardinal Bernardin defended his position on abortion and reprimanded Mrs. Hackett and her committee for resorting to "divisive tactics [that] only serve to damage the credibility and effectiveness of all who represent the Pro-Life movement." In a rejoinder dated March 26, Mrs. Hackett and a colleague named Bonnie Quirke told the cardinal that "a more appropriate response from you would [have been] to tell us why daily prayer for the unborn and the end of abortion is such a radical suggestion that it cannot be implemented. . . . When we asked for bread, you gave us a stone." And Cardinal Bernardin, on May 12, replied once again, "I am saddened that at a critical time in the pro-life movement, when so much needs to be done to build unity among pro-lifers and increase credibility for our cause, you have chosen to focus your time and efforts on attacking me and the priests of the Archdiocese."[40]

This correspondence conveys something of the contempt with which many (especially radical) Catholic pro-lifers have come to regard their bishops over the past decade or so. Indeed, there are relatively few bishops today who command genuine respect from the anti-abortion movement as a whole. One of them is Austin Vaughan, auxiliary bishop of New York, who has actually been arrested for publicly protesting abortion.[41] Another is Bishop René H. Gracida of Corpus Christi, Texas, who has gone so far as to excommunicate Catholic directors of abortion clinics. Cardinal John O'Connor, archbishop of New York, has won national notoriety for his public feuds with New York governor Mario Cuomo, among others. Cuomo argues that in a pluralistic democracy such as the United States, one cannot enshrine the religious values of any particular group or groups into public law. And Cardinal O'Connor's position, which he has articulated time and again over the past several years, is that Catholic politicians behave neither as good Catholics nor as good politicians when they relegate their church's teaching on abortion to the domain of merely private moral preference.[42]

Conclusion

Throughout the 1980s and early 1990s, anti-abortion protest in the United States assumed a progressively more militant (and desperate) tone. Religious passions which had previously been shielded—though never quite entirely—from public view were given full play, and efforts at persuasion were increasingly set aside for open confrontation. Nowhere at present is such passion and confrontation more clearly evident than on the doorsteps of abortion clinics across the country.

As part of their ongoing campaign of public protest, radical Catholic activists (and quite a few Protestants as well) regularly participate today in what they often refer to as "public witness." Depending on the occasion, public witness may range from peaceful picketing outside abortion clinics to flagrant acts of civil disobedience. In almost every case, however, it conveys an unmistakably religious flavor. Many Catholic activists pray the rosary incessantly, some carry statues or other devotional artifacts, and Catholics and Protestants alike join in chanting hymns and reciting Scripture. To the outside observer, in fact, it sometimes seems that public witness is governed more by an expressive than an instrumental logic. When praying the rosary or singing Marian hymns on the picket line, activists seem primarily concerned with expressing their religious convictions and solidarity, sometimes without reference to anticipated results. Public witness, in other words, is important as much for its spiritual gratifications and symbolic meaning as for its possible political effectiveness.[43]

Moderates within the pro-life movement continue to be deeply troubled by public witness. In their view, the dramatic and overtly religious activities with which it is chiefly associated have succeeded only in reaping for the larger movement public scorn and political impotency. With this in mind, I recently asked a number of radical Catholic activists if they themselves had considered the possibility that public witness, and especially the intensive Marian piety that seems so central to it, might actually be damaging to the anti-abortion cause.[44]

John Cavanaugh-O'Keefe summed up the sentiments of most of those with whom I spoke in this regard when he described public witness as a spiritual calling that transcended any ordinary calculus of success or failure. "It's true that our public protests are potentially disastrous in terms of public image," he told me at his home in rural Maryland. "All of us have a very strong Marian piety which we bring to the streets with us, and of course this allows the enemy to label us as fanatical Catholics. But we can't worry about that. We're called to witness to the truth, and our Marian piety is the truth and the source of our strength. Mary's role in creation is immense, and she is a feminist model for today. After all, Mary said Yes at the Annunciation."[45]

Julie and Steve McCreevy are a thirtyish couple who have been involved with public witness since the late 1980s. At least twice a week they carry a life-sized, gold-framed image of Our Lady of Guadalupe to the picket line outside a busy abortion clinic in downtown Chicago. And like Cavanaugh-O'Keefe, they define anti-abortionism in manifestly supernatural terms. "For the first decade after *Roe*," Julie McCreevy told me in July, "pro-lifers attempted a strategy based on scientific evidence. They didn't realize the dimension of evil involved—that abortion couldn't be eradicated by appealing to people's good nature. This thing is straight out of hell, and you can't combat it without supernatural agency." I asked Steve McCreevy if he and his wife ever questioned the political value of their expressly religious form of protest. "Occasionally we do," he said, "but we believe that only God—through the intercession of Mary—can melt hearts and change people's minds on this issue. If we were to throw out our rosaries and statues, then we'd be playing by Satan's rules. We'd be throwing away our strength. This is exactly what our enemies would love us to do. Plus we suffer enormous abuse and ridicule at the abortuary—the blasphemy against our faith is horrible—and we need Mary to sustain us through this. What we are involved with here is a sacred crusade."[46]

Indeed, almost all of the radical Catholic activists I interviewed similarly characterized the battle against abortion as a sacred crusade. American society, they are convinced, has been almost entirely overtaken since the 1960s by a grave spiritual affliction—an affliction they variously refer to as secularism or moral relativism—and liberalized abortion is its most egregious symptom. Moreover, and perhaps as important, they are equally convinced that American Catholicism itself has been grievously infected by secularism as well. With the rise of theological liberalism after the Second Vatican Council and the corresponding decline of moral and doctrinal certitudes, the American church seems to them to have become virtually indistinguishable from the broader secular culture. It is little wonder, according to pro-life radicals, that the vast majority of American Catholics—including most priests and nuns—stand serenely aloof from the struggle over abortion. In just a few short decades, they have become full participants in a culture that is antithetical to the values and aspirations of authentic Catholicism.

Public witness, then, may be understood as a protest simultaneously against abortion and against the moral softness of mainstream Catholicism in the United States. At a time when the institutional church seems largely absorbed by the dominant culture, and most criteria of Catholic distinctiveness seem cast into doubt, it affords the stalwart faithful an opportunity to demonstrate unqualified religious virtue. Public witness, viewed in this light, is a ritual of cultural defiance and a medium for the assertion of a heroic and contracultural piety.

"When we're on the street, praying our rosaries and singing and getting arrested," Joseph Scheidler told me, "we're fighting abortion and we're also making a powerful religious statement. Most Catholics and even most bishops might have sold out, but there are still some of us who are fully prepared to pay the price for our religious convictions. If Catholics don't take a stand on the sanctity of life, there is nothing left to take a stand on. I'm convinced that most of us would actually sacrifice our lives for the cause. I've been arrested fifteen times, and if the situation arose, I'd pray for the strength to die for my faith."[47]

As the larger church wallows in secularism, claims Mary Anne Hackett of Illinois Right-to-Life, Catholic pro-lifers represent the advance guard of a revitalized and militantly faithful American Catholicism. "We are the activist arm of orthodox Catholicism in the United States. It's our responsibility to speak the truth on contraception and abortion, regardless of public abuse and abuse from our own religious leaders. It's up to us to keep genuine faith alive, and to rejuvenate the American church. Above all else, we are soldiers of Jesus Christ."

For such Catholics, then, pro-life activism is a manifestly vocational enterprise, an imperative of faith; and through it they aspire toward precisely the sort of religious virtuosity that most of them find lacking in the mainstream church. The fetus, in their view, is a reflection of transcendence, an unassailable symbol of divinity; and the failure of most American Catholics—including bishops, priests, and nuns—to protest abortion with unstinting passion is regarded by them as a betrayal of the highest order.[48]

At the present, in fact, such Catholics may be said to constitute a distinctive subculture within American Catholicism: they have their own networks of piety, their own publications, and, to at least some extent, even their own schools.[49] Fiercely loyal to Rome, and unrelentingly conservative in devotional practice, they see themselves as a conventicle of heroic faith—an "ecclesiola in ecclesia"[50]—called to rescue (if rescuing is possible) the American church from servitude to the dominant secular culture.

NOTES

1. For the movement's early history, see Faye D. Ginsburg, *Contested Lives* (Berkeley: University of California Press, 1989), chap. 2; Connie Paige, *The Right to Lifers* (New York: Summit Books, 1983); James R. Kelly, "Learning and Teaching Consistency: Catholics and the Right-to-Life Movement," in Timothy A. Byrnes and Mary C. Segers, eds., *The Catholic Church and the Politics of Abortion* (Boulder, Colo.: Westview Press, 1992), chap. 9; James R. Kelly, "Beyond the Stereotypes: Interviews with Right-to-Life Pioneers," *Commonweal*, November 1981, pp. 653–57; James R. Kelly, "Toward Complexity: The Right-to-Life Movement," in Monty L. Lynn and David O. Moberg, eds., *Research in the Social Scientific Study of Religion* (Greenwich, Conn.: JAI Press, 1989), chap. 5; and Kristin Luker, *Abortion and the Politics of Motherhood* (Berkeley: University of California Press, 1984). My historical account is based partly on these sources, partly on interviews I conducted with movement activists at the 1986 National Right to Life Committee Convention in Denver, and partly as well on conversations with James R. Kelly of Fordham University, who is the movement's foremost social historian.

2. The Court declared abortion to be virtually an unfettered right during the first and second trimesters of pregnancy. For a more extensive discussion of the *Roe* opinion, see Lawrence H. Tribe, *Abortion: The Clash of Absolutes* (New York: W. W. Norton, 1992), pp. 11–13. For appraisals of *Roe*, see John T. Noonan, Jr., *A Private Choice* (New York: The Free Press, 1979), and Ronald Dworkin, *Life's Dominion* (New York: Knopf, 1993).

3. See Paige, *The Right to Lifers*, p. 84ff.

4. See Kelly, "Learning and Teaching Consistency," pp. 156–57.

5. Byrnes and Segers, *The Catholic Church and the Politics of Abortion*, includes relevant essays on anti-abortion activism in New Jersey, Florida, Illinois, Pennsylvania, Louisiana, Connecticut, and New York. For a discussion of lobbying at the federal level, see Tribe, *Abortion*, and Roger Rosenblatt, *Life Itself: Abortion in the American Mind* (New York: Vintage, 1992).

6. The most famous pro-life handout during this period was a pictorial display entitled *Life or Death* (Cincinnati: Hayes Publishing Co., n.d.).

7. Bernard N. Nathanson, "Deeper into Abortion," *New England Journal of Medicine* 291 (28 November 1974): 1189. This and the following paragraph borrow heavily from my *Catholics against the Church* (Toronto: University of Toronto Press, 1989), p. 45.

8. Bernard N. Nathanson (with Richard N. Ostling), *Aborting America* (Garden City, N.Y.: Doubleday, 1979), pp. 187–217; and Nathanson, *The Abortion Papers* (New York: Frederick Fell, 1983), pp. 177–209.

9. Dave Andrusko, ed., *To Rescue the Future: The Pro-life Movement in the 1980s* (Toronto: Life Cycle Books, 1983), p. 162.

10. Andrusko, *To Rescue the Future*, p. 16.

11. William Brennan, *The Abortion Holocaust* (St. Louis: Landmark Press, 1983). For James Burtchaell's observation, see his *Rachel Weeping* (Kansas City, Mo.: Andrews and McMeel, 1982), p. 141.

12. Quoted in Paige, *The Right to Lifers*, pp. 61–62.

13. On Ireland, see John A. Hannigan, "Containing the Luciferine Spark," in Roger O'Toole, ed., *Sociological Studies of Roman Catholicism* (Lewiston, N.Y.: E. Mellen Press, 1989), pp. 71–84. On Canada, see my "Keepers of the Faith: Lay Militants, Abortion, and the Battle for Canadian Catholicism," pp. 127–42 in the same volume.

14. For a more detailed discussion of these initiatives, see Timothy A. Byrnes, "The Politics of Abortion: The Catholic Bishops," in Byrnes and Segers, *The Catholic Church and the Politics of Abortion*, pp. 14–26.

15. For discussion of the public opinion data, see Rosenblatt, *Life Itself,* pp. 183–89, and Elizabeth Adell Cook, Ted G. Jelen, and Clyde Wilcox, *Between Two Absolutes: Public Opinion and the Politics of Abortion* (Boulder, Colo.: Westview Press, 1992).

16. Donald DeMarco, *The Contraceptive Mentality* (Edmonton: Life Ethics Centre, 1982), p. 3; Joseph Boyle, "Contraception and Natural Family Planning," *International Review of Natural Family Planning* 4, no. 4 (1980): 311–12. For a similar discussion of the contraceptive mentality thesis, see my *Catholics against the Church,* pp. 35–39.

17. DeMarco, *The Contraceptive Mentality,* p. 12.

18. Author interview, Stafford, Virginia, 10 August 1993. All subsequent quotations attributed to Judie Brown are derived from the same interview.

19. *HLI Reports,* the organization's principal informational organ, is published seventeen times annually, and the *Population Research Institute Review,* its most ambitious scholarly organ, is published bimonthly. See also Fr. Paul Marx, *The Death Pedlars* (Collegeville, Minn.: Saint John's University Press, 1971). For background information on HLI, I interviewed Vernon Kirby, the organization's public relations officer, in Gaithersburg, Maryland, on 17 June 1993.

20. Author interview, 18 June 1993. All subsequent quotations attributed to Fr. Paul Marx are derived from the same interview.

21. See Ginsburg, *Contested Lives,* p. 260. For an account of congressional testimony given by Archbishop John R. Roach and Cardinal Terence Cooke in support of the Hatch Amendment, see Patricia Beattie Jung and Thomas A. Shannon, eds., *Abortion and Catholicism: The American Debate* (New York: Crossroad, 1988), pp. 10–43.

22. I use *evangelicalism* here as a shorthand designation for conservative Protestantism in the United States more generally.

23. On Prolifers for Survival, see the following brochures written by Juli Loesch, all published in Chapel Hill, North Carolina, in 1985: *Acts of Aggression, Imagining the Red,* and *On Nuclear Weapons.* See also the bimonthly newspaper *P.S. (Prolifers for Survival).*

24. Rosemary Bottcher, "Modern Feminism Bewitched by Abortion," in Andrusko, *To Rescue the Future,* p. 175. See also Gail Grenier Sweet, ed., *Pro-Life Feminism* (Toronto: Life Cycle Books, 1985), and the newsletter *Sisterlife,* which is published by Feminists for Life of America from the organization's main office in Kansas City, Missouri.

25. For a provocative history of the alliance, see Michele McKeegan, *Abortion Politics: Mutiny in the Ranks of the Right* (New York: The Free Press, 1992).

26. Kelly, "Learning and Teaching Consistency," pp. 159–61.

27. Tribe, *Abortion,* p. 23.

28. Kelly, "Learning and Teaching Consistency," p. 160. On the "worldwide pattern" noted by Kelly, see Colin Francome, *Abortion Freedom* (Boston: Allen and Unwin, 1984).

29. The first Birthright center was opened in Toronto, Ontario, in November 1968. See Louise Summerhill, *The Story of Birthright* (Libertyville, Ill.: Prow Books, 1973). The following quotation is taken from an interview I conducted with Mrs. Summerhill in Toronto on 17 June 1986.

30. On Conrad Wojnar's ministry, see Joe Gulotta, *Pro-Life Christians: Heroes for the Pre-Born* (Rockford, Ill.: TAN Books, 1972), pp. 111–15. Altogether, there are almost five thousand crisis pregnancy centers in the United States today. For the most comprehensive listing of these centers, see *Life—What a Beautiful Choice: Resources* (Valley Forge, Pa.: Arthur S. DeMoss Foundation, 1993), and the *1991–92 Pro-Life Resource Directory* (Los Angeles: International Life Services, Inc., 1993). One of the better-known ventures in the crisis pregnancy field is the Nurturing Network (see Gulotta, *Pro-Life Christians,* pp. 74–79). Founded by Mary Cunningham Agee in 1985, and based in Boise, Idaho, the Network has received extensive (and generally favorable) media coverage over the past several years. Mention should also be made of groups such as Women Exploited by Abortion and American Victims of Abortion, which provide counseling to women who have already undergone abortions. See Marshall Fightlin, "Post-Abortion Counselling: A Pro-Life Task," in Andrusko, *To Rescue the Future,* pp. 273–79.

31. (Gaithersburg, Md.: Prolife Nonviolent Action Project, 1984), p. 15. See also, in a related vein, John Cavanaugh-O'Keefe's *Nonviolence Is an Adverb* (Gaithersburg, Md.: Prolife Nonviolent Action Project, 1985).

32. Quoted in E. Michael Jones, "Abortion Mill Rescue: Are Sit-ins the Answer?" *Fidelity* 6, no. 8 (July–August 1987): 34.

33. It is unlikely that anyone is more admired by militant Catholic activists than Joan Andrews, who has spent five years in prison (mostly in solitary confinement) for acts of civil disobedience at abortion clinics. See Richard Cowden-Guido, ed., *You Reject Them, You Reject Me: The Prison Letters of Joan Andrews* (Manassas, Va.: Trinity Communications, 1988).

34. Scheidler's remark, which was reported to me by several activists, has attained almost canonical status among militant Catholic pro-lifers. Moreover, it was Scheidler's 1985 book, *Closed: 99 Ways to Stop Abortion* (Toronto: Life Cycle Books), that inspired Randall Terry, a Pentecostal minister based in Binghamton, New York, to found Operation Rescue, the organization that is most commonly identified today with civil disobedience at abortion clinics. On Operation Rescue, see Marian Faux, *Crusaders: Voices from the Abortion Front* (New York: Carol Publishing, 1990), pp. 116–72. For profiles of conservative Protestant activists, see Paul deParrie, *The Rescuers* (Brentwood, Tenn.: Wolgemuth and Hyatt, 1989).

35. John C. Willke, M.D., "From the President's Desk: A Place for Public Witness?" *National Right to Life News*, 15 May 1986, pp. 3, 8; John C. Willke, M.D. (NRCL President), *1986 Convention Hand-out*, Denver, 27 May 1986.

36. I witnessed these events while doing field research at the convention. On the Pro-Life Direct Action League, see *The Unborn Speak . . . "Doesn't My Life Count for Something?"* (St. Louis, n.d.), and *Because ACTION Speaks Louder Than Words* (Chicago, n.d.)

37. Cardinal Joseph Bernardin, "A Consistent Ethic of Life: An American Catholic Dialogue," Fordham University Gannon Lecture, 6 December 1983.

38. Author interview, Milwaukee, Wisconsin, 30 June 1993. See Monica M. Migliorino, "Report from Rats' Alley: Down and Out with the Unborn in Chicago and Milwaukee," *Fidelity* 6, no. 8 (July–August 1987): 38–45.

39. Author interview, Chicago, Illinois, 29 June 1993. The quotation attributed to Mary Anne Hackett in the final section is derived from the same interview.

40. Letter from Committee of Pro-Life Catholics to Joseph Cardinal Bernardin, 17 February 1993; letter to Mrs. Hackett and Mrs. Quirke (Committee of Pro-Life Catholics) from Joseph Cardinal Bernardin, 4 March 1993; letter from Mary Anne Hackett and Bonnie Quirke to Joseph Cardinal Bernardin, 26 March 1993; letter to Mrs. Hackett and Mrs. Quirke (Committee of Pro-Life Catholics) from Joseph Cardinal Bernardin, 12 May 1993.

41. See Gulotta, *Pro-Life Christians*, pp. 96–98.

42. See Timothy A. Byrnes, "The Cardinal and the Governor: The Politics of Abortion in New York State," in Byrnes and Segers, *The Catholic Church and the Politics of Abortion*, pp. 137–51. For Cuomo's position, see "Religious Beliefs and Public Morality: A Catholic Governor's Perspective," in Jung and Shannon, *Abortion and Catholicism*, pp. 45–96. For Cardinal O'Connor's perspective, see "Abortion: Questions and Answers," *Catholic New York* (Special Edition), 14 June 1990. See also Nat Hentoff, "Profiles (Cardinal O'Connor—Part II)," *The New Yorker*, 30 March 1987, pp. 37–52, 73–92.

43. For a fuller discussion of these themes, see my "Soldier of Orthodoxy: Revivalist Catholicism in North America," *Studies in Religion/Sciences Religieuses* 17, no. 3 (1988): 347–63.

44. During the summer of 1993, I interviewed a total of twenty Catholic activists (all of whom are involved in militant forms of anti-abortion protest) in the metropolitan areas of New York City, Chicago, and Washington, D.C.; and in the spring of 1994, I interviewed an additional fifteen in the New York City/New Jersey area. The findings rehearsed in this concluding section are based almost entirely upon these interviews.

45. Author interview, Laytonsville, Maryland, 17 June 1993.

46. Author interview, Chicago, Illinois, 29 June 1993. Julie and Steve McCreevy are pioneer leaders of Our Lady of Guadalupe Rosary Crusade for Life.

47. Author interview, Chicago, Illinois, 28 June 1993.

48. The passionate protest of militant pro-lifers, Catholic and Protestant, has lately been hampered by injunctions and lawsuits. Over the past year, both Operation Rescue and Joseph Scheidler have been sued under the provisions of the federal RICO (Racketeer Influenced and Corrupt Organizations) law, and it remains to be seen how such litigation will affect street protest against abortion clinics. For a fuller discussion of this issue, see Philip F. Lawler, "Are We Really Losing?" *The Catholic World Report,* March 1994, pp. 44–53.

49. For the most part, militant Catholic pro-lifers have what may be described as a concentrated devotional life, with heavy emphasis upon conventional (or church-approved) Marian piety. Their publications would include *Fidelity Magazine* (South Bend, Indiana); *The Wanderer* (St. Paul, Minnesota); *Catholic Eye,* a monthly newsletter published by the National Committee of Catholic Laymen, Inc. (New York City); and *Free Speech Advocates,* a monthly report published by Catholics United for Life (New Hope, Kentucky). Some of the newer and more doctrinally rigorous Catholic colleges, and especially in this regard Christendom College in Front Royal, Virginia, have actively encouraged their students to participate in street protest against abortion.

50. Joachim Wach employs the concept of "ecclesiola in ecclesia" to characterize nonschismatic groups that protest against apparent compromise and laxity within the larger ecclesiastical body. And this is precisely the situation of the militant Catholic pro-lifers under discussion here. See Wach, *Sociology of Religion* (Chicago: University of Chicago Press, 1994), pp. 173–205.

12

Self-Consciously Countercultural
Alternative Catholic Colleges

MARY JO WEAVER

Prologue

This essay on newly founded conservative Catholic colleges presents
one stage in the complex evolution of American Catholic higher education.
In many ways, the very existence of these new colleges is symptomatic of a
crisis, focused on the issue of formation. What does it mean to be educated
"as a Catholic" in the modern world? Is it possible to get a Catholic education in mainstream Catholic universities after the Council? Has the influx
of courses on Eastern religions, history of religion, and new religions,
along with a pastiche of new methods, pedagogies, and theological assumptions, led to a troubling departure from core Catholic courses and a
common Catholic religious identity?

On the one hand, the very phrase "Catholic higher education" may
seem oxymoronic to some academicians in secular universities who believe
that education should not be compromised by denominational markers.
On the other hand, presidents and faculties of institutions such as Notre
Dame, Georgetown, Boston College, and Fordham believe that genuine
education—including open-minded and confident debate about opposing
and unsettling viewpoints—can occur within a broad-based imperative to
form young Catholic men and women through liturgies, service activities,
and opportunities for spiritual growth.

From John Henry Newman's *The Idea of a University* (1850) to Theodore M. Hesburgh's *The Challenge and Promise of a Catholic University* (1993), Catholics have struggled to define Catholic education. For the last thirty years in particular, members of Catholic colleges and universities have been engaged in spirited disputes about the means and ends of Catholic higher education. As we will see, the Land O' Lakes conference in 1967 was a turning point in this discussion and, obliquely, a stimulus for the formation of alternative Catholic institutions.

Although everyone involved in Catholic education is concerned to maintain and to foster the "Catholicity" of their various institutions, there is vigorous disagreement about what constitutes the very Catholic identity that educators, students, parents, bishops, and the Vatican hope to promote. To put the question in its starkest terms: What gives a university the right to be called *Catholic?* Must it demand and enforce "orthodox" Catholic beliefs and behavior? If so, can a Roman Catholic institution qualify as a university?

Pope John Paul II joined this discussion in the 1980s through a series of documents and directives. *Ex Corde Ecclesiae* (15 August 1990), his most explicit statement on the relationship between Catholic institutions of higher learning and the hierarchical church, has provoked significant debate and hardened liberal and conservative positions within Catholic colleges, universities, and professional societies. The "Proposed Ordinances for Catholic Colleges and Universities in the United States" (October 4, 1990) was issued by the American Catholic bishops to guide local ordinaries in their dealings with schools of higher education in their dioceses. The document evoked grateful thanks from those Catholics broadly dissatisfied with the present state of Catholic higher education. But it also stimulated critical responses from Catholic institutions of higher learning; indeed, it was tabled in 1994.

The new Catholic colleges that are the subject of this chapter, as if anticipating Vatican directives, are models of papal educational policy. As such, they tell us something about the anguish some conservative Catholics have felt in relation to Catholic higher education and their inability to counteract dominant trends. Despair about the state of Catholic education and determination to respond creatively to the situation have not been limited to colleges. Indeed, disgruntlement with Catholic education, from preschool through college, has led to increased involvement of Catholics in home schooling, the founding of new high schools, the revitalization of old colleges, the establishment of conservative institutes within Catholic universities, support for graduate institutes to promote the defense of the papal prohibition on artificial birth control as articulated in *Humanae Vitae,* and professional associations for conservative Catholic intellectuals.

Although none of these initiatives will be treated in this chapter, they form part of the larger context. For example, Catholics have recently become enthusiastic members of the home schooling movement: organizations such as Seton Home School (Front Royal, Virginia), and Our Lady of the Rosary Home School (Bardstown, Kentucky), created to assist parents in educating their children at home, have grown dramatically in recent years. They offer phone-in help lines, testing services, textbooks, and general support. In addition, organizations such as Catholics United for the Faith (profiled in this book by James Sullivan) have been publishing textbooks for use by Catholic parents dismayed by the lack of traditional teachings in local Catholic schools.

Catholic secondary education is being reshaped by such experiments as the Trinity Schools in South Bend, Indiana, and St. Paul, Minnesota. Sponsored by Catholic charismatic renewal, Trinity School in South Bend has been nationally recognized for the high quality of its humanities education. Catholic charismatic renewal must also be credited for the revitalization of the Franciscan University of Steubenville, an institution that deserves a chapter of its own. No longer a floundering diocesan college, today the Franciscan University of Steubenville is a thriving Catholic university explicitly shaped by its fidelity to the magisterium and inspired by the combination of orthodoxy and Catholic charismatic spirituality. The fact that Catholics United for the Faith is moving its national headquarters to Steubenville, and that various conservative groups find it a congenial place for annual meetings, is one small testament to its growing importance.

In addition to home schooling, new high schools, and renewed colleges, conservative Catholic efforts to create orthodox enclaves within Catholic universities—the St. Ignatius Institute at the University of San Francisco, for example—also testify to a desire to turn current educational policy in a different direction. Graduate programs such as the John Paul II Institute for Studies on Marriage and Family—it occupies part of a floor of the Dominican House of Studies in Washington—promote the defense and promulgation of *Humanae Vitae* as a primary basis for the renewal of the Catholic family. If Catholic colleges were teaching "orthodox Catholicism," it is implied, such institutes would not be necessary. Finally, one can find professional societies such as the Fellowship for Catholic Scholars (described in this book by James Hitchcock) and newly galvanized groups such as the Society of Catholic Social Scientists founded by

Dominic Aquila (Steubenville) and Joseph Varacalli (Nassau Community College), social scientists who hope to provide objective social research to assist the Catholic Church in reconstructing the social order along Christian principles.

All of these initiatives indicate where some of the educational energy and vitality of conservative Catholics has been invested. This chapter focuses exclusively on alternative Catholic colleges founded since the Council. They are all small, slow-growing institutions with modest goals and a kind of sectarian spirit. As such, we cannot expect them to have more than a limited impact, however remarkable their individual stories.

Catholic Colleges before the Council

Catholic colleges in the aftermath of World War II could not compete with great American universities in terms of scholarship, but enrollments were up, morale was high, and there was a general sense that Catholic intellectuals had a special mission to a fractured world. Carried along on the waves of "the Catholic revival," a cultural and intellectual rebirth rooted in Thomism, Catholic Action, and Mystical Body theology, Catholic educators and their students were supremely self-confident. They believed that their tradition contained the best answers for a world crippled by secularism.

When the system worked ideally, students in Catholic colleges were keenly aware of their heritage. They had undeclared minors in theology and philosophy and a passable understanding of Catholic doctrine. If they did not take actual courses on Catholic aesthetics, they might well have been in an undergraduate discussion group that featured Catholic novels and poetry. In preparation for parenting large families, they packed courses on marriage and family that deepened their convictions and seemed to make them immune to divorce. Although they were the first generation of upwardly mobile young Catholics who would work and live in friendly proximity to Protestants, these college graduates knew their faith and could defend it.

Their teachers belonged to Catholic professional societies, published in Catholic journals, and knew their way around Catholic movements designed to provide practical training in the lay apostolate. Many were members of religious orders, but increasing enrollments necessitated the hiring of young Catholic laymen.[1] Whether these newly hired professors were family men or single, their dedication to their institutions and to their students often had the power and enthusiasm of a religious vocation.

The physical plants of these Catholic colleges and universities varied enormously in size and style, but one could always find chapels where daily mass, devotional opportunities, and regular confession marked the days and the years. Strolling through campus could be religiously inspiring since the grounds, buildings, and classrooms were decorated with the artistic and statuary reminders of the Catholic world. The hours of the day and night were carefully supervised, and it was not unusual to have a few days set aside for an annual college retreat.

This idyllic account may describe Catholic colleges through the 1940s, but by the mid-1950s there was a rising level of self-criticism in Catholic higher education. For a number of complex reasons—upward social mobility, changes in the culture, the hiring of new young professors who had obtained degrees from "non-Catholic" institutions, the desire to take part in a world of academic discourse that was not totally shaped by a religious perspective—Catholic educators willingly dropped what they saw as a ghettoized and intellectually inferior approach to education.[2] A momentous change that also served as a clarion call of crisis for conservatives was the issue of academic freedom.

Academic Freedom in the Catholic University

The forces that changed the character of Catholic higher education were felt most keenly in the universities, and were perhaps most clearly articulated at the University of Notre Dame under the leadership of Theodore M. Hesburgh, president of that institution from 1952 to 1987. At the heart of the debates was the nature of the Catholic university: What made it Catholic, and what made it a university? A pivotal issue in these questions was academic freedom and its relation to education. In the opinion of Damien Fedoryka, former president of Christendom College, Catholic university presidents in general, and Hesburgh in particular, destroyed the metaphysical foundation of Catholic education in 1967 when they no longer wished to invoke the religious exemption clause in the AAUP academic freedom guidelines.[3] Up to that time, nearly all universities in the country subscribed to an "Academic Freedom and Tenure" statement that allowed this exception: "Limitations of academic freedom because of religious or other aims of the institution should be clearly stated in writing at the time of the appointment."[4] Religious colleges and universities welcomed this exclusion because it allowed them to impose ecclesiastical limitations on their faculty members and to enact policies that abolished dissent.

In 1967, when he was president of the International Federation of Catholic Universities, Hesburgh organized a set of meetings on the idea of the Catholic University to be held at the Notre Dame conference center at Land O' Lakes, Wisconsin. In July, at the end of the second day, twenty-six Catholic college presidents, deans, and advisors from the United States and Canada signed the document that changed the face of Catholic higher education. They relinquished the AAUP exemption, thereby making Catholic universities liable to the same rules of academic freedom that governed other institutions of higher learning.[5] For good or for ill, therefore, Catholic universities now play on the same field as their secular counterparts. They neither ask for exceptions nor conform to external authority. As it says in the Land O' Lakes statement: "The Catholic university must have a true autonomy and academic freedom in the face of authority of whatever kind, lay or clerical, external to the academic community itself."[6]

The Land O' Lakes group was convinced that the Catholic university "must be a university in the authentic sense of the word, both traditional and modern."[7] They were concerned to promote academic excellence in an atmosphere of true autonomy and to foster ecumenical and interdisciplinary dialogue with no theological or philosophical imperialism. Critics of the Land O' Lakes statement, who believe that *Catholic* means orthodox conformity with the teaching of the magisterium, say that great universities do not have to relinquish their heritage in order to achieve greatness. As it says in the foundational principles of Thomas Aquinas College, "Rather than supposing that men can attain the truth by the exercise of freedom, they [the Christian faith and the tradition of the church] teach that men become free by finding, or being found by, the truth and abiding in it."[8] Hesburgh's notion that a Catholic university has within it a "Catholic presence" is, to the minds of its critics, simply inadequate. "I believe that *Catholic* makes more of a difference than that," Fedoryka told me when I brought up the notion of the Catholic presence. "Historically, universities sprang from the heart of the church, and a Catholic university has to commit itself to Catholicism in every way."[9] Ralph McInerny, a professor of philosophy at Notre Dame, agrees with Fedoryka on this point: "The real problem with American Catholic universities is not that they *cannot* be both Catholic and universities, but that they no longer *wish* to be."[10]

The conservative case as manifest in the founding of new colleges is a response to what their founders see as the educational crisis resulting from denying the magisterium any effective role in Catholic higher education. Whether they are talking about home schooling, more traditional catechetical efforts, or the bankruptcy of liberalism and secularism, conservative critics of Catholic education long for a return to a system that is authentically Catholic.[11] The founders and administrators of the alternative colleges established in the last twenty years stress obedience to the pope. Thomas Aquinas College (Santa Paula, California), Christendom College (Front Royal, Virginia), Magdalen College (Warner, New Hampshire), and Thomas More College (Merrimack, New Hampshire), together constitute a fascinating chapter in the history of Catholic higher education, and a countercultural voice in contemporary American Catholicism.

In seeking to shape a true Catholic identity in conformity with Rome, these new institutions of higher learning have been encouraged recently by the apostolic constitution *Ex Corde Ecclesiae*, which calls for all Catholic teachers to be faithful to "Catholic doctrine and morals in their research and teaching."[12] *Ex Corde Ecclesiae* says that a Catholic university carries out its research, teaching, and service missions "with Catholic ideals, principles, and attitudes."[13] Of course, all Catholic institutions claim to be operating under Catholic ideals, and all hope that they are helping to shape a "Catholic identity": they differ radically in defining that identity and in the means they choose to inform it, which is why there is almost constant debate and dialogue about Catholic education.

Not all critics of Catholic higher education are conservatives. Kenneth L. Woodward, a Notre Dame graduate and religion editor of *Newsweek* magazine, is distressed that today's Catholic college graduates have very little sense of their own identity. They do not "realize what treasures lie in their own tradition," he says. "There is no religious tradition that speaks more critically, more coherently, and yes, more controversially to our sorely afflicted society than that tradition to which we are all the unworthy heirs. It is far from perfect, and necessarily incomplete. But I ask: Must our Catholic college and university students be the last to notice that it exists?"[14] Woodward would not, I hazard to guess, send his children to one of the new conservative Catholic colleges, but he might be impressed with the attempts that these institutions are making to shape a Catholic identity in an atmosphere redolent of the rigor of the medieval university and the mythic innocence of the 1950s. Although these colleges do not replicate their preconciliar cousins and are significantly more innovative in their curricula, there is something about them that evokes nostalgia. Thomas Aquinas College focuses on the philosophy of its namesake with passion and self-assurance; Magdalen puts an emphasis on formation;

Christendom "places the Catholic faith at the heart of the entire curriculum";[15] and Thomas More is an experiment in Catholic community.

Thomas Aquinas College

The largest and most physically impressive new Catholic college was founded in southern California in 1971 with 33 students and a budget of $150,000. Today it has a multi-million-dollar budget and more than 200 students—on the way to an optimal number of 350—nestled into the mountains near the sleepy little town of Santa Paula, California. A few miles north of the campus is the vista that was used in the 1937 version of *Lost Horizon* to represent "Shangri La," the elegant Himalayan utopia of eternal life stumbled into by Ronald Colman. With its unusual atmosphere—a mixture of dreaminess, intensity, orthodoxy, and community—TAC is rather like Shangri La.

In contrast to other Catholic universities, says Ralph McInerny, students at TAC "learn the perennial philosophy and sacred theology of the Church, in conformity with the *magisterium.*"[16] In a glowing appraisal of this new institution, Michael Platt says that "the school seems to know that the secret of youth (as of life) is learning to live fulfilled lives with unfulfilled desires."[17] Its admirers are not wrong to praise doctrinal orthodoxy and character development, but the real secret of the college, according to its faculty and students, is pedagogy. As it says in one of its routine advertisements in *The Wanderer,* "We offer a coherent curriculum based on the accumulated wisdom of our Christian and Western civilization. Your sons and daughters will be introduced to philosophy and theology through the liberal arts—the arts of learning: grammar, logic, music, geometry, and astronomy."[18]

When I asked president Thomas Dillon why he chose to come to TAC, he said, "I love this kind of [Great Books] education." He denied that TAC was trying to replicate the Catholic colleges of the 1950s, saying that he did not think such colleges existed in the 1950s. "Then there was a greater reliance on textbooks and manuals rather than a teaching of students to work it out for themselves . . . we strive for real knowledge."[19] Ron McArthur, one of the founders and clearly the inspiration behind TAC, told me that for education, "the only answer lies in the Great Books. They are worth everyone's time. If people read the same texts and discuss the same texts, there is a way they talk to each other about serious things, and that is the way to go in education."[20] When I asked Peter De Luca, one of the tutors, why students were not encouraged to use lexicons and commentaries in Scripture classes, he said, "We realize that what we are trying to do is to get them to *think*. It kills that purpose if an expert tells them that this is so. When that happens, they cannot discuss it. If someone presents an opinion of the experts, then they have to present his argument to prove it."[21]

The students I interviewed raved about the sense of intellectual community they find at TAC. Some of them had been at Catholic and secular universities and quit because they were not learning anything. At TAC they are plunged into the intellectual life by way of primary texts that they are expected to unpack and discuss among themselves. Most of them mentioned an amazing sense of coherence in the program, the integration of the moral, intellectual, and spiritual life. When I asked them the same question about not using commentaries in Scripture classes, one student told me: "It is a gradual process of trusting yourself with the text. You start saying you cannot do it, but you gradually get into it. One of the natural reactions is to go to other sources . . . but it is counterproductive. We are trying to get the ability to understand the arguments and to come to terms with them."

Tutors at Thomas Aquinas College are all expected to teach the entire curriculum, a four-year Great Books program with no electives. They need not be experts. In fact, one of the founders told me, "We don't see the tutor as anything more than a good amateur. He doesn't sit there as a source of wisdom, but as a lover, a more advanced student who can turn others on to questions."[22] At the end of four years, everyone has worked through Euclid as well as Aquinas, Copernicus as well as Chaucer, and the experience of a totally shared set of texts provides a common bond among students and faculty past and present. The demands on faculty members, therefore, are uncommon. As Ron McArthur told me, "Young faculty members here have to give up traditional goals. They will not become specialists in their own field here and will not publish a great deal. They will not get the kind of credentials that will make them a success in the world."[23]

The curriculum, the students, and the tutors are dedicated to a view of Catholic education quite in line with *Ex Corde Ecclesiae,* which in turn stands in the tradition of the great medieval universities. According to Pope John Paul II, every Catholic university has four essential characteristics: a Christian inspiration, fidelity to the Christian message as it comes through the church, an institutional commitment to serving the human community on its way to a transcendent goal, and "a continuing reflection in the light of the Catholic faith upon the growing treasury of human knowledge."[24] For Ron McArthur and other tutors at TAC, "liberal education" means getting students interested in great things: "Liberal education has always been known to be concerned with ends that are not monetary and not having to do with being known or having power, but with living a life of reason, habituated to what you learn in theology."[25]

The library is well stocked with classics and with sets of the Great Books, which, of course, contain no women authors: Jane Austen's *Emma* is the only female-authored book recommended on this campus. When I asked various students and tutors about this, they were surprised that I saw it as a problem. "Tell me a woman author who is good and we will consider her," I was told more than once.[26] There were few new books in the library, very little written in the last twenty-five years, and although they had a *Jerome Biblical Commentary*, very little biblical criticism graced their shelves. The periodical section comprised mostly newspapers and magazines—*The Wanderer, The Twin Circle, This Rock*, e.g.—and few journals. Although they hope to build a new library soon, it will probably be stocked with rare editions of the classics. TAC offers its students the perennial philosophy; most new books do not.

The chapel resembles an old-fashioned Catholic church with the exception of an altar facing the congregation. The kneelers, when I was there, were hard and narrow, which might be a metaphor for the Christian life as they understand it. Daily Latin Mass *(Novus Ordo)* and Sunday High Mass with a well-rehearsed schola mark the regular liturgical life. I attended Sunday Mass there on the feast of St. Bruno, founder of the Carthusians. Members of the congregation sang the ordinary parts of the Mass while the schola managed the Gregorian chant of the propers. The sermon focused on the constancy of the cross and the fact that life is about suffering. Students admitted that they found "a certain mystique about the Latin Mass, a sense of awe and mystery."[27] Generally, students and tutors agree that "Latin is a better vehicle for the liturgy, more fitting. It tends to elevate the mind more."[28]

TAC is a friendly and quite serious place. The students and staff are engaged with each other and with their common task of learning together: everyone seems to have a sense of purpose. The admissions director told me that the school "does not suit students for the world very well,"[29] but I do not think he meant that to be a criticism. If there is a bottom line in the approach at TAC, it is argumentation: supplied with the "lost tools of learning," the school's graduates are skilled in dialectic and rhetoric and know the value of definitions, distinctions, and logic. Their curriculum does not conform to the more generally accepted guidelines in contemporary universities, but students leave TAC having read through a number of difficult primary texts, and with a great deal of confidence in their ability to reason through any situation.

Magdalen College

Magdalen began its 1991–92 school year on a new campus architecturally designed to resemble a New England village. Fifty students and seven faculty members work together in elegant surroundings on 135 acres located about thirty miles northwest of Manchester, New Hampshire. Everything is pristine: the seven new buildings are beautifully appointed, the grounds immaculately kept, the students impeccably dressed and unfailingly polite. One has a sense of order here, as if every possible contingency had been anticipated. Founded by John Meehan (its current president), Francis Boucher (a local businessman), and Peter Sampo (who later left to found Thomas More College), Magdalen puts its main emphasis on formation in order to train young people to be Catholic lay leaders. The catalogue placards the purpose of the college on its cover: "forming Catholic leaders for the 21st century to rebuild the family in America."

If the purpose has always been clear, the surroundings have not always been so posh. Magdalen opened in 1974 in an abandoned motel south of Manchester; that first semester it had thirteen students and four faculty members who doubled as staff. The location and the buildings were never ideal, and the college grew very slowly. A decade later, just as things began to turn around for the fledgling institution, there was a major confrontation between two groups of faculty members over the no dating rule. "Two different philosophies developed. . . . In the aftermath of that division, four people were dismissed from the college. . . . Finally we lost about *half* the student body over this and were plunged into a financial disaster from which we are now rebuilding."[30] A generous financial contribution gave the school a new lease on life and enabled it to construct its ideal campus.[31]

Two related features distinguish Madgalen from the other new Catholic colleges: its comprehensive approach to ecclesiastical documents, and its emphasis on formation. Meehan believes that young people aiming toward apostolates in the world need solid moral teaching and spiritual formation. Magdalen teaches the lay vocation to its students through a modified Great Books program augmented with a full year's immersion in the documents of Vatican II in an atmosphere where that vocation can be fostered. As Paul

Sullivan told me, "Magdalen's emphasis is on the whole life of the student, not just on the academics. We deal with formation here, a school for laymen where there are certain things demanded of students."[32]

Students who attend Magdalen have a personal interview with the admissions director before matriculation because life in this small, ordered community appeals to a self-selected few. A typical day begins with Mass at 6:45 A.M., breakfast at 7:30, and classes from 8:45 until noon. Students are involved in work projects or study all afternoon, with some leisure activity time set aside an hour or so before dinner. My conversations with students there were informal and perfectly pleasant, and a senior thesis defense I attended was an impressive example of academic give and take. I did not find the students as philosophically sophisticated as the students at TAC, but they are not trying to be. "We're trying to get away from the layman who can argue about St. Thomas Aquinas and discuss philosophical matters in the abstract," said Paul Sullivan in a recent interview. "The church is urging the layman to get back in the temporal world. We're calling our students to a life of service, to be a leaven in the world and society."[33] Like their counterparts at Bob Jones University—which Magdalen resembles in its clean-cut men and women, its regimented daily schedule, and its enthusiastic participation in the formation of new apostles—Magdalen students appear to be perfectly happy and spiritually sure of themselves.

Magdalen is the only one of the four new colleges that has its own free-standing chapel.[34] Mass is said in English or in Latin *(Novus Ordo),* and on Sundays the choir sings parts of the Mass in Latin. All students participate in the college choir and learn Gregorian chant. Magdalen operates with a fairly small faculty, who are expected to teach the whole program and to be very involved in shaping the lives of their students. Since the program at Magdalen, unlike those at other colleges, is very heavily invested in formation, the recruitment of faculty members is particularly difficult. Predictably, perhaps, many of the Magdalen faculty are graduates of the college.

Students and faculty at Magdalen operate under the aegis of three public documents: the "Program of Studies," the "Student Handbook," and "The Formation Handbook," by far the heftiest of the three. Studies at Magdalen are devoted primarily to a Great Books program offering tutorials in social thought, philosophical thinking, scientific reasoning, mathematical reasoning, creative arts, language (Latin), and catechesis. Student life is structured around the common good, with the rights, policies, and expectations of the college spelled out in some detail. The most extensive document—three times longer than either of the other two—is devoted to formation and is based on a comprehensive view of obedience meant to awaken the apostolic spirit in young people. Christ as an obedient servant is a model for the obedience owed to institutional authorities. As it says in the handbook, "the order of obedience is essential."[35] The concept of formation is based on "paternal rule" since "according to Nature, and therefore God, the man (male) is the giver of life."[36] Paternal rule is "grounded in virtue (manliness)," whereas "everything to which the Devil invites and urges, regardless of sex, is effeminacy."[37] The model is grounded on and fostered by the family, a manageable unit where each person knows his or her faith and understands the right order of things. As John Meehan said in a junior seminar I attended, "The family is a model of unity based on love, hope, and faith. Only the laity can have families. How will I know when Magdalen is a success? When we have wall-to-wall kids from our alumni."[38]

Magdalen is the most separatist of the new colleges, not inclined to associate with other experiments in "orthodox" Catholic education. The bottom line is formation: Magdalen spends its time and energy tempering and directing the affections of its students, showing them that the principle of paternal rule is good, and urging them to see that the Catholic family is an apostolic vocation. Faculty members and administrators take an oath of fidelity to Christ and His Church every year to acknowledge their solemn obligation to pass on the faith. This college teaches its students to be loyal to the magisterium and clear about their vocation to bring the Gospel to the temporal order.

Christendom College

Like Magdalen, Christendom College was founded in response to the call of Vatican II for the laity to take a greater role in the mission of the church. Its name is reminiscent of the time when the Catholic faith profoundly influenced the public life of the Western world. Warren Carroll, a former *Triumph* staff member and the founder of Christendom, was particularly interested in a fully integrated Catholic curriculum. "I believe that the Catholic faith is objectively true, and that is the way it should be taught," he told me. "Catholic history is about the importance of Christ, the reality of the soul and its struggles. Those things are what is most important and what we want to convey when we teach history here." When I asked him if this approach was the one being used by Catholic colleges in the 1950s, he said, "No. In the 1950s they taught religion all right, but they taught all other subjects just as they were being taught in secular schools. That was the mistake. Everything in a Catholic university should be taught from a Catholic perspective."[39]

The connections between Christendom and *Triumph* magazine are worth noting, especially since anti-abortion activism is part of the world-engaging work of Christendom students. Patrick Allitt, summarizing the arguments that led Brent Bozell to leave the *National Review* (edited by his brother-in-law, William F. Buckley) in order to found *Triumph* magazine, says that the precipitating factors were the volatile aftermath of Vatican II, which Bozell thought needed to brought under control; the abortion question and the sexual revolution; and dissatisfaction with the *National Review*'s policy-oriented conservatism.[40] In many ways, *Triumph* became the rallying point for Catholic intellectuals who were opposed to the so-called "spirit of Vatican II."

Through Warren Carroll, Christendom stands in that stream of Catholic intellectual life that disagrees with the ways in which the documents of Vatican II have been interpreted. More important, however, Christendom sees itself as responsive to the crisis in higher education that resulted from allowing dissent from church teaching to have a place on a Catholic college campus. As Mark McShurley told me, "We felt that many Catholic institutions of higher learning were losing their identity as Catholic institutions . . . were not keeping their corporate commitment to the church. So, Christendom is a clear response to that as well."[41] When an interviewer asked Damien Fedoryka if colleges such as Christendom were founded for more traditional, pre–Vatican II families, he said, "No. The reason Christendom was founded was not for these orthodox, traditional families. It was a response to the crisis in education—the truths of the Church were not being taught."[42] Like the other new Catholic colleges, Christendom began in a small way: it opened in 1977 in an unused parish hall in Triangle, Virginia, with twenty-six students and about $50,000. Today it is located on 150 acres in the Shenandoah Valley, with a multi-million-dollar budget and 140 students, hoping eventually for 450 resident students. Its seventeen faculty members and its administrators are Catholics, as are all of its students. Christendom has its own press, which publishes books and pamphlets as well as the college newsletter. Each year the school sponsors a summer institute—in 1992 cosponsored by Human Life International—on Catholic apologetics. Christendom is different from the other new Catholic colleges in two ways: its curriculum is more like that of a regular university, and it offers distinctive political action opportunities as part of its program. Christendom does *not* take a Great Books approach. Instead it offers an eighty-one-hour core curriculum (for freshmen and sophomores) and six majors (classical and modern languages, English, history, mathematics, political science, and theology). An hour's drive from Washington, D.C., Christendom is unique in offering a "politics program," to teach students how to shape the political future of the nation. The practicum for this course consists of seminars, lectures, and workshops in Washington on such topics as abortion, taxes, judicial power, foreign policy, and the everyday workings of politics. The internship is a six-week summer position on a congressional staff or a political action committee meant to provide students with an inside look at the shaping of public policy. The politics program is described in extensive terms, but is aimed foremost at anti-abortion activity.[43]

Christendom has been successful in building up a student body, fostering vocations, and establishing "undiluted Catholicism at its core,"[44] but the college is not without its critics. A former faculty member wrote a highly negative article on alternative Catholic colleges featuring Christendom, though not by name. Obviously disenchanted by what he hoped would be an atmosphere of "confidence in the Faith" which would allow everyone "to explore the great questions freely and energetically," he found instead anti-intellectualism, isolationism, and a "tendency to reduce a liberal education to catechetics and apologetics" which finally is "producing not Catholic leaders, but sectarian followers."[45] If such criticisms were ever true, they seem to be an inaccurate description of the current situation, partly because of some recent administrative changes.

In the summer of 1992, Christendom got a new president (Timothy O'Donnell), a new vice-president for development (Peter Lemon), and a new director of admissions (John Ciskanik). They are young, energetic men who have generated successful fund drives, quadrupled the number of applicant inquiries, and succeeded in bringing an expansive vision to the college. They combine Mother Teresa's dictum—"We are called to be faithful, not successful"—with a flair for public relations. In 1992 they broke ground for a new chapel and multipurpose building.

Christendom is sometimes compared to the Franciscan University of Steubenville, which, with its 1,800 students and 130 faculty members, is an upgraded, revised edition of the old diocesan college. Steubenville has its vital center in the charismatic vision and energy of its president, Michael Scanlon, and has typically appealed to charismatic Catholics. In the past few years, however, Steubenville has consciously made a much broader outreach, promising sound, orthodox teaching and theology. It may be the only university in the country to offer a major in "humanities and Roman Catholic culture."[46] Administrators at Christendom see Steubenville as its major competitor, since both of them offer traditional college majors in an institution whose primary selling point is fidelity to church teaching.

The differences between the two are in many ways related to size. Christendom is housed in what used to be an AFL-CIO training center and resembles a summer camp more than a college campus. Its library is sparse but growing—from 27,000 to 40,000 volumes in the last two years—and its student body is small, given to more traditional expressions of style and prayer than one would find at Steubenville. One does not have to be a charismatic to attend Steubenville, but it probably helps. At Christendom, students attend a Latin Mass *(Novus Ordo)* daily and on Sunday with a choir adept at Gregorian chant. Mark McShurley told me that the Latin Mass is a new experience for some of the students, and that some come to Christendom preferring the old Tridentine Mass. Also, "There is some nostalgic traditionalism. Some have come through a post-conciliar experience and their parents have looked for something else for themselves and for their children."[47]

Thomas More College of Liberal Arts

The youngest of the new Catholic colleges, lying in the hills of southern New Hampshire, was founded in 1978 by Peter Sampo (president) and Mary Mumbach (dean) with some program design help from Donald and Louise Cowan at the University of Dallas. The Dallas connections are strong: Mumbach, faculty members Glen and Virginia Arbery, and staff member Mary Bonifield were all shaped by the educational and intellectual vision of the Cowans, whose educational philosophy emphasizes heroic vision and the centrality of poetry.[48] Their approach to education places learning beyond liberal or conservative categories in order to stress visible and invisible transformation of the person. Perhaps that is why Thomas More presents itself as a community where students can engage "concepts of risk, daring, and hope about life," rather than as an institution concerned primarily with orthodoxy. "We think orthodoxy is in service to something much greater, which is, finally, the transformation of human society so that it can conform to the ultimate good."[49]

Thomas More has three distinguishing features: it offers a "Rome program" for its sophomores; its inspirational debt to the Cowans is significant; and its "Great Books" approach is unique. The sophomore semester abroad, a mixture of cultural and religious experience, is an integral part of the curriculum meant to "evoke new sensibilities and depth in the students."[50] The Rome program is a particular embodiment of Louise Cowan's approach to literature through Aristotelian genres of poetry: the sense that life begins, falls, endures, and struggles can be recapitulated in lyric poetry, tragedy, comedy, and epic. In Rome, students are immersed in the classical works of the Roman republic on the transcendent terrain of Augustine, Aquinas, and Dante.

The overall curriculum is also indebted to Louise Cowan, as well as to her husband, Donald, who believes that humanity is at the end of the modern age and must be prepared for what is to come. Thomas More does not want to be understood as a Catholic Great Books program: its curriculum "is organized according to a study of major cultures in the history of Western civilization,"[51] and unlike most Great Books programs, it does not rely on a strict seminar approach. Students at Thomas More attend a two-hour humanities lecture each morning, part of a four-year cycle shared by the faculty and divided according to historical periods. When I visited the campus, they were all immersed in the Enlightenment. The humanities lecture focused primarily on literature, using *Moby Dick* and *Don Quixote* to raise questions. The Great Books part of the curriculum that semester also featured Enlightenment thinkers—Hobbes, Locke, Rousseau, Descartes—and was augmented by modern critical works and literature *(Lord Jim,* for example, and *Madame Bovary)*. Peter Sampo says that their curriculum "has time for discussing only the most significant human experiences: of pilgrimage, of suffering, of community, of death and resurrection . . . indeed, the curriculum prefigures fundamental experiences that the student will undergo throughout his life."[52] When I asked how Thomas More students compared to TAC students, Glen Arbery told me that their students were encouraged to develop different skills. "At Thomas Aquinas they concentrate on dialectic and rhetoric," he explained, whereas "our students are really not encouraged to be argumentative."[53] Indeed, the whole Thomas More curriculum is aimed toward *communal* thinking, a working together toward a unitive truth. "Literature, in terms of the shared experience of the narrative, can work that way, whereas an emphasis on philosophy or theology might not."[54] All students participate in a core curriculum before choosing one of three majors (political science, philosophy, or literature).

Thomas More began with ten students in classroom space leased from Daniel Webster College. It had twelve students when it moved to its present location—the old Bowers family farm just outside of Merrimack, New Hampshire—in 1981. The old white farm house (present administration building) and red barn look like a postcard vision of rural New Hampshire, a picture not marred by the addition of a new dormitory building (opened in 1986) and library (opened in 1990). Growth has been sporadic but relatively steady—from twelve to seventy-eight students in the last thirteen years—with its largest freshman class (thirty) entering in 1993. Having impressed Russell Kirk, among others, Thomas More is recommended in the *National Review College Guide*.

The chapel, a relatively modern-looking space with some traditional touches, was designed by Lyle Novinski, a liturgical artist. It is located in the student center (the old red barn) and gives the impression of airy, welcoming space. Mass is celebrated daily in English, and students may attend a rosary and/or the liturgy of the hours daily as well. The library, like its counterparts on other new college campuses, has very few new books, and the periodical collection is inadequate by even minimal standards. It is an elegant building which houses seminar rooms and a large lecture hall.

The faculty, with degrees from places such as Notre Dame, Oxford, Michigan, and Louisiana State, as well as from the University of Dallas, is well diversified. Although some of these new colleges—Magdalen, for example—draw heavily on their alumni to fill the ranks of their faculty and staff, Thomas More does not. I did not talk to students at Thomas More except informally over lunch, which was perfectly pleasant and uneventful. Students at all of these colleges are "normal-looking," in contrast to the stereotype that pictures them as if they were preparing to ferret out heretics for a living. The students at Thomas More are perhaps somewhat more mainstream in their approach to fashion.

The bottom line at Thomas More is community and culture. Its founders wanted a small Catholic college that could achieve a mean between popular heterodoxy and what they saw as overly defensive apologetics. Celebrating the Greco-Roman tradition as it has been embraced and transformed by Christian experience, Thomas More tries to balance a recognition of modern intellectual achievements with the return to the sources that one finds in any Great Books curriculum. The emphasis at this small college is less theological than at Christendom, Magdalen, or TAC. "We are certainly a Catholic school," Glen Arbery told me, "but our patron is Thomas More, who was very witty and not the kind of person to strain grace, to force it on people, or to make it exclusive."[55]

Conclusions

All of these new Catholic colleges are recent, lay-founded, lay-administered experiments in Catholic education. They are small in size, and often hire their own graduates for staff and faculty positions. Linked by a shared belief in objective truth and the means to attain it, they are in many ways heroic responses to a perceived crisis in higher education. At the same time, they appear to be tilting at windmills and are deeply involved in the paradoxical disjunctions between their hopes and their abilities to achieve them.

Thomas Aquinas College, for example, hopes to change the face of Catholic higher education through its Great Books approach, but places its faculty in a position where they can have no real impact on any larger debate. Since its faculty members do not publish in scholarly journals, attend academic meetings, or engage in disciplinary discourse, they restrict their ability to influence Catholic higher education by the very nature of their approach. None of their faculty, so far as I can tell, belong to the Fellowship of Catholic Scholars, where they might at least find some fellow travelers. It is not clear to me that their graduates move out into a wider world of intellectual conversation. Indeed, the few I have met tend to find one another in urban locations where they gather for mutual support and liturgical celebration.

Magdalen College takes seriously the directives of the Second Vatican Council that encourage laymen and -women to take up vocations in the world that will support the work of the church, but they do so in a way that is so ideologically remote from the world in which they wish to participate that it is hard to imagine them being effective. The *in loco parentis* style of the campus—the heavy stress on a "moral atmosphere" where dress, manners, and conduct are closely supervised—removes them from the world. Finally, the fact that obedience to the magisterium is a keystone of their foundation may be a problem when graduates are ready to participate in ordinary parish life. Since many conservative Catholics today are much bolder in their criticism of the hierarchy than they would have been thirty years ago, this stress on obedience could raise an interesting question, viz., whether a student body taught to be obedient would passively support the "new church" found in most American dioceses.

Christendom College teaches everything from a Catholic perspective and offers its students a chance for political engagement in Washington, D.C. It prides itself on offering real majors and on being realistic in terms of the future activism of its graduates. It is not clear, however, that its students are genuinely active in anything beyond public anti-abortion protest marches in the capital. Conservative Catholic think tanks, such as those headed by George Weigel or Michael Novak, do not employ Christendom graduates or use their students as interns.

Thomas More hopes to create a community with a literary approach to culture where education is directed at heroism. Christopher Dawson's suggestion that the curriculum of Catholic colleges be constructed around the notion of Christian *culture,* which was not taken up with much enthusiasm when it was proposed, is alive and well at Thomas More. The celebration of Catholic culture and its role in shaping a curriculum and major courses of study is a foundational principle of the institution. Its goals are the most modest and most attainable of all these colleges. Since graduates of Thomas More do not hope to change the world or save the church, the school is free to pursue its dream to form a caring community through a highly interactive curriculum. Since the student body is necessarily small, their contribution is small as well.

All of these new colleges are responses to an intellectual identity crisis among Catholics which, as Philip Gleason has perceptively argued, follow the complex logic of assimilation.[56] As American Catholics integrated themselves into their society, they were tossed on the horns of a painful dilemma: too much assimilation could lead to total absorption by the dominant culture and thus to the erasure of Catholic distinctiveness, yet too much attention to Catholic particularity could result in protective isolation and social retardation. The question of Catholic identity as it reverberated in academic circles widened a discussion that had begun in the nineteenth century and that reached a crisis point in the 1960s: What makes a college or university "Catholic"?

On this volatile question, the pope, the American bishops, theologians, Catholic college presidents, alternative college founders, and students—disgruntled and satisfied—all have something to say about what Catholic education should be.[57] The new colleges hope to respond to some of the arguments in Catholic education that were raised in the post–World War II era, when American Catholic colleges and universities began to experience the sweet smell of success. They testify to a belief that there is a Catholic culture that colleges must pass on to the next generation. As they see it, the debates of the 1950s and 1960s about Catholic intellectual leadership and prestige led to a conclusion that they find patently absurd: that there is no such thing as a Catholic university. On the contrary, they say by their presence, Catholicism brings a much-needed perspective to the intellectual community.

It is hard, on the one hand, to argue with their claims, since by some measures they are successful. Thomas Aquinas College and Magdalen have been in operation for more than twenty years, while Christendom and Thomas More have been in business for more than fifteen years. They have all had charismatic founders and dedicated faculties, and they have doubled or quadrupled in size. On the other hand, their decision to remain small and to keep themselves away from the mainstream mutes any voice they might raise in the debates about Catholic higher education. Instead, they tend to glory in the fact that they are not successful by worldly standards and that they do not suit their students for conventional lives in a troubled world.

NOTES

1. It does not serve history well to use sex-inclusive language here, since a majority of all lay faculty members in Catholic colleges—including women's colleges—were, until well into the 1970s, lay *men*. Many of them were a kind of bachelor don whose social lives intersected most easily with those of the campus priests. The NCWC "Summary of Catholic Education" for faculty in 1956 shows a total of 2,528 laywomen overall and 10,438 laymen.

2. The famous indictment of Catholic education by John Tracy Ellis, "American Catholics and the Intellectual Life," *Thought* 30 (Autumn 1955): 351–88, moved many Catholic educational reformers to drop the "siege mentality" and "get out of the ghetto." The best account of this period is that of Philip Gleason, "American Catholic Higher Education, 1940–1990: The Ideological Context," in George M. Marsden and Bradley J. Longfield, eds., *The Secularization of the Academy* (New York: Oxford University Press, 1992), pp. 234–58.

3. I interviewed Fedoryka twice at Christendom College, in September 1991. Both times we spoke at some length about academic freedom. The 1967 conference was held at Land O' Lakes, Wisconsin, and the statement is usually referred to as the "Land O' Lakes Statement." Conservative critics often turn to this statement to argue for "truth in packaging" for Catholic higher education. See, for example, Frank Morris, "Time to Demand that Catholic Colleges and Universities Be What They Claim," *The Wanderer* (1992).

4. American Association of University Professors, *Policy Documents and Reports*, 1984 ed. (Washington, D.C.: AAUP, 1984), pp. 3–9, quotation from p. 3. This historic statement was designed "to promote public understanding and support of academic freedom and tenure." College and university teachers are entitled to full freedom of research and publication, and full freedom of discussion within the classroom. In religious institutions, however, that freedom did not apply in cases where church teaching or discipline was ignored or violated. Although the AAUP accepted this interpretation of the clause for many years, its 1970 interpretation of the guidelines says: "Most church-related institutions no longer need or desire the departure from the principle of academic freedom implied in the 1940 *Statement,* and we do not now endorse such a departure" (p. 5). The implications of this policy—specifically the notion that exceptional (religious) institutions perforce forfeit the moral right to proclaim themselves institutions of higher learning—are outlined and criticized in George Marsden's "The Ambiguities of Academic Freedom," *Church History* 30 (July 1993): 221–36.

5. The "Statement on the Nature of the Contemporary Catholic University" can be found in the pamphlet *The Idea of the Catholic University,* published under the auspices of the North American Region of the International Federation of Catholic Universities. For a fuller explication, see Neil G. McCluskey, *Catholic Education Faces Its Future* (Garden City, N.Y.: Doubleday and Co., 1968), pp. 215–55. For Hesburgh's enthusiastic interpretations of contemporary Catholic university life, see *The Hesburgh Papers: Higher Values in Higher Education* (Kansas City, Mo.: Andrews and McMeel, 1979), pp. 36–67. Also Theodore M. Hesburgh, "The Work of Mediation," *Commonweal* 74 (1961): 33–35.

6. "Statement on the Nature of the Contemporary Catholic University," paragraph 1. It should be noted from the preamble to this statement that the authors meant to speak only to "university-level problems, the nature and role of the Catholic liberal arts college or of the smaller university were not considered."

7. "Preamble," *The Idea of a Catholic University.*

8. *A Proposal for the Fulfillment of Catholic Liberal Education,* privately printed by Thomas Aquinas College, 1981 ed., p. 12. This thirty-page booklet, referred to by TAC tutors reverently as "the blue book," was drafted in 1967 as a statement of purpose for a new kind of Catholic college. Its drafters held a conference to discuss it in 1968, and published it as a booklet in 1969. This charter document is driven by two ideas: a discussion of the "crisis in the Catholic college," which argues that faith can illumine understanding and that academic freedom as understood by the AAUP leads necessarily to tyrannical governance; and a defense of "liberal education" as the soul of higher education necessarily governed by theology.

9. Personal interview with the author, 19 September 1991.

10. Ralph McInerny, "Starting Over: Catholic Higher Education Flourishes in California," *Crisis* 5 (March 1987): 11. For McInerny, as for many others, orthodoxy ought to be a criterion for hiring and firing in a Catholic university.

11. Edmund Miller, "Truly Catholic Education," *The Wanderer* 125 (17 September 1992): 4.

12. "Ex Corde Ecclesiae: Apostolic Constitution on Catholic Universities," *Origins* 20 (4 October 1990): 266–76. The relation between Catholic theology and the Vatican is the bottom-line issue and is an important part of this constitution. The Land O' Lakes statement stressed the Catholic character of universities precisely through departments of theology but at the same time declined to bow to authorities external to the university itself. The Vatican document insists that "Catholic theology [be] taught in a manner faithful to Scripture, tradition, and the church's magisterium" (p. 270). Theology used to be a *seminary* business and as such was more under the supervision and control of Roman officials. Such is no longer the case, and the relationship between the institutional church and departments of theology is not always cordial. See Alice Gallin, ed., *American Catholic Higher Education: Essential Documents, 1967–1990* (Notre Dame, Ind.: University of Notre Dame Press, 1992), and also John P. Langan, ed., *Catholic Universities in Church and Society: A Dialogue on Ex Corde Ecclesiae* (Washington, D.C.: Georgetown University Press, 1993). For some perceptive questions in this area, see Robert J. Wister, "The Teaching of Theology 1950–90: The American Catholic Experience," *America* 162 (3 February 1990): 88–93, 106–109.

13. Ibid., p. 274.

14. "Catholic Higher Education: What Happened?" *Commonweal*, 9 April 1993, pp. 13–18.

15. The words of Warren G. Carroll, founder of Christendom College. Personal interview conducted on the campus of Christendom, 19 September 1991.

16. McInerny, "Starting Over," p. 11.

17. "Thomas Aquinas and America," *Crisis*, July–August 1991, pp. 21–25, 42; quotation from p. 23. The panegyric nature of this article is contained in the subtitle: "How One College Might Strengthen the Souls of Youth and Reinvigorate the Republic."

18. One can see a homage to the medieval syllabus, divided into the *Trivium* (skills training as found in grammar, dialectic, and rhetoric) and *Quadrivium* (particular subjects; in the Middle Ages they were arithmetic, music, geometry, and astronomy). TAC students and tutors have no doubt read Dorothy L. Sayers, *The Lost Tools of Learning* (London: Methuen, 1948) (pamphlet).

19. Personal interview with Thomas Dillon, president of Thomas Aquinas College, 7 October 1991. Dillon has a Ph.D. in philosophy from the University of Notre Dame and came to Thomas Aquinas when he was twenty-six years old. He earned his B.A. from St. Mary's (Oakland) in 1968, where he was introduced to the Great Books idea and to Ron McArthur, the founder of TAC.

20. Personal interview with Ron McArthur conducted at Thomas Aquinas College, 8 October 1991. McArthur earned his B.A. from St. Mary's College (1949) and a Ph.D. from Laval in 1956, studying with Charles De Koninck. He taught at St. Mary's from 1958 to 1971, when he resigned to help found Thomas Aquinas College. McArthur, a charismatic figure, personally and intellectually, is the heart of Thomas Aquinas. His passion for a Great Books curriculum and his position at St. Mary's brought together the core group that founded and now sustains TAC. His study of Aquinas with De Koninck links him with another De Koninck student, Ralph McInerny, Michael P. Grace Professor of Medieval Studies at Notre Dame. Thomas Dillon, current TAC president, studied with McArthur as an undergraduate and with McInerny as a graduate student. Peter De Luca, a TAC tutor who resigned from the private sector in 1969 to spearhead the fund drive for seed money to start TAC, was a St. Mary's graduate and, in his terms, "was very much influenced by Dr. McArthur." Several of McArthur's colleagues at St. Mary's—Marcus Berquist, e.g., and John Neumayr—studied at either Laval or Notre Dame and were active in the Great Books program at St. Mary's.

21. Personal interview conducted on campus at TAC, 7 October 1991.

22. Personal interview with Peter De Luca, 7 October 1991.

23. Interview, 8 October 1991. Paradoxically, by emphasizing teaching to the extent that their faculty will not publish much, the neo-Catholic colleges in effect forfeit broader leadership in the conservative Catholic intellectual movement.

24. *Ex Corde Ecclesiae,* p. 269.

25. Personal interview, 8 October 1991.

26. Patricia Pucetti Donohoe, a graduate of Thomas Aquinas College, disagrees with the tone of my observations on this matter. The limitations of the TAC curriculum tend to privilege ancient sources, she explains, and there is no reason to think that TAC faculty and students are *against* female authors.

27. Sean Kelsey, who graduated in 1992, in a group interview with students, 8 October 1991.

28. Interview with Tom Susanka, admissions director, 7 October 1991.

29. Ibid.

30. Personal interview with Jeffrey J. Karls, executive vice-president of Magdalen College, conducted on campus, 17 March 1992. Younger faculty members thought that students would learn best through experience and so were opposed to college regulations that forbid dating among the students. The administration, however, believes that students should "aim toward a healthy friendship without the selfishness that tends to be in young people's dating relationships." Quotation from a personal interview with admissions director Paul Sullivan.

31. The new campus, built within an hour's drive of the White Mountains, is meant to accommodate 120 students. There are two dormitories, a chapel, two classroom buildings, a multipurpose center, and a learning center housing the administrative offices and library. It is not clear how much money Magdalen received—somewhere between $8 and $11 million—but most of it came from a single source. According to Paul Sullivan, admissions director, "We were helped by Jack Bisgrove, a businessman from upstate New York. . . . He has been involved in Catholic causes for the past ten years." Personal interview conducted at Magdalen College, 17 March 1992.

32. Personal interview conducted on the Magdalen campus, 17 March 1992. According to the *Student Handbook,* all students at Magdalen work at least one hour a day on the grounds or in the buildings. They have mandatory study hall, a dress code, and a nightly curfew. Distractions are virtually eliminated: no student may have a radio, television set, or any kind of stereo equipment, and none may listen to rock music. Punctuality, quiet, and personal neatness are not just encouraged, they are rules.

33. John Paul Arnerich, "Three Views of a Truly 'Catholic' Education," *The National Catholic Register,* 16 February 1992, p. 8.

34. "Magdalen College Chapel Consecrated; Faculty Takes Oath of Fidelity," *The Wanderer,* September 1991, p. 11.

35. Draft copy of "The Formation Handbook of the Magdalen Program of Studies," 25 January 1991, p. 27. I was given a copy of the handbook when I visited there in March 1992.

36. Ibid., p. 52.

37. The distinction between manliness and effeminacy is not meant to divide men and women. Using Catherine of Siena as an example, the authors of the Formation Handbook argue that anyone can be "manly." The "effeminate are vague and vacillating. . . . Those who dare not act justly and punish injustice . . . have a timid need of living in peace and on good terms with all the world." All quotations from p. 53.

38. From my notes taken in a junior seminar, 17 March 1992. Meehan's enthusiastic support of the lay vocation is grounded on a clear sense of the order of things. Priests and laity have different missions in life. "The clerical task is to aspire to personal holiness and preach the Gospel whereas the laity is to restore all creation to Christ."

39. From a personal interview with Carroll (19 September 1991) on the Christendom College campus. He is a convert to Catholicism, received into the church in 1968. Although he has a Ph.D. in history from Columbia, he did not teach until he founded Christendom. He told me

that he was "pretty dissatisfied with higher education" and spent most of his life working for the government. He was on the staff of *Triumph* magazine from 1973 to 1975, when he got the idea for Christendom, using the *Triumph* mailing list as an initial source for start-up donations. Carroll considers Christendom "the greatest accomplishment of my life," but stepped down in 1985 to write a six-volume history of Christendom (the historical reality, not the college; see the review of his *Isabel of Spain: The Catholic Queen* in *Reflections,* a Wanderer publication, Fall 1991, p. 8). His wife, Anne Carroll, is associated with Seton Home School and has written many of he books they use, including *Christ the King, Lord of History.*

40. *Catholic Intellectuals and Conservative Politics in America, 1950–1985* (Ithaca, N.Y.: Cornell University Press, 1993), p. 141. *Triumph* magazine ran from October 1966 until midyear 1975.

41. Personal interview with Mark McShurley, 17 September 1991. McShurley was then the director of admissions for the college.

42. Arnerich, "Three Views of a Truly 'Catholic' Education," p. 9.

43. Their advertising flyer summarizes the politics program by saying that the practical knowledge gained in the program "is especially needed today by the student aspiring to join the dramatic fight to protect the inalienable right of life for the unborn child." Damien Fedoryka, president of Christendom 1985–92, is a nationally known anti-abortion activist. His small book *Abortion and the Ransom of the Sacred* was published by Christendom Press in 1991. Every year Christendom closes the campus so that faculty, staff, and students can participate in the Annual March for Life in Washington, D.C.

44. From an article in the *Richmond Times Dispatch,* 12 May 1991. For statistics on vocations, see "Many Religious Vocations Spring from Christendom College," *The Wanderer,* November 1992.

45. Gregory Wolfe, "Killing the Spirit," *Crisis,* September 1991, pp. 19–24. Wolfe, a convert to Catholicism, taught at Christendom. In recent years he has begun a journal of Christian aesthetic criticism, *Image,* which is published from his base at Kansas Newman College in Wichita.

46. Catholic colleges and universities in the 1940s and 1950s were intent on building their curricular offerings around scholastic philosophy and/or theology. Christopher Dawson argued against that program and hoped to see a Catholic college education shaped around culture, as it has sustained and been sustained by Christianity. See his *The Crisis of Western Education* (New York: Sheed and Ward, 1961).

47. Personal interview, 17 September 1991.

48. Donald Cowan has a Ph.D. in physics from Vanderbilt and has done research on nuclear theory. As a founding member of the Dallas Institute of Humanities and Culture, he has devoted his energies to clarifying the connections among history (memory), poetry (imagination), and science (reason). *Unbinding Prometheus: Education for the Coming Age* (Dallas: The Dallas Institute Publications, 1988) is a collection of his essays on education delivered as speeches while he was president of the University of Dallas (1962–77). Louise Cowan (Ph.D., Vanderbilt), whose interest in liberal education is as powerful as that of her husband, was a distinguished professor of literature at the University of Dallas. Her book *The Terrain of Comedy* (Dallas: The Dallas Institute of Humanities, 1984) captures her literary approach to culture.

49. Virginia Arbery, former director of admissions, in an interview by Arnerich, "Three Views of a Truly 'Catholic' Education," p. 8.

50. 1991–92 catalogue, p. 22.

51. Ibid., p. 4.

52. In May 1993 the Fellowship of Catholic Scholars posed the following question to Catholic college presidents: "What is Catholic about a Catholic college?" The quotation is part of Sampo's reply and will be published in the 1993–94 version of the college catalogue. Sampo's statement is clear about what a Catholic college is *not:* "Its purpose is not to save souls since such a presumption would make it a rival to the Church. . . . Its purpose is not to save the Church since the Church is to save us. Were its purpose to save a culture or a civilization, it would take on an impossible task. . . . The purpose of a Catholic college is both more modest and more

ambitious: it is to help transform the heart and mind of each student who, almost miraculously, appears in the classroom."

53. Personal interview with Glen Arbery conducted on the Thomas More Campus, 16 March 1992. Arbery and his wife (former director of admissions) came to Thomas More in 1986.

54. Ibid. As he understands it, students at TAC are "more interested in distinctions and definitions and the development of certain arguments," whereas Thomas More students should be more interested in penetrating literature, in being "open to mystery, having a capacity to wonder."

55. Ibid. James Hitchcock reminded me that although Thomas More was considered very witty, he also burned heretics as lord chancellor of England.

56. "Immigrant Assimilation and the Crisis of Americanization," in *Keeping the Faith* (Notre Dame, Ind.: University of Notre Dame Press, 1987), pp. 58–81.

57. The drafts of *Ex Corde Ecclesiae* and the responses from American bishops and Catholic college presidents constitute a regular part of *Origins* from 1985 to the present. Whether Catholic colleges are in more danger from external critics—Robert Wolff of Columbia, e.g., wrote in 1970 that the phrase "Catholic university" is a strict contradiction in terms—or from their internal reformers is an issue taken up by George A Kelly, ed., *Why Should the Catholic University Survive?* (New York: St. John's University Press, 1973). One can see from this book why many conservatives prefer a more aggressive expression of Catholic identity to an attempt to make room for all voices in Catholic education. Theologians have been engaged in a very serious argument about the nature of Catholic theology in the United States. See Matthew L. Lamb, "Will There Be Catholic Theology in the United States?" *America* 162 (26 May 1990): 523–25, 531–34; Thomas O'Meara, "Doctoral Programs in Theology at U.S. Catholic Universities," *America* 162 (3 February 1990): 79–84, 101–103. From both sides of the Atlantic, students have registered serious criticisms about their failure to get a truly Catholic education in Catholic institutions. Louise Bagshawe, "The Smack of Firm Doctrine," *The Tablet* 244 (10 February 1990): 162, and Nancy W. Yos, "Teach Me: A Catholic *Cri de Coeur*," *First Things* 22 (April 1992): 23–28, write about secondary education, but their criticisms could be applied to colleges as well. Patrick J. Reilly ("Catholic Universities Espouse Stale Liberal System," *The Wanderer* [1991]) is a Fordham graduate who founded PACT (Preserving a Catholic Tradition) to call attention to what he perceived as a serious sellout on the part of Catholic universities. Paul Scalia, in "How Catholic Are America's Catholic Colleges?" *Campus Magazine,* Winter 1992, condemns Holy Cross College for taking Catholicism out of a priority position and placing it on a level with secular humanism.

Epilogue

What Difference Do They Make?

R. SCOTT APPLEBY

This volume represents the first phase of a project designed eventually to provide a map of postconciliar American Catholicism. Inspired in part by an awareness that contemporary Catholic intellectuals and activists often seem more comfortable with their ideological counterparts in other denominations than with their fellow Catholics, the project asks of Catholics along a spectrum of belief and practice: What do we have in common? On what fundamental points do we disagree?

Thus we assume the reality of ideological fragmentation in the church after the Second Vatican Council and recognize that people have embraced various points of view along a spectrum of belief and practice. Although the project directors intend the mapping to be a descriptive task, normative questions—e.g., who represents "authentic Catholicism"?—inevitably creep in, especially when the conversation takes a polemical turn. Such questions seem to demand simple resolutions to complex issues of obedience, authority, dissent, and other divisive matters. For those concerned with preserving a catholic approach to Catholic identity, Gene Burns is reassuring when he asserts that "historically it is quite clear that Rome, Catholic conservatives, Catholic socialists, and Catholic feminists all inherit a truly Catholic legacy. They emphasize different aspects of that legacy, but because the legacy is multifaceted and partly ambiguous, they all can point to true historical precedence for their beliefs."[1]

Burns is reassuring, but is he correct? This kind of claim seems particularly objectionable to the self-styled conservative and neoconservative American Catholics whose self-descriptions form the core of this volume. There is a tendency among some conservative activists, for example, to draw the map in such a way that Catholic feminists, not to mention "radical feminists," appear on the borders or, in less generous mappings, seem to lurk in the primeval swamps, where the ancient cartographers warned: "here be monsters." Generally, conservative activists complain that liberal or progressive Catholics have assumed control of the diocesan and national bureaucracies, where they rigorously attempt to exile conservatives, neoconservatives, and traditionalists off the map. Some conservatives and neoconservatives, it must be noted, are quite willing to join the liberals in consigning the traditionalists to the margins.[2]

In mapping projects, it is probably impossible to avoid right-left directions or labels altogether. Furthermore, a clear view of the terrain in its complexity requires a map with overlapping circles and changing configurations depending on the question being posed. If one asks about loyalty to the papacy, for example, the configurations are different from those visible when one asks about loyalty to American values and institutions. Finally, since maps usually orient the traveler according to directions on a compass, they are organized around the identification of a center and its peripheries. Mapping contemporary American Catholicism can be especially frustrating in this regard because most of those who know the terrain fall into one of two categories: (1) those many rivals with little in common other than the claim of each to sole possession of the center, and (2) those who claim that there is no center.

Is there a center to contemporary American Catholicism? Or, as many of those represented in this book lament, has the center disappeared? Does the diversity of ideology in the contemporary Catholic community extend to the underlying basis of the faith, to the fundamental affirmations and truth claims of Catholicism? Do Catholics agree in naming the authoritative sources of Catholic belief and practice, and in identifying the locus of moral, spiritual, and religious authority? Are there Catholic nonnegotiables, principles or doctrines or practices which are constitutive of the Catholic faith, elements without which the ideological formations make little sense? Is there consensus about what used to be called the *preambula fidei:* the role of the will and intellect in the act of faith, and the relationship between faith and reason, between revealed truth and natural law? We wonder, in short, where the ecclesial and religious boundary lines might be discerned thirty years after Vatican II.

Consensus on the Right

This volume provides some answers to these questions by identifying common ground shared by the large and somewhat amorphous group of Catholics on the right. Mary Jo Weaver, in the introduction, imagined a monologue by a "representative" conservative Catholic complaining about the loss of certainty and certainties in the postconciliar church. The monologue was based on our experience listening to self-styled conservative Catholics, all of whom agree that the authority of the magisterium has been compromised by theological dissent and inadequate catechesis—and that this challenge to papal-episcopal authority and traditional teaching is indisputably a bad thing.

They agree, further, that there has been an erosion of the preconciliar culture of the supernatural, and that this erosion is somehow connected to the church's new relationship to modernity (often described as capitulation or accommodation). In this view the once-vibrant American Catholic religious imagination—resplendent with angels, devils, saints, purgatory, hell, heaven, mortal and venial sins, actual and prevenient graces—has been replaced with bland formulae, empty symbols, and "conventional wisdom" drawn from the secular culture. "Pseudo-Catholics" proliferate in the brave new world—people who have abandoned the great tradition in favor of a superficial blending of religious sensibilities with the worldview of twentieth-century scientific culture.

Finally, conservative Catholics agree that the most powerful threat to Catholicism comes from within the church, from dissidents, feminists, liberal clergy, and laity who refuse to stand and be counted as opponents of moral evils such as abortion, and who undermine Catholic unity by suggesting that Catholics are individual moral decision-makers just like other Americans.

To put these points of consensus positively, we may say that conservative Catholics prefer: (1) pluralism narrowly defined and regulated by authority, (2) a religious identity and practice rooted in a traditional, supernatural worldview, and (3) a consistent expression of "private" religious belief in "public" behavior, be it moral, social, or political behavior. It will be interesting to discern if Catholics on the left agree about the priority or even salience of such concerns. Only then, perhaps, may we speak compellingly of a recognizable "core" of American Catholic beliefs, attitudes, and practices.

Divisions on the Right

Despite these attitudes held in common, conservative Catholics do not adopt the same approach to other fundamental questions of Roman Catholic identity. They do not agree among themselves, for example, about the desirability of forming religious and/or political alliances with non-Catholics. The neoconservatives described by George Weigel are noted for their coalitions with Orthodox Jews and evangelical Protestants who share a common social agenda and biblical faith. For the traditionalists profiled by Bill Dinges, however, ecumenism of all kinds, even for the sake of joining forces to battle abortion, is a symptom of the malady affecting the church, and thus to be studiously avoided.

As Joseph Komonchak demonstrated in chapter 1, conservatives also disagree among themselves about the meaning of Vatican II and the status of the church that implemented its decrees. Weigel, who sees the Council as a glorious watershed in the history of the church's increasing realization of the Gospel, is not a conservative in the same sense as the far-right sedevacantist, who sees the Council as the work of apostates and thus null and void. Nor is James Hitchcock, who welcomed Vatican II but was disappointed by its uneven and undisciplined implementation. They occupy different positions along a conservative spectrum.

Nor do conservatives uniformly celebrate the United States as a benevolent home for orthodox Catholicism, as I demonstrated in chapter 2. On this point, neoconservative Weigel and liberal-turned-conservative Hitchcock have more in common with liberal Catholics, who embrace church-state separation and religious liberty as goods in themselves, than with traditionalists or other European-inspired conservatives. The farther right one moves along the conservative spectrum, the less likely is one to meet the Catholic who is entirely approving of "the American experiment in ordered liberty." Is it appropriate to include in the category "conservative Catholics" both David Schindler, editor of *Communio* and an ardent critic of Americanist-style Catholicism, and Michael Novak, the neoconservative intellectual who celebrates *The Spirit of Democratic Capitalism* as being compatible with his religious identity?

World-Transformers and World-Renouncers

At the root of these divisions among conservative Catholics is a fundamental difference in orientation toward the world. By "world" I mean the reality that exists outside of the conservative movement, group, association, college, fellowship, or think tank in question. In addition, the world of some conservatives is much smaller than the world of others. Some conservative Catholics interact primarily with the church, or a corner of it (e.g., the Congregation for the Doctrine of the Faith), while others engage the larger, non-Catholic world beyond the church (e.g., American culture).[3]

To simplify the picture, we can speak of two basic conservative Catholic orientations to the world, however it is defined. Toward the far right on the spectrum one finds the *world-renouncers,* Catholics who reject Vatican II without qualification, who feel that the world and perhaps even the church has been given over to Satan, and who despair of an immediate deliverance within history. As one moves away from the far right, one finds conservative Catholics willing to live within the church and world, however disappointed or disheartened they may feel about the prospect of doing so. In this volume, moral theologians such as Father Benedict Ashley and his colleagues represent this middle position, as does the Fellowship of Catholic Scholars, depicted herein by one of its leaders, James Hitchcock, as a fairly phlegmatic bunch. These conservatives are deeply troubled by a perceived loss of theological unity in the post-Thomist Catholic intellectual world, and seem resigned to a fate as witnesses to a glorious age which has passed.

Ashley, Hitchcock, and their colleagues might be *world-transformers* were they more willing to adapt to late modern theological trends such as ecumenism, or to adopt some American–cum–Vatican II democratic values and procedures. Jim Sullivan suggests that Catholics United for the Faith, in borrowing lobbying techniques from the republic and lay theology from Rome, are very much in the spirit of what I am calling the world-transformer. CUF sees itself as the vanguard of the new laity heralded by Vatican II, men and women actively involved in defending and promoting the teaching of the magisterium. Thus they get involved in Catholic education and catechesis, entering the fray on matters of curriculum and textbook approval. They promote their own brand of lay spirituality and adult formation, taking their cues from preconciliar authorities such as Cardinal Newman, packaged in a postconciliar style. Some CUF chapters, Sullivan acknowledges, have also been known to hound liberal and even moderate bishops who prove themselves to be feckless guardians of orthodoxy. In a church threatened by liberal drift, CUF is fighting the good fight, it believes, with full hope of containing the momentum of reform within the boundaries supposedly recognized by Vatican II. Helen Hull Hitchcock's report on the organization she founded, Women for Faith and Family, suggests a similar formula for vigorous lay action in direct engagement with church and world. Feminism is the specific threat to which WFF responds, but the inspiring animus seems to be that of CUF: both groups seek to defend the postconciliar church from itself. In so doing, they are very much engaged with the politics of this world and its trappings, including direct-mail surveys, phone and fax networks, and coalition-building conferences.

Like CUF and WFF, the ecumenical-minded Catholic activists presiding over the think tanks dotted along the country's northeastern corridor seek to change the situation in the church. But the neoconservatives described by George Weigel also want to change the nation. Thus they gather allies, like-minded Protestant and Jewish religious conservatives, in the hope of wielding socio-moral influence. Weigel and company rub elbows with secular policymakers and conduct fruitful, often critical, conversations with politicians, church leaders, media elites, and prominent academics. In terms of sheer impact on the world outside their immediate circle, the neoconservative Catholics are arguably the most effective of the would-be world-transformers. By virtue of their prominence outside the church, they enhance their reputations and influence within it. Despite their occasional posturing to the contrary, the neoconservatives share a well-developed vision of church and society, and they have made significant progress in the 1980s and 1990s in fostering this vision among conservative thinkers in general. Unlike some of the conservative Catholic organizations studied in this volume, they are imaginative, energetic, politically savvy, well-funded, and exceedingly well-organized. One need only read Weigel's essay in this volume to grasp the extent of their ambition and their sophistication, especially in comparison with other conservative Catholics, in articulating and pursuing their goals.

By contrast, the "remnant faithful," as traditionalists call themselves, are the most obvious exemplars of the world-renouncer orientation. Updating his previous research on anticonciliar groups, Bill Dinges reports that familiar world-renouncing and apocalyptic themes have become even more prominent in traditionalist literature since the mid-1980s, when schismatic leaders were forced to justify their renunciation of the church itself. He notes the traditionalists' "escalating denunciations" of John Paul II, especially on occasions when the pope voices support for ecumenism and religious liberty. Something new has appeared, however, in the traditionalists' repertoire—"a growing critique of American political institutions and democratic ideology"—and it underscores their deepening sense of siege and alienation from the modernist and Americanist church and world.

Another relatively clear example of the world-renouncing position is found in elements of the postconciliar Marian movement, which has been invigorated by the reported appearances of the Blessed Virgin at Medjugorje and, subsequently, at several sites in the United States. Like the traditionalists, many devotees of Mary embrace "an apocalyptic end-time scenario" purportedly revealed or suggested by the Medjugorje messages. Their fervor deepened through a growing network of Marian groups and conferences, and by a cottage industry in pamphlets and prophecies, the devotees ponder the ten secrets told to the visionaries by the Virgin. Thus they hold the key to the meaning of imminent, catastrophic events of cosmic significance. "Ordinary" history is ended; we live in extraordinary times in which the one, true church, embodied by the Blessed Mother, will vanquish the apostate church on earth. As in traditionalist envisionings, a purified, sacred remnant awaits vindication by a force acting beyond a "fallen" place and time.

Sandie Zimdars-Swartz honors the complexity of the movement, noting that these apocalyptic, cosmic themes often find local and very personal appropriation, as in the case of women visionaries who are dealing with intimate social and cultural anxieties. In other words, apocalyptic world-renouncing Catholicism may also be a way of coping with the world as it is. Zimdars-Swartz traces the steps of Marian visionaries and their followers down paths leading from alienation to some form of connectedness with a movement or group that does not think the world is entirely lost. Of course, many Marian enthusiasts explicitly reject such social expressions of their deepest convictions; presumably they prefer the isolation of the pew, grotto, or personal shrine, there to await the fulfillment. But some of the people who visit the sites of recent apparitions or who participate in the prophecy networks become affiliated with the charismatic movement, while others join the anti-abortion movement. They may still be renouncing the world in doing so, but they have not separated themselves entirely from the world, either.

In a unique blending of religious revivalism with politically calculated social activism, the anti-abortion activists portrayed in this book provide an even better example of the commingling of world-renouncing and world-transforming modes. In the words of the conservative Catholics interviewed by Michael Cuneo, one finds a bitter denunciation of tepid episcopal leadership and an institutional church that has lost its moorings. But in the same interviews one also discovers an almost poignant hope for the renewal of that church—a renewal that will result, the activists believe, from concrete, radical, prophetic action on behalf of the unborn. In this sense the conservative Catholic pro-lifers condemn the world in order to save it, here and now.

Ironically, perhaps, given their far different behavioral profile, the founders, faculty, and students of the postconciliar Catholic colleges are attempting precisely the same feat. They retrieve a partially forgotten intellectual tradition in the hope of providing an alternative vision for contemporary Catholic youth. These colleges are not monasteries or even seminaries; purportedly they are preparing students for positions in the workaday world, as lawyers, teachers, and other would-be professionals possessed of a sound liberal-arts education. The adminstrators and faculty of these colleges wish, at the very least, to sustain a worldview and way of life that mainstream Catholic colleges and universities once provided but have largely abandoned in the postconciliar era. As Mary Jo Weaver notes, however, these nascent institutions of higher education are pathetically ineffective in exercising any real influence on the world beyond their walls. To remain intellectually "pure," they isolate their faculty from the professional meetings and associations of the mainstream and their students from the latest pedagogical and substantive developments in their respective fields of inquiry. In short, the new Catholic colleges seem to be preparing students for a world that no longer exists.

Making a Difference

"Preparing people for a world that no longer exists." Is this a suitable slogan—some might call it an epitaph—for conservative Catholics thirty years after the close of the Second Vatican Council? If it were, we might have borrowed the title of Bill Dinges's essay on the traditionalists—"We Are What You Were"—for the title of this book. But conservative Catholics, the vast majority of whom are not traditionalists or apocalyptic believers, have not repudiated the present world. Nor do they despair of seeing the church move gradually back to their sense of a center. Conservatives point to hopeful signs in the recent past, including the success and popularity of a pope who has declared war on various expressions of religious liberalism and who has filled the hierarchy with like-minded bishops. Many recent appointments to American sees suggest that the Vatican values unity and obedience over ideological pluralism and pastoral flexibility. Seminaries are hardly overflowing, but the percentage of conservative-minded candidates for ordination has increased dramatically during John Paul II's pontificate. In short, conservative American Catholicism cannot be counted on to fade away, at least in the foreseeable future.

Liberals might read some of the chapters in this book and think otherwise. After all, what real hope has the Fellowship of Catholic Scholars for reversing the tide of liberalism in the Catholic Church? In fact, what real hope does it have even of perpetuating itself for the next generation? How will a small outfit such as Women for Faith and Family, organized originally around a housewife's kitchen table, make any difference in the long term, when many religious orders and even the Catholic universities seem to advance a feminist agenda for a democratic church and nonpatriarchal society? When one visits the offices of Catholics United for the Faith or attends a conference on the latest Marian apparition, the impression is hardly one of long-term staying power. Is contemporary conservatism the last spasm of a dying breed of orthodox believers? If not, how will such "movements" prevail in a cultural and religious climate that seems increasingly liberal?

The chapters of this book suggest a starting point for reflection upon these questions. To put the matter succinctly: the conservative Catholics who *adapt* to postconciliar America are poised to continue to thrive and grow, while those who merely *react* seemed doomed to increasing irrelevance (to anyone but themselves) or even to extinction.

It is difficult to predict a fate other than gradual or immediate decline for the reactionary conservatives—the world-renouncing traditionalists and other "remnant faithful"—who continue to focus on the struggle with Vatican II and its implementation. Zimdars-Swartz's essay is instructive on this point in noting that the Marian devotees who see no obstacle, and even a boon, in the Council are increasing in number, while the apocalyptic nay-sayers, those who continue to seek revenge for the supposed conciliar slight of Mary, are no longer the most prominent members of the movement. The charismatic movement co-opts some of the more open-minded Marianists, while parish renewal and devotional programs draw upon the good will of others. Dinges likewise sees nothing in the recent developments in traditionalist circles to suggest that they are emerging from the margins of Catholic life, where they inhabit a few chapels, publish poorly circulated pamphlets, and hope for a widespread revival of the Tridentine liturgy.

Engagement with others is the predominant pattern of American social history and the key to growth in American religion. Pluralism, which is at the very heart of the nation's "ordered experiment in liberty," is an insistent—traditionalists might say "insidious"—formative force, calling forth traditional believers from their enclaves and urging them toward the toleration, if not the celebration, of diversity. Recruitment depends heavily on such engagement with the culture.

The Catholic Church once provided an enclave, buttressed by a coherent supernatural worldview, that effectively and dramatically resisted the incursions of outsiders who were not orthodox Catholics, but who instead blended their religious faith with political or cultural sensibilities derived from a godless economy or rationalist system of higher education. Some conservative Catholics mourn the loss of that enclave, it seems, because its passing has left them unprotected from the encroachments of the unbelievers. Groups such as the Fellowship of Catholic Scholars, for example, attempt to preserve intellectual traditions without the support once provided by the enclave in the form of devotional and catechetical networks, sodalities, vigorous lay associations, and the like. The lack of support undermines their educational and apostolic efforts and lends their protestations a melancholy if not defeatist tone.

For better or worse, the conservative Catholic future seems to belong to the world-transformers, and it could be a promising future indeed. These are the Catholics who seem annoyed but undaunted by too-liberal renderings of Vatican II or the materialism of American society. These are the Catholics who thrive on enagagement with their opponents as well as their allies—the mostly lay activists of CUF, WFF, the anti-abortion movement, and the neoconservative intellectuals. One perceives decline in these groups only when they fail to connect with a larger "public" outside their inner core; CUF, for example, could face a dismal organizational future if its battles on the textbook and curricular front fail to engage the sympathies of Catholic parents and the organization turns inward as a result, nurturing its own esoteric worldview. This is why so many of these movements become politicized: engagement with church or world is a recipe for growth and a token of relevance.

What, then, becomes of Mary Jo Weaver's original intention in pursuing a serious and respectful study of Catholics who seem to have been overlooked by mainstream scholars of religion? It may be said that our book simply confirms the cynical judgment that Catholic traditionalists and "ultraconservatives," as well as those unaffiliated individuals intensely devoted to a preconciliar piety and worldview, are irrelevant and perhaps more than a bit out of touch with the world as it is. The "interesting" subjects of this study would therefore be the neoconservatives and the activists who are capable of effecting change in the church and world.

Yet it must be remembered that most of those whom we have described as existing on the margins have self-consciously *sought* the margins. As an act of faith or conscience, they intentionally avoid the mainstream. As a result of their reading of the signs of the times, they perceive little choice but to reject a world, and much of a church, that has capitulated, they are convinced, to the enemies of Roman Catholicism—liberalism, modernism, and, ultimately, atheism—about which popes have warned the faithful since the French Revolution. To be rejectionists in such a situation is a response bespeaking great integrity and courage. If they are correct in their analysis of the current state of affairs, the world-renouncers' prayers and fidelity to "the true church" may turn out to be far more "transformative" in the long run than any adaptive program of their fellow conservatives who are so much engaged with the world.

NOTES

1. Gene Burns, *The Frontiers of Catholicism: The Politics of Ideology in a Liberal World* (Berkeley: University of California Press, 1992), p. 2.

2. For a discussion of the tendency of advocates on both sides to accuse the other side of malevolent intent, see Margaret O' Brien Steinfels, "The Unholy Alliance between Right and Left in the Catholic Church," *America* 166 (2 May 1992): 376–82.

3. We do not know of conservatives who focus exclusively on the world beyond the church, evincing no preoccupation with ecclesial affairs; and this may turn out to be a distinctive mark of conservative Catholics.

APPENDIX

Conservative Catholic Periodicals

JOHN H. HAAS

Being Right: Conservative Catholics in America focuses in large part on intellectuals and activists whose connections to the lives of "ordinary" American Catholics may not always be evident. At the same time, it is probable that the periodical literature reviewed here reflects many of the pressing concerns of most traditional Catholics. Some are served by quarterlies and monthlies representing divergent points on the ideological map; others subscribe to newspapers, Marian magazines, and a variety of newsletters. Although I cannot say that I have listed (or even found) every conservative Catholic periodical in the country, I believe that this short survey is typical and fairly inclusive. I have divided the material into newspapers, quarterlies, monthly magazines and journals, and newsletters. I have also included generic categories to introduce the large number of independent periodicals published by those American Catholics with Marian or traditionalist interests.

Newspapers

The Wanderer, founded in 1867 as a German-language newspaper, has been published and edited by the Matt family of St. Paul, Minnesota, since 1897. Although an English edition was initiated in 1931, the German edition was not discontinued until 1957. Proud of its uncompromising opposition to liberalism in all forms, *The Wanderer* combines theological orthodoxy, laissez-faire economics, and midwestern agrarian populism. Over the years it has vigorously opposed Americanism, modernism, and many of the theological and liturgical innovations introduced in the wake of Vatican II. It has been no less vocal in its criticism of socialism, the New Deal, the Kennedy administration, and liberal social policies in general, including secularism and feminism. *The Wanderer* was a consistent supporter of Senator Joseph McCarthy during the 1950s, and opposes communism and socialism in all its forms. Current contributors include Joseph Sobran and Patrick Buchanan. Circulation is estimated at 35,000.[1]

Our Sunday Visitor offers an expression of popular or localized religious conservatism. Widely distributed through parishes, it is a family newspaper that mixes practical issues such as parenting, everyday spirituality, and question-and-answer columns with strategies for renewing parish life according to a conservative or "strict constructionist" reading of Vatican II documents. The current editor-in-chief, Greg Erlandson, continues a tradition of mild advocacy. The weekly began in 1912 and has grown in the postconciliar years to its current circulation of approximately 155,000.

Catholic Twin Circle is a weekly family newspaper edited by Loretta G. Seyer. Subtitled *Parents and Pastors Working Together,* it engages youth and family issues, providing instruction on personal devotions and critical perspectives on popular culture. Founded in 1964, the newspaper provides its 52,000 subscribers with regular reports on pro-life activities around the nation and stresses the centrality of the abortion issue to Catholic identity.

The *National Catholic Register,* established in 1921 and presently edited by Joop Koopman (with contributing editors Dale Vree, Peter Kreeft, and Philip Lawler), offers a conservative Catholic perspective on national politics and world events; its circulation stands at 57,000.

Quarterlies

Communio: International Catholic Review first appeared in 1974 as the American version of Hans Urs von Balthasar's *Internationale Katholische Zeitschrift.* James Hitchcock was its editor until 1982, when his assistant editor, David L. Schindler (currently professor of fundamental theology at the John Paul II Institute for Studies on Marriage and the Family), took direction of the journal. *Communio* provides a forum for theologians and philosophers influenced by the work of European thinkers such as Balthasar, Henri de Lubac, Joseph Ratzinger, and Antonio Sicari. *Communio* seeks to lay the theological foundation for a uniquely Catholic oppositional culture. Schindler maintains, for example, that the ontology presupposed by the American system of government is fundamentally incompatible with Catholic theology. This conviction has led him and other journal contributors to question the validity of John Courtney Murray's attempts at reconciling Roman Catholicism and American political philosophy, and has also led to some spirited criticism of neoconservatives such as George Weigel and Michael Novak. Circulation for *Communio* is approximately 2,700.

Faith and Reason, a quarterly sponsored by Christendom College, combines scholarship and polemics on a variety of theological and topical issues. Begun in 1975, the journal is edited by the Reverend James McLucas, S.T.D., who succeeded Timothy O'Donnell when the latter became president of Christendom in 1992. The editorial board includes Germain Grisez, Robert A. Herrera, Charles Rice, James V. Schall, S.J., and Frederick D. Wilhelmsen. Recent contributors include Stanley L. Jaki, Msgr. George A. Kelly, and Peter Kreeft. O'Donnell's question "Can a culture and society still be formed by the fullness of the truth brought to man by the Incarnate Word?" expresses the distinctive theme of the journal. Like *Communio, Faith and Reason* offers a forum for Catholic intellectuals who are skeptical about any ultimate compatibility between Catholicism and the American experiment, as in William A. Marshner's article *"Dignitatis Humanae* and Traditional Teaching on Church and State," or Robert A. Herrera's essay "Should the Catholic Church Secede from the Union?" Circulation runs about 1,000.

Human Life Review was founded in 1975 by its present editor, J. P. McFadden. The quarterly is far from being exclusively Catholic, either in its presentation of the pro-life position or in the religious affiliations of its contributors: while well-known Catholics such as Joseph Sobran, James Hitchcock, Thomas Molnar, and the late Malcom Muggeridge have published in the journal, evangelicals such as Harold O. J. Brown, C. Everett Koop, and John Warwick Montgomery have also written for the *Review,* as has Nat Hentoff. The journal provides its 14,000 or so readers with analyses of the social and ethical implications of abortion, euthanasia, and fetal research, proposals for a human life amendment, criticisms of Supreme Court decisions, and withering dissections of pro-choice arguments.

Caelum et Terra, established in 1991, is edited by Daniel Nichols. Although not a conservative Catholic publication as such, *Caelum et Terra* operates in the tradition of Ruskin, Morris, and the Southern Agrarians and thus shares important perspectives with some segments of the conservative Catholic community. The writers gently promote an alternative way of life more in harmony with Catholic conviction and piety than that which they believe has resulted from a rationalized, spiritually debased, consumption-oriented capitalism. Articles explore issues such as the psycho-spiritual effects of electronic media, Christian environmentalism and agrarianism, resources within the Catholic tradition for resisting the dominant culture, the sacramentality of creation, and Catholic perspectives on community, marriage, nonviolence, and technology. Circulation runs around 1,000.

The *Dawson Newsletter,* which first appeared in 1981, is edited by John J. Mulloy of the Society for Christian Culture. This magazine-size quarterly offers a Catholic critique of contemporary culture. Joining the intellectual battle against "the secular ideologies—Marxism, feminism, multiculturalism, the idea of Progress, idealization of non-Christian religions and cultures, religious syncretism"—the magazine takes its inspiration from British historian Christopher Dawson, reprinting selections from his work in every number. Writers and advisors have included Russell Hittinger, Jude Dougherty, Russell Kirk, and Alphonse Matt. Dedicated to defending the Judeo-Christian tradition in the midst of what it perceives as an American Kulturkampf, Mulloy et al. criticize the "standardized consumer culture of the democracies" and "the homogenizing pressure of secular society" for undermining the development of the human person no less thoroughly than would any totalitarian regime. Using Dawson's philosophy of history as a template for its cultural analysis, the newsletter combines a populist indignation at the machinations and greed of corporate elites with an outré aestheticism that considers wearing blue jeans "a jarring note against the dignity of the human person . . . a witness to the cheapness and vulgarity which is at the heart of modern society." It has a circulation of approximately 800.

Monthly Magazines and Journals

The *Homiletic and Pastoral Review* is the oldest of the theologically conservative monthlies, appearing initially as the *Homiletic and Monthly Catechist* in 1900. Originally designed for priests, this journal has established a reputation for an uncompromising conservatism regarding ecclesiastical issues. It is currently edited by Fr. Kenneth Baker, S.J. (author of *Fundamentals of Catholicism,* 3 vols., 1982–83). Rejecting the softer forms of ecumenism found in some of the more recent neoconservative periodicals, the *Review* presents the distinctives of the church in a parochial and sometimes triumphalist spirit reminiscent of the "ghetto Catholicism" of the 1950s. Political and cultural topics—with the notable exception of abortion—find little space in this journal. The format and art work are indicative of the intentionally unfashionable ethos the *Homiletic and Pastoral Review* seeks to cultivate: it has changed little, if at all, since the early 1970s. Circulation stands at approximately 14,500.

Triumph, founded in 1966 by William F. Buckley's brother-in-law, L. Brent Bozell, occupies a unique place in the history of modern conservative Catholic journalism. In "The Confessional Tribe" (July 1970), Bozell announced his rejection of the conservatism that accepted the American pluralist framework, answering the question, "Is it not time to make America a Christian country?" with a definite "no . . . that time has passed." Among its editors and writers were Thomas Molnar, Frederick Wilhelmsen,

Christopher Dawson, Jeffrey Hart, Russell Kirk, Gerhart Niemeyer, and the Protestant theonomist Rousas John Rushdoony. Warren Carroll, who worked for *Triumph* for a while, later founded Christendom College. Aiming to unite writers and readers in "a movement dedicated to laying the foundations of a new Christendom," *Triumph* became the standard-bearer of a radical Catholicism that was culturally and ideologically separatist yet militantly engaged in pro-life direct-action campaigns. At its peak, its circulation approached 10,000. It ceased publication in 1976.

Fidelity appeared in 1981 and is in many ways the ideological successor to *Triumph*. *Fidelity* is the brainchild of E. Michael Jones, the zealous and indefatigable polemicist and author. Among other books, Jones has written *Degenerate Moderns: Modernity as Rationalized Sexual Misbehavior* (1993) and *Dionysos Rising: The Birth of Cultural Revolution out of the Spirit of Music* (1994). Among Jones's original editorial advisors were James Hitchcock, Alphonse Matt, Jr., and Notre Dame law professor Charles Rice. *Fidelity* surveys and analyzes current developments in society, culture, politics, and the church with an eye toward assessing their impact upon the family. Supporting the magisterium and opposing the intrusions of the federal government, Jones insists that the West, having turned its back on the asceticism requisite to spiritual health, is sick with economic and sensual luxury. *Fidelity* is known for its frequent attention to the sexual immorality that Jones believes is central to the ills afflicting society, and articles have applied this particular critique to a host of events and movements, from Wagnerian opera to the civil rights movement, from abstract expressionism to liberalism in theology. *Fidelity*, which claims a circulation of 10,000, has also leveled its sights on other segments of conservative Catholicism with which it disagrees, including the Lefebvrists and other traditionalists, as well as members of the Marian movement and the promoters of visionary phenomena such as those associated with Medjugorje.

Catholicism in Crisis was begun in 1982 by Michael Novak of the American Enterprise Institute and Notre Dame philosophy professor Ralph McInerny. Claiming to be a response to the eclipse of the voice of the laity by overweening clerics, particularly in economic policy and foreign affairs, it established itself as the voice of Catholic neoconservatism in the 1980s. In 1986 it changed its name to *Crisis*. Under both titles, it has been conspicuous in offering a Catholic defense of conservative positions in articles such as "The Morality of Deterrence" and "The Morality of Capital Punishment." Contributors include George Weigel, Dinesh D'Souza, James V. Schall, S.J., James Hitchcock, Thomas Pangle, Anne Husted Burleigh, Thomas Molnar, and recently Eugene D. Genovese. William Bentley Ball, Zbigniew Brzezinski, Alexander Haig, Eugene J. McCarthy, Paul Weyrich, and James Q. Wilson lend their names to the masthead. Although the circulation figure is not impressive—it hovers around 8,000—the journal editors claim that its elite readership constitutes an influential bloc of opinion-makers.

First Things is a relatively recent addition to the neoconservative ranks. Founded in 1990 by the prominent author and Lutheran pastor Richard John Neuhaus (who subsequently converted to Roman Catholicism), *First Things* provides an ecumenical forum for conservative intellectuals dedicated to advancing the possibilities for a renewed public religious consciousness in a "transmodern" or "postmodern" context. The writing is lively and disputatious, the conflicts usually occurring between one or more members of the select *First Things* crowd and its liberal opponents. Readers are occasionally treated to symposia and declarations from the former on controversial topics such as affirmative-action proposals for homosexuals. Published by Neuhaus's

Institute on Religion and Public Life, this opinion journal appeals to readers interested in establishing the relevance of religion to morality, public policy, and civil society. Editors and advisors include Peter Berger, Midge Decter, Jean Bethke Elshtain, Mary Ann Glendon, Stanley Hauerwas, Gertrude Himmelfarb, George Weigel, and the late Christopher Lasch. Circulation has grown steadily, with reports ranging from a low of 15,000 to a high of 25,000 in 1994.

The *New Oxford Review* represents that segment of the Catholic community that seeks to combine theological conservatism with cultural radicalism. Founded in 1977 and edited by political scientist Dale Vree, this journal specializes in offering trenchant, theologically informed critiques of contemporary American culture: it has discussed sexual morality, abortion, contraception, and feminism, and at times it has offered negative appraisals of the theory of evolution, biblical criticism, and liberal theology. Like many of the Catholic neoconservative publications, *New Oxford Review* combines criticism of secular and hedonistic trends in American culture with an ecumenical approach to moral reform. It parts company with neoconservatives, however, on several important issues deriving in large part from the personal background of the editor. Vree comes from a working-class family and was himself a Marxist living as an expatriate in East Germany when he converted in 1966. Unlike many ex-radicals, however, Vree did not swing to the opposite ideological pole: *New Oxford Review* exhibits a communitarian orientation in its social criticism and has at times offered scathing criticisms of neoconservative attempts at harmonizing Catholicism and laissez-faire economics. Contributing editors have included Robert N. Bellah, L. Brent Bozell, Robert Coles, Peter Kreeft, Christopher Lasch, Walker Percy, and Sheldon Vanauken. Circulation is approximately 9,000.

30 Days: In the Church and in the World is basically independent of American influence. The English-language edition of this Italian monthly first appeared in 1988, edited by Joseph Fessio, S.J., founder and publisher of Ignatius Press. *30 Days* offers its readers a European perspective on church and world affairs, influenced by theologians such as Hans Urs von Balthasar, Msgr. Luigi Giussani, and Cardinal Joseph Ratzinger. In November 1990, Antonio Socci became editor-in-chief of the international edition. By early 1991, Fessio voiced concern over recent changes in the content of the magazine that he thought might be related to Socci's editorship (e.g., articles asserting an international Masonic conspiracy, ambiguous references to something identified as "the power," detailed analyses of Italian politics, and the increased promotion of Giussani's organization, Comunione e Liberazione). The March 1991 issue of *30 Days*, with its vigorous opposition to the Gulf War and uncompromising criticism of the United States' role in that conflict, coincided with and exacerbated the growing alienation of many American readers from the magazine. When Fessio ceased publication of the English-language *30 Days* with the April 1991 issue, Italcoser Corporation took over distribution in September. Circulation is estimated to stand at 27,000.

Catholic World Report was founded by Fessio in 1991 after he severed connections with *30 Days*. Fessio's new magazine is currently edited by Philip Lawler of the Catholic League for Civil and Religious Rights. Published in cooperation with I. Media of Rome, *Catholic World Report* focuses primarily on international news of Catholic interest: it also features editorials on current events—Fessio has recently criticized the Curia, for example, for its decision to allow female altar servers—and polemical responses to challenges to orthodoxy. The magazine is an ardent opponent of sex-inclusive language and a defender of the new *Universal Catechism of the Catholic Church*, the traditionalist translation of which Fessio advocated. Its circulation runs at approximately 20,000.

This Rock: The Magazine of Catholic Apologetics and Evangelization was launched in 1990, in part as a response to the challenge of fundamentalist Protestantism. Published by Catholic Answers, Inc., it is edited by Karl Keating. Scott Hahn of the Franciscan University of Steubenville, a well-known convert from evangelicalism (and coauthor, with his wife, of *Rome Sweet Home*, 1993), is a frequent contributor. *This Rock* specializes in the methodical dismantling of Protestant objections to traditional Catholic teachings, and often goes on the offensive with articles such as "Logic and Protestantism's Shaky Foundations." Keating admits that the tone of the magazine is sometimes "strident and sarcastic." Dissent and innovation in the church are addressed in a similar spirit: a recent article asked, "Are the sacraments you receive valid?"; theologians not fully in accord with the Vatican are described as "the Dead See." Circulation stands at about 8,000.

Catholic Heritage, edited by Robert P. Lockwood and published by Our Sunday Visitor Press, was begun in 1992 as an educational magazine for Catholics increasingly out of touch with the ideas and practices of their own tradition. It generally features stories about saints, liturgical seasons, and Catholic practices. Its circulation stands at 23,000.

Lay Witness, the newsletter of Catholics United for the Faith, was established as a monthly publication in 1968. Currently edited by James Sullivan, it has a circulation of 20,000, and has become a handsomely produced, glossy newsletter aimed at a wider audience than CUF members. It features reviews and articles on Catholic tradition, spirituality, and history, along with news about local and regional CUF chapters and meetings. Its circulation is 20,000.

A traditionalist publications sampler: A number of traditionalist publications deserve mention as representative of a distinctive location on the conservative Catholic landscape. *The Angelus*, perhaps the best known of these periodicals, is the magazine of the International Society of Saint Pius X; it is edited by Fr. Kenneth Novak. Others include the *Roman Catholic*, edited by the Rev. William Jenkins, and *The Athanasian*, the newsletter of the sedevacantist organization Traditional Catholics of America, edited by Fr. Francis E. Fenton. All have been publishing since the late 1970s. Older publications such as Walter Matt's newspaper, *The Remnant*, and the magazine of the Congregation of Mary Immaculate Queen, *The Reign of Mary*, edited by Fr. Casimir Puskorius, CMRI, along with newer additions such as *The Latin Mass*, edited by Jeffrey Rubin, and the *Catholic Voice*, the newsletter of the Society of Traditional Roman Catholics, are important indicators of the depth and breadth of traditionalist disaffection from the postconciliar church. A small, privately printed newsletter, *Vox Sacerdotalis: A Magazine for Priests*, began in England in 1983 and is published on an irregular basis (about three times a year). Although it is not an American periodical, it takes most of its substance from American conservative publications and finds most support for its pamphlet series—for example, "Women Priests: The Devil's Final Attack"—from American readers.

A Marian publications sampler: Many of the Marian publications are relatively unknown outside that movement. They include *Garabandal: The Message of Our Lady of Mount Carmel*, edited by Joseph Lomangino; *Maryfaithful*, the publication of the Marian Hour Radio Rosary Broadcast; and the *Fatima Family Messenger*, edited by

Fr. Robert J. Fox. Much better known and widely circulated is *Soul,* the magazine of the World Apostolate of Fatima (the Blue Army), which has been published since 1950 and reports a circulation of 115,000. The *Marian Helpers Bulletin,* which was founded in 1944, has a circulation of 1,127,342 and is edited by the Reverend Gerald Ornowski.

Newsletters

Newsletters serve the in-house needs of a variety of organizations, alerting members to upcoming events, reporting on conference activities, announcing and describing useful publications, and so forth. For example, the new Catholic colleges (see chapter 12) all publish newsletters which are sent to alumni and friends to keep them informed about the institution and its future. The Fellowship of Catholic Scholars (see chapter 8) publishes a newsletter edited by Ralph McInerny with a circulation of 3,000.

Some newsletters serve as platforms for the opinions of their editors and are sent out nationally to subscribers. For example, Jim McFadden's *Catholic Eye* is a monthly four-page newsletter begun in the mid-1980s by the founder of the *Human Life Review.* Each issue includes a short editorial on some (usually lamentable) aspect of the contemporary Catholic scene, followed by a running commentary on two or three news stories, with a guest essay by the likes of Francis Canavan, S.J., or Anne Roche Muggeridge. Witty, hardboiled, and feisty, McFadden eschews ecumenism, dialogue, and nuance as symptoms of compromise. *Eye* is fond of contrasting the flaccid Catholicism promoted by the theologians and bishops it considers "Ultramundane" with the vigorous Catholicism of yesterday, with its demanding asceticism, its rigorous standards of belief, and its ornate devotionalism—including the Tridentine Mass. It is published by the National Committee of Catholic Laymen.

Newsletters can provide a glimpse into conservative Catholic activity by showing that various organizations exist and have enough interest and support to maintain a publication. Most of these newsletters are brief—no more than a few pages—and some are produced more professionally than others, but they all serve a discrete segment of the American Catholic population and draw attention to a particular set of ideas.

Free Speech Advocates is the newsletter of Catholics United for Life, an organization chaired by Charles E. Rice and Thomas P. Monaghan. Catholics United for Life provides legal counsel for anti-abortion activists being prosecuted for their activities.

Christifidelis reports the activities of the St. Joseph Foundation, directed by Charles Wilson. The foundation, established in 1984, has devoted itself to alerting ecclesiastical authorities to liturgical and doctrinal deviations that may be proscribed by canon law.

Catalyst is the new name for the *Catholic League Newsletter,* a publication of the Catholic League for Religious and Civil Rights, begun in 1973. The current president of the league is sociologist William A. Donohue, and the current editor is John Pantuso. The league, founded by Virgil Blum, S.J., is a watchdog organization dedicated to exposing anti-Catholic and antireligious activities. The newsletter has reported on events such as judicial decisions that affect religious schools or restrict pro-life demonstrations, school board deliberations on sex education curricula, government-sponsored commercials that promote the use of condoms, examples of media bias against the church, and art exhibits that are offensive to religious sensibilities. Circulation is 25,000.

CCL Family Foundations has been published since 1974 by the Couple to Couple League to promote noncontraceptive family planning. Edited by Ann M. Grundlach, the newsletter is published by John F. Kippley (author of *Sex and the Marriage Covenant: A Basis for Morality*, 1991), who with his wife, Sheila, founded the league in 1971. CCL advocates the sympto-thermal method of birth control through its publications and the hundreds of teaching couples who lead parish-sponsored marriage preparation courses. CCL promotes a *Humanae Vitae*–based theology of sexuality that insists upon the incompatibility of artificial birth control with respect for the body, disciplining the will, obedience to God, and the total giving of the self to the spouse. According to Kippley, "The acceptance of marital contraception is the heart and core of the sexual revolution" and has produced the moral chaos of our time, including abortion, promiscuity, adultery, homosexuality, pornography, divorce, drug addiction, and crime. Many of the CCL publications are taken up with explaining and defending the biological-technical aspects of the method; other articles present empirical confirmations of the technique's effectiveness and scientific data on the harmful side effects of artificial methods.

Religious Life, a monthly newsletter published by the Institute for Religious Life, was begun in 1976. The institute, founded as an alternative to the Leadership Council for Women Religious, promotes the wearing of the religious habit, full obedience to the pope, and fidelity to the original charism of the community. It claims that traditional orders of sisters are receiving new vocations because they have remained faithful to the teaching of the church. In addition to news about the institute or reports on regional and national meetings, *Religious Life* usually features articles on traditional Catholic beliefs such as purgatory. Although most of the news is about sisters, there are regular articles on missions, protecting the rights of the unborn, and evangelization.

The *Forum* is the quarterly newsletter published by the Wanderer Forum Foundation and the Forum Affiliates under the editorial direction of Frank Morriss, a regular columnist for *The Wanderer.* The *Forum* produces reviews and opinions much like the ones found in its parent newspaper. Its self-description on the masthead reads: "A network of lay Catholics who have banded together to promote and defend Catholic teaching, and to infuse principles based on that teaching into the social consciousness of this nation."

NOTE

1. Circulation figures for the periodicals described in this essay have been taken from the periodical or from Karen Troshynski-Thomas and Deborah M. Burek, eds., *Gale Directory of Publications and Broadcast Media* (Detroit: Gale Research, Inc., 1994), and/or Theresa Glynn Beauchamp, ed., *Catholic Press Directory* (Rockville Centre, N.Y.: Catholic Press Association, 1993).

CONTRIBUTORS

R. Scott Appleby is the director of the Cushwa Center for the Study of American Catholicism and associate professor of history at the University of Notre Dame. His books include *"Church and Age Unite!": The Modernist Impulse in American Catholicism* and five volumes of the American Academy of Arts and Sciences' Fundamentalism Project, which he coedited with Martin E. Marty.

Benedict M. Ashley is a Dominican priest and moral theologian who recently taught at the John Paul II Institute for Marriage and Family in Washington, D.C. He now teaches at the Aquinas Institute of Theology in St. Louis.

Michael W. Cuneo is associate professor of sociology and anthropology at Fordham. His most recent book, *Catholics against the Church*, is a study of pro-life activism among conservative Catholics in Canada.

Allan Figueroa Deck is a Jesuit pastoral theologian who coordinates Hispanic pastoral studies at Loyola Marymount University in Los Angeles. His research and publications combine his interests in Latin American studies and missiology.

William D. Dinges is an associate professor of religions and religious education at the Catholic University of America. His research and publications for the last several years have been devoted to traditional Catholicism, specifically Lefebvrist groups, in the United States.

Helen Hull Hitchcock is the founder of Women for Faith and Family. She lives in St. Louis and has become one of the most prominent spokeswomen for "orthodox" Catholic women in the United States.

James Hitchcock is a professor of history at St. Louis University, one of the founders of the Fellowship for Catholic Scholars, and the author of such books as *The New Enthusiasts* and *Catholicism and Modernity: Confrontation or Capitulation?*

Joseph A. Komonchak is a priest from the New York Archdiocese and an associate professor of theology at the Catholic University of America. With Giuseppe Alberigo and Jean-Pierre Jossua, he edited *The Reception of Vatican II*.

James A. Sullivan was the vice-president of Catholics United for the Faith, and editor of their newsletter, *Lay Witness*, when he wrote this essay. He is now a development director for Thomas More College.

Mary Jo Weaver is professor of religious studies and women's studies at Indiana University. She has been engaged in research on conservative American Catholics for the past five years. Her most recent book is *Springs of Water in a Dry Land: Spiritual Survival for Catholic Women Today.*

George Weigel is president of the Ethics and Public Policy Center, an ecumenical and interreligious research institution in Washington, D.C. Among his nine books are *The Final Revolution: The Resistance Church and the Collapse of Communism.*

Sandra L. Zimdars-Swartz is a professor of religious studies at the University of Kansas. Her first book, *Encountering Mary: From La Salette to Medjugorje*, tracked Marian apparitions in Europe from the mid-nineteenth century to the present time.

INDEX

Abortion rights: conservative Catholic groups organized to oppose, 8–10; Catholic feminists and, 164–65. *See also* Anti-abortion movement

Academic freedom: Fellowship of Catholic Scholars and, 198; in conservative Catholic colleges, 304–307, 320n.3, 320n.4

Academy of Catholic Hispanic Theologians of the United States (ACHTUS), 91

Aeterni Patris (Leo XIII), 65, 67, 69

Affirmation for Catholic Women (WFF), 163–64, 167–68, 177–78

Amaladoss, Michael, 104n.39

American Association of University Professors, 198, 320n.4

Americanism, conservative Catholics and, 37–59

American Life League (ALL), 280, 282–83

American Revolution, 25, 255

Andrews, Joan, 133n.8, 298n.33

Andrusko, Dave, 276

Angelus, The (magazine), 342

Anti-abortion movement: Catholics United for the Faith and, 108, 125, 133n.8, 135n.21; neoconservative Catholics and, 156; Women for Faith and Family and, 169; Marian revival and, 226, 229; traditionalist movement and, 269n.81; Catholic militancy and, 270–96; conservative Catholic colleges and, 313, 318

Anti-Semitism, of conservative Catholics, 36n.27, 263

Apparitions, Marian, 214–15, 218, 227–33

Appleby, R. Scott, vii–xi, 13, 92

Arbery, Glen and Virginia, 315, 316, 317

Aristotelian Thomism, 72–74

Arnold, Patrick M., 134n.20

Ashley, Benedict M., 13, 38, 329

Athanasian, The (magazine), 342

Atwater, Lee, 286

Bainvel, Jean, 121

Barrera, Mario, 89

Baum, William W., 142

Benedict XIV, 141

Berger, Peter, 148

Bernardin, Cardinal Joseph, 176, 291, 292

Berrigan, Dan, 142

Bevans, Stephen B., 103n.18

Bevilacqua, Cardinal Anthony, 195

Bianchi, Eugene, 49, 51

Birth control, and agenda of anti-abortion movement, 274, 278–82. See also *Humanae Vitae*

Birthright pregnancy centers, 287

Bishops, U.S.: pastoral letter on peace, 59n.10, 161n.25; on sex education, 136n.40; anti-abortion movement and, 277–78, 290–93. *See also* National Conference of Catholic Bishops (NCCB)

Blue Army of Mary, 7

Boff, Leonardo, 175

Bombings, of women's health clinics, 289

Bonifield, Mary, 315

Bottcher, Rosemary, 285

Bozell, L. Brent, 135n.23, 313

Brandi, Salvatore, 46–47

Brennan, William, 277

Brown, Judie, 280–81, 283, 287

Brown, Michael, 223–25

Brown, Raymond, 193

Brunelli, Lucio, 159n.5

Buckley, William F., 188

Burns, Gene, 58, 59, 325–26

Burtchaell, James, 277

Caelum et Terra (quarterly), 339

Canadian Catholic Conference of Bishops, 165

Canon, literary, 309

Carroll, John, 40–41

Carroll, Warren, 312, 313, 322–23n.39

Catalyst (newsletter), 343

Catherine of Siena, 322n.37

Catholic Answers, 109–10

Catholic Charismatic Renewal, 10–11

Catholic Eye (newsletter), 343

Catholic Family Life Bureau, 273

Catholic fundamentalism, vii–xi

Catholic Heritage (magazine), 342

Catholicism, contemporary American: traditional and conservative organizations in, 6–8; map of, 13–14, 34, 325–26; "crisis" in, 37–38; Americanism and form of public, 55–59; impact of Hispanics on, 88–93; liberal and conservative labels in, 140–44; opposition to traditionalist movement in, 259–61; influence of conservative Catholics on future of, 332–35. *See also* Conservative Catholics

Catholicism in Crisis (magazine), 340

Catholic League for Religious and Civil Liberties, 7, 108–109